WORKERS IN IMPERIAL GERMANY

GERMANY

The Miners of the Ruhr

—

S. H. F. HICKEY

CLARENDON PRESS · OXFORD
1985

Oxford University Press, Walton Street, Oxford OX2 6DP
Oxford New York Toronto
Delhi Bombay Calcutta Madras Karachi
Kuala Lumpur Singapore Hong Kong Tokyo
Nairobi Dar es Salaam Cape Town
Melbourne Auckland

and associated companies in
Beirut Berlin Ibadan Nicosia

Oxford is a trade mark of Oxford University Press

Published in the United States
by Oxford University Press, New York

© S. H. F. Hickey 1985

British Library Cataloguing in Publication Data
Hickey, S. H. F.
Workers in Imperial Germany: the miners of
the Ruhr.—(Oxford historical monographs)
1. Coal miners—Germany (West)—Ruhr (Region)
2. Ruhr (Germany: Region)—Social conditions
I. Title
305.9'622   HD8039.M62G3
ISBN 0-19-822935-6

Library of Congress Cataloging in Publication Data
Hickey, S. H. F.
Workers in Imperial Germany.
(Oxford historical monographs)
Bibliography: p.
Includes index.
1. Coal miners—Germany (West)—Ruhr (Region)—
History.   2. Ruhr (Germany: Region)— Social conditions.
3. Trade-unions—Coal miners—Germany (West)—Ruhr
(Region)—Political activity—History.   I. Title.
HD8039.M6152G34 1985   331.7'622334'094355   85-15564
ISBN 0-19-822935-6

Typeset by Joshua Associates Limited, Oxford
Printed in Great Britain
at the University Press, Oxford
by David Stanford
Printer to the University

To my parents

Acknowledgements

A book of this nature would not be possible without the support and help of many people. Here I can only mention some of them.

Particular thanks are due to the Warden and Fellows of St. Antony's College, Oxford, to Professor Hans Mommsen of Bochum University and to the staff of the several archives used—especially the Bochum *Stadtarchiv* and the Münster *Staatsarchiv*. Together with the financial support generously provided by the Department of Education and Science and the *Volkswagen Stiftung*, they enabled the original research on which the book is based to be conducted—and for it to be done in stimulating and congenial settings.

Special debts are due to Tim Mason, who first stimulated my interest in this field of history and made helpful comments on an earlier draft; and to Tony Nicholls of St Antony's College who gave sustained and invaluable help, advice and encouragement over many years. Amongst others whose help, support, and constructive criticism has been of particular importance are Professor F. L. Carsten, David Crew, Geoff Eley, Richard J. Evans and Hans-Dieter Kreikamp. Thanks also to Katie Gibson, who typed the manuscript, and the staff of the Oxford University Press who prepared it for the press. The deficiencies which remain are entirely my own.

Finally, I would like to record special thanks to my wife and family for their remarkable patience in the face of the unrelenting demands of the Ruhr mineworkers.

London, 1984

Contents

Abbreviations

BA	Bergbau Archiv
HKB	Handelskammer zu Bochum
IGBE	Industriegewerkschaft Bergbau und Energie (Archiv)
IISG	International Instituut voor sociale Geschiedenis (Amsterdam)
IZF	Institut für Zeitungsforschung (Dortmund)
KA	Krupp-Archiv (Bochum)
KLB	Königliche Landrat Bochum
RPA	Regierungspräsident Arnsberg
StAB	Stadtarchiv Bochum
STAM	Staatsarchiv Münster
WWA	Westfälisches Wirtschaftsarchiv (Dortmund)

Tables

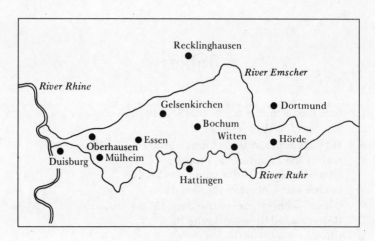

1. Ruhr District

2. Bochum

Introduction

THE organized labour movement has long played a central role in Germany. Despite the efforts of Bismarck and his successors to ban or undermine it, by the First World War the Sozialdemokratische Partei Deutschlands (SPD) and the trade unions constituted the largest political party and the largest mass organizations in the country. Although deeply divided within itself, it was the labour movement which had to take the lead in re-forming the German polity after the collapse of 1918: Weimar was largely its creation. Unable to defend itself or the democratic system it had helped to form, the labour movement was crushed by Hitler; despite twelve years of repression, however, it was one of the first forces to re-emerge after his defeat. The German Democratic Republic has since been dominated by communists who trace their history back to the same origins as the social democrats who form one of the pillars of the Federal Republic. Understanding the history of labour is therefore central to any understanding of the shaping of modern Germany.

Until recently, however, most writing on the labour movement concentrated on a narrow field, particularly the ideological and organizational development of the SPD. Other areas were relatively neglected. Above all, ordinary workers—the people for whom the labour movement existed and on whom it depended for support—hardly got a look in. In this respect the historiography of labour tended to mirror the overriding concern of most historians of Germany with 'high' politics at the expense of the underlying social developments.

In recent years the balance has begun to change. In a growing stream of publications, previously neglected areas in the history of nineteenth and twentieth-century Germany have begun to be explored. In Germany as in Britain, social history has moved from a backwater to become one of the more vigorous fields of historical research. One effect has

been to shift some attention away from national political
and institutional developments and towards what has been
termed 'history from below'. This has involved a greater
willingness to view ordinary people as active agents in their
own historical experience, rather than simply as passive
recipients of influences from above. It has led to a new
interest in regional and local affairs. Perhaps most strikingly,
it has seen the emergence of *Alltagsgeschichte*—the history
of everyday life—almost as a new sub-discipline in its own
right. Through such developments whole areas of previously
neglected historical experience have begun to be addressed.
Leisure and recreational activities, family life and roles,
migration and housing—these topics and more have begun
to command significant historical attention.[1]

Much, however, remains to be done. The relationship
between the 'social' history of labour and the 'political'
history of the labour movement remains ambiguous. Not
all recent studies have avoided the danger of going from the
previous narrow preoccupation with politics almost to the
opposite extreme, so that formal political and organizational
developments, if addressed at all, seem to have only secondary significance.[2] Moreover, several issues of central importance to an understanding of the character and development
of the labour movement remain to be explored in depth.
One is the experience of work itself. This was clearly a decisive part of most people's lives, taking up their time and
energies and providing a vital source of social identity and
social experience. It was also a point at which differing
aspirations and interests met and were resolved, sometimes
harmoniously and sometimes through conflict: it was therefore a focal point for the establishment and expression of
power relations within society. Despite its crucial role,
however, our knowledge of the actual experience of work
in nineteenth and early twentieth-century Germany remains

[1] For a general discussion of these trends see R. J. Evans, 'Introduction:
the Sociological Interpretation of German Labour History', in R. J. Evans (ed.),
The German Working Class 1888-1933: the Politics of Everyday Life (London,
1982).

[2] G. Eley and K. Nield, 'Why does social history ignore politics?', in *Social
History* V. ii (May 1980), pp. 249-71; Evans, 'The Sociological Interpretation
of German Labour History'.

very limited. The same applies to the trade union movement. It has long been recognized that the unions were of decisive importance to the labour movement in Germany; yet little is known, for instance, about the history of many individual trade unions, the role they played in the work-place and the local community, their successes and failures, the constraints under which they were forced to work, and their internal dynamics and conflicts. This in turn makes it hard to assess the strengths and weaknesses of the labour movement as a whole. Similarly, the role of religion within the working class has barely begun to be addressed—despite the fact that Germany spawned not one but two major labour movements, divided primarily on religious lines.[3] With topics as important as these still largely under-researched, it might be argued that recent advances have served almost as much to highlight the gaps in our knowledge as actually to fill them.

The central issue for the labour movement was power. Individual workers were weak in the face of established economic and political forces: the *raison d'être* of the labour movement was to create new forms of power, to enable workers collectively to realize aims and aspirations which as individuals they were too weak to achieve. This required solidarity. Only through shared loyalties and common action could workers hope to challenge and defeat their powerful and well-organized opponents. But solidarity was not a constant, immutable factor in working-class life. The forms it could take and its strength and durability varied—for example, with the nature of the industry, the state of the economy, the attitude of the Government, and the strength of rival organizations. Nor was the relationship between the solidarity of industrial disputes and that of organizational or political action necessarily straightforward: the striker and industrial militant did not necessarily become the political radical, and apparent political success, for example in elections, was not always underpinned by a dependable economic power. The dynamics of the labour movement

[3] A convenient introduction to recent writing on work and trade unionism is provided by W. Conze and U. Engelhardt (ed.), *Arbeiter im Industrialisierungsprozess. Herkunft, Lage und Verhalten* (Stuttgart, 1979). Several of the contributors have presented more detailed findings in book form. On religion see *European Studies Review* XII. iii (July 1982).

and the factors which affected its success or failure were
therefore rooted in its specific historical circumstances.

The present study aims to contribute to the understanding
of the German labour movement by examining its emerging
character in the Ruhr during the formative period before
1914. It looks in particular, although not exclusively, at the
coal-miners in the Bochum electoral district—encompassing in
addition to Bochum the towns of Gelsenkirchen, Herne, Witten,
and Hattingen and several smaller villages—lying at the heart
of the Ruhr complex. This area was of particular importance
for German labour. It represented the heartland of German
industry, the main centre of coal, steel, and engineering. It
was the most heavily proletarian region.[4] And it was dominated
by miners—a group long noted for their solidarity and
militancy. Twice in the Wilhelmine period the Ruhr mines
were the stage for the biggest strike movements yet seen in
Germany; in the revolutionary period after 1918 the district
saw some of the biggest and bitterest industrial and military
confrontations. On the face of it, therefore, the Ruhr should
have formed a corner-stone of the German labour movement.
As Rosa Luxemburg wrote: 'The misery of the miners, with its
eruptive soil which even in "normal" times is a storm centre of
the greatest violence, must immediately explode, in a violent
economic socialist struggle . . .'.[5]

Certainly there is a long international literature which
has stressed the militancy and solidarity of mineworkers.
In international comparisons mining stood out as amongst
the most strike-prone industries.[6] The reasons are not hard
to grasp. The official inquiry into the British miners' strike
of 1972 observed: 'Other occupations have their dangers and
inconveniences, but we know of none in which there is
such a combination of danger, health hazard, discomfort in
working conditions, social inconvenience and community

[4] Ruhr cities occupy the first five places in Guttsman's index of proletarianization in Germany, based on the 1907 census. W. L. Guttsman, *The German
Social Democratic Party 1875–1933* (London, 1981), p. 91.

[5] R. Luxemburg, *The mass strike, the political party and the trade unions*
(London, n.d.), p. 56.

[6] C. Kerr and A. Siegel, 'The Interindustry Propensity to Strike—an International Comparison' in A. Kornhauser, R. Dubin, and A. M. Ross (ed.), *Patterns
of Industrial Conflict* (New York, 1954); P. N. Stearns, *Lives of Labour* (London,
1975), p. 316.

isolation.'[7] The industry has been described as one in which 'the habit of solidarity . . . suggests itself naturally'.[8] Phrases like 'isolated mass', 'separatist group', and 'occupational community' have been used in attempts to systematize the complex of ties which bound miners together in their work, their homes, and their communities, and which stimulated both a deep mutual loyalty to each other and endemic conflict between them and their employers.[9] Historians of the Ruhr have also highlighted the factors which fostered miners' militancy. In his monumental study of Ruhr miners in the mid-nineteenth century, Tenfelde has stressed the 'unifying factors' which heightened their cohesiveness and solidarity and culminated in 1889 in their first general strike. Brüggemeier has emphasized the importance of 'informal' ties between miners—their shared housing, their multifarious contacts at work and away from it—which enabled them to cope with their harsh conditions and gave a basis for a solidarity and militancy which ran ahead of the more cautious approach of their trade unions. Lucas has focused on the 'radicalism' of Hamborn miners, particularly in the revolutionary period of 1918 to 1920, and has contrasted its particular forms with the different character of metalworkers' radicalism in Remscheid. Crew has contrasted miners' militancy in the Ruhr with the passivity of metalworkers in the same district; the discrepancy can best be understood, he argues, in terms of the 'occupational community' which embraced most miners and their families but which had no equivalent among the metal-workers:

. . . the miner's residential and marriage patterns reinforced the solidarity that was created, in the first instance, by the structure of his work. Since the miner's personality and his occupation were so intimately associated, it was predictable that grievances experienced individually would be expressed in collective protest.[10]

[7] M. P. Jackson, *The Price of Coal* (London, 1974), p. 141.

[8] E. J. Hobsbawm, *Labouring Men* (London, 1968 edition), p. 9.

[9] Kerr and Siegel, 'The Interindustry Propensity to Strike'; G. V. Rimlinger, 'International Differences in the Strike Propensity of Coal Miners: Experience in Four Countries', in *Industrial and Labor Relations Review* XII. iii (1959); M. I. A. Bulmer, 'Sociological Models of the Mining Community' in *Sociological Review* xxiii (1975).

[10] D. F. Crew, *Town in the Ruhr: a Social History of Bochum 1860–1914*

There is no doubt that the Ruhr miners did show, on occasion, an impressive level of solidarity. But for the labour movement in Germany their history is much more ambiguous. For despite so many apparent advantages the labour movement which emerged in the Ruhr proved to be neither radical nor strong. In fact several apparently contradictory trends coexisted together: industrial militancy with political conservatism, unparalleled mobilizations of workers with unyielding and unbowed employers, a Government sometimes harshly repressive but occasionally imposing conciliation and concessions. Far from fulfilling Rosa Luxemburg's hopes, the labour movement as it developed in the years before 1914 proved to be conservative, divided, and above all weak.[11] The present study aims to explore the reasons for this by considering the labour movement itself against the background of workers' social and industrial experience: only in this way is it possible to appreciate the parameters within which the movement appeared and developed, the issues and problems which it faced, and the factors which shaped its character and historical development. The aim is to assess not merely the roots of militancy and radicalism but also the constraints and limitations on it: were the factors which united miners always so much more important than those which divided them? Were strikes in fact the most typical or the most salient of the miners' responses to their situation —or were absenteeism or job-changing, or even passive acceptance, just as characteristic? What were the results —as distinct from the causes—of their strikes? Did they succeed or fail, and why? Above all, did the labour movement succeed in creating effective forms of working-class power?

The answers were important not just for the Ruhr but for the general development of the labour movement in Germany.

(New York, 1979), p. 194; K. Tenfelde, *Sozialgeschichte der Bergarbeiterschaft an der Ruhr im 19. Jahrhundert* (Bonn-Bad Godesberg, 1977); E. Lucas, *Arbeiterradikalismus: Zwei Formen von Radikalismus in der deutschen Arbeiterbewegung* (Frankfurt a. M., 1976); F. J. Brüggemeier, *Leben vor Ort. Ruhrbergleute und Ruhrbergbau 1889–1919* (München, 1983). The latter study includes a useful overview of the historiography of the Ruhr miners.

[11] See also the discussion in Barrington Moore, *Injustice. The Social Bases of Obedience and Revolt* (London, 1978), pp. 227-74.

For although the Ruhr was not straightforwardly 'typical' of the German industrial districts, it was not wholly unique. One of the main lessons of recent work has been that no single locality was quintessentially typical: Germany was a highly diverse society and much of its history was shaped by this fact. Within this diversity the Ruhr was of particular importance in its own right as a major industrial region, a huge concentration of workers, and a prime centre of coal-miners—so often a leading force within labour movements. In addition, however, many of the social and industrial factors which were important there—population growth and geographical mobility, social and cultural divisions within the working class, the character and role of heavy industry, the experience of industrial conflict, and the factors which made for success or failure—were present elsewhere, albeit in different forms.

Nor was the character of the labour movement as it emerged in the Ruhr far out of line with national trends: explicit revisionism was rejected but energies were devoted to building organizations and winning elections, not to making revolution. While the specific causes of the labour movement's pragmatic, non-radical character in the Ruhr doubtless had few exact parallels elsewhere, comparable factors may well have been at work. In contrast, the strength of radicalism in other localities may perhaps be explained by the very different industrial and social patterns which prevailed there.[12] It is not least through the building up and contrasting of such locally-based studies that our understanding of German labour and the German labour movement will be advanced.

[12] See the contrasts drawn in Lucas, *Arbeiterradikalismus* and M. Nolan, *Social democracy and society: working class radicalism in Düsseldorf, 1890–1920* (Cambridge, 1981), pp. 291–3, 305.

1

The Creation of the
Ruhr Working Class

A natural starting-point for any analysis of the social transformation of Germany in the nineteenth century is the
growth of the population. In 1820 the lands which later
comprised the German Empire had some 25 million inhabitants. By the mid-century the figure stood at 34 million and
in 1871 nearly 41 million. By 1890 the population had
reached almost 50 million and by 1910 almost 65 million.
This increase—160 per cent in ninety years—was proportionately slightly less than that of Great Britain over the
same period (190 per cent) but far higher than that of Italy
(83 per cent) or France (30 per cent).[1] It provided the pre-
condition for the economic and social transformation of
Germany in the period.

Such a growth in the number of people living in the same
area naturally created problems for agriculture, their chief
means of support. The problem took two forms. The most
immediate was the simple one of producing sufficient food
for the larger numbers. This did not prove too difficult, at
least in the long run. The output of grain crops in Germany
grew from 123 million quintals per year on average in 1845-54
to 458 million in 1905-14; the total value of agricultural output, expressed in constant (1913) prices, rose from about
4.2 billion marks to 11.2 billion over the same period.[2] In
addition there was the possibility of importing food from
more efficient or larger-scale producers such as America and
Russia providing, of course, that sufficient foreign currency
could be earned in other ways to pay for it.

[1] B. R. Mitchell, *The Fontana Economic History of Europe: Statistical Appendix, 1700-1914* (London, 1971), p. 14; W. R. Lee, 'Germany' in W. R. Lee (ed.), *European Demography and Economic Growth* (London, 1979).
[2] Mitchell, *Economic History of Europe*, pp. 19, 33.

The second problem was that agriculture could no longer provide virtually the whole population with a livelihood. This was clearly felt first in south-western Germany. Here partible inheritance played an important part in reducing peasants' holdings to very small sizes with the result that as the population grew increasing numbers farmed dangerously near the subsistence level. At times of bad harvests, as in the disastrous years of 1816 and 1817, there was serious and widespread distress. Many peasants were forced to leave the land and seek their fortunes elsewhere. For some the situation was worsened by the terms of the emancipation of the peasantry. Fiscal taxes or compensation frequently had to be paid. In areas where partible inheritance was not the rule, money had to be raised to provide for younger sons. This meant borrowing and debts and encouraged peasants to sell out.[3]

In Mecklenburg and Prussia east of the Elbe the rural scene was dominated by large estates. Here the problems of overpopulation was manifested differently. In Mecklenburg the obligation on the local community to provide for the poor relief of its inhabitants, combined with the political control which the big estate-owners exercised over their localities, meant that it was difficult for young men to settle and raise families. Marriage was dependent on the production of a certificate of domicile and this could only be provided by the lord. He in turn tried to keep down potential poor relief costs by ensuring that only those with a clear right to live there or those who were absolutely essential for the estate received such certificates. There was therefore pressure for 'surplus' people to leave the area. In eastern Prussia peasant emancipation was accompanied by an expansion of agricultural production which ensured continued employment for the first decades of the century. It was only in the 1860s that the capacity of agriculture to absorb labour in this area reached an end. In 1868 the Ministry of Commerce was actively seeking job opportunities to relieve distress. The 1870s saw the appearance of cheap foreign grain in bulk, and

[3] I. Ferenczi, 'International Migration Statistics', in W. F. Willcox (ed.), *International Migrations* (New York, 1929) i 116; P. Marschalck, *Deutsche Überseewanderung im 19. Jahrhundert* (Stuttgart, 1973), p. 61; W. Conze, 'Vom Pöbel zum Proletariat', in H. U. Wehler (ed.), *Moderne deutsche Sozialgeschichte* (Köln, 1970), p. 116.

precipitated rationalization and a large-scale exodus from the land.[4]

Agriculture was not the only traditional livelihood which suffered in the nineteenth century. Cottage industries like spinning and weaving were hit by competition from mechanized sources, at first from England but later from within Germany itself. Cottage industry was of importance to many agricultural workers and smallholders who used it to supplement their family's income. The collapse of one source of income could force them to leave the land entirely.

The nineteenth century thus saw a very considerable expansion of the population in Germany and a failure of the traditional means of support—primarily agriculture—to provide employment for them. As a result millions of people left the land and their homes and moved in search of work. Many left Germany entirely. In 1818 an official reported:

The craze to emigrate to America has become an epidemic in the two counties of Wittgenstein and is arousing our special concern . . . . In the neighbouring Hesse-Darmstadt the same wandering spirit is said to have erupted. It is true that invitations from earlier emigrants have arrived in these parts with fair promises of better conditions in America; the local authorities, however, see the main cause for emigration not in these attractions but in poverty and the recent severe difficulties in gaining a livelihood.[5]

There was substantial emigration from Germany throughout the century. After rising sharply after the Napoleonic Wars the rate declined in the 1820s but then rose again. Bad harvests and depression led to large-scale emigration in the 1830s, 1840s, and 1850s. Agricultural depression likewise precipitated the peak emigration of the years 1880 to 1895. After this it fell and there may have been some net immigration into Germany in the remaining years before 1914. Over the period 1840 to 1910 Germany lost around five million emigrants, net of immigrants. The loss caused political concern since the emigrants came in the main from the rural population who were thought by many to represent

[4] Marschalck, *Deutsche Überseewanderung*, pp. 64–6; Tenfelde, *Sozialgeschichte* p. 239.

[5] W. Köllmann, 'The Population of Germany in the Age of Industrialism', in H. Möller (ed.), *Population Movements in Modern European History* (New York, 1964), p. 101.

the strength and core of the nation: Bismarck denounced the emigrant 'who discards his country like an old coat; for me [he] is no longer a German'.[6]

However, not all migrants went abroad. Even more moved to new homes within Germany, to industry and the towns. The latter expanded enormously. In 1850 only four urban centres—Berlin, Hamburg, Breslau, and Dresden—had over 100,000 inhabitants; in 1871 there were eight such centres, and by 1910 the number had risen to 48. Migration was not simply a one-way movement from country to town: there were also patterns of seasonal migration, and considerable movements of people back from the towns to the country-side and from one town to another. Nevertheless, the main overall trend was towards industry and towards the towns.[7] In 1871, 24 per cent of the population lived in towns of 5,000 or more; by 1910, 49 per cent did so, despite the massive increase in the total size of the population in the meantime. Not all the migrants succeeded in finding jobs, particularly in the 1870s and 1880s when the depression was at its height, but industry was eventually able to absorb most of them and from the 1890s Germany ceased to be a net provider of emigrants: 'Through the rise of manu-factures . . . it was possible to retain in the country those surplus workers from the rural districts who had furnished most of the emigrants.'[8] This did not happen in some other parts of Europe: 'In contrast to Ireland . . . a demographic catastrophe [in Germany] was avoided by industrialization.'[9]

This vast upheaval was arguably the most important social

[6] H. U. Wehler, *Bismarck und der Imperialismus* (Köln, 1969), p. 157; F. Burgdörfer, 'Migration across the frontiers of Germany', in Willcox (ed.), *International Migrations* ii 316; Marshalck, *Deutsche Überseewanderung*, pp. 35–7; Lee, 'Germany', pp. 160–1, 192.

[7] W. Köllmann, 'Industrialisierung, Binnenwanderung und "Soziale Frage" ', in *Vierteljahresschrift für Sozial- und Wirtschaftsgeschichte* (1959); D. Lange-wiesche, 'Wanderungsbewegungen in der Hochindustrialisierungsperiode. Regionale, interstädtische und innerstädtische Mobilität in Deutschland 1800–1914', in ibid. (1977).

[8] Burgdörfer, 'Migration', p. 344; W. Köllmann, 'Urbanization in Germany at the height of the industrialization period', in *Journal of Contemporary History* (July, 1969).

[9] Köllmann, 'The Population of Germany in the Age of Industrialism', p. 102. See also Conze, 'Vom Pöbel zum Proletariat'; W. Köllmann, *Bevölkerung in der industriellen Revolution* (Göttingen, 1974), pp. 61–90.

change in nineteenth-century Germany and greatly affected both the economic and social conditions under which industrialization took place. To simplify broadly, the material standards offered to a new labour force were unlikely to be particularly high when the underlying labour market was characterized by a significant and continuing labour surplus and at a time when industrialists were seeking to establish themselves in the face of strong external competition. Indeed, the availability of cheap labour was perhaps a prerequisite for investment in the early stages of industrialization, when risks were high and profits far from assured. On the other hand, with a tight labour market and substantial existing investment in industry, wages and other incentives for labour might be expected to rise. Germany was characterized more by the first than the second condition for most of the century, although towards the end the underlying labour market began to change.

Beyond these economic effects, the migrations created a new social environment and unprecedented problems in all areas of people's lives. The failure of agriculture adequately to support the population and the resultant movements of people from the land eroded the authority of the traditional social élites associated with it: the aristocracy, the churches, and the traditional state structures. Old loyalties and methods of social control ceased to be adequate for the new situation of large masses of people gathered together in towns and working in industry. New social forces appeared to fill the vacuum—employers, trade unions, political parties, and pressure groups; and with them updated manifestations of the older élites—church organizations and political groups which, while continuing to look to the past, adapted to the new conditions in their methods and in so doing helped to further many of the very developments which they sought to obstruct and reverse.

The Ruhr was one district where the problems associated with industrialization appeared in marked form in the later nineteenth century. There had been coal mining in the area for many years, mainly in the south near the river Ruhr itself where the coal lay near the surface. Nevertheless, until the mid-century Bochum and the surrounding area could be described as 'primarily a farming district' which exhibited 'a quite rural character'.[10] The growth of the mining industry was the chief motor behind the industrial transformation of the district in the following years. Despite cyclical fluctuations the demand for coal maintained a rapid growth and production expanded accordingly. The enormous scale of the Ruhr mining industry's expansion is clear from Table 1. The only index which did not maintain its growth was that of the actual number of mines. This was the result of the increasing size of the pits and a growing concentration of production in the hands of relatively small numbers of companies who rationalized production, closed the smaller and less economic mines, and concentrated production at the large ones.

TABLE 1
Coal production in the Ruhr, 1800–1913[a]

Year	No. of mines	Output (000 tons)	Value of output (000 Marks (current))	No. of miners
1800	158	230	1,039	1,546
1850	198	1,666	10,385	12,741
1870	220	11,813	67,626	51,391
1890	177	35,469	282,442	127,794
1913	167	110,812	1,282,013	394,569

[a] M. J. Koch, *Die Bergarbeiterbewegung im Ruhrgebiet zur Zeit Wilhelms II* (Düsseldorf, 1954), p. 139.

One important factor behind the expansion of the industry was the advance in mining technology. The richer coal-seams lie to the north of the river Ruhr itself, indeed in the Emscher rather than the Ruhr basin. However, the further north they lie the deeper they are. This made them virtually unusable until satisfactory solutions could be found to drainage and ventilation problems. It was only in the mid-century that deep-level mining became technically possible in the Ruhr. One of the first deep pits in the eastern district was *Präsident*, opened in 1841 just outside Bochum. The following years

[10] StAB, HKB *Jahresbericht*, 1857; A. Heinrichsbauer, *Industrielle Siedlung im Ruhrgebiet* (Essen, 1936), p. 7.

saw a spate of new deep-level pits: around Bochum, *Baaker Mulde* was sunk in 1855–60, *Dahlhauser Tiefbau* in 1858, *Dannenbaum* in 1859–61 and *Hasenwinkel* in 1860–2.

A further critical factor was a change in the ownership and control of the industry. Until the mid-century the Prussian state had exercised close day-to-day control of the industry, including the details of production, marketing, and labour. The liberalization of the post-1848 period—culminating in a new legal framework in the *Allgemeine Berggesetz* of 1865 —led the state to disengage and leave the private mine-owners to run the Ruhr mines largely—although never entirely—as they wished. It was not until after the turn of the century that growing concern about the concentration of economic power in the hands of the increasingly mono-polistic private companies led to some regrets about the extent of the disengagement and to attempts to regain a direct stake for the state. However, the grandiose plans of Theodor Möller, Prussian Trade Minister, to purchase the third largest coal company in 1904 came to naught and the state's direct ownership in the Ruhr remained limited and uninfluential.[11]

The Ruhr coal industry—in contrast to the position in the Saar, where the state continued to play a dominant role— thus lay in private hands, and although this may not have been an essential prerequisite for exapansion there can be little doubt that the economic liberalization encouraged the speed and scale of the growth. Most companies were owned by shareholders: the most important exception was Krupp, a family concern whose prime interest lay in the metal indus-try but which also had substantial coal interests. Such family companies produced less than 10 per cent of Ruhr coal. Much more important were those owned by a number of shareholders. Increasingly the *Aktien-Gesellschaft* displaced the more traditional *Gewerke* as the predominant com-pany form. Its main advantage was that it facilitated the introduction of external capital—essential to finance the

[11] D. Baudis and H. Nussbaum, *Wirtschaft und Staat in Deutschland vom Ende des 19. Jahrhunderts bis 1918/19* (Berlin-Ost, 1978), p. 171; C. Medalen, 'State Monopoly Capitalism in Germany: the Hibernia Affair', in *Past and Present* lxxviii (1978), p. 109.

heavy investment which the expanding industry required. The result was that ownership commonly lay outside the industry itself: in particular, the banks played an increasingly important role.[12]

Private ownership was not the only significant feature of the control of the coal industry. The later nineteenth and early twentieth centuries saw three important trends: concentration, cartelization, and integration. The concentration of ownership was dramatic: whereas in 1885 only seven companies owned more than one mine, by 1910 a mere nine firms were producing around two-thirds of the Ruhr's total coal output. The three biggest companies—the Gelsenkirchener Bergwerks AG, the Harpener Bergbau AG, and the Bergwerksgesellschaft Hibernia—each produced over five million tons.[13] Concentration of ownership in fewer hands was accompanied by a parallel process of cartelization, enabling closer co-operation between rival companies and minimizing the impact of cyclical fluctuations. Attempts by companies to work together found their first lasting expression in the foundation in 1858 of the Verein für die bergbaulichen Interessen im Oberbergamtsbezirk Dortmund, generally known as the Bergbau Verein. This organization soon included all the major Ruhr mines amongst its members and acted as the industry's spokesman—a position formally recognized by the Government in 1893. It was a member of the national employers' organization, the Zentralverband deutscher Industrieller, and a co-founder of the regional Verein zur Wahrung der gemeinsamen wirtschaftlichen Interessen in Rheinland und Westfalen. A more strictly social forum was provided by the 'Coal Club', founded in 1880 and patronized by many of the leading individuals within the industry.[14]

Perhaps the most significant step, however, was the

[12] Baudis and Nussbaum, *Wirtschaft und Staat*, p. 132; F. Schunder, *Tradition und Fortschritt. Hundert Jahre Gemeinschaftsarbeit im Ruhrbergbau* (Stuttgart, 1959), pp. 62, 226; Tenfelde, *Sozialgeschichte*, p. 198.

[13] Baudis and Nussbaum, *Wirtschaft und Staat*, p. 132; Schunder, *Tradition und Fortschritt*, pp. 213–14.

[14] Schunder, *Tradition und Fortschritt*, pp. 33–4, 48, 214; M. Kealey, 'Kampfstrategien der Unternehmerschaft im Ruhrbergbau seit dem Bergarbeiterstreik von 1889', in H. Mommsen and U. Borsdorf (ed.), *Glück auf, Kameraden! Die Bergarbeiter und ihre Organisationen in Deutschland* (Köln, 1979), pp. 175–97.

establishment of the Kohlen-Syndikat in 1893. This represented a substantial step towards the full cartelization of the industry. Members undertook to sell all their coal to the Syndikat which in turn handled the marketing. Since the great majority of those companies producing for the market (as distinct from those who produced coal only for their own internal use) were soon members of the Syndikat, the new organization rapidly achieved a near-monopolistic position in the market-place. In order to sustain prices and even out fluctuations in demand, members were assigned coal quotas which they were not to exceed. The result was a reduction in price fluctuations and more assured markets for the producers—but at the cost of significant constraints on their freedom to expand their output. This created difficulties for certain companies who were unable to expand production to the optimum technical and commercial levels: larger companies sought to overcome these difficulties by buying up smaller and less efficient mines in order to close them and transfer their quotas to their own more efficient pits. The creation of the Syndikat thus gave added impetus to the concentration of production at the newer and larger pits and in the hands of the giant companies. A further important development was the foundation in 1908 of the Zechen-Verband, with the aim of improving the employers' co-ordination of labour market and industrial relations policies.[15]

Although coal was the largest it was not the only major industry in the district. The high cost of transport encouraged coal-consuming industries to base themselves nearby. The chief customer was the iron and steel industry, and several large plants developed during the second half of the century. In Bochum the major firm was the Bochumer Verein, founded in 1845 by Jacob Meyer and Eduard Kühne with around fifty workers. Meyer provided the technical direction until his death in 1875 but the chief architect of the firm's expansion was Louis Baare. Baare, a former director of the Cologne-Minden Railway, joined the company in 1854 and ran it until 1895, when his son Fritz succeeded him as general director. The work-force rose to 300 in 1855, over

[15] See chapter 5 below.

2,000 by 1870, and over 7,500 by 1913.[16] The company specialized in railway equipment and heavy items such as cylinders for hydraulic machinery, ships' screws, and bells. Unlike its Essen rival, the family firm of Krupp, the Bochumer Verein was not noted for military production. One Cologne paper commented on the two companies: 'Both firms may look each other in the eye confidently and without envy; and, as Goethe observed of Schiller, the older Essen may say of the younger Bochum: "The Germans should consider themselves fortunate to have two fellows such as us." '[17]

In addition to giant companies such as Krupp, Thyssen, Hoesch, and the Bochumer Verein there were a plethora of smaller firms, many of them providing specialist services or products, or subcontracting for their large neighbours. Between them the coal and steel industries overshadowed the economic landscape, so that in 1899 the Bochum Chamber of Commerce could observe that 'in this district [they] are completely dominant in their economic significance. They also dominate the activity of the other branches of industry and commerce and the great mass of the population is directly or indirectly dependent on their prosperity.'[18]

One characteristic of these industries, however, was their tendency to ever-closer integration. 'Vertical integration', whereby a single company undertook all the processes from the mining of the coal, the smelting of the steel, through to the making and marketing of the finished product, was a long-standing practice in the Ruhr. Most of the large steel companies owned one or more mines for their in-house coal needs. The creation of the Syndikat encouraged this trend. The *Hüttenzechen*, as the mines owned and used by the steel companies were known, were not at first members of the Syndikat and hence remained unaffected by quotas and unrestricted in their production. Any coal they produced which was surplus to their company's in-house needs could be sold freely on the open market. They could therefore

[16] The figures relate only to those in the metal-works, not those employed on the company's mines. W. Däbritz, *Bochumer Verein* (Düsseldorf, 1934), Table 8; K. Brinkmann, *Bochum* (Bochum, 1968), pp. 181–4.

[17] *Kölnische Zeitung* (n.d.), quoted in Däbritz, *Bochumer Verein*, p. 177.

[18] StAB, HKB *Jahresbericht*, 1898/9, p. 17.

be run more flexibly and more efficiently than those mines which were members of the Syndikat, which were constrained by quotas. At the same time steel companies without their own pits found themselves at a disadvantage, since the Syndikat's restrictions on output led to coal shortages when demand was high. The result was to increase the attractions of vertical integration and to sharpen the conflict of interest between *Hüttenzechen* and the members of the Syndikat. In 1903 the *Hüttenzechen* were admitted to the Syndikat, but on favourable terms which permitted them to continue to produce unlimited coal for their own steel plants. Existing Syndikat members now also found the creation of close links —or even amalgamation—with steel companies an attractive means of expanding their output beyond their quotas: the pressures are illustrated in a report in 1909 that in the Hordel area the *Hüttenzechen* were working consistently, whereas the 'pure' coal mines were obliged to limit their production and work short time.[19] The last years before the war saw a further burst of integration. The Gelsenkirchener Bergwerks AG, under the direction of Emil Kirdorf, bought up two steel companies and by 1913 was not only Germany's largest single coal producer but also her largest producer of pig-iron. Other newly expanding 'mixed' enterprises included the Deutsch-Luxemburgische Bergwerks und Hütten AG, created by Hugo Stinnes, and the Phönix AG für Bergbau und Hüttenbetrieb. Conversely Hoesch AG, formerly purely a steel company, now acquired coal and other interests. Not all the major mining companies joined the trend: among those which did not do so were Harpen, Haniel, and Hibernia, although even here there were signs of diversification: Harpen bought two shipping firms, giving it the largest coal fleet on the Rhine.[20]

If coal and steel—increasingly concentrated under the control of a handful of giant companies—dominated the economy of the Ruhr, their impact on the physical landscape was no less marked. 'Anyone who knew Bochum, its situation and setting twenty, thirty, forty or fifty years ago and was

---

[19] StAB, 481, *Amt* Hordel to KLB, 17. 8. 1909.
[20] Baudis and Nussbaum, *Wirtschaft und Staat*, p. 150; Schunder, *Tradition und Fortschritt*, p. 224; Medalen, 'State Monopoly Capitalism', pp. 83–4.

to visit her again today and look around after a long absence would hardly know her', wrote the town's mayor during the 1880s, well before the process of change was anything like complete.[21] In 1903 another observer described the new industrial landscape:

Virtually the entire Ruhr mining district between Oberhausen and Dortmund, Duisburg, Hattingen, and Recklinghausen, already has the appearance of a continuous giant city, its individual parts linked by a thick network of electric trams, state railways, and spurs to individual mines, vibrating above and below ground with the most vigorous industrial and mining activity and teeming with a giant army of workers. It is the main artery and workshop of the German coal and iron industry. Everything lives from and for these two products and everything is touched by them. Wherever one looks there are winding towers and the broad outlines of waste-tips, chimneys, and smoking furnaces. The whole scene is enveloped and covered by a misty, gassy, dusty, dirty veil which often scarcely allows the blue sky to be seen and which falls on the rows of houses, churches etc. as a coating of dirt.[22]

Small semi-rural towns became industrial cities and rural hamlets became centres of mining or industry. Even where industry did not settle the side effects were felt. The pastor of Harpen, a village just east of Bochum, described the transformation of his village:

When the *Harpen Gesellschaft* started with the workings people in the parish of Harpen dreamt of a golden economic future and a great development of the village. Unfortunately this did not occur. Even in the vicarage one could hear the miners below the earth firing the coal free. But apart from the old *Karoline* shaft, no great mining establishment ensued. Instead, as if by a frost in a spring night, the aspirations of the parish were dashed. The lovely water meadows in the Wiescher-mühlenbach became boggy, the growth of the trees suffered, nature receded, the potatoes no longer thrived, the song-birds became fewer and the vermin more numerous. A lovely and entirely rural parish with pure air became a country industrial parish. But the worst was that thoroughout Harpen the wells, springs, and ponds dried up. A court action for compensation, brought by the church, was lost. Harpen had the disadvantages but not the advantages of industry.[23]

[21] C. Lange, 'Die Wohnungsverhältnisse der ärmeren Volksklassen in Bochum', in *Schriften des Vereins für Socialpolitik* (Leipzig, 1886), xxx 73.

[22] L. Pieper, *Die Lage der Bergarbeiter im Ruhrgebiet* (Stuttgart and Berlin, 1903), p. 214.

[23] *Pfarrer* Leich, *Harpen und Harpener Bergbau* (Bochum, 1937), p. 11.

The social effects of coal and steel were no less marked than the physical. In the first place, they created a great demand for labour. Despite the considerable capital investment needed to sink mines and build steel mills, both industries were highly labour intensive. However, the labour required was primarily manual. The need for white-collar skills was much more limited, with the result that in the Ruhr workers formed—at least in numerical terms—the dominant social class. In 1907 three-quarters of the economically-active population of both Dortmund and Bochum were classified as manual workers. In the mining villages the proportion was even higher: 'It is in the nature of coal mining that there is, even today, little if any middle-class employment.'[24] Workers formed a higher proportion of the population in the Ruhr than anywhere else in Germany. Moreover, the chances of rising socially out of the manual working class were slim: a few, particularly in the metal industry, were able to rise to supervisory or management jobs; for others, particularly the miners, the best hope was to open a small shop or bar. Overall, however, the number of workers able to find a nonmanual livelihood was very small.[25]

Coal and steel needed male, not female workers. This meant a sharp differentiation of sexual roles. The small textile industry in the area, which had provided women with some earning opportunities, declined and disappeared during the 1870s and 1880s.[26] The 1907 census showed only five Bochum women working in the mining industry, compared with 15,000 men, and seven women employed in foundry work, compared with over 2,500 men. The main jobs open to women seem to have been in shops, domestic service, the garment trade, and 'agriculture'—presumably the cultivation of small plots and allotments. Women comprised only 12 per cent of those classified as economically active in Bochum;

---

[24] R. T. Jackson, 'Mining Settlements in Western Europe', in R. P. Beckinsale and J. M. Houston (ed.), *Urbanization and its Problems* (Oxford, 1968), p. 157; *Statistik des deutschen Reiches* (Berlin) ccvii 152; R. Lützenkirchen, *Der sozialdemokratische Verein für den Reichstagswahlkreis Dortmund-Hörde* (Dortmund, 1970), p. 122; see also I. D. Wolcke, *Die Entwicklung der Bochumer Innenstadt* (Kiel, 1968), pp. 143–5.

[25] Crew, *Town in the Ruhr*, chapter 3; Guttsman, *German Social Democratic Party*, p. 91.

[26] WWA, HKB *Jahresberichte*.

among workers they formed an even smaller proportion—
10 per cent.[27]

The shortage of jobs for women contributed to the persistent numerical predominance of men. Between 1875 and 1905 women represented only around 46–48 per cent of the population of Bochum. This in turn encouraged early marriage —a further reinforcement to the domestic role which women played in the area.[28] Domestic work was hard and unrelenting. The mines operated with two main shifts (normally starting at 6.00 am and 2.00 pm) and a smaller night shift. If, as was common, the men in the house worked different shifts, someone would be setting off for work or returning home, tired and hungry, at all hours of day and night; their patterns differed again from those of the children. Nevertheless, despite the importance of women's work for the family, few working-class women were able to contribute a cash income to the household, unless they took in lodgers or worked at an allotment. There was thus normally no safety-net of women's earnings such as existed in such diverse areas as contemporary London or the Oxfordshire countryside; the general lack of experience even of domestic service meant that workers' wives in the Ruhr were less able to help out their families in times of need by taking in washing or ironing or by doing cleaning than were women in longer-established and more socially mixed towns such as Remscheid.[29]

The growth of the Ruhr industries required a huge increase in the size of the work-force. Some of the demand was met

[27] *Statistik des deutschen Reiches* ccvii. 152, ccix. 329–32.

[28] H. Silbergleit, *Preussens Städte* (Berlin, 1908), pp. 8–9; IZF, *Arbeiter Zeitung* 30. 6. 1914; Pieper, *Lage der Bergarbeiter*, p. 225.

[29] On the position of working-class women in the Ruhr, see L. Fischer-Eckert, *Die wirtschaftliche und soziale Lage der Frauen in dem modernen Industrieort Hamborn im Rheinland* (Hagen, 1913); Lucas, *Arbeiterradikalismus*, pp. 57–70. On women in English mining communities, see N. Dennis, F. Henriques, and C. Slaughter, *Coal is our Life* (London, 1969 edition), chapter V; D. Douglass, 'The Durham Pitman', in R. Samuel (ed.) *Miners, Quarrymen and Saltworkers* (London, 1977), p. 267; B. Williamson, *Class, Culture and Community: a Biographical Study of Social Change in Mining* (London, 1982). For other English examples of the vital role of women's earnings in the working-class family economy, see A. S. Jasper, *A Hoxton Childhood* (London, 1971); R. Samuel, 'Quarry Roughs' in R. Samuel (ed.), *Village Life and Labour* (London, 1975), p. 181.

by seasonal recruitment and migration. In the 1850s many factory workers only worked during the summer months and returned home for the winter. The building trade remained highly seasonal in character, due mostly to the practical difficulties of construction work during the winter: in the winter of 1904 union activity amongst building workers was reported to be spreading from Bochum to Hesse, Eichfeld, and the Paderborn area, 'because the building workers here mostly have their homes in those parts'. Coal-mining also made use of seasonal labour: in the winter of 1889 the *Shamrock* mine near Herne was hiring workers from Hesse-Nassau who worked in agriculture during the summer months and in industry in the winter. Building workers sometimes worked in the mines during the winter. Seasonal labour thus provided a margin to meet the peaks of demand for labour. It also helped cope with the troughs: during the economic downturn of 1902 both miners and laid-off metal-workers were reported to be returning home to work on the farm.[30]

Nevertheless, seasonal migration alone was quite inadequate to meet the voracious demand for labour. Much more important was the general increase in the population of the area. While in the first half of the nineteenth century the population of the Rhineland and Westphalia had hardly increased faster than that of Germany as a whole, during the second half the picture changed radically: between 1880 and 1910 their populations rose by 75 and 102 per cent respectively while that of Germany rose by only 44 per cent.[31] In the industrial areas themselves the growth was even more dramatic. The population of Bochum and the surrounding *Landkreis* rose from under 19,000 in 1855 to nearly 82,000 in 1880 and 256,000 in 1910. Most of the increase came not in the Bochum old town (*Altstadt*) but in the surrounding suburbs and villages. This reflected the importance of the mines in

[30] STAM, RA I 96, *Stadt* Bochum to RPA, 10. 10. 1904; Däbritz, *Bochumer Verein*, p. 86; StAB, 462, *Amt* Herne to KLB, 8. 12. 1889; StAB, *Magistratsbericht*, 1898/9, p. 21; H. Münz, *Die Lage der Bergarbeiter im Ruhrrevier* (Essen, 1909), p. 29; WWA, K2 857, HKB to RPA, 27. 9. 1902, *Gelsenkirchener Gusstahl- und Eisenwerke* to HKB, 20. 9. 1902.

[31] W. Köllmann, 'Die Bevölkerung Rheinland-Westfalens in der Hochindustrialisierungsperiode', in *Vierteljahresschrift für Sozial- und Wirtschaftsgeschichte* (1971); N. J. G. Pounds, *The Ruhr* (London, 1952), p. 89. See also Lee, 'Germany', p. 178.

providing jobs: only one pit—*Präsident*—was situated in close proximity to the town itself.

Some of the population growth came from indigenous causes. The annual birth-rate in Bochum reached over 60 per thousand in the mid-1870s and although it fell to under 50 per thousand by 1882, it was not until 1911 that it fell below 40 per thousand. The death-rate was considerably lower: between 1875 and 1886 it fluctuated between 35 and 28 per thousand; between 1887 and 1903 it was between 29 and 21 per thousand; between 1905 and 1912 the figure lay between 20 and 15 per thousand.[32] As Table 2 demonstrates, the surplus in Bochum and other Ruhr towns was far higher than in Germany as a whole.

TABLE 2

Surplus of births over deaths, per thousand inhabitants[a]

	Germany	Bochum	Essen	Dortmund	Witten	Gelsenkirchen
1865–7	9.3	7.1	9.6	18.0	19.1	–
1868–71	9.0	10.8	19.7	16.9	16.2	–
1872–5	12.1	26.6	28.2	18.9	–	–
1876–80	13.2	26.0	20.6	22.3	21.4	–
1881–5	11.3	21.6	17.3	19.8	19.4	–
1886–90	12.1	19.5	18.1	18.3	16.2	24.5
1891–5	13.0	20.3	20.6	20.0	15.9	25.8
1896–1900	14.8	17.9	22.3	21.9	16.7	22.3
1901–5	14.4	20.3	27.9	22.2	16.3	33.9

[a]P. Wiel, *Wirtschaftsgeschichte des Ruhrgebietes* (Essen, 1970), p. 77.

Births and deaths, however, do not tell anything like the full story of the population increase. We have already seen that vast numbers of people in nineteenth-century Germany moved in search of new opportunities: the Ruhr was one of their main destinations. In Bochum the new arrivals numbered between twenty and thirty per cent of the existing population almost every year during the 1890s and 1900s, and even when the considerable numbers leaving the town were discounted most years saw a significant net surplus.[33] Moreover, the fact that migrants tended to be younger

[32] StAB, *Magistratsberichte.*
[33] *Statistisches Jahrbuch deutscher Städte* (Breslau).

people of child-bearing age itself helped to boost the birth-rate. Migrants formed an actual majority of the population. Even in 1871 only five out of 22 Bochum *Gemeinden* had more natives than immigrants and only one-third of the inhabitants of the town were actually born there. In 1907 over 63 per cent of Bochum's inhabitants were immigrants—a slightly higher proportion than in some other Ruhr towns: in Gelsenkirchen the figure was 61 per cent, in Dortmund 58 per cent. In the western Ruhr the proportion fell to 53 per cent in Essen and 51 per cent in Duisburg. The proportion of immigrants was even higher in the surrounding *Landkreise* than in the towns themselves. As Köllmann has observed: 'the decisive element in the formation of the population of the large cities was immigration.'[34]

If migration was an essential factor behind the growth of the population as a whole, it was particularly so for the working-class section of society. In 1907 some 63 per cent of Bochum's population were immigrants and 24 per cent had come long distances (i.e., from beyond the Rhineland and Westphalia). Table 3 shows, however, that amongst the workers in almost all the main occupational groups the proportions were far higher. When we speak of the working class in the Ruhr at this time, therefore, we are referring to a group composed overwhelmingly of people who had moved to a new home, frequently over long distances.

This fact had major implications for the character of the newly forming working class. In the first place, since many had come to escape from bad conditions at home, their aspirations may have been relatively modest—at least by the standards of the society to which they moved if not in comparison with what they had left behind. As one contemporary noted:

[34] W. Köllmann, 'Binnenwanderung und Bevölkerungsstrukturen der Ruhrgrossstädte', in *Soziale Welt* ix (1958), p. 220; Westfälischer Verein zur Förderung des Kleinwohnungswesens, *Ergebnisse der Wohnungsaufnahme in westfälischen Städten vom 1. Dez. 1905* (Münster, 1907/1909) ii 10–11; H. Croon, 'Studien zur Sozial- und Siedlungsgeschichte der Stadt Bochum', in P. Busch, H. Croon, and C. Hahne (ed.), *Bochum und das mittlere Ruhrgebiet* (Paderborn, 1965), p. 122.

TABLE 3

Migrants as percentage of manual workers, Bochum 1907[a]

Workers in occupational group:	*Immigrants*	*Long distance immigrants*
Quarries	98	84
Mines	84	37
Construction	83	50
Transport	82	31
Food	77	19
Engineering	71	40
Metals	69	42
Timber	68	36
Commerce	61	20
Total population	63	24

[a] *Statistik des deutschen Reiches* ccx. ii. 194 ff.

The cause of their mass migration to the west is to be found in the bad economic and social position in which they find themselves at home. The critical relations east of the Elbe make it explicable that the Poles find earnings in the west extremely high and enticing and that they move there in large numbers.[35]

Despite such motivation, however, the demand for new labour in the Ruhr was so great that employers sometimes had to resort to recruiting campaigns. Early attempts to attract workers from Upper Silesia were made during the boom years of the early 1870s and the practice of sending recruiting agents to the east became common from the late 1880s. High wages and cheap housing were the main inducements. Sometimes the promises exceeded the reality: in 1896 advertisements appeared in the *Zwickauer Wochenblatt* promising wages of up to six marks per shift at the *General Blumenthal* pit near Recklinghausen, when in practice the average wage for hewers there was only 3.80 marks. The mine management denied that they had endorsed the advertisements and said that they had not produced many applicants.[36]

[35] Pieper, *Lage der Bergarbeiter*, p. 16.
[36] STAM, *Oberbergamt* Dortmund 1400; L. Schofer, *The formation of a modern labor force: Upper Silesia, 1865-1914* (Berkeley, 1975), pp. 73-7.

A similar occurrence in 1910 led to a near riot at the *Rhein-Elbe* pit near Gelsenkirchen: men had been recruited from the Hohensalza area on promises of five marks a shift and company housing; when they arrived, however, they found that the wages were only 3.80 marks and that the homes were not available; around 100 men gathered angrily together and in a violent mood demanded their papers back; the police were brought in to preserve the peace and a large number of the disillusioned men eventually returned to their homes.[37]

Despite such incidents the tide of immigration continued. One result was that many workers did not have deep roots in the district or a commitment to any one locality within it. Some saw their time in the Ruhr as a temporary phase, designed to earn sufficient capital to buy land or a small business back home. Families were often left behind initially, until the migrant had had a chance to establish himself and perhaps to realize what a long haul his stay might be. Post offices were full after pay-days with migrants sending money home, and a high proportion of the deposits in Polish banks in the east came from migrants in the west. The Poles, it was claimed, 'almost without exception return home as soon as they have accumulated a substantial sum of money'.[38] One such was Antoni Podeszwa, born in Upper Silesia, who in 1889 followed his six brothers to the Ruhr in search of work: after seventeen years, during which he was active in the Polish miners' union, he returned home with savings of 4,000 marks and set himself up as a farmer. Such success was no doubt unusual: not only was it far from easy to save such sums, but land prices in the east were rising under the pressure of demand. Finally, in 1904 a change to the law made it far more difficult for Poles henceforth to buy small-holdings in the east.[39]

[37] STAM, *Oberbergamt* Dortmund 1840, *Arbeiter Zeitung*, 11. 1. 1910. See also chapter 2 below.

[38] StAB, 450, *Amt* Bochum I to KLB, 27. 7. 1899; Pieper, *Lage der Bergar-beiter*, pp. 246–7; Koch, *Bergarbeiterbewegung*, p. 72.

[39] Schofer, *Formation of a modern labor force*, p. 52; Fischer-Eckert, *Lage der Frauen*, pp. 83 ff.; H. Linde, 'Die soziale Problematik der masurischen Agrar-gesellschaft und die masurische Einwanderung in das Emscherrevier' in Wehler (ed.), *Moderne deutsche Sozialgeschichte*, p. 469; G. Kliss, *Die Wanderung der*

The continuing demand for labour throughout the Ruhr, combined with the widespread absence of strong local roots and commitments, meant that there was also considerable movement within the district. Internal mobility and job-changing were facilitated by the removal, during the liberalization period of the 1850s and 1860s, of restrictions on the freedom of employees to change their place of work. The merger of the individual miners' social and insurance organizations—the *Knappschaften*—also reduced the impediments to movement.[40] The rate of annual departures from Bochum, like the rate of arrivals, was high. Crew found that from a sample of Bochum miners in 1880, only 39 per cent remained in the town ten years later and only 19 per cent in 1901. The figures for factory workers and day-labourers were broadly comparable; skilled builders and artisans, on the other hand, were much more stable.[41] Table 4 illustrates the high and persistent overall level of job-changing in the mining industry.

Occasionally, large groups moved together from one pit and one locality to another. In 1905 the *Deutscher Kaiser* mine near Oberhausen tried to recruit men in Langendreer, outside Bochum. The *Deutscher Kaiser* manager, who had formerly worked at *Neu Iserlohn* near Langendreer, offered wages of 5.50 marks at a time when average earnings for hewers in the Ruhr stood at 4.86 marks a shift. In the end around 300 Langendreer men took up the offer. Many were Poles or Italians, and about half were married. A Dortmund paper commented;

The reason why the miners change their homes so easily is to be found in the conditions offered to them. They receive a good wage, free transport of their belongings, and the rent they owe here is covered.

Ostpreussen nach Bochum um die Jahrhundertwende in Zuge der Ost–West–Wanderung (Seminararbeit, Bochum, 1971), p. 8; C. Klessmann, *Polnische Bergarbeiter im Ruhrgebiet 1870–1945* (Göttingen, 1978), p. 65.

[40] The three Ruhr *Knappschaften* finally merged in 1890. Tenfelde, *Sozialgeschichte*, pp. 177–91, 282–91; Schofer, *Formation of a modern labor force*, pp. 79 ff. On the establishment of the labour market in the Ruhr, see K. Tenfelde, 'Arbeiterschaft, Arbeitsmarkt und Kommunikationsstrukturen im Ruhrgebiet in den 50er Jahren des 19. Jahrhunderts', in *Archiv für Sozialgeschichte* xvi (Bonn, 1976), pp. 30–8.

[41] Crew, *Town in the Ruhr*, p. 168.

TABLE 4

Hirings and departures as percentage of all miners
employed, Ruhr mines, 1896–1913[a]

	Hirings	Departures		Hirings	Departures
1896	49	40	1905	38	34
1897	59	45	1906	57	49
1898	59	49	1907	71	56
1899	63	51	1908	63	58
1900	68	52	1909	52	51
1901	54	47	1910	50	58
1902	48	44	1911	62	59
1903	58	48	1912	69	61
1904	54	48	1913	78	69

[a] Figures from the *Allgemeine Knappschaftsverein*, printed in Koch, *Bergarbeiter-bewegung*, p. 24. They do not agree exactly with those published in the official *Zeitschrift für das Bergbau-, Hütten- und Salinenwesen*, but the differences are minor. 'Departures' includes deaths.

In addition, the director of the *Deutscher Kaiser* pit, where the men have found work, is well liked by the miners since he used to be mine manager of Shaft I [of *Neu Iserlohn*].

Most of the migrants left together on 31 August:

This morning there was a great deal of activity in the streets leading to the station, with miners carrying packed suitcases. With a few exceptions these men have left the mines here and will take up work in the Oberhausen area. The departure of so many workers is a hard blow for the locality.[42]

But such mass movements were not the normal form of internal migration within the Ruhr. More common was the individual miner or relatively small group who became dissatisfied with the earnings or conditions at one pit and sought something better elsewhere. At the *Mons Cenis* mine near Herne the coal was particularly difficult to work and in the 1880s miners left so frequently that the very existence of the pit was in question.[43] Others left involuntarily:

[42] STAM, RA I 1485, *Dortmunder Zeitung*, 20. 8. 1905, 2. 9. 1905; KLB to RPA, 1. 9. 1905.
[43] *Festschrift zum 100-jährigen Bestehen der Gewerkschaft ver. Constantin der Grosse* (Essen, 1948), p. 32.

particularly in the aftermath of strikes 'agitators' were liable to dismissal.

Job-changing did not necessarily involve moving house. The mines of the Ruhr were often near enough to make it possible for a man to find a new job within walking distance of his home. In 1893 the young August Schmidt (later chairman of IG Bergbau und Energie) and his father were sacked from the *Germania* pit near Dortmund after participating in a strike; they eventually found work at *Graf Schwerin* near Castrop, two hours walk away.[44] Nevertheless, it was frequently necessary or convenient for a man who wished to take a new job to find a new home at the same time. If he had lived in a company home he had no choice.

Not all those who left one pit immediately sought a job at another. Some left the industry completely, because of invalidity or because they found a different job elsewhere. Others left the mines for a while but returned later: some, as we have seen, worked in the building industry or agriculture during the summer months and returned to the pits in the winter when those trades became slack and demand for coal was high. At the large *Hannover* and *Hannibal* pits to the north of Bochum between 60 and 80 per cent of those who left each year went straight on to another mine.[45]

The overall level of job-changing in the industry fluctuated with cyclical economic changes. During upswings—culminating in 1900, 1907, and 1913—turnover increased, reflecting the growing demand for labour and the opportunities for individual miners to find alternative work at other pits. When the economy faltered—as in 1901 and 1908—turnover fell. Nevertheless, between 1896 and 1913, 1905 was the only year in which the numbers starting and leaving jobs both fell significantly below half of the total number of men employed at the time. (1905 was abnormal because of an industry-wide strike, followed by severe restrictions on

[44] A. Schmidt, *Lang war der Weg* (Bochum, 1958), pp. 18–19.
[45] BA, 20/C 116, 117, 119 *Hannibal* and *Hannover Jahresberichte*. The figures cover the years 1900–1910. The later *Arbeitsnachweis* indicated that only around half the miners who left one pit went on directly to another, with a third of the remainder returning to the industry later; however, these statistics were probably incomplete. Koch, *Bergarbeiterbewegung*, p. 121.

job-changing.) Despite cyclical fluctuations, high labour turnover was endemic in the mines throughout this period.[46] Nor was job-changing limited to the mining industry. Even in 1877 and 1878, during the depths of the depression, the Bochumer Verein had around 2,200 hirings and resignations each year at a time when the total work-force stood at between 2,500 and 2,700. The Chamber of Commerce commented:

It is self-evident that with such a constant coming and going thorough training for the individual workers in their tasks is made extraordinarily difficult and the productivity as well as the prosperity of a large works is severely affected. In this respect the English and Belgian firms, who enjoy a much more stable and better-schooled work force, have a great advantage over us. The reason for this turnover of workers lies essentially in their low incomes, which they hope to improve in some other job— usually without success. The less productive older workers stay true to the company, while the younger ones are encouraged to leave by the necessary wage reductions.[47]

Normally, however, high labour turnover was particularly prevalent during economic booms. In 1899, for instance, the Westfälische Stahlwerke in Weitmar, to the south of Bochun, experienced very high turnover. In March alone it was reported that nearly 200 workers had left, when the total work-force stood at some 1,540. The company concluded that they would have to introduce a system of one month's notice on both sides.[48] The following year saw the end of the boom. The Chamber of Commerce reported:

Industrial relations were generally satisfactory this year [1900]. There were no stoppages. There were frequent complaints about the high turnover of workers and also about a noticeable drop in productivity, particularly from the smaller firms. With the change in the economic cycle, the end of the labour shortage, and the possibility of laying off inefficient workers, there has been an improvement . . .[49]

[46] Turnover appears to have been somewhat higher in the Ruhr than elsewhere in Germany, although it was none the less high in Upper Silesia. Tenfelde, *Sozialgeschichte*, p. 231; H. G. Kirchhoff, *Die staatliche Sozialpolitik im Ruhrbergbau* (Köln and Opladen, 1958), p. 161; Schofer, *Formation of a modern labor force*, pp. 124–31; Langewiesche, 'Wanderungsbewegungen'.

[47] StAB, HKB *Jahresbericht*, 1878, pp. 5–6. This report was almost certainly written by Louis Baare.

[48] IZF, *Volksblatt*, 25. 3. 1899.   [49] StAB, HKB *Jahresbericht*, 1900.

The next boom reached its peak in 1907 and again there was a spate of complaints about job-changing. One large engineering firm (not named) claimed that on the monthly pay-days up to one-third of the workers gave notice.[50] One Gelsenkirchen firm with around 890 workers saw 375 departures in 1906 and 750 in 1907. The problem was common throughout the region and some firms resorted to special premium payments to discourage job-changing and poor working. The 1907 factory inspectorate report for the eastern Ruhr confirmed these stories:

> The labour turnover in the industrial works was unusually great in most areas up to around the end of the year. It degenerated into a disaster for some works. The great turnover of the first three quarters, following cyclical conditions, is the result of the fact that the workers easily change their place of work during upswings when there is a general demand for labour. The dismissals resulting from the slackening business situation evidently played a part in the turnover of the last quarter. Those works employing a large number of unskilled workers have had the greatest part of the turnover. The large iron and steel works have particularly suffered. Up to 135 per cent of their average work force have given notice in these works.[51]

In 1913 too a Bochum employer complained about the way in which his workers would not settle down:

> As a result of plant expansion I had to take on more workers. But to an extraordinary degree the men lack a sense of duty and a concern for lasting employment, so that of the many I have taken on only a very few stay permanently or for a long time and the turnover is very high. It was certainly encouraged by the fact that I operated without a system of mutual notice, so that the workers could leave when they liked. After the introduction of a requirement of two weeks' notice the turnover has not been so great.[52]

The turnover figures conceal some differences between groups of workers. One observer reported: 'The fluctuation is particularly prevalent amongst the unmarried workers and the Poles.'[53] The official *Zeitschrift für das Bergbau-, Hütten- und Salinenwesen* commented in 1909: 'As in the past, the turnover came less from the older hewers and more from the

[50] ibid., 1907.
[51] STAM, RA I GA 493, *Gewerbeaufsicht* report for *Regierungsbezirk* Arnsberg, 1907, p. 28.   [52] StAB, HKB *Jahresbericht*, 1913, p. 13.
[53] Pieper, *Lage der Bergarbeiter*, p. 126.

younger, single men, the apprentice hewers, the hauliers (*Schlepper*) and brake-boys (*Bremser*), who are inclined to leave their former places of work for trivial reasons.'[54] These comments were supported by the results of an official inquiry into pit closures in 1904: in the first six months some 28 per cent of the men employed at the six Bochum pits affected had left for new areas; but while this included 39 per cent of the single men, only 16 per cent of the married men had gone and hardly any of those married men who owned their own homes. The higher mobility of the young workers and to a lesser extent of recent immigrants reflected their fewer ties and responsibilities.[55] Job-changing does not, however, appear to have varied significantly from one part of the Ruhr to another. While the young, the single, and immigrants may have been more disposed to move than other workers, we should not forget that these groups between them comprised a substantial majority of the whole labour force. Movement can fairly be described as a general characteristic of working-class life in the Ruhr—as indeed it was elsewhere in industrializing Germany.[56]

A consequence of this widespread movement of people into and within the Ruhr was the creation and strengthening of cultural and ethnic divisions within the emerging working class. The hostility and suspicion which many natives felt towards newcomers was reflected in a report in 1881 by the Bochum Chamber of Commerce which claimed that the increase in 'bodily injuries, moral offences, resistance to state authority and general actions and crimes stemming from rough dispositions was undoubtedly a consequence of the renewed influx of many dubious elements into our district'.[57] We shall see in the next chapter how housing patterns helped to reinforce social and cultural divisions, particularly

---

[54] *Zeitschrift für das Bergbau-, Hütten- und Salinenwesen im Preussischen Staate*, 1909, p. 233. On the categories of mineworker, see chapter 4 below.

[55] WWA, K2 213, *Denkschrift betr. die Stillegung verschiedener Steinkohlen-zechen des Ruhr-Reviers*. See also Crew, *Town in the Ruhr*, pp. 62-4.

[56] *Zeitschrift für das Bergbau-, Hütten- und Salinenwesen* 1907, p. 609. On the high degree of working-class mobility in Germany generally, see L. Niethammer and F. Brüggemeier, 'Wie wohnten Arbeiter im Kaiserreich? ', in *Archiv für Sozialgeschichte* xvi (Bonn, 1976); Langewiesche, 'Wanderungsbewegungen'; Brüggemeier, *Leben vor Ort*, p. 61.

[57] StAB, HKB *Jahresbericht*, 1881.

between natives and immigrants. But the newcomers themselves were also far from united. Most came from the Rhineland or Westphalia but a substantial minority (a quarter of the entire population of Bochum in 1907) came from further afield. Half of these came from the north-east provinces of East and West Prussia and Posen, 11 per cent from Hessen and Waldeck, and a third from other parts of Germany. Six per cent came from abroad, chiefly from Austria, the Netherlands, and Italy. It was estimated that over twenty 'languages and idioms' were spoken in the Ruhr.[58]

The most distinctive single group of immigrants was the Poles. Because of the partition of the historical kingdom of Poland they were not classified as a distinct national group: most of those in the Ruhr were German citizens. Consequently there are no exact figures for the number of Poles in the area. The usual index used is the number of Polish speakers, although this creates problems since it includes Masurians who, although generally Polish-speaking, were Protestant and strongly anti-Polish and pro-German in outlook; it could also include those with two languages. Different censuses give very different results. According to the official Prussian statistics, while there were only sixteen Polish speakers in the Rhineland and Westphalia in 1861, the number had grown to over 33,000 by 1890, and reached 131,000 in 1900 and 279,000 in 1910. In the town of Bochum it was estimated that Polish speakers formed 2 per cent of the population in 1890 and nearly 5 per cent in 1910; the proportion in the *Landkreis* in the latter year was said to be 9 per cent. According, however, to the biennial census carried out in Westphalia, from 1904 onwards Polish speakers formed around a fifth of the population of the *Landkreis*. Of these Polish speakers around two in five were Masurians.[59]

---

[58] Köllmann, 'Binnenwanderung und Bevölkerungsstrukturen', p. 220; *Statistisches Jahrbuch deutscher Städte* xi; StAB, 481, RPA to *Minister des Innern*, 28. 11. 1907.

[59] H. U. Wehler, 'Die Polen im Ruhrgebiet', in Wehler (ed.), *Moderne deutsche Sozialgeschichte*, pp. 437–55; R. T. Schnadt, *Bochum. Wirtschaftsstruktur und Verflechtung einer Grossstadt des Ruhrgebietes* (Bochum, 1936), p. 13; Kliss, *Wanderung der Ostpreussen*, p. 9. See also Croon, 'Studien', p. 99; Klessmann, *Polnische Bergarbeiter im Ruhrgebiet*, pp. 37–43.

Whatever the precise numbers the impact of these immigrants was considerable. All the major shops displayed a sign:
Ustaja polski—Polish spoken here.[60] Like other immigrants
the Poles tended to live amongst and marry others from their
homeland. It was reported that the Poles in south Bochum
'almost all teach their children to read and write Polish.
They stay more and more together and avoid everything
German.'[61] Polish social and religious clubs proliferated and
there were Polish shops, banks, and building societies. The
Poles tended to concentrate in certain geographical districts:
in 1899 Horsthausen, near Herne, was described as 'populated
predominantly by Poles' and in 1910 areas such as Bergen
and Gerthe (both to the north of Bochum) had well above
the average number of Poles while Querenburg (to the south)
and Harpen (to the east) had very few. The concentrations
were often around particular mines: as early as 1899 it was
claimed that 'nineteen pits can practically be described as
Polish mines, since more than half their workers are Poles
or German-Poles.'[62] The tendency to create a largely autonomous Polish sub-culture within the Ruhr was vigorously
encouraged by the Polish nationalists, who became an
increasingly powerful cultural and political force. In 1898
their paper urged: 'Polish parents! Teach your children to
speak, read and write Polish! He who allows his offspring
to become German is no Pole'; in the following year the
Poles were warned of the dangers of marrying non-Poles
and urged to reflect on the exemplary Princess Wanda of
Cracow, who had killed herself rather than marry a German
prince.[63]

The historical circumstances in which it emerged thus had
significant effects on the character of the working class in
the Ruhr. Throughout the pre-1914 period it was a class
in the very process of formation, with its numerical growth
fuelled both by the need of people in many parts of Germany

[60] Pieper, *Lage der Bergarbeiter*, p. 241.

[61] StAB, 482, *Amt* Bochum II to KLB, 13. 8. 1914; Croon, 'Studien', p. 95.

[62] Pieper, *Lage der Bergarbeiter*, p. 20; Croon, 'Studien', p. 99. See also
W. Brepohl, *Der Aufbau des Ruhrvolkes im Zuge der Ost–West Wanderung* (Recklinghausen, 1948), pp. 244–5.

[63] *Wiarus Polski*, 4. 1. 1898, quoted in *Westfälische Allgemeine Zeitung*,
30. 5. 1972; StAB, 450, *Wiarus Polski*, 15. 7. 1899.

to find new sources of livelihood and by the voracious demand for labour from the expanding Ruhr industries. The nature of these industries fostered a rigid differentiation of sex roles, making the 'work' area virtually a male preserve and rendering families crucially dependent on the men's wages. Numerically the workers formed the dominant social class with few opportunities for advancement into non-manual work; yet because so many were recently arrived from different parts of Germany and abroad they had no common cultural or social background and a significant minority did not even speak German. Internal migration and job-changing was common and contributed further to the unsettled nature of the new society. In Germany as a whole it has been suggested that up to one-third of rented dwellings were vacated within one year, while only a small minority were inhabited by the same person for longer than five years: it was common in many towns to see a relatively settled bourgeoisie contrasting with 'a constantly mobile working class'.[64] The Ruhr was clearly no exception. The 'working class', therefore, was not an established, settled, cohesive community; instead, we see a class numerically strong but socially disorientated, geographically unsettled, and culturally diffuse.

[64] Niethammer and Brüggemeier, 'Wie wohnten Arbeiter? ', p. 84; Lange-wiesche, 'Wanderungsbewegungen', p. 10.

2

Housing

The transformation of the Ruhr threw up new issues and problems. One was housing. Difficulties first appeared in Bochum in the 1860s, under the impact of the growing population. In 1861 the town authorities complained:

With the rapid population growth of the last few years the housing question has also appeared here in an acute form. The rents rise quite enormously, often up to three times their former levels, and the housing shortage nonetheless remains very great.[1]

Three years later the problem seemed even worse:

One evil from which the labouring classes here also suffer and which becomes worse from day to day is the lack of sufficient housing. A walk amongst our workers' homes again and again reveals a situation which is not worse in the largest cities. A large number of families share their limited accommodation with one or with several lodgers. The same rooms often serve for living, sleeping, cooking, washing, and for all other domestic activities. People of all ages and both sexes are not separated.[2]

Nevertheless, building did go ahead to try to meet the increasing demand for housing. The boom of the early 1870s led to a growth in speculative house building, often by small builders. The Griesenbach quarter in the south-west of Bochum saw the most new building, with entire streets being laid down. The area was not very suitable, being poorly drained and sometimes afflicted with standing water. The quality of the new buildings was often poor. Despite their limitations, however, the new houses eliminated the worst of the shortage: 'At the beginning of 1873 there was a definite shortage of homes, especially medium and small ones; by the end of the year, however, this had essentially been overcome.'[3]

[1] StAB, *Magistratsbericht*, 1861, p. 8.
[2] ibid., 1864, p. 4.
[3] ibid., 1873, p. 13; Croon, 'Studien' p. 92.

The depression of the 1870s meant that wages fell and the town's population ceased to grow. The bottom dropped out of the housing market. In 1875 the first effects were felt: 'There was a definite surplus of homes, especially in the south-west of the town and in the new streets in other parts, and as a result the rents have fallen, sometimes quite markedly compared with last year.'[4] A year later the situation was even more dramatic: 'Whole rows of houses are standing empty, particularly at the edge of town, and rents are still falling rapidly, particularly in the more outlying parts.'[5] By the late 1870s new building had come to a virtual halt.[6]

The crash of the 1870s implanted a lasting caution in the minds of private builders in Bochum. Henceforth, before committing themselves they were more careful to ensure that demand was strong and likely to last. This was particularly the case with cheaper accommodation, of the sort that working-class families could afford, since it was they who were most vulnerable to economic fluctuations. Building for the more expensive market was a safer bet:

Our housing situation has shown an astonishing elasticity, when one recalls that in 1876, with a population of around 28,000, there were just about as many homes available as in 1882 with a population of around 38,000. Even today [1883], when there has been a definite improvement in the rent situation, at least as far as the landlord is concerned, it is still true that despite the years of stagnation in private building there is no shortage of good and medium class housing, whereas there is a need for workers' houses—a need which grows more and more with the expansion of industry.[7]

The Chamber of Commerce noted 'a particular shortage of suitable accommodation for workers, because practically all new building is concerned exclusively with providing larger homes'.[8]

The 1880s saw the start of economic recovery and a revived demand for labour. Population growth resumed its hectic path. This, combined with the reluctance of private

[4] StAB, *Magistratsbericht*, 1874, p. 25.
[5] ibid., 1876, p. 15.
[6] Lange, 'Wohnungsverhältnisse', p. 78.
[7] StAB, *Magistratsbericht*, 1881/2.
[8] WWA, HKB *Jahresbericht*, 1884.

builders to build appropriate housing, created a veritable
housing crisis. Workers' housing conditions became much
worse even as the worst of the slump (and with it unemployment and low wages) ended. This was reflected in the growth
of homelessness in the early 1880s: in 1883 it became so
significant a problem that for the first time the town authorities were compelled to intervene, putting some homeless
families in the isolation hospital. In summer 1884 fear of
a possible cholera outbreak meant that the hospital was
needed for its proper function and a special barracks was
built for homeless and destitute families. By October, 20
families were living there paying a rent of one mark a week,
which they earned by breaking stones for the town. The
town's annual report emphasized the moral failings of those
needing help:

> The families who have been helped belong to the dregs of society,
> though only two of them are being permanently helped from public
> poor relief. Drink and idleness were for most of them the cause of
> their homelessness. Landlords would not accept them even when
> rooms were free because they could not rely on the rent being paid.[9]

But the mayor of Bochum also pointed out in a special study
that the situation was primarily the result of the housing
shortage. Even when rent was guaranteed and even when
the poor relief authorities had made the 'greatest conceivable
efforts' to find private accommodation, no result was achieved
'because due to the immigration from outside all the accommodation in the town was occupied; and because there was
an absolute shortage of homes for the working population
of the town, as has been confirmed by official researches'.[10]

Homelessness and destitution remained major problems
throughout the 1880s. In 1885 a second barracks was opened,
and in 1889 the isolation hospital also had to be brought
back into service:

> Because of the high rents, particularly for small homes, and the most
> varied factors which must mostly be blamed on the unreliability and
> unsoundness of the persons concerned, homelessness was suffered by
> various families. Even though various workers' houses have been built

---

[9] StAB, *Magistratsbericht*, 1884, pp. 44–5.
[10] Lange, 'Wohnungsverhältnisse', p. 88.

their number stands in no relation to the growth of working-class families.[11]

Building did not keep pace with the need. There was particularly little speculative building, and what there was was aimed primarily at the richer market. In 1890 the town authorities could report that, thanks to the building of the previous two years, 'the demand for better and medium class housing can be regarded as adequately met for the immediate future, while housing for workers remains in short supply and relatively expensive.'[12] The number of homeless people accommodated by the poor relief authorities did not reach its peak until 1891, when over 300 people were housed in the barracks. The figure dropped subsequently, fluctuating in the region of 100 to 170 until 1909, after which it fell still lower.[13]

The 1890s saw an increase in the amount of housing available. In 1900 the Chamber of Commerce estimated that in its district (including Gelsenkirchen, Witten, Hattingen, and Herne in addition to Bochum) the population had grown by around 40 per cent between 1892 and 1899, while the building licences issued for housing increased by nearly 70 per cent: 'in general there is no longer a real shortage of housing'.[14] Homelessness did not reappear before the war as a major social problem. The reports on housing in the town's annual reports became brief. When, following the example of other cities, a 'building advisory office' was established in Bochum in 1911, its main concern was with the aesthetics of new buildings.[15]

Nevertheless, although absolute destitution and homelessness declined, the underlying situation remained gloomy. Rents were high. In the early 1880s many working-class families were thought to be paying over a fifth of their

[11] StAB, *Magistratsbericht*, 1889/90, p. 53.

[12] ibid., p. 43.

[13] StAB, *Magistratsberichte*.

[14] WWA, HKB *Jahresbericht*, 1899. In Duisburg too the overall situation, which had worsened during the 1880s, eased after 1890: J. H. Jackson, 'Overcrowding and Family Life', in R. J. Evans and W. R. Lee (ed.), *The German Family* (London, 1981), p. 207.

[15] StAB, *Magistratsbericht*, 1911, p. 109.

income in rent.[16] In 1905 a housing association, the West-fälischer Verein zur Förderung des Kleinwohnungswesens, made an extensive survey of housing standards in several Westphalian towns, concentrating on the small dwellings of up to five rooms in which the bulk of the population lived. They regarded fifteen per cent of a family's income as a reasonable rent but concluded that in Bochum and most Ruhr towns a great many families were paying above this level. Average annual earnings for mineworkers in the Ruhr in 1905 were slightly under 1,200 marks and average earnings in the Bochumer Verein's steel and engineering works were about 1,270 marks. Average annual rents in Bochum varied according to the size of the dwelling—150 marks for a two-room dwelling, 225 marks for three rooms, 275 for four rooms, and 333 marks for five rooms. Clearly, family circum-stances differed considerably and the data do not permit a detailed comparison of family income with expenditure on rent. Nevertheless, we are justified in concluding that many families were compelled either to live in extremely cramped conditions or pay a rent high in relation to their income —or both.[17]

Many families did indeed live on top of one another. The Verein took as their measure of overcrowding a density of over two people per room (including the kitchen). Table 5 illustrates the extent of overcrowding in a number of Ruhr towns, taking both this and the less extreme density of over one person per room as criteria. Münster and Arnsberg repre-sent non-industrial controls.

The survey related only to small homes, those of up to five rooms. But even from this it is clear that a very substantial proportion of the housing stock was severely overcrowded. The proportion of people who were living in such cramped accommodation was even larger. In Bochum nearly 30,500 people—or 40 per cent of those covered by the survey— were living at densities of over two persons per room and almost 70,000—84 per cent—were living with more than one person per room. These figures indicate that even if

[16] Lange, 'Wohnungsverhältnisse', p. 95.
[17] Westfälishcher Verein, *Ergebnisse* i 29–30; Koch, *Bergarbeiterbewegung*, p. 149; Däbritz, *Bochumer Verein*, Table 4.

TABLE 5

Overcrowding in urban housing, 1905[a]

	Total homes	Homes with over 2 persons per room		Homes with over 1 person per room	
Münster	7,783	531	(7%)	3,539	(45%)
Arnsberg	1,074	143	(13%)	543	(51%)
Bochum	17,041	4,124	(24%)	11,952	(70%)
Recklinghausen	7,301	1,806	(25%)	5,275	(72%)
Herne	4,700	1,135	(24%)	3,374	(72%)
Hörde	5,024	1,198	(24%)	3,608	(72%)
Witten	6,466	1,621	(25%)	4,679	(73%)
Hattingen	1,681	256	(15%)	1,028	(61%)

[a]Westfälischer Verein, *Ergebnisse* ii. 27–31.

acute homelessness had declined there was still a severe underlying housing shortage.[18]

Overcrowding was more common in smaller homes. Table 6 illustrates this by comparing the proportion of small (one- to three-room) dwellings with over two inhabitants per room with the proportion for homes with four or five rooms. There were some extreme cases: in Bochum in 1905 there were reckoned to be no fewer than 33 one-room dwellings with ten or more people living in them and there were similar instances in the other towns surveyed. The Verein concluded that their investigation showed 'how large groups of the population are concentrated in the narrowest living space in these towns. The needs of the workers' families for air and space are not usually too highly estimated. These figures reveal the unhealthy housing conditions in which large masses of the population live.'[19]

In practice it was common for one room to serve as living-room, kitchen, wash-room, and bedroom. Some craftsmen, such as tailors and shoemakers, would also use it as work-room.[20] Of more general significance was the widespread

[18] ibid. The situation was comparable with that in the East End of London in the 1890s: G. Stedman-Jones, *Outcast London* (London, 1976 edition), pp. 219–20.

[19] Westfälischer Verein, *Ergebnisse* ii 6; StAB, *Magistratsbericht*, 1871; Lange, 'Wohnungsverhältnisse', p. 87.

[20] Lange, 'Wohnungsverhältnisse', p. 87; Pieper, *Lage der Bergarbeiter*, p. 215.

TABLE 6

Overcrowding by size of dwelling, 1905[a]

	1–3 room dwellings with over 2 persons per room	4–5 room dwellings with over 2 persons per room
	per cent	*per cent*
Münster	16	3
Arnsberg	22	4
Bochum	30	10
Recklinghausen	30	11
Herne	27	12
Hörde	27	12
Witten	29	7
Hattingen	19	7

[a]Westfälischer Verein, *Ergebnisse* ii. 27–31.

practice of taking in lodgers or boarders. In Bochum nearly ten per cent of the homes surveyed in 1905 had one or more boarders, mostly in the larger dwellings but a substantial number in the one- or two-room homes. Even in the larger homes boarders caused drastic overcrowding since there was frequently more than one in the household. In each of the Ruhr towns surveyed around half of all the families with boarders took more than one. The Verein commented: 'There is a direct connection between boarding and the overcrowding of small homes in these areas. An improvement in conditions in this respect would therefore only be achieved if good and inexpensive accommodation outside family housing were provided for single workers.'[21] The Verein recommended that the taking of lodgers in one-room homes be made illegal but it is doubtful whether such measures could ever have had more than a marginal impact on the problem. The excessive taking of boarders was a direct reflection of the deeper problem of insufficient and therefore too expensive housing at the cheaper end of the market. The high cost of housing forced poor families either to squeeze into cramped accommodation or to sublet some of their home to lodgers. In the most extreme cases they did both.

[21] Westfälischer Verein, *Ergebnisse* ii 17, 32–8.

After the war the Bochum local authority accepted that prior to 1914 the population had been outstripping the growth of the housing stock:

The incomes of large sections of the population were such that with the rents of the time many families were unable to rent a home suitable and large enough for their needs. Where necessity did not stand in the way there was frequently a false sense of economy and the importance of good accommodation was seriously undervalued. The result was that in Bochum many homes—particularly the smaller and cheaper ones— were overcrowded and left much to be desired in relation to hygiene and morality.[22]

Housing and public health

The shortage of good housing and the resultant overcrowding had several undesirable results. In the first place it fostered disease. Lack of proper sanitation, the proximity in which people lived in these overcrowded conditions, and the slow development of public health measures all played their part. Cholera appeared in Bochum in 1849 and returned with disastrous force in 1866. The 1866 outbreak was worst around Essen and at the *Zollverein* pit alone 80 miners died.[23] In Bochum 230 people were affected by the disease and 86 of them died. The town authorities reported:

The disease was present virtually throughout the town but was most virulent in parts where bad housing and unhealthy neighbourhoods generally favoured the spread of epidemics ... The disease appeared in the Gerberstrasse, and just as this street has been particularly badly affected by epidemics once they are established so this time it was the disease's focus. The poor state of the land evidently played an essential part. It is therefore our intention to secure improved drainage of the Gerberstrasse and nearby streets.[24]

The outbreak coincided with a smallpox epidemic. Smallpox had appeared in Bochum in the 1850s and reappeared in

---

[22] StAB, *Magistratsbericht*, 1913/24, p. 107. Standards in the Ruhr were by no means the worst in Germany: see Niethammer and Brüggemeier, 'Wie wohnten Arbeiter?', pp. 96-101.

[23] M. Seippel, *Bochum Einst und Jetzt* (Bochum, 1901), p. 181; Verein für die bergbaulichen Interessen, *Die Entwicklung des Niederrheinisch-Westfälischen Steinkohlen-Bergbaues* (Berlin, 1904), xii 94.

[24] StAB, *Magistratsbericht*, 1866, pp. 26-7.

December 1865. In the year 1866 1,347 cases were reported
and 143 died. From nearly two thousand schoolchildren in
the town 420—more than one in five—were hit by the
disease and 36 died. The death-rate in the town, which had
been fluctuating around 31 per thousand in previous years,
stood at almost 73 per thousand in 1866 under the impact
of this combination.[25]

Despite these outbreaks little was done to improve the
town's sanitation. The collection of refuse was improved but
little else was achieved. In 1871 smallpox returned, even
more disastrously than before. This time 2,719 people
—or almost 13 per cent of the town's population—were
affected by the disease, and 333 died. All children under
twelve were vaccinated and there was a general disinfection
campaign.[26]

This epidemic seems to have stimulated the town's
authorities to take action to improve public sanitation. In
1872 an engineer was brought in from Berlin to devise
a drainage plan for the entire town. His proposals were only
partially approved, but despite the limited scale of the
programme it did mark the start of sustained efforts to
improve the town's sanitation. Work continued in subsequent
years to improve the water supply and drainage. In 1886
the mayor could write that 'virtually all the houses in the
town are supplied with the necessary water by the town
water supply.' Nevertheless, there was opposition: 'complaints have come from individual house owners who still
use wells with bad water or let their tenants use them to
avoid the water charge. Thanks to the energetic action of the
police such wells have been closed off and these houses
connected to the water supply.'[27] By 1895 it was reported
that nearly all the more populous parts of the town were
effectively drained. Other improvements were being made
at the same time. By the end of the century virtually all the
town's streets had been paved and the number of gaslights

---

[25] StAB, *Magistratsbericht*, 1866, pp. 26-7. Verein für die bergbaulichen Inter-
essen, *Entwicklung des . . . Steinkohlenbergbaues* xii 94. The sanitary situation in
Bochum and other Ruhr towns was compared unfavourably with London and
Manchester: StAB, *Magistratsbericht*, 1868.

[26] StAB, *Magistratsbericht*, 1867, p. 23; ibid., 1871, p. 55.

[27] Lange, 'Wohnungsverhältnisse', p. 86; StAB, *Magistratsbericht*, 1873, p. 14.

increased from 70 in 1860 to 877; 355 of these lights burned all night.[28]

Despite these improvements, however, sanitation in Bochum was far from adequate by the turn of the century. Potentially dangerous wells were still in use and seem to have been a contributory cause of typhus outbreaks in 1906 and 1907. Domestic toilets were not linked up with the main drainage system. Many homes still did not have their own toilet: the 1905 housing survey revealed that in 44 per cent of the homes covered the family had to share with one or more others; 273 dwellings were found without apparent access to any toilet at all. It was only in 1908 that approval was given to comprehensive plans to incorporate domestic sewage with the general drainage system. As late as 1924 a great deal remained to be done to equip the town with a modern sewage disposal system.[29]

Improved drainage and sewage disposal were not the only measures taken to try to improve the general health of the area. In 1892 an office was established to test the quality of food sold in the town and from 1895 the inspection was extended to the surrounding *Landkreis*. In the early years between 20 and 30 per cent of the food tested was below standard; by the early 1900s the proportion had fallen to around 10 per cent in the town, although it remained higher in the *Landkreis*. Other health measures included hospital building (there were three major ones in Bochum in 1901, and a further one was founded in 1910) and the subjection of prostitutes to regular health checks. However, by 1907 Bochum was one of the few Prussian towns still without an official school doctor.[30]

Improved sanitation and public health was accompanied by a gradual decline in the death-rate and an end to disastrous epidemics such as those experienced in the 1860s and early 1870s. The overall death-rate in Bochum fell from between 35 and 28 per thousand in 1875–86 to between 20 and 15 per thousand in 1905–12. The proportion of deaths

[28] StAB, *Magistratsbericht*, 1895/6, p. 50; Seippel, *Bochum Einst und Jetzt*, pp. 154, 163.

[29] StAB, *Magistratsberichte*; Westfälischer Verein, *Ergebnisse* ii 43.

[30] StAB, *Magistratsberichte*; IZF, *Tremonia*, 28. 5. 1910; Silbergleit, *Preussens Städte*, p. 260.

during the first year of life also declined. Cholera did not
reappear in Bochum, although in 1884 preparations were
made to deal with a possible outbreak. The only reappearance
of smallpox was in 1904, when it was probably introduced
by a Belgian woman. It did not have the virulence of earlier
outbreaks. Twenty-five cases were identified in Bochum itself,
four in the *Landkreis*, and one in Witten. Four people died.
All the sick were isolated and their homes closed up. There
was a general disinfection and 50,000 people were vaccinated.
In a few months the outbreak was eliminated.[31]

Despite these improvements, however, the area was far
from healthy. Typhoid was endemic and caused more deaths
in relation to the size of the population in the Ruhr than in
Prussia as a whole. Three hundred died in an epidemic in
Gelsenkirchen in 1901. This led to the first serious efforts
to clean up the Emscher. In Bochum 76 cases were reported
in 1904 and between 1906 and 1911 the number fluctuated
between 33 and 84 each year: over these six years there were
320 cases and 46 deaths from typhoid. The cause was impure
water and foodstuffs, and cases tended to concentrate in the
less salubrious districts of the town. The outbreak in the
summer of 1906, for instance, centred on the Bruchstrasse
and its side streets. In 1908 it reached epidemic proportions
in the Thomasstrasse and nearby streets where there were
54 cases, while only 27 cases were reported in the rest of
the town. Eleven died in this outbreak. In 1909 dysentery
was again concentrated in the older parts of the town, the
Thomasstrasse, Gerberstrasse, and Bruchstrasse. Scarlet
fever and diphtheria were also common: in 1904 scarlet
fever was reported to be 'epidemic' in Bochum; the disease
was reported to be most common in working families with
many children. In 1905, when both scarlet fever and
diphtheria increased, it was reported that 'chronic centres
of disease are formed in streets heavily populated with large
families.'[32]

---

[31] See chapter 1 above; *Statistisches Jahrbuch deutscher Städte* ; StAB, *Magistratsbericht*, 1884/5, p. 45; ibid., 1904/5, p. 81.

[32] StAB, *Magistratsberichte*; A. Heinrichsbauer, *Industrielle Siedlung im
Ruhrgebiet* (Essen, 1936), p. 11; Brüggemeier, *Leben vor Ort*, p. 52. On Germany
generally see Niethammer and Brüggemeier, 'Wie wohnten Arbeiter?', pp. 92–4.

There were occasional epidemics of less common diseases, again probably worsened by overcrowding. One such was cerebrospinal meningitis, a vicious disease which attacks the fluid around the brain. It appeared in Bochum in 1907 and from 77 reported cases 50 died. Again it was concentrated in a few streets in the old town. The following year it appeared in some of the outer areas: from 56 cases there were 31 deaths. Further cases were reported in 1909 and 1910.

The most common illnesses were connected with the respiratory organs. In 1893, a year without any major outbreak of disease, it was estimated that 13 per cent of the deaths in the town were due to 'consumption' (*Lungenschwindsucht*—tuberculosis). A further 20 per cent were caused by 'inflammatory diseases of the respiratory organs'. These diseases were constantly mentioned in subsequent years as the biggest single killers. In 1912 there were 7 deaths from typhus in Bochum, 33 from diphtheria and 56 from scarlet fever; but 243 died from tuberculosis and 406 from other respiratory diseases. Consumption was popularly— although incorrectly—believed to be caused by the sharp east winds. In fact tuberculosis was caused by an inhaled or ingested organism but, like influenza and bronchitis, was fostered by overcrowded, damp, polluted, and poorly ventilated conditions.[33]

All these diseases were general in their scope and were not limited to particular occupational groups: they thus differed from afflictions like the worm disease which was rampant amongst the miners in the early 1900s.[34] They demonstrated that despite the non-recurrence of epidemics on the scale of 1866 and 1871 and despite the substantial drop in the overall death-rate, disease was still a serious scourge. Although not the only factor involved, the incidence of disease was frequently closely related to inadequate and overcrowded accommodation. Poor housing was not merely inconvenient: it was often dangerous.

[33] StAB, *Magistratsbericht*, 1893/4, p. 35; ibid., 1897/8, p. 41. Tuberculosis was the most lethal disease in Germany throughout most of the nineteenth century, affecting both urban and rural areas; Lee, 'Germany', p. 157.
[34] See chapter 4 below.

Housing and families

The housing shortage had important social as well as physical effects. One of the main working-class reponses to the shortage, as we have seen, was for families to share their homes with lodgers. This had important benefits for both parties, despite the undoubted drawbacks of yet further crowding in already cramped conditions. Taking in lodgers was one of the few ways open to many families of earning extra cash. This was particularly important at the more vulnerable phases of the family life-cycle—when the main breadwinner was sick or unemployed, for example, or when there were many children below working age to feed, or following bereavement. For the lodger—particularly newcomers to the district —the system gave somewhere to sleep and eat together with flexibility so that he could, if he so wished, easily move on. In addition it provided newcomers with ready access to the family and social life of the community.

Lodging was widespread in the Ruhr: in the early 1890s it was estimated that around twenty per cent of miners were lodgers and the proportion was almost certainly maintained in later years.[35] It thus represented a very common working-class response to the housing shortage. It had certain social implications. Many families shared their homes with non-family members—a situation which has been described by historians as 'semi-open' family structure. The term suggests the limited scope for personal or family privacy in such conditions and an unusual degree of openness and interaction beween the family and the wider community. The lodging system, it has been suggested, thus helped to reinforce non-familial ties and loyalties and provided one of the social bases for group or class solidarity. However, the significance of the system should not be overstated. Fischer-Eckert noted that in Hamborn the turnover of population and the mixing of people from different backgrounds meant that many women lived rather isolated lives with little real contact with neighbours. Even where lodging opened up the immediate nuclear family it would be wrong to assume that social solidarity thereby extended to the working class generally:

---

[35] Münz, *Lage der Bergarbeiter*, p. 136.

it may have been extended only to kin, friends, and new-comers from the same home area. Moreover, such living arrangements were not necessarily very novel: in some ways they represented a new manifestation, in an industrial setting, of a long-established peasant and plebeian system.[36]

Some contemporaries were more concerned with the moral threats which the lodging system seemed to pose. It reinforced the independence of the young: 'in this industrial district the sons not infrequently depart their parents' home practically as soon as they have left school and get a little money in their hands', reported one local official gloomily.[37] The ease with which they could find alternative accommodation was thought to undermine parental control and social discipline. Another official regretfully concluded that parents could not be made responsible for their sons' behaviour at work, since 'unfortunately most of the young miners around here do not live at home.'[38] The resulting moral decay threatened the state itself:

The social democrats here [Hofstede] are almost all young, immature persons who are misled into wasting their money in bars and music halls through their high earnings and the lack of home supervision. The families of the long-established workers (*Stammarbeiter*) and the rural families are the only ones who can provide a morally healthy new generation of industrial workers. The rising licentious generation, however, form the overwhelming majority, and are thus a danger to state order. This danger will continue to grow so long as high

---

[36] Fischer-Eckert, *Lage der Frauen*, p. 133. On the 'semi-open' family in the Ruhr, see Niethammer and Brüggemeier, 'Wie wohnten Arbeiter?'; L. Niethammer and F. J. Brüggemeier, 'Schlafgänger, Schnapskasinos und schwerindustrielle Kolonie. Aspekte der Arbeiterwohnungsfrage im Ruhrgebiet vor dem Ersten Weltkrieg', in J. Reulecke and W. Weber, *Fabrik, Familie, Feierabend. Beiträge zur Sozialgeschichte des Alltags im Industriezeitalter* (Wuppertal, 1978), pp. 135–64; Brüggemeier, *Leben vor Ort*, pp. 62–8, 73; F. J. Brüggemeier, ' "Volle Kost voll". Die Wohnungsverhältnisse der Bergleute an der Ruhr um die Jahrhundertwende', in Mommsen and Borsdorf (ed.), *Glück auf, Kameraden!*, pp. 151–73; F. J. Brüggemeier, 'Ruhr miners and their historians', in R. Samuel (ed.), *People's History and Socialist Theory* (London, 1981), pp. 326–32. For reservations about the concept, see D. Groh, 'Base-processes and the problem of organization: outline of a social history research project', in *Social History* (May 1979), p. 274. See also M. Anderson, *Approaches to the History of the Western Family 1500–1914* (London, 1980), pp. 75–84.

[37] StAB, 441, *Amt* Bochum I to KLB, 24. 9. 1889.

[38] ibid., *Amt* Herne to KLB, 25. 9. 1889.

earnings continue and the employers continue to take on every dubious person because of the labour shortage.[39]

Some employers provided hostels for single workers. In the Bochumer Verein it was obligatory for single employees to live in the company hostel if they were not at home. In most cases, however, such hostels involved fairly stringent rules and were rejected by the young men in favour of the greater freedom and independence of lodging. One commentator reported:

It is a well known fact that the single workers only avoid the official establishments and dormitories provided by the companies because if they used them they would be compelled to adopt punctual and orderly behaviour. They sacrifice the higher cost of alternative lodgings to secure independence—which only too often leads to the worst moral failures. It frequently happens that half-grown youths leave their parents' home and take lodgings in the same area just because they feel their 'freedom' too restricted when under their parents' eye.[40]

The lodging system was not only blamed for moral decay by freeing the young from parental control. The host family was also thought to be at risk. Police regulations attempted to lay down minimum conditions for boarders: in 1879, for example, regulations for Dortmund, Bochum, and Hagen decreed that the lodger's bedroom was not to link directly with the family's living- or bedroom; there was to be at least one bed and one set of washing equipment for every two lodgers; mixing of the sexes in one bedroom was forbidden; there was a minimum size of room allowed per person. These regulations were amended from time to time but it is doubtful whether they were ever effective.[41] It was inevitable that the host family and the lodger(s) should live in close proximity to one another. Some observers stressed the threat to family life which this entailed. Mayor Lange of Bochum claimed that promiscuity, drunkenness, and crime was the result: lodging 'has created a situation which from the moral point of view causes the greatest concern and which must be eliminated by all legally acceptable means if

[39] StAB, 479, *Amt* Hofstede to KLB, 31. 7. 1900.

[40] Münz, *Lage der Bergarbeiter*, p. 137.

[41] Lange, 'Wohnungsverhältnisse', pp. 93–4; WWA, K2 342; Niethammer and Brüggemeier, 'Wie wohnten Arbeiter?', p. 119.

complete brutalization and degeneration is to be avoided .... This lodging system, which has spread wider like a contagion the more that industry has grown, has caused, apart from the ruin of many families, multifarious crimes, even assault and murder.'[42] This was a somewhat fevered overstatement. In many cases the boarder shared a room with the host's son of about the same age—'a custom which is certainly quite unobjectionable'.[43] Nevertheless, strains must have existed in such cramped conditions and naturally worried workers as well as bourgeois observers. Max Lotz, a miner from the Rhineland, wrote of 'the misery of the lodging system' which, in his view, led to the break-up of marriages; in similar terms Heinrich Münz, a sympathetic bourgeois commentator, described lodging as 'a great danger to the worker's family life.'[44]

Company housing

In some societies the need for cheap yet salubrious housing for industrial workers has been met in part by the develop-ment of publicly owned housing. This possible resolution of the Ruhr housing crisis was ruled out in the pre-war years. Local authorities, on which the working-class voice was virtually non-existent, refused to contemplate undertaking building work themselves, partly because they did not see this as a proper function of local government and partly because of the cost.[45] This did not mean, however, that

[42] Lange, 'Wohnungsverhältnisse', pp. 92–3.

[43] WWA, K2, HKB to RPA, 17. 6. 1907.

[44] A. Levenstein, *Aus der Tiefe; Arbeiterbriefe* (Berlin, 1909), p. 19; Münz, *Lage der Bergarbeiter*, p. 136. See also Pieper, *Lage der Bergarbeiter*, pp. 239–40. According to Georg Werner, chairman of the Overmen's (*Steiger*) Association, there were three categories of boarding in the Ruhr: 'half-board' (bed and limited food provided), 'full-board' (bed and food), and 'full-full-board' (bed, food, and the housewife's favours). The latter was rarer than the concern which it aroused in bourgeois circles implied. Niethammer and Brüggemeier, 'Wie wohnten Arbeiter? ', p. 118 ff; Brüggemeier, ' "Volle Kost voll" ', p. 161 ff; Lucas, *Arbeit-erradikalismus*, p. 71; Brüggemeier, *Leben vor Ort*, p. 68.

[45] Kirchhoff, *Sozialpolitik*, p. 126; Crew, *Town in the Ruhr*, pp. 150–1; Tenfelde, *Sozialgeschichte*, p. 333; Niethammer and Brüggemeier, 'Wie wohnten Arbeiter? ', p. 107; Niethammer and Brüggemeier, 'Schlafgänger, Schnapskasinos und schwerindustrielle Kolonie', pp. 145–8; Brüggemeier, *Leben vor Ort*, pp. 38–46. On the origins of local authority housebuilding in Germany, see C. J. Fuchs, *Zur Wohnungsfrage* (Leipzig, 1904), p. 47.

non-workers in the Ruhr could totally ignore the problem: employers found the housing shortage an important obstacle to labour recruitment. Their response was to undertake a substantial building programme for their own employees.

The pressure on employers to build for their workers started early. In 1868 the Bochum Chamber of Commerce observed that 'the larger firms will have to go over to building workers' housing on a larger scale if they want to secure a steady and reliable work force.'[46] The collapse of private speculative building in the 1870s made the need even more urgent:

With the great increase in the working population which has taken place in the last years, private speculative building has not been able to satisfy the demand for workers' housing, partly because of the unprofitability of such housing in relation to its costs, and partly because of the nature of our industrial conditions whereby mass redundancies are not uncommon. It will therefore have to be left chiefly to industry to meet the housing needs of a growing number of workers.[47]

The *Hannover* and *Hannibal* mines built their first houses in 1864 in an attempt to alleviate a shortage of labour. The Harpener Bergbau AG found in 1870 that at their *Heinrich Gustav* pit they were only able to employ 720 men, although they could have used up to 1,800. The main problem was a shortage of accommodation, despite a company building programme dating from 1863. As the economy boomed the labour shortage was felt more acutely, and in 1872 the company decided to launch a major new building programme. Some of the 'colonies', as the mine-owned estates were known, were large. The *Constantin* colony in Hofstede, built between 1869 and 1874, had 65 houses with 123 homes and was larger than the original village.[48]

Despite these early beginnings the real growth in company housing came much later. As Table 7 illustrates, the most dramatic expansion took place in the decade before the outbreak of war. This expansion largely reflected the growth

[46] StAB, HKB *Jahresbericht*, 1868, p. 12.

[47] StAB, *Magistratsbericht*, 1882/3, p. 34.

[48] *Festschrift zum 100-jährigen Bestehen der Zechen Hannover und Hannibal* (Bochum, 1947), pp. 12, 16; A. Heinrichsbauer *Harpener Bergbau AG* (Essen, 1936), p. 159; Croon, 'Studien', p. 97.

TABLE 7
Homes owned by mines in the Ruhr[a]

1873	6,772
1893	10,376
1901	26,250
1907	52,900
1912	81,870
1914	94,027

[a]Heinrichsbauer, *Industrielle Siedlung*, p. 44; G. Adelmann, *Die soziale Betriebsverfassung des Ruhrbergbaues* (Bonn, 1972), pp. 163–4; Verein für die bergbaulichen Interessen, *Entwicklung des . . . Steinkohlenbergbaues* xii. 188; *Glückauf* 23. 5. 1914.

of mining in the undeveloped northern parts of the Ruhr. The *Rheinisch-Westfälische Zeitung* commented in 1904:

Finally, and this is the crux of the matter in the development of all mines in the underpopulated north, the achievement of such production demands a suitable work-force. The mines north of the Cologne-Minden railway have almost without exception had to resort to large scale building of 'colonies' to attract the necessary workers.[49]

This was reflected in the spread of mine housing around Bochum and neighbouring districts. Even as late as 1912 some pits there had little or no housing but they were mainly to the south of the town. At the south Bochum mines with one exception the proportion of men in company housing lay between 11 and 19 per cent. In the north Bochum district there was one pit, *Präsident*, which had less than one per cent of its workers in mine accommodation but this was because the mine lay within the town itself. All the rest had far higher proportions, ranging up to *Lothringen* with 36 per cent. In the Herne district *Julia* had 35 per cent of its workers in company accommodation, *Recklinghausen II* had almost 46 per cent, and *Viktor* had 67 per cent. Similarly in the Gelsenkirchen district one mine had 19 per cent, three had 32 to 35 per cent and one (*Königsgrube*) had over 56 per cent; only the long-established *Hibernia* had virtually no housing. Even further north, amongst the Recklinghausen pits, there were several mines where over half the workers

[49] WWA, K2 213, *Rheinisch-Westfälische Zeitung*, 2. 4. 1904.

lived in company housing. In the Ruhr as a whole the proportion of miners living in such housing rose from under 20 per cent in 1901 to 33 per cent in 1912 and about 37 per cent in 1914. While most miners and their families continued to depend on the private housing market, a substantial and rapidly growing minority were thus provided for by their employer.[50]

Company housing was not limited to the mines. Krupp in Essen was perhaps the most famous builder of housing for his workers. The Bochumer Verein built a home for 126 single workers and another building for ten foremen and their families in the 1850s. In the following decades they established the Stahlhausen colony near the factory, to the west of the town. The first houses were of the 'Mühlhausen' type, comprising a living-room and kitchen downstairs, a bedroom upstairs, and cellar, wash-room, a small garden, and shed for pigs or hens. From these small beginnings the company's housing provision expanded so that by 1900 some 5,000 people lived in Stahlhausen and a further 1,000 in the boarding home for single men. In Gelsenkirchen the Schalker Gruben- und Hüttenverein provided housing for 628 families in 1901. Smaller firms too sometimes provided accommodation: in 1901 the Bochumer Eisenhütte Heintzmann und Dreyer, which employed 170 workers, had ten houses (each probably with more than one flat) providing 'large, cheap homes'. Breweries also provided housing for some of their employees: the Glückauf brewery in Ueckendorf provided it free and in Dortmund a major demand by brewery workers in their boycott of 1905 was that they should not be obliged to live in the brewery. While the provision of housing was most marked and carried furthest by the northern mines and the large steel and engineering firms, it was therefore not exclusive to them and can be seen as a general characteristic of the area.[51]

[50] STAM, *Oberbergamt* Dortmund 1837; Heinrichsbauer, *Industrielle Siedlung*, p. 44; *Glückauf*, 23. 5. 1914; Koch, *Bergarbeiterbewegung*, p. 139.

[51] W. Fischer, *Herz des Reviers* (Essen, 1965), p. 266; Däbritz, *Bochumer Verein*, p. 86; Wolcke, *Entwicklung der Bochumer Innenstadt*, p. 45; Brinkmann, *Bochum*, p. 183; Heinrichsbauer, *Industrielle Siedlung*, pp. 26–7; IZF, *Volksblatt*, 9. 5. 1900; WWA, K2 522, Schalker Gruben- und Hüttenverein to HKB 4. 5. 1901; Seippel, *Bochum Einst und Jetzt*, p. 260; STAM, RA I 76, *Landrat* Gelsenkirchen

Company housing offered a number of advantages to employees. It was usually close to the work-place and thus reduced the daily walk to and from work. It was generally of better quality than local private accommodation. Most had three or four rooms, compared with two to three in the private market. Most company homes also had at least some garden and facilities for livestock. Rents were considerably lower than in comparable housing in the neighbourhood: a survey in 1901 revealed that the cost of similar private housing was almost everywhere at least 20 per cent more and sometimes double that of company housing.[52] In 1906 the Bochumer Verein's housing favourably impressed a visiting delegation of English workers:

We next came to the colony of workmen's dwellings at 'Stahlhausen' . . . . In our opinion the dwellings are quite up to the standard of work-men's requirements and in regard to some of their sanitary arrange-ments they are highly creditable. There is plenty of air and plenty of room. The houses stand apart and there is no overcrowding. The rent is less than what is asked in the town. In the town the average price of a flat is calculated at from 76 to 90 shillings per annum per room; whereas in the Colony it is 50/-. No comparison between the two sorts of dwellings, however, can be made as regards space and good air and general comforts. . . . Each flat has a cellar attached to it and most of them have also a small garden, and a little shed. A special system of ventilation is here used for the closets which answers well. The Firm has set apart about forty acres of land which is let to the workmen in small allotments as kitchen-gardens for growing their vegetables and potatoes.[53]

This happy picture was not the universal experience. Sometimes the need for labour was so pressing that firms cut corners in building and put in tenants before the houses were ready. The *Lothringen* pit in Gerthe was said in 1907

to RPA, 25. 5. 1901; STAM RA I GA 493, *Gewerbeaufsichtsbericht* for *Reg. Bezirk* Arnsberg, 1905. Company housing existed, of course, in other German industrial centres: a national survey in 1898 suggested that on average around 18 dwellings had been built for every thousand workers in plants with twenty or more workers. Fuchs, *Zur Wohnungsfrage*, p. 44; Schofer, *Formation of a modern labor force*, pp. 84–91.

[52] Verein für die bergbaulichen Interessen, *Entwicklung des . . . Steinkohlen-bergbaues* xii 192–7; Westfälischer Verein, *Ergebnisse* ii 27–31; R. Hundt, *Berg-arbeiter-Wohnungen im Ruhrrevier* (Berlin, 1902), pp. 18–21.

[53] Gainsborough Commission, *Life and Labour in Germany* (London, 1906), pp. 25–6.

to be building homes in about eight weeks and bringing in
tenants before the windows and footpaths were complete.
The estate was deep in mud and standing water. The houses
were not given time to dry out and many of the internal
walls were damp and even mouldy. The building inspectors
turned a blind eye. The mine gave the tenants free coal and
charged no rent for the first three months: the arrange-
ment nevertheless provided them with labour for this period
and saved them the expense of drying out the house themselves.[54] The *Arbeitsmarkt-Korrespondenz* described graphically the situation near booming Oberhausen:

The number of workers there is continuously rising. Some days see the
arrival by train of hundreds of Slav workers. The sudden and enormous
flood has caused a dreadful housing calamity. Hundreds live in simple
barracks. The company colonies are literally packed with people. Even
though building is unusually brisk the supply of housing does not
remotely meet the need. The houses are scarcely plastered before they
are occupied. . . . Packing together so many workers in barracks and
scantily equipped houses is a public danger, particularly since they are
foreign and from a less cultivated background. Were an epidemic to
break out—the horror of the situation does not bear consideration.[55]

When firms provided housing they generally aimed at more
than simply accommodation for their workers. They tried
to build not just homes but communities. Houses were
normally built in closed groups, known as 'colonies', physically separate from the others in the village or town. Of 858
dwellings owned by mines in the south Bochum area in 1901
all but 65 were in colonies; in north Bochum 691 of the
1,038 mine-owned dwellings were in colonies. In the Herne
area 576 of the 1,203 mine-owned dwellings were in colonies
and in the Gelsenkirchen area the figure was 1,783 out of
2,125. The proportions were lower in the older mining areas
where, anyway, company housing was not increasing at the
same pace: in the Witten district only 96 of the 426 company dwellings were in colonies and in the Hattingen area
only 108 out of 302. Many other dwellings, while not in
'colonies' were in what the surveyors described as 'enclosed

---

[54] IISG, *Volksblatt*, 28. 12. 1907.
[55] STAM, RA I 98, *Polizei-Commissar* Gelsenkirchen to RPA, 31. 8. 1906.

localities'.[56] Thus one significant characteristic of company housing was that it tended to isolate its inhabitants from the rest of the community.

This tendency was reinforced by the provision of other facilities in addition to housing. The Bochumer Verein ran a co-operative store with seven branches for its employees. The colony also had a kindergarten for young children and a training school for adolescent girls to teach them 'female handicrafts'. The same pattern was found at the Krupp-owned mines at *Hannover* and *Hannibal* to the north of Bochum. By 1889 *Hannover* had three separate colonies, each providing housing for between 18 and 76 families. Each home had three to five rooms. *Hannibal* had one colony of 88 homes, each with four rooms and some land. By 1901 *Hannover* had dwellings for 381 families and *Hannibal* enough for 102 families. All these homes had gardens and facilities for livestock attached. The company also financed a kindergarten run by three women, one of whom also ran the Günningfeld colony's medical service. The number of such schools grew in the following years so that by 1907 there were five schools in the various Krupp colonies, two Catholic and three Protestant. In addition there was a company store.

Despite these benefits, however, the firm found that it was not attracting sufficient labour to take full advantage of the economic boom; this failure was being compounded by high levels of labour turnover, which in turn had bad effects on productivity. In 1905, therefore, Krupp decided to expand the supply of housing radically and work on a new colony on the Dahlhausen heath started in 1906. In eight years 715 homes for workers and officials were constructed. This was a model colony: the houses were not identical or set out in straight rows as in the earlier ones. There was considerable greenery. There was both a Catholic and a Protestant elementary school and two schools for very young children. For the girls there were sewing, domestic work, and cookery classes. In 1907

[56] Verein für die bergbaulichen Interessen, *Entwicklung des . . . Steinkohlenbergbaues* xii 192-7; Hundt, *Bergarbeiter-Wohnungen*, pp. 18-21; Wolcke, *Entwicklung der Bochumer Innenstadt*, p. 54.

a branch of the Krupp library was opened in Hordel and there was also a company savings institute. Finally, in December 1913 a large hall for 800 people was opened with billiard and reading rooms, a bowling alley, and rooms for clubs, small meetings, and festivities.[57]

The Krupp and Bochumer Verein colonies were unusual in the extent of their social provision. Greater resources were brought to bear by these large firms than most others could contemplate. The official investigation which followed the 1889 miners' strike described the provisions at the *Hannover* pit and those of the Bochumer Verein at *Maria-Anna und Steinbank* as 'exemplary'. But these firms only carried out in a large and systematic manner a policy which was common throughout the area. As the number of company houses increased many companies provided other facilities with them. As early as 1889 a number of pits owned or ran stores for their workers, in a few instances giving credit and deducting bills from wages. Other mines—for example, *Vollmond*, *Unser Fritz*, and *von der Heydt*—bought potatoes and sometimes other foodstuffs to sell to the workers at cheap rates. In the 1900s almost all the major companies in and around Bochum purchased foodstuffs in bulk and sold them at cost price to their workers. The Gussstahlwerk Witten provided a bath-house, a workers' restaurant, and a store in addition to its houses while the Gewerkschaft Orange, a firm which only employed 140 workers at the time, was reported in 1882 to have 'tried to improve the lot of its workers by the renovation of its workers' dwellings, by paving the streets of the colony and planting them with trees, by establishing an evening school, and by granting free medical treatment and medicines to their wives and children'.[58]

[57] Lange, 'Wohnungsverhältnisse', p. 80; Gainsborough Commission, *Life and Labour*, p. 28; StAB, 442, 'Ergebnisse der Untersuchung der Betriebs- und Arbeitsverhältnisse auf den Kohlengruben'; Verein für die bergbaulichen Interessen, *Entwicklung des . . . Steinkohlenbergbaues*, xii 194–5; BA, 20/A 45, 'Geschichte der Zeche Hannover'; BA, 20/C 116–18, *Hannover* and *Hannibal, Jahresberichte*; BA, 20/C 56a, *Krupp'sche Mitteilungen*, 3. 1. 1914; Croon, 'Studien', pp. 105–6.

[58] StAB, 445, *Denkschrift über die Untersuchung der Arbeiter- und Betriebs-Verhältnisse in den Steinkohlen-Bezirken* (Berlin, 1890), p. 41; StAB, 442, 'Ergebnisse der Untersuchung der Beitriebs- und Arbeitsverhältnisse auf den Kohlengruben'; WWA, K2 816; WWA, HKB *Jahresbericht*, 1882; Tenfelde,

Gardens and allotments were very popular in the Ruhr, in part because they enabled working-class families to limit their dependence on the man's wages. The mining companies recognized this and were at pains to provide not only gardens but also facilities for the keeping of animals. Goats were popular and were known as 'the miner's cow'. A recruitment advertisement distributed in East and West Prussia in 1908 by the *Viktor* mine (situated near Rauxel) stressed that with every colony dwelling there was 'a sizeable shed, where each person can keep his pig, his goats, or his hens. So the worker does not need to purchase every pound of meat or litre of milk'; each home also had a garden so that 'everyone can grow his own vegetables, his cabbage, and his potatoes which he needs for the summer. Anyone who needs more land can lease it cheaply nearby. In addition the mine supplies potatoes cheaply in the winter.' Of the 858 mine-owned dwellings in the south Bochum district in 1901 all had facilities for livestock and 768 had gardens. In the north Bochum area the figures were respectively 958 and 937, from a total of 1,038 dwellings.[59]

Medical insurance was another important service which most firms offered their employees, even before it was legally obligatory for them to do so. The miners were in any event covered by the special occupational scheme, the *Knappschaft*. This institution covered all the pits in the area, so that when a man moved from one to another he did not lose his insurance cover. Non-miners were generally covered by company schemes, particularly those who worked for large firms, and contributions were usually lost if the man left the firm. In 1901 seven Bochum firms ran their own health insurance schemes. Only the worker himself, however, was covered by compulsory insurance: the legislation did not extend to his family. Some firms therefore started on their own initiative to extend cover to dependants. The *Hibernia* mine introduced free medical treatment for miners' families in 1897 and the following year the Harpener Bergbau AG could report that 'free medical treatment has been introduced at

Sozialgeschichte, p. 361; *Gussstahlwerk Witten AG, 1854–1954* (Witten, 1954), p. 76.

[59] Fischer-Eckert, *Lage der Fauen*, p. 59; Hundt, *Bergarbeiter-Wohnungen*, pp. 18–21.

all the company's mines for members of workers' and officials' families'.[60]

Company housing was therefore part of a wider system of social provision by Ruhr firms. The benefits—known collectively as *Wohlfahrtseinrichtungen*—were usually a source of great pride to the companies concerned. Not untypical was the description of Louis Baare in a document drawn up—probably within the Bochumer Verein—for the *Deutscher Handelstag* in 1910:

> As manager, he demonstrated his concern for good relations between employer and worker through a warm concern for his employees. Baare established a beautiful and lasting memorial to his activity in the workers' colony of Stahlhausen with its pleasant houses, shady alleys, gardens, playgrounds, and creche. He created a very beneficial institution in the comfortable home for single workers. He cared for the workers' well-being through numerous relief funds and other socially beneficial arrangements, the last one being on his retirement as general director when he donated a large capital sum, the interest on which was to be used to support needy wives and the widows of employees. That the workers felt satisfied under his directorship is demonstrated by the fact that over 300 of the firm's employees have been over 25 years in its service.[61]

Similarly the Gelsenkirchener Bergwerks AG, on the fortieth anniversary of its foundation, described housing as the chief example of its social policy: the aim was 'not just to provide needed accommodation for the necessary manpower but above all to create healthy and cosy homes. . . . All these institutions demonstrate that the Gelsenkirchener Bergwerks AG has remembered the social obligations which have been brought to the consciousness of our age more than ever before.'[62]

Notwithstanding the undoubted benefits to workers, company housing and other provisions were also of considerable advantage to the firms. The official mining journal noted that 'in the majority of cases the employer who institutes *Wohlfahrtseinrichtungen* serves not only the wellbeing of his

[60] *25 Jahre Bergwerksgesellschaft Hibernia* (Düsseldorf, 1898), p. 76; *Glückauf*, 29. 10. 1898; Seippel, *Bochum Einst und Jetzt*, p. 191; IZF, *Volksblatt* 7. 4. 1900.

[61] WWA, K2 92.

[62] *Gelsenkirchener Bergwerks AG 1873–1913* (Düsseldorf, n.d.), pp. 23–4.

workers but also—consciously or unconsciously—his own interest.'[63] This was very clear in areas where without company housing the pits simply would not have been able to recruit sufficient labour. In such situations the costs of building the houses and charging rents below the market rate were subsumed by the expanded production which only an increased work-force allowed. Most companies did not need to create an entirely new labour force in this way: but they were often faced with a substantial problem in recruiting for expansion and in keeping the workers that they had. As we have seen, labour turnover was a perennial difficulty for employers throughout this period. It restricted productivity and tended to force up wages as employers competed with each other for workers. Company housing and other benefits could help in this situation. At the Bochumer Verein's 1899 AGM Fritz Baare (the son and successor of Louis) stressed the important role of housing in creating a settled and contented work force and the advantages which this gave in the competition for labour:

It is clear that because of the generally increased activity in the foundries and the mining industry there have been temporary shortages of able workers. This was felt here less than elsewhere. I believe that I can explain this through the fact that we are in the happy position of being able to offer a large part of our work-force good, healthy, and cheap accommodation—for the single worker in our lodging house which is recognized for its excellent installations, and for the married in suitably built family homes. That our efforts for the benefit of our employees have fallen on good soil is probably best demonstrated by the fact that at present the number of officials, foremen, and workers who have belonged to our concern for over 25 uninterrupted years has risen to about 700.[64]

The number of workers who had stayed with the firm for twenty-five or more years was a favourite measure of the success of companies' social policies. Such men were lauded at company festivities and other workers were encouraged to emulate their loyalty and years of hard work for the company. The Gelsenkirchener Bergwerks AG listed

---

[63] *Zeitschrift für das Bergbau-, Hütten- und Salinenwesen*, 1906, p. 3.

[64] STAM, RA I GA 355. In 1898 the company employed 9,221 men in the metal works and 3,221 in the mines.

its social spending in its own twenty-five-year anniversary publication and commented:

The company can partly attribute to these institutions the fact that a substantial number of its officials and workers have already celebrated or are celebrating their 25-year anniverary of activity at the company's mines. This will be a good omen for the continued growth, blossoming, and prosperity of the firm, which now enters its 26th year in the old miner's calling.[65]

The costs, on the other hand, were not necessarily high despite the initial capital expenditure. In 1888 the board of the Bochumer Verein decided to embark on a new house-building programme, 'in consideration of the fact that the rents for workers' accommodation are considerably more expensive in the town than in Stahlhausen, that there is a constant and very high demand for them, and finally that the Stahlhausen houses, which are better and healthier than the average of the town, are profitable in spite of the low rents . . .'.[66]

Company housing did greatly reduce the willingness of workers to leave their job and seek work elsewhere. Homes were always given strictly on condition that the tenant worked for the firm or pit concerned. To leave his job, therefore, meant also leaving his home. As Table 8 illustrates, colony dwellers were far less mobile than workers at the same mines living in private accommodation. Job-changing amongst colony dwellers does seem to have increased in later years, reaching 25 to 30 per cent in 1908–10; but even at this level it remained well below the turnover rates for miners generally.[67]

The economic advantages of reduced labour turnover were recognized. A settled and loyal labour force was clearly more productive than one which was constantly changing. The Gelsenkirchener Bergwerks AG's first annual report commented:

The increase in our workers' housing, particularly through the establishment of the Ottiliene colony, plays a vital role. The expansion of our

[65] *Zur Feier des 25-jährigen Bestehens der Gelsenkirchener Bergwerks AG 1873–1898* (Düsseldorf, n.d.).

[66] KA, 129 00, *Verwaltungsrathssitzung*, 16. 2. 1888.

[67] Heinrichsbauer, *Industrielle Siedlung*, p. 52.

TABLE 8
Labour turnover at Bochum mines, 1900[a]

Mine	Turnover of all workers (per cent)	Turnover of colony dwellers (per cent)
(South Bochum)		
Dannenbaum	54	0
Prinz Regent	54	1
Prinz v. Preussen	17	0
Heinrich Gustav	58	3
Vollmond	37	6
Friederica	54	0
(North Bochum)		
Constantin	49	0
Hannibal	51	2
Carolinenglück	75	3
Hannover	33	2
Lothringen	49	9

[a]Hundt, *Bergarbeiter Wohnungen*, pp. 34–5. 'Turnover' is quantified by adding the number of workers leaving and taken on.

work force through settled workers and the resulting considerable increase in productivity is mostly a result of this. This factor, as well as the increase and improvement of our other building investments, will in future be of increasing benefit to production.[68]

It is not possible to quantify the productivity loss through job-changing since other factors also affected output, but it took some time for a worker new to a pit to adjust fully to the new conditions and achieve his full potential. This was particularly important when—as was often the case in the Ruhr—there were wide variations in such crucial factors as the hardness of the seams between one pit and another. In the 1930s, however, one knowledgeable writer observed: 'Before the war every new miner's house was reckoned to be worth an increased production of 450 tons.'[69] The mines inspector Robert Hundt commented in 1902:

[68] *Zur Feier des 25-jährigen Bestehens der GBAG.*

[69] Heinrichsbauer, *Industrielle Siedlung*, p. 42. See also E. Oberschuir, *Die Heranziehung und Sesshaftmachung von Bergarbeitern im Ruhrkohlenbecken* (Düsseldorf, 1910), pp. 14–15; M. Metzner, *Soziale Fürsorge* (Jena, 1911), p. 8; Pieper, *Lage der Bergarbeiter*, p. 124.

The provision of good housing for the workers is the best and only means in the Ruhr coal-mining district to settle the workers and limit the extremely strong labour turnover. The low interest on the capital outlay is only illusory. In reality the higher productivity of a settled work-force who understand the character of the coal seams will soon more than compensate for the lack of interest on capital. The building of good housing is thus as much to the economic advantage of the employer as to that of the workers.[70]

Some employers, particularly the larger ones, probably drew little distinction between enlightened self-interest and a responsible concern for their employees' well-being. They would not have rejected the title 'paternalist' since they saw the firm very much as a kind of extended family. All worked for the common good, each according to his ability and station. It was the duty of the more fortunate to care for their more lowly brethren; but equally it was the duty of the head of the 'family' to ensure that the overall good took precedence. No challenge to their steward-ship was to be tolerated but so long as everyone willingly accepted his place within the hierarchy they could be genuinely munificent. The notion of the firm as a family community reached its apogee in the periodic company anniversary celebrations, particularly in the large engineering firms. At the Bochumer Verein's anniversary celebration of 1894 the twin notions of life-long commitment to the firm and firm's duty to care for its employees were expressed by Engineer Capelle:

It is frequently asserted that in modern industrial works the old dependence and the former good and to some extent patriarchal relationship between employer and employee has been lost. In some places this may be true. But the large number of men celebrating their jubilee with us proves that this is not the case with the *Bochumer Verein.* Here the initiative of the general director and the willingness of the board to provide the means have created a profusion of *Wohlfahrt-seinrichtungen* which I do not need to enumerate since they are known to all of us. We cannot better express our thanks for everything which has been done for us in this way in the past and particularly today than to make a solemn vow to stay true in future to the flag around which we gathered 25 years ago or more. We wish to do our duty and fulfil

[70] Hundt, *Bergarbeiter-Wohnungen*, p. 39.

our obligations until a higher Power orders: 'Now is the time for rest'.[71]

The provision of housing and other social benefits was thus presented as an expression of duty, a natural responsibility of those at the head of the company community to those below them. Although in no sense economically irrational—on the contrary, *Wohlfahrtseinrichtungen* provided powerful support to companies in coping with a difficult labour market—they served also a moral function, legitimizing power, offering a sense of identity and a focus for loyalty in a rapidly changing society. They thus provided psychological as well as material bonds between all those serving 'die Firma'. As Crew has observed, they represented an 'attempt to create a community both physically and morally insulated from the wider society'.[72]

Company social provisions thus gave tangible expression to the firm as a community of interest. Many workers were provided by their employer with homes and other facilities the like of which they had never before enjoyed and had little likelihood of finding elsewhere. Loyalty and good service clearly could pay dividends. Although company propaganda doubtless greatly exaggerated it, there is no reason to doubt that many workers were effectively encouraged to see their real support in their firm and to have their hopes and aspirations concentrated primarily on it. The appeal of company, as against class, was thus appreciably strengthened.

Company housing, particularly in the form of colonies, also helped to preserve and consolidate divisions amongst the workers. The status of those who lived in the colonies seems to have differed between the large engineering firms such as the Bochumer Verein or Krupp on the one hand, where to be accepted by the firm as a permanent employee and given a company home was a sign of skill and standing, and the mines on the other, where colony dwellers were often seen as socially inferior. This was partly because most mineworkers were relatively unskilled anyway but also because the pit colonies were largely inhabited by recent immigrants—in

---

[71] Bochumer Verein, *Bericht über die Jubel-Feier des Bochumer Vereins* (Bochum, 1894), p. 7.   [72] Crew, *Town in the Ruhr*, p. 149.

later years particularly immigrants from the east. The physical
and social isolation of the colonies meant that such immigrants enjoyed relatively little contact with other workers.
One contemporary observer reported the social isolation of
a Hamborn colony, particularly as it affected the children:

In the schools the children of officials, prosperous artisans, and workers
sit together in a healthy mix and learn from one another. But whereas in
the privately rented dwellings this coexistence continues at play, in the
colonies the [workers'] children only have each others' company in
their free time. There is a complete lack of mutual influence with other
social classes. One mother of seven, whose friendly, clean household
I admired with delight, complained to me: 'It is good to live here;
in the town we would get nothing with seven children. But the colony
is still the colony and for the children it is worthless. They neither see
nor hear anything better and the bad example makes them forget all
my exhortations'.[73]

This social isolation could be reassuring to some, particularly those new to industrial society. In 1908 the *Viktor* pit's
advertisement for workers, circulated in East and West
Prussia, specifically sought to reassure potential Masurian
immigrants that they would not need to mix with non-
Masurians:

Masurians! The mine seeks honest, decent families for this quite new
colony. If possible only Masurian families will inhabit the colony, so
they may live entirely amongst each other and need have nothing to do
with Poles, East Prussians, etc. Everyone will be able to imagine that he
is in his Masurian home-land.[74]

In 1902 the *Frankfurter Zeitung*'s correspondent described
the Polish colonies:

At least sixty per cent of the Polish immigrants are in the colonies and
have no steady communication with the natives. In my neighbourhood
there are great colonies with several hundred households. If anyone
wants convincing, let him go there: he would imagine he was in
'Greater Poland'. Not only the adults but also the children speak
Polish. These extensive company colonies are thus Polish enclaves
on German soil. The pit managements are naturally perfectly aware
of this development, but do nothing to alleviate it in an '*alldeutsche*'
spirit . . .[75]

---

[73] Fischer-Eckert, *Lage der Frauen*, pp. 35–6.
[74] ibid., p. 61.
[75] *Frankfurter Zeitung*, 1902 Nr. 35, quoted in Pieper, *Lage der Bergarbeiter*,
p. 242.

The gap between the immigrant colonies and other workers
was reinforced by the contempt with which the immigrants
—particularly taken *en masse* in colonies—were regarded.
Germans often found their manners rough and their homes
squalid. Colonies with a preponderant Polish element were
known as 'Polack colonies'. One German from Datteln told
a later researcher:

The pits needed men. So all sorts of riff-raff came who could not find
work elsewhere, the 'dryers' who only lived in the new houses until
they were dried out, many Italians, Croats, and Poles. When the Poles
arrived they were still servile and kissed one's shoes. But when they had
had three pay-days that was all over; then they became brazen. There
was disorder and quarrelling in these new houses. What did they have?
They got beds from the mine and then some boards and crates, that was
all. On pay-days there were regular punch-ups.[76]

The inhabitants of such colonies were popularly referred to
as the 'rabble'.[77]

The colonies thus helped to preserve ethnic and regional
differences between workers in the new industrial environment. This naturally helped the employers to preserve their
authority from serious challenge. The colonies were also of
more direct assistance to them in this. Residents were subject to strict rules and were more generally exposed to the
power of the employer. Thus the 'House Rules' of the
Bochumer Verein's home for single workers decreed that
'every inhabitant must obey unconditionally the directions
of the adminstrator and the supervisor' and provided detailed
rules about what was and what was not allowed. Some laid
down elementary common-sense practices of good social behaviour: if a fire broke out anywhere on the firm's premises
the men had to help put it out; they were not to lie in bed
with dirty clothing and smoking in bed was forbidden;
drunkenness and fighting were not to be tolerated. Other
rules appear more restrictive: visitors were only allowed
with the administrator's permission; the men could not
visit each other's rooms; they had to attend lunch . . .

[76] H. Croon and K. Utermann, *Zeche und Gemeinde* (Tübingen, 1958), p. 18.
[77] Kliss, *Wanderung der Ostpreussen*, p. 22. Even Dr Pieper, a defender of the
Poles, agreed that the Silesian and Bohemian miners 'are generally on a lower level
of living'. Pieper, *Lage der Bergarbeiter*, p. 215.

These restrictions were resented by many of the young men. The Gainsborough Commission commented that 'it is true that many of the men do not like the clause in their contract compelling them to lodge and board with the Firm; but it is impossible to contest the advantages that accrue to them from the system.'[78]

Most colonies had at least some similar rules, designed to suppress uncleanliness, drunkenness, and other behaviour ⅄ which was regarded as anti-social and to which the raw immigrant was sometimes felt to be particularly susceptible. Tenants would be issued with a list of rules on arrival and fined if they lost them. Such rules extended into the home some of the discipline of the work-place; they represented a part of the process by which a largely new, first-generation work-force was re-orientated and subordinated, psychologically as well as economically, to the demands of industrial labour and production. Thus Robert Hundt considered the colonies particularly useful for preserving law and order and acclimatizing newcomers to the new environment:

The settlement of workers in colonies has at least this advantage—not to be underestimated—over the building of scattered housing that it facilitates the maintenance of order and adequate cleanliness. All mines which own a large number of workers' dwellings have appointed housing administrators who are solely concerned with the control of such dwellings. . . . Tight supervision of workers' dwellings is particularly necessary for that large proportion of immigrant miners who have previously without exception lived in much worse housing and who only gradually learn to value the advantages of order and cleanliness.[79]

However, the really vital power which the colonies gave to employers stemmed from the link they created between a man's home and his job. These homes were only let on condition that the tenant—and often his able-bodied sons and lodgers—worked for the relevant company. His home was effectively tied to his job. If—for any reason—he left the

[78] Gainsborough Commission, *Life and Labour*, p. 26; Lange, 'Wohnungsverhältnisse', pp. 83–5. See also Fischer-Eckert, *Lage der Frauen*, pp. 32–6.

[79] Hundt, *Bergarbeiter-Wohnungen*, pp. 30–1. On the cultural acclimatization of first-generation workers to industrial labour in America and Britain, see H. G. Gutman, *Work, Culture and Society in Industrializing America* (Oxford, 1977); E. P. Thompson, 'Time, work-discipline and industrial capitalism', in M. W. Flinn and T. C. Smout (ed.), *Essays in Social History* (Oxford, 1974), pp. 33–77.

job or was sacked he had normally a couple of weeks to evacuate his home too. If he were to stop work without giving the obligatory two weeks' notice—and most strikes fell into this category—he could be required to leave his home immediately. We shall see later that this was a power which employers were sometimes willing to use. Perhaps more important than the occasions when men were actually thrown out of their homes, however, was the general vulnerability of large numbers of workers to their employers, a vulnerability which exerted its influence at all times, not just when the power was actually invoked. The miners' union paper described company housing as 'the worker's chains, which bind him to the employer':

For the inhabitant of such dwellings, which are in fact relatively cheap, this advantage is lost twice over through the dependence in which he is placed. He allows a small reduction of wages to take place without protest, simply with the thought that the advantage of a better wage he might obtain elsewhere will be lost through the higher rent he would have to pay there. He will usually submit to the most unworthy treatment, in the knowledge that otherwise he may be ejected from his cheap home and that any dismissal involves the danger of suddenly finding himself on the pavement with his possessions.[80]

[80] IZF, *Deutsche Berg- und Hüttenarbeiter Zeitung*, 2. 7. 1898. See also Fischer-Eckert, *Lage der Frauen*, p. 30.

3

Religion

Information on the religious beliefs and behaviour of workers in industrializing Germany is disappointingly limited. Recent historical attention has focused on the 'secularization' of the working class in the nineteenth century, under the twin influences of industrialization and urban growth. This meant not simply that intellectual commitment to the Christian faith declined but, more crucially, that social activities and behaviour commonly ceased to contain a specifically religious form and orientation. By the early twentieth century the contacts between the Churches and many of the millions of workers now gathered together in industrial cities were few and tenuous. The ordinary activities of work, family, leisure, and even politics took place increasingly in a world where religion played little or no overt role and seemed largely irrelevant to daily life. In some working-class circles religion as such was explicitly renounced and rejected.

Despite the long-term trend towards a more secular society, however, it would be wrong to describe the role of religion, even in the industrializing areas of Germany, simply in terms of marginalization and decline. The reality was more complex. Anti-clericalism, scepticism, and even disbelief were by no means unknown in pre-industrial Europe, and the novelty of 'secularization' should therefore not be overstated. Conversely, religion sometimes continued to play an important and influential role within working-class life well into the twentieth century. In Germany, as elsewhere, Catholics tended to remain more clearly under Church influence than Protestants, and women more than men. Even among Protestants the situation was far from uniform. Individual workers varied in their beliefs and behaviour from devout and loyal Church-members at one extreme, through degrees of nominal belief and indifference to outright atheism at the other.[1]

[1] V. L. Lidtke, 'Social Class and Secularisation in Imperial Germany', in *Year*

In the Ruhr as elsewhere rapid social change seemed to threaten the Churches and even religion itself. As early as 1867 the Protestant Synod in Bochum bemoaned the 'materialist spirit of the times, the estrangement from the church and its means of grace, the often horrible ignorance of religious things'.[2] Longer working-hours and shift-work made religious observance more difficult and turned Sunday for many into a day for sleep, rest, and recuperation rather than worship. Catholic saints' days were increasingly treated as working days. The local custom of starting the shift with a hymn or a prayer declined. Rival attractions, including inns and secular clubs, competed for the worker's few leisure hours. Little hard information is available about the level of church attendance, but it was certainly regarded as unsatisfactory—particularly among Protestants. In the early 1880s not more than ten to twenty per cent of Protestants seem to have attended church on a regular basis. In the more northern areas, such as Gelsenkirchen, the vast scale of immigation meant that churches remained full to bursting; but even here complaints began after the turn of the century that church attendance was no longer what it should be. Among Catholics church attendance was almost certainly higher: even in the 1920s over forty per cent of adult Catholics were attending mass in Schalke. In both cases, however, it was boosted by the influx of immigrants; without them the decline in regular contact between Churches and people might have been both more obvious and more rapid.[3]

Book of the Leo Baeck Institute xxv (1980), pp. 21–40; R. J. Evans, 'Religion and Society in Modern Germany' and H. McLeod, 'Protestantism and the Working Class in Imperial Germany', in *European Studies Review* XII. iii (1982), pp. 323–44; W. Schieder, 'Religionsgeschichte als Sozialgeschichte', in *Geschichte und Gesellschaft* iii (1977), pp. 291–8; R. Marbach, *Säkularisierung und sozialer Wandel im 19. Jahrhundert* (Göttingen, 1978). See also J. Sperber, 'Roman Catholic religious identity in Rhineland-Westphalia, 1800–1870', in *Social History* VII. iii (1982), pp. 305–18; K. Thomas, *Religion and the Decline of Magic* (London, 1982 edition), pp. 205–6, 764.

[2] A. Kraus, 'Gemeindeleben und Industrialisierung', in Reulecke and Weber (ed.), *Fabrik, Familie, Feierabend*, p. 274.

[3] ibid., pp. 277–8; O. Neuloh and J. Kurucz, *Vom Kirchdorf zur Industriegemeinde. Untersuchungen über den Einfluss der Industrialisierung auf die Wertordnung der Arbeitnehmer* (Köln, 1967), pp. 49–55; H. J. Brandt, 'Kirchliches Vereinswesen und Freizeitgestaltung in einer Arbeitergemeinde 1872–1933: Das Beispiel Schalke', in G. Huck (ed.), *Sozialgeschichte der Freizeit* (Wuppertal,

By the early twentieth century many Ruhr workers were disenchanted with the Churches and some even with belief in Christianity itself. Shortly before the war Adolf Levenstein asked over 800 Ruhr miners whether they believed in God and whether they had officially ceased to be members of their Church. The sample was unrepresentative since those questioned were generally social democratic sympathizers and because the response rate was poor.[4] Catholics were probably heavily under-represented. Nevertheless, Levenstein did obtain some striking results. Of the 436 Ruhr miners who actually answered this question, no fewer than 369 said that they did not believe in God.[5] Some who did profess to believe in God also showed a strong anti-clericalism. One 35-year-old replied: 'Yes, I believe in a God and in an afterlife. But not in the priests. I have not been to the black brothers for the last decade.'[6] But the number who had actually taken the public step of leaving their Church was much smaller—only 103.[7] The reason that some gave was concern for their family. As one put it: 'The dear Lord did me so much harm in my youth, and gave me so many sleepless nights on the way to socialism, that I banished him in retaliation. I have not yet broken with the form (Catholic), since it cannot hurt me and in order not to give my boys trouble at school.'[8]

It is clear that Levenstein did tap an important vein of anti-religious feeling amongst at least some Ruhr workers. Nevertheless, its extent should not be exaggerated. The question was stark, with little room for gradations of belief: the effect was to polarize responses, when the true feelings

---

1982), p. 221; W. Brepohl, *Industrievolk Ruhrgebiet* (Tübingen, 1957), p. 132. It was only in 1895 that the Bochumer Verein decided that the less important Catholic holy days should be treated as ordinary working days—in line with such firms as Krupp, Phönix, Rheinische Stahlwerke etc., most of which operated in more heavily Catholic areas. Tenfelde has suggested that the pre-shift hymn or prayer (which had a safety role as well as religious significance) persisted in some places until after the Second World War. KA, 129 00 20 *Verwalthungsrathssitzung*, 27. 7. 1895; Tenfelde, *Sozialgeschichte*, p. 95.

[4] The original response rate was 63 per cent, including 810 miners, but only 436 answered this question. Levenstein, *Arbeiterfrage*, pp. 10, 13, 334. See also Barrington Moore, *Injustice*, p. 193.

[5] Levenstein, *Arbeiterfrage*, p. 334.

[6] ibid., p. 330.   [7] ibid., p. 335.   [8] ibid., pp. 331-2.

of many respondents may have been a rather ill-defined indifference towards religion rather than a clearly articulated belief or disbelief. This may in part explain the poor response rate which the question evoked. Moreover, even among these workers—who by their selection were unusually amenable to anti-religious arguments and feelings—many continued to profess a faith and only a small minority actually left their Church.[9]

It has been suggested that one of the major effects of industrial and urban development in modern Europe has been the removal of the need for supernatural aid during most people's working life: 'a largely mechanised economy dependent on humanly controllable factors no longer requires prayers for rain.'[10] This change, it is argued, removed one of the fundamental social bases for the religious and quasi-religious thought-patterns and behaviour of pre-industrial times. Miners, however, remained clearly and immediately vulnerable to the forces of nature and may therefore have retained a greater respect than most for the role of the supernatural. Although any conclusion must remain speculative, it may be that such feelings were expressed as much through popular superstitions as through conventional religious behaviour and belief. Otto Hue, himself a social democrat miners' leader, observed:

Very few miners are complete atheists. Many claim to be, but if one looks more closely one discovers that the apparent denier of God is an unconscious pantheist who sees God in every expression of nature . . . . The average miner is deeply religious, even when—as is very common—he attends no church. And the man who disputes God out of existence lets him in again through a back door. However, the collier does not generally dispute about abstract matters; he is taciturn, a result of his long work in the lonely depths.[11]

[9] Leaving the Church may have offered some tax advantages; on the other hand, it could involve expensive legal processes. Only 17 of the 103 Ruhr miners who told Levenstein that they had left the Church said that they did so for tax reasons. Levenstein, *Arbeiterfrage*, p. 335; Nolan, *Social democracy and society*, p. 48.

[10] H. McLeod, *Religion and the People of Western Europe 1789–1970* (Oxford, 1981), pp. 93–4. See also Thomas, *Religion and the Decline of Magic*.

[11] O. Hue, *Neutrale oder parteiische Gewerkschaften?* (Bochum, 1900), pp. 90–1. Minework has often been accompanied by superstitions—not surprisingly, in view of the dangers and the evident vulnerability of men in the

The pervasiveness of religious models of thought, even amongst avowed non-believers, was illustrated by Peter Klein, a social democrat miner from the Saar, who described his adoption of socialism in the following terms: 'When I was a soldier at Metz I got to know a very able comrade from Nuremberg called Auer. He showed me what I was then lacking and freed me from the delusion of religious fanaticism by explaining to me the new religion of socialism. Since then I have taken this religion as my rightful inheritance.'[12]

The most active opponents of religion amongst the workers were the social democrats. The anti-clerical and atheistic views of many of their leaders were well known and actively propagated. The identification of the Churches, particularly the official Protestant Church, with the state, the employers, and the upper classes generally, made it easy to combine a political critique with an attack on religion as such. There were occasional organized campaigns against the Churches. In 1890 it was reported that the party was trying to weaken the Catholic Church's influence, particularly among workers' wives. A campaign in Hörde, near Dortmund, in 1905 and 1906 resulted in over 150 people leaving the Church. At social democrat meetings in Gelsenkirchen in the following year supporters were urged to leave the Church on the grounds that it constituted an important prop to capitalist society. In 1910 the SPD persuaded around 70 people in Weitmar to leave the Church, but the priest managed to get at least some of them to return. In Langendreer too a campaign was mounted, although 'the general feeling is against it'. By 1912 the agitation was said to have virtually ceased.[13] Such campaigns confirmed the Churches in their view that social democracy was bitterly hostile to religion and the Churches as such and gave local political conflicts a signifi-

face of nature. For contemporary examples, see D. Douglass and J. Krieger, *A Miner's Life* (London, 1983), pp. 15–16.

[12] A. Levenstein, *Aus der Tiefe: Arbeiterbriefe* (Berlin, 1909), p. 115. See also McLeod, *Religion and the People of Western Europe*, p. 45.

[13] STAM, *Oberpräsidium* 2694 Bd. I, RPA. to *Minister des Innern*, 24. 12. 1890; StAB, 481, RPA to *Minister des Innern*, 10. 12. 1906; STAM, RA I 99, *Stadt* Gelsenkirchen to RPA, 14. 9. 1907; StAB, 482, *Amt* Weitmar to KLB, 8. 8. 1910; StAB, 482, *Amt* Langendreer to KLB, 12. 8. 1910; StAB, 482, KLB to RPA, 27. 8. 1912.

cant religious dimension. However, their importance to the working class as a whole, and even to the social democrats themselves, should not be exaggerated. The campaigns seem to have formed relatively minor and intermittent features of social democratic activity in the Ruhr. Moreover, they need to be seen against the other main element in the party's approach to religion—its espousal of toleration. In principle, the SPD regarded religion as a private matter to which the party was officially indifferent. Criticism was therefore supposed to be directed primarily at the political and social behaviour of the Churches, not at religious belief as such. Indeed, the social democrats prided themselves on showing greater tolerance than most of differing religious views. August Bebel, in a speech in Bochum in 1890, declared that although an atheist himself he believed in religious freedom for all and had opposed the expulsion of the Jesuits from Germany in the 1870s; social democracy, he claimed, was more tolerant in this area than the other political parties. In similar vein the regional party paper assured its readers in 1893 that the party was not opposed to religion as such and that everyone was free to believe what he wished.[14]

Even the social democrats thus showed some hesitation and ambivalence in criticism of the Churches and religion. Behind their concern was an awareness of the continuing underlying strength of religious loyalties within the working class generally. These were not necessarily greatly weakened by a decline in religious observance or even in conventional religious belief. As Joyce has noted with regard to nineteenth-century Lancashire, religion could continue to play a critical part in the social and political life of a community, even when formal religious belief and practice appeared weak and lukewarm: despite the trends there towards a more 'secularized' society, religion still provided an important basis for social identity and communal loyalties.[15] In the Ruhr too religion continued to be of major importance.

[14] IZF, *Westfälische Freie Presse* 30. 12. 1890; IZF, *Rheinisch-Westfälische Arbeiter Zeitung* 14. 6. 1893. For the party's general approach to religion see V. L. Lidtke, 'August Bebel and German Social Democracy's Relation to the Christian Churches', in *Journal of the History of Ideas* (1966).

[15] P. Joyce, *Work, Society and Politics. The Culture of the Factory in later Victorian England* (London, 1982 edition), p. 176.

One reason for this was the lack of alternatives. For some the 'religion of socialism' might offer a rival appeal but for many others, despite misgivings about conventional religion, the leap was simply too great or perhaps too unconvincing. One such was Bruno Bittner, a miner originally from Silesia, whose views were described by his colleague Max Lotz:

> His beliefs are very puzzling. He is no longer able to feel enthusiasm for the Christian lullaby of the spiritual perspective, as well as the renunciation of earthly pleasure which always accompanies it. He sees wealth piling up on one side and the severest poverty on the other, sees how the Christian priesthood supports this 'God-willed order', and cannot then understand how the thoroughly charitable and loving 'Creator of the world and of men' willed this shrill disharmony or wills it still. It also nags at him—and he often talks of this—that lightning can strike the church and the tabernacle (this actually occurred near his former Silesian home), and he regards it as folly that God should drive himself out of his own house. One cannot deny him a certain power of observation. He has not yet managed to paint a coherent picture of the world. He just believes in nothing in particular because many others do likewise. He does not have an independent view or an alternative to the usual concept 'God'.[16]

The role of religion in the ritual life of the community was one source of the sustained strength of its appeal. Even secular celebrations often had a religious element with the Protestant Church prominently involved in the great public celebrations of the Emperor's birthday and the commemoration of the battle of Sedan. By the 1880s Catholic organizations were also participating in these patriotic festivities. The Catholic Church also organized public celebrations, notably the Corpus Christi processions which became more popular during the 1880s. The social democrats' main regular public festival was May Day. This was clearly non-religious in character but, as we shall see in a later chapter, it was normally fairly modest in its size and appeal. Where the Churches maintained a virtual monopoly, however, was in the rituals surrounding the main life-cycle events—the 'rites of passage'

[16] Levenstein, *Aus der Tiefe*, pp. 36–7. In his study of religion in nineteenth-century London, McLeod points out the importance of having 'an alternative system of belief' available if religious ties are to be broken. There is scope for debate about the extent to which social democracy really offered an equivalent in terms of intellectual, emotional, and social provision. H. McLeod, *Class and Religion in the Late Victorian City* (London, 1974), p. 79.

associated with birth, marriage, and death. Church baptism, marriage, and burial remained almost universal. Occasionally even these ceremonies would be given a broader social or even political significance: funerals, in particular, were often accompanied by a turn-out of the deceased's fellow club-members, sometimes with flags and uniforms. The social democrats sometimes tried to emulate this, with red flags and a socialist oration, but such efforts were relatively infrequent. After one such incident, the Protestant Synod in Bochum threatened not to carry out the burial in the case of a repeat. Social democrats seem almost always to have had their children baptized even though they occasionally failed to attend the service themselves. For most people religion provided the only available language and forms through which to mark these landmarks in their own lives and those of their families and immediate community.[17]

Religious loyalties were further fostered by the Churches' influence on the young. In part this was direct, through their influence on elementary education and through the establishment of church clubs and organizations aimed specifically at young people. In addition, even parents who paid little attention to religious matters themselves sometimes insisted that their children should do so. In the 1920s church attendance among young Catholics in Schalke was significantly higher than amongst adults. This may also have reflected the place of religion in the sexual division of labour within families. In Germany, as elsewhere in Europe, religious observance was seen by many as primarily a women's responsibility. It was part of their 'private' sphere, separate from the 'public' sphere of men. In Hamborn in 1913 it was reported that most Catholic women followed the priest's instructions to attend church regularly—although they showed little enthusiasm about it—while Polish women attended more frequently than was strictly required; the few

[17] P. Pieper, *Kirchliche Statistik Deutschlands* (Freiburg, 1899), pp. 211, 241, 266-7; Kraus, 'Gemeindeleben', pp. 275-6; Tenfelde, *Sozialgeschichte*, p. 392; K. Tenfelde, 'Mining Festivals in the Nineteenth Century', in *Journal of Contemporary History* xiii (1978). For May Day in the Ruhr, see chapter 6 below. A suggestive account of the importance of ritual in the struggle between Catholicism and Communism in modern Italy is provided in D. I. Kertzer, *Comrades and Christians. Religion and Political Struggle in Communist Italy* (Cambridge, 1980).

Protestant women, on the other hand, seem to have stayed aloof. Catholic women there were almost all members of the Mothers' Union, one of the main concerns of which was the last rites of deceased members. Bochum Protestant leaders saw the wives as one of the best defences against anti-church agitation and the social democrats seem to have taken the same view. In 1890 workers' wives responded to one anti-church campaign by refusing to let the distributors of social democratic papers into their homes. The effect of such attitudes was that most children, including the children of many social democrat supporters, continued to be brought up with a set of assumptions in which religion was an important and potent element.[18]

The role of religion was reinforced by some of the very changes which were transforming the Ruhr in the nineteenth century. The constant influx of migrants meant that many workers were fresh from non-urban environments where the priest or minister still carried a traditional authority. Religion offered symbols and a language which enabled people in an utterly novel social setting to establish and express a new collective identity. As we shall see, the Poles afforded the most striking example of this: for many, their commitment to Roman Catholicism was scarcely distinguishable from their commitment to the Polish language or even to political Polish nationalism.[19] In such circumstances 'religion' sustained a social meaning and significance far deeper than the evidence of secularization alone would suggest.

Indeed, in the Ruhr the divisions between Christians and non-Christians were less significant than those between, and even within, the denominations themselves. The region was denominationally divided, predominantly Catholic in the west—in towns such as Duisburg, Hamborn, and Essen—and mainly Protestant in the east, around Dortmund. Bochum

[18] Kraus, 'Gemeindeleben', p. 288; STAM, *Oberpräsidium* 2694 Bd. I, RPA to *Minister des Innern*, 24. 12. 1890; Fischer-Eckert, *Lage der Frauen*, p. 135. R. J. Evans, 'Politics and the Family: Social Democracy and the Working-Class Family in Theory and Practice before 1914', in Evans and Lee (ed.), *German Family*, p. 270; McLeod, 'Protestantism and the Working Class', pp. 337–9; Marbach, *Säkularisierung*, p. 50.

[19] Discussing the Irish in nineteenth-century Lancashire, Joyce comments that, 'the identification of Irishness and Catholicism was well nigh absolute.' Joyce, *Work, Politics and Society*, p. 252.

was fairly evenly balanced. In 1907 some 47 per cent of the town's population were Catholic but amongst the workers the proportion was 51 per cent. As Table 9 suggests, the denominational split amongst workers varied from one industry to another. In addition to the two main denominational groups, Roman Catholics and Lutherans, there were small numbers of Jews and members of other Protestant sects.[20]

TABLE 9

Catholics as a proportion of workers by industry,
Bochum, 1907[a]

Timber	61 per cent	Mining	50 per cent
Construction	60	Engineering	49
Foodstuffs	57	Quarries	47
Transport	53	Hostelries	47
Commerce	53	Metals	36

[a] *Statistik des deutschen Reiches* ccvii. 608 ff.

Protestants and Catholics were not spread evenly geographically. In 1871 Catholics comprised 46 per cent of the population of Bochum and its surrounding *Landkreis*; but within individual *Gemeinden* the proportion varied from 79 per cent (Grumme) to 7 per cent (Harpen). In 1912, after 40 years of population growth, Catholics comprised 43 per cent of the total population with the highest proportional (not absolute) concentration in Riemke (61 per cent) and the lowest still in Harpen (9 per cent). The range had thus narrowed. Moreover, whereas in 1871 there had been three *Gemeinden* in which Catholics comprised over 60 per cent of the population and eight where they were fewer than one-quarter, by 1912 the number of such unbalanced *Gemeinden* was down to one and two respectively. We see something of

[20] In 1900 the Bochum *Altstadt* was said to contain, in addition to nearly 35,000 Catholics and 29,500 Lutherans, 933 Jews, 212 Baptists, 94 *Dissidenten* and 31 Old Catholics. Ten years later it was claimed that these official estimates understated the number of non-Lutheran Protestants, and that there were approaching 2,000 Methodists, Baptists, Adventists, etc. in the town. Either way, they represented a small minority. Seippel, *Bochum Einst und Jetzt*, p. 51; Kraus, 'Gemeindeleben', p. 286.

the same trend towards greater geographical mixing of denominations within Weitmar, where 45 per cent of the population were Catholics. In 1909 73 per cent of them lived in streets where between 30 and 60 per cent of the inhabitants were Catholic but by 1913 the proportion had risen to 80 per cent. The large and growing majority of Weitmar Catholics thus lived in streets which, in basic numerical terms at least, were fairly well mixed.[21]

While not as deep and bitter as in, say, Ireland, sectarian divisions persisted in many areas of life. The *Kulturkampf* —the anti-Catholic state measures of the 1870s—increased tensions and a sense of isolation among many Catholics. Paradoxically, the effect of repression was to strengthen Catholics' sense of religious identity and to radicalize some Catholics' political and social perspectives so that they came close to those of the social democrats themselves. In later years relations between the two main Churches seem to have been uneasy. Occasionally Protestants and Catholics would join together in popular celebrations. At other times, however, there were signs of hostility: Catholic street processions might be seen as provocative and sometimes lead to Protestant attempts to restrict their route. The schools were divided on denominational lines. In 1886 and 1896 there were six Catholic and six Protestant primary schools in Bochum: with the exception of one Catholic pupil at a Protestant school in 1896, none took any children from the other creed. Ten years later each denomination had 19 schools but there were still no Protestants at the Catholic schools and only three Catholic children in the Protestant ones. Hospitals, old-people's homes, and orphanages were also denominational in character. Perhaps most important, intermarriage between Catholics and Protestants remained exceptional: even when it occurred it was liable to promote not denominational harmony but rival sectarian claims for the allegiance of the ensuing children.[22]

[21] S. H. F. Hickey, *Class conflict and class consciousness: the emergence of the working class in the Eastern Ruhr 1870–1914* (D.Phil. thesis, Oxford, 1978), p. 106. Bochum town and *Landkreis* covered 18 *Gemeinden* in 1912, and the 1871 figures cover the same ones. WWA, K2 359.

[22] Brepohl, *Industrievolk Ruhrgebiet*, pp. 133–4; Kraus, 'Gemeindeleben', pp. 281–5; Silbergleit, *Preussens Städte*, pp. 216–18; Tenfelde, *Sozialgeschichte*, pp. 493–7; Tenfelde, 'Mining Festivals in the Nineteenth Century', pp. 400–1.

The social and community life of the area thus embraced important denominational divisions. Religious labels provided a ready shorthand for community loyalties and conflicts. In Bochum the division between 'black' (Catholic) and 'blue' (Protestant) seems to have permeated both economic and social life in the 1880s. When neighbouring Langendreer, traditionally a Protestant village, experienced an influx of propertyless Catholic workers, friction at once ensued with the Protestant craftsmen, shopkeepers, and businessmen who dominated local life and paid local taxes and who saw little reason to provide funds for Catholic religious and social needs.[23] Young people often divided on sectarian lines: Otto Hue recalled his youth in Hörde, near Dortmund, in the 1870s and 1880s:

Sectarian hatred is so profoundly imparted to school children that as a school kid I was involved in the most murderous fights with the 'blacks'. Later I and many of these 'blacks' worked together at the foundry in a perfectly friendly spirit and we looked back with bitter scorn at the time when fanatical self-interested politics had incited us youngsters against each other.[24]

Such conflicts did not always bear religious labels: at Datteln ('Steinfeld') the stream between the old village and the new colony formed a frontier where the boys from the two communities—both of which contained Catholics and Protestants —fought each other.[25] In Witten, on the other hand, youthful sectarianism flourished at least until the 1920s. As one inhabitant of this mainly Protestant town recalled:

The intolerant—but generally popular—description of the area from Kronen— and Kesselstrasse to Crengeldanzstrasse, and beyond to the Marienstrasse and the beginning of the Ardezstrasse, as the 'Nigger Village' [*Negerdorf*]—because of the predominantly 'black' voters there—was quite current during my school years in the 1920s; and was now and then a willingly utilized reason to provoke strong disputes even amongst grammar school students.[26]

---

[23] Crew, *Town in the Ruhr*, pp. 129–30; Croon, 'Studien', p. 89. The predominantly Catholic area around Langendreer station became known as the 'Catholic station'.

[24] Hue, *Neutrale oder parteiische Gewerkschaften?*, p. 111.

[25] Croon and Utermann, *Zeche und Gemeinde*, pp. 19–20.

[26] W. Nettmann, *Witten in den Reichstagswahlen des Deutschen Reiches 1871–1918* (Witten, 1972), p. 104.

The identification between denominational and community loyalties created problems within as well as between the Churches. Immigrants, particularly those who had come long distances from a quite different social environment, saw the maintenance of their religious practices as a central part of their attempts to preserve their language, customs, and sense of community in the new setting. Protestant Masurians and Catholic Poles did not feel at home in the established German Churches which they found in the Ruhr. Indeed, to the embarrassment of their respective hierarchies they insisted on having their own ministers and priests. Masurians, for example, demanded a far more vocal and ostentatious style of worship than their German co-religionists—with much emphasis on singing, genuflection, and the sign of the cross. The language barrier was another major problem. In the 1890s a Masurian minister travelled around the Masurian groups in the Ruhr and in 1887 and 1891 the first special Masurian ministries were established in Gelsenkirchen and Bochum. In the 1890s a Polish-speaking Protestant minister in Gelsenkirchen was receiving financial support from a number of large employers. However such measures were not always sufficient. The Protestant Church lost credibility in the eyes of many workers through its identification with the ruling establishment, both national and local. Indicative of certain Protestant attitudes was the reluctance of the school authorities in Herne in 1878 to support the creation of new schools for miners' children. Similarly, Masurian immigrants in Langendreer found little welcome or sympathy in the local Church. Such attitudes, based on political conservatism, ethnic suspicion, and social contempt, led some Protestants to seek a more sympathetic religious life in one of the nonconformist sects. For others, particularly in the second generation, the result was disillusion with the Churches and a weakening of religious loyalties.[27]

The Poles, with their large numbers and their sense of distinctive nationhood, posed even bigger problems for the Catholic hierarchy. The first Polish priests appeared in the

---

[27] Kraus, 'Gemeindeleben', pp. 286–7; Tenfelde, *Sozialgeschichte*, pp. 383–4; Croon, 'Studien', p. 103; Neuloh and Kurucz, *Vom Kirchdorf zur Industriegemeinde*, p. 49; KA, 129 00 Nr. 20, BVG *Verwaltungsrathssitzung*, 28. 10. 1894.

Ruhr in the 1870s and 1880s. Despite the insistence by Dr Franz Liss, the most prominent of them, that 'a good Pole is a good Catholic', their activities contributed powerfully to the emergence within the Ruhr of a distinct Polish-Catholic sub-culture with strong nationalist overtones. The first Polish Catholic Congress was held in Bochum in 1894 and issued a strongly-worded demand for more Polish priests in the district. The embarrassed Church authorities—with encouragement from the state—responded by sending Liss back to the east and restricting the duration of other Polish priests' ministries in the west. Despite the introduction of Polish language classes at the Paderborn and Münster seminaries and a gradual growth in the number of Polish-speaking German priests, the conflict continued throughout the pre-war years. The Church refused to allow baptisms, communion lessons, marriages, or burials to be conducted in Polish—and even the occasional Polish-language mass provoked strong German criticism. In 1906 there were renewed calls by the Poles for more Polish priests and talk—which came to nothing—of a petition to the Pope. At the local level a 'Polish Committee to Obtain Better Spiritual Care' was established in Baukau: at a meeting in January 1908 'the bishops and priests were generally very sharply criticized because they did not want to fulfil the justified demands of the Poles' and it was agreed to write to the local priest and urge him to approach the bishop. By 1913 there were 75 Polish-speaking priests active in the Ruhr, all but three of them of German nationality, and a number of churches had regular Polish sermons and hymns; but these concessions in no way resolved what had become a source of festering discord within Catholicism in the region.[28]

[28] Klessmann, *Polnische Bergarbeiter im Ruhrgebiet*, pp. 58, 137–41; Wehler, 'Polen im Ruhrgebiet', pp. 445–51; StAB, *Westfälische Allgemeine Zeitung*, 26. 5. 1972; StAB, 464, *Polizei* Baukau to KLB, 6. 1. 1908; StAB, 482, *Amt* Langendreer to KLB, 8. 8. 1911. The Irish in America and England posed similar problems for the Catholic Churches there. One American noted: 'I have never had reason to believe that the mass of the Irish are attached to the Roman Catholic religion as a matter of faith. It is a matter of national pride, and of the gallantry of those who lived where it has been persecuted. A Catholic congregation here, under the charge of an English or French priest, is almost always restless. They want an Irish priest, for their interest in their faith is, that it was their faith in their oppressed home.' T. Coleman, *Passage to America* (London, 1974),

Despite the growth of towns and industry, therefore, religion continued to act as an important focus for the beliefs, loyalty, and communal self-awareness of many workers and their families. Nevertheless the position of the Churches was not secure. It was increasingly necessary for them to find new ways of maintaining their links with and appeal to the industrial workers who now dominated the district.

Social Catholicism

The Catholics were the first to develop a distinctive progressive and socially-orientated interpretation of their creed. Bishop Ketteler of Mainz, the main spokesman of 'social Catholicism' in Germany, wrote in the 1860s: 'Efforts to improve the wretched conditions which the principles of the modern economic system have imposed on the workers . . . are certainly not in contradiction to the spirit of Christianity but to the contrary are in complete accordance with it.'[29] It was a view which could easily attract sympathy from Catholics in the Ruhr where large numbers of Catholic workers had their lives dominated by Protestant employers. Many Catholics there were ready and willing to campaign to defend the interests of workers against what they saw as rapacious and often un-Christian employers.

The Church and the lay Catholic establishment in Germany adopted a cautious approach towards such views. The need to improve the conditions of workers was broadly accepted. But, at least for the Church, this was a secondary aim: defence of the faith came first. Thus the Prussian bishops in their pastoral letter of August 1890 conceded the need for special church clubs specifically for industrial workers but cautioned:

These clubs must be truly Christian. . . . They must all have religion, sincere and living Christianity, as their basis and religious morality as their rule. Where this is lacking clubs will not only be unfruitful and decay but will easily degenerate and make the evil worse. It is therefore better to begin with a small number of truly religious

pp. 204–5. On the Irish in England, see McLeod, *Class and Religion*, and footnote 19 above.

[29] A. Erdmann, *Die christlichen Gewerkschaften* (Stuttgart, 1914), p. 9.

members and gradually to expand than to introduce the germ of corruption into the club through some kind of indulgence towards the secular spirit with the aim of size.[30]

The Church's most significant statement on the social question came the following year in the papal encyclical 'Rerum Novarum'. This argued vigorously against the alleged socialist solution to the social question, 'the transference of all property from individuals to the community'. Private property was defended as a natural right, as being to the ultimate advantage of the worker himself and as a defence of the family. Inequality and burdensome work were inevitable but harmony between property owners and the propertyless was possible and it was the Church's duty to foster it. The aim therefore was to avoid unnecessary conflict within society through fair and Christian behaviour on all sides. In this context workers' clubs were permitted but with the defence and propagation of the faith as their primary aim:

The religious element must be the basis of the association. The faith of the members should be the most important aim, and the Christian faith must permeate the entire organization. Otherwise the association would soon lose its original character; it would become the same as those other associations which exclude religion from their ranks. But what does it profit the worker to win from the association advantages for his earthly comfort, if his soul comes into danger through lack of spiritual nourishment? [31]

The Church's attitude was clear: social concern was a proper part of Christianity; but it was to be expressed not through class conflict but through greater harmony and more Christian behaviour within the given, and inevitably unequal, society. The greatest help to the worker was to strengthen his faith.

The lay Catholic hierarchy, particularly the Centre party, was also cautious in its attitude towards social issues. Few party leaders were themselves of working-class origins. Politically, the party was committed to the defence of private property and was thus suspicious of those whose radicalism might seem to threaten it. Within the Ruhr this approach led

[30] ibid., p. 24.
[31] ibid., p. 31; G. Brakelmann, *Die soziale Frage des 19. Jahrhunderts* (Witten, 1962), pp. 217–26.

to conflicts within the party. In the 1874 *Reichstag* election in Essen Laaf, a priest and leader of radical Catholics, urged that the miners should support the party as 'the lesser evil' but promised that next time they would put up their own candidates. The Centre party candidate, Forcade de Biaix, won but was subjected to attacks from Laaf and the miner Rosenkranz over the next few years on the grounds that he did not sufficiently understand or support the workers' interests. In the 1877 election a workers' candidate, Stötzel, was put up against the Centre candidate and won.[32]

The *Kulturkampf* helped to strengthen the radicals within the Centre party in the 1870s. In Dortmund Lambert Lensing, the editor of *Tremonia*, the leading Catholic paper, was outspoken in championing the workers against the employers. In 1900 'an old miner' writing in the Bochum socialist press recalled the mood of those years:

When I got involved in the miners' movement twenty years ago, it was through a Catholic miners' association. In those days there was a quite different life in those associations. The money snobs were told the truth straight, and our chaplain was one of the most vociferous in the struggle against the factory owners. . . . One comrade at the end of the 1870s wanted to work at the *Centrum* mine; he was chased away by the mine manager: the poor man was an ultramontane; had he merely been a social democrat he could have worked. At that time it was more dangerous to be an ultramontane than a socialist. Lambert Lensing was one of the most radical. I was regularly intoxicated with the agitation speeches against Capital which he delivered. The *Tremonia* wrote more bitingly against the employers than the socialist press does today. In consequence the factory workers were forbidden to read *Tremonia* and other similar ultramontane papers! When today I remember how sharply and maliciously Lensing spoke and wrote against the capitalists at that time, I simply cannot understand how a man can change so much. Bölger, Dietrich, Tölcke, and other socialist agitators were young innocents compared with Lensing, at least as far as fighting the owners was concerned. Today one does not see the Lambert of those days any more. Nor does one recognize his colleagues, the 'red Johannes' [Johannes Fussangel, a Catholic miners' leader] or Stötzel who spent the '70s constantly in court for slander against the police or the owners.[33]

There were two main expressions of 'social Catholicism' in the Ruhr, although both were to some extent muted as a result

---

[32] Hue, *Bergarbeiter*, ii 317–19.
[33] IZF, *Volksblatt*, 14. 3. 1900.

of the cautious attitude taken by the Church and lay Catholic establishment. These were the Catholic working mens' clubs (*Arbeitervereine*) and the (predominantly Catholic) 'Christian' trade unions. The first Catholic *Arbeitervereine* in the Ruhr were formed in the 1860s and 1870s; although their growth was hindered by the *Kulturkampf* and the early days of the anti-socialist law, the papal encyclical 'Humanum genus' of 1884, which supported them, marked the beginning of a further expansion.[34] The aims and activities of one club, founded in 1870, were expressed in its first two statutes:

1. The main aim of the society is to raise the religious and moral standards of the workers, starting from the conviction that the social question can only be resolved in a peaceable manner through Christianity. Another aim is the material improvement of the workers; in particular, members who have fallen into need through no fault of their own should be supported, as far as the society's resources allow.
2. These aims will be followed: (a) through pleasant and useful diversions, through monthly public lectures on practical and social issues, through suitable literature, singing and the enjoyment of Christian and congenial society; (b) through mutual friendly and helpful behaviour in civil life.[35]

The club thus provided a focus for social life and fostered mutual help and self-improvement with a general emphasis on religion. It was a combination which characterized the Catholic clubs generally. The club for young Catholics from Gelsenkirchen and Bulmke met every Sunday and Monday evening: 'On Sunday evenings religious, social, and historical talks are held and on Monday evenings there are lessons in religion, writing, book-keeping, and drawing. There is a large library. And for amusement there are chess, billiards, and bowling.'[36] In Wanne the Church provided two clubs for young men; the aims of one, in the words of the priest, were 'to sustain them in their religion and love of their fatherland and to protect them from the manifold dangers which attend this age. This is achieved through edifying and instructive talks, through discussions and through singing.'[37] The clubs

[34] H. Krauss and H. Ostermann, *Verbandskatholizismus?* (Kevelaer, 1968), pp. 28–32; Tenfelde, *Sozialgeschichte*, pp. 361 ff.
[35] A. Kalis, *Kirche und Religion in Revier* (Essen, 1968), p. 49.
[36] STAM, *Landratsamt* Gelsenkirchen 48, *Amt* Bismarck to *Landrat* Gelsenkirchen, 30. 9. 1902.
[37] ibid., *Pfarrer* Schnettler to *Amt* Wanne, 12. 9. 1902.

often had good facilities: in Witten in 1897 the Catholic workers' club had a library of 210 volumes while the parallel apprentices' club had 650.[38] In Schalke, where the Catholic Church had formed over thirty clubs aimed at different social groups by 1912, a large communal building was established to house them: the facilities included bowling, billiards, a large library, meeting rooms, and rooms for dances and shows. It also provided lodging rooms for around thirty young workers. The Bochum Catholic Apprentices' Club also had its own building: like the others it saw its aim as to 'protect native and travelling apprentices from moral dangers', and sought to achieve this through lectures, singing, and speaking classes.[39]

The clubs were generally presided over by non-workers, usually the priest but sometimes other local notables, including even employers. One club, founded at Werden near Essen in 1880, had an honorary committee of 25 including the chairman of a mining company, doctors, officials, priests, and teachers.[40] The Church's role was strengthened in the 1880s by a general requirement that the clubs have a priest, nominated by the bishop, at their head—although a worker should be chairman.[41]

The opportunities which these clubs gave for promoting opposition both to Protestant liberalism and to 'atheistic' social democracy are clear. In the 1870s and 1880s many Catholics saw liberalism as the chief threat. With the re-emergence of social democracy in the 1890s and the gradual improvement in relations between the Catholic establishment and the state, more of the rhetoric was directed at the social democrats. The Church's attitude was expressed uncompromisingly by the Bishop of Münster in 1890:

The social democrats aim at nothing less than the total dissolution of the existing order of society, the overthrow of the throne and the

[38] StAB, 479, *Bürgermeister* Witten to KLB, 6. 4. 1897.

[39] STAM, RA I 103, *Bürgermeister* Bochum to RPA, 10. 11. 1892; Brandt, 'Kirchliches Vereinswesen'.

[40] Kalis, *Kirche und Religion*, p. 49.

[41] Krauss and Ostermann, *Verbandskatholizismus?*, p. 31; R. J. Ross, *Beleaguered Tower: the Dilemma of Political Catholicism in Wilhelmine Germany* (Notre Dame, 1976), p. 85.

extirpation of Christianity with all its institutions and creations. They demand the abolition of marriage, the dissolution of property—even each individual's personal property—and the introduction of the socialist republic. Denial of God and unbelief should become general and rule, according to their views.[42]

The equation of Catholic faith with militant anti-socialism was common throughout this period. At a Polish meeting at Castrop in 1891 the speaker declared:

Christ be praised! (Response) Dear brothers! It pleases me greatly to be able to greet so many of you. I come at once to the question—what do the socialists want? How should we protect ourselves from their attacks? The socialists . . . want no religion, no church, and no throne. What belongs to one should also belong to the rest. That is not right. We must believe in God because the Holy Book tells us so. If we had no Church millions of soldiers would be of no help to us. The schools would become Godless since the priests would not be allowed to educate the children in religion. The social democrats want neither king nor Kaiser, they want a republic. We have seen how they do not hold back even from the murder of kings and they have even murdered priests. . . . The socialist says that you should not listen to the priests and tries to take from us our most holy possession, our religion.[43]

Attempts by the social democrats to show that they meant nothing of the sort merely provoked further denunciations. During the 1898 *Reichstag* election the SPD issued leaflets in Polish explaining that the party viewed religion as a private issue. The (Catholic) *Wittener Volkszeitung* denied this:

The social democrats want to rob us of our religion so as to use us more surely for their own ends. So, Polish workers, do not give your votes to the candidates of a party which wishes to take away the religion of your fathers and only follows goals which can never be achieved![44]

Even if the social democrats had convinced the Church that they were truly neutral on the question of religious belief, it is doubtful whether this would have removed the profound distrust between them. For the view of the Pope and the bishops, as we have seen, was that strengthening

---

[42] STAM, *Oberpräsidium* 2693 (Bd. 2), *Germania*, 2. 12. 1890; J. K. Zeender, 'The German Centre Party 1890-1906', in *Transactions of the American Philosophical Society* LXVI. i (1976), p. 54.

[43] Quoted in Klessmann, *Polnische Bergarbeiter im Ruhrgebiet*, p. 212.

[44] Nettmann, *Witten in den Reichstagswahlen*, p. 141, *Wittener Volkszeitung* 16. 6. 1898.

the faith was the prime aim and took precedence over any secular venture in which Catholics and non-Catholics might otherwise co-operate. Religious neutrality was not enough; the only organizations approved were those with a positive Catholic content. This exclusiveness extended even to reading matter. *Wiarus Polski*, the Polish nationalist paper in the Ruhr, declared:

No true Catholic can maintain that he can read whatever he wishes since if the Church forbids any particular book everyone must follow its guidance. We have a great selection of Polish-Catholic books and writings and only such things may be read. Members of a Catholic club too should not conclude that everyone may read what he wishes; the conclusion can only be that a Catholic may read only Catholic newspapers.

Seven years later the paper was urging its readers to burn any copies of socialist papers they found.[45]

It should not be supposed that by providing church-based social facilities the priests were invariably able to impose their political views on their flock. Through the clubs, indeed, some workers learned the basic skills of public life which they might later use in support of causes which the priests found distasteful. During the 1889 miners' strike some priests used their pulpits and the clubs to oppose the stoppage, but with little success. They also failed to prevent Polish Church clubs from becoming centres of Polish nationalism.[46] However this does not detract from the importance of the denominational orientation of these clubs. They built a confessional element into the very basis of much of the social life of the district and did much to consolidate the social isolation of Catholics from non-Catholics.

Catholic trade unionism

Church clubs were only one manifestation of 'social Catholicism'; a second, and from the Church's point of view less welcome one, was the 'Christian' trade union movement.

---

[45] StAB, 450, *Wiarus Polski*, 1. 7. 1890; StAB, 479, *Oberbürgermeister* Bochum to RPA, 31. 7. 1897, *Gazeta Robotnicza*, 31. 7. 1898.

[46] STAM, *Oberpräsidium* 2828 Bd. 3, *Landrat* Gelsenkirchen to *Oberpräsident.* 12. 5. 1889; STAM, RA I 94, *Landrat* Gelsenkirchen to RPA, 24. 2. 1899; Tenfelde, *Sozialgeschichte*, pp. 395–6.

Militant involvement by Catholics in miners' strikes and in trade union activity dated back to the earliest industrial conflict in the Ruhr. A miners' strike in 1872, starting near Essen, was supported by radical Catholics and was popularly known as the 'Jesuit strike'. The strike failed but was rapidly followed by an attempt to form a miners' union. Its executive consisted of two Catholics, two Protestants, and one Lassallean socialist. The union aimed to further the material interests of the miners and not to concern itself with religious or political affairs. But it never appears effectively to have got off the ground and disappeared soon after its foundation. A further attempt to form a union was made in 1878 by the Catholic miner Rosenkranz, a supporter of Laaf in his conflict with the Centre party establishment in Essen. He too sought a non-denominational and non-political organization and was willing to work with socialists to this end. However, the socialist influence became too marked for even the radical Catholics, and the 'Rosenkranz Union' was denounced not only by the Catholic clergy but also by Laaf who called for a specifically Christian union. As one Catholic paper put it:

As soon as you [workers] become social democrats your souls will suffer undoubted harm. You plunge yourselves in the greatest danger of being for ever lost, of forfeiting salvation for yourselves and perhaps for your wives and children, without having the least hope of achieving happiness here on earth through social democracy. Now choose between the dubious hope of improving your earthly situation and the virtually undoubted certainty of everlasting ruin![47]

The inability of even radical Catholics to work with socialists in one union was to be a perennial theme. A united miners' union was formed in 1889 following the great strike of that year which miners of both denominations and all political persuasions had supported. This union too was supposed to be politically and religiously neutral but disputes soon broke out and only five months after its foundation the 'Christians'——mainly Catholics——seceded and formed

---

[47] Tenfelde, *Sozialgeschichte*, p. 516; M. Schneider, *Die Christlichen Gewerkschaften 1894-1933* (Bonn, 1982), p. 56; Hue, *Bergarbeiter* ii 306-27; Koch, *Bergarbeiterbewegung*, pp. 25-7; STAM, RA I 82, *Reg. Präsident* Düsseldorf to RPA, 1. 5. 1906.

their own rival organization. This did not last long—largely because of the economic slump—but in 1894 the Christlich-soziale Gewerkverein der Bergarbeiter was formed. Although smaller than the socialist-dominated 'old' union (now known as the Alter Verband) the Gewerkverein was a lasting and successful organization: by 1910 it had nearly 83,000 members compared with the Alter Verband's 123,000.

The Gewerkverein, although vehemently anti-socialist and 'Christian' in its views and predominantly Catholic in membership, was largely independent of Church control. In contrast to the prime importance, in the view of the Church hierarchy, of the defence of the faith, the union saw as its main concern the defence of workers' interests in industry. Although dominated by Catholics it was in theory non-denominational and always contained a minority of Protestants. This policy of non-denominationalism, which applied to the Christian trade union movement generally in Germany, was deplored by many of the German bishops and was the subject of much controversy within the Church, particularly when in 1900 most (but not all) the bishops publicly came out in support of denominational craft associations under close clerical supervision and against the interdenominational independent Christian trade unions. The Gewerkverein did not hesitate to denounce the bishops' views.[48] The union—despite its avowed commitment to the maintenance of good relations between employers and employees—also alientated some powerful Catholic opinion through its readiness if necessary to resort to strike action. The *Rheinisch-Westfälische Zeitung*—which generally reflected employers' opinion—commented that 'it is hard to find a material difference between the demands of the social democratic miners and those of the Christians'.[49] The Gewerkverein

[48] StAB, 479, RPA to *Minister des Innern*, 24. 11. 1900; Ross, *Beleaguered Tower*, chapters 5–7; Koch, *Bergarbeiterbewegung*, p. 64; H. Mommsen, *Bergarbeiter; Ausstellung zur Geschichte der organisierten Bergarbeiterbewegung in Deutschland* (Bochum, 1969); H. J. Wallraff, 'Die Belastung einer Gewerkschaft durch ideologische Differenzen', in H. O. Vetter (ed.), *Vom Sozialistengesetz zur Mitbestimmung* (Köln, 1975); Schneider, *Die Christlichen Gewerkschaften*, p. 62.
[49] Schneider, *Die Christlichen Gewerkschaften*, p. 68; W. Loth, *Katholiken im Kaiserreich. Der politische Katholizismus in der Krise des wilhelminischen Deutschlands* (Düsseldorf, 1984), p. 93.

co-operated fully with the Alter Verband and other unions in the 1905 miners' strike and occasionally—for example in 1909 on the question of labour exchanges—even adopted a more militant stance than its socialist rival. Even when in 1912 the Gewerkverein refused to join the other unions in strike action, and thereby undermined any hope of success that the strike might otherwise have had, the refusal was ostensibly on tactical grounds rather than because of any rejection of strikes in principle.

Despite the Gewerkverein's genuine independence, however, important links did exist between the union and the Catholic establishment. Some churchmen were sympathetic towards the Christian trade unions. Even the Papacy, when in 1912 it declared its view on the trade union question, adopted an ambiguous approach which left the unions free to continue and develop their work.[50] Until 1905 the union had, in addition to its executive committee, a 'Council of Notables' which acted as a final court of appeal and had a general supervisory function. In addition to some members of the executive itself this body included two Catholic priests (one of whom eventually resigned and was replaced by a professor), a Protestant minister, and a Protestant layman. At the local level there were often close links between the union and leading Catholics. The first branches were often formed from members of Catholic workers' clubs. When the Wiemelhausen branch was formed the guest of honour was the local priest and the union's aims were explained by a teacher. The Centre party sympathies of many leading figures in the union were also well known. August Brust, the union's main founding figure and leader until 1904, became a Centre party deputy in the Prussian *Landtag* and later leaders such as Johann Effert, Hermann Köster, and the Imbusch brothers were also supporters of the party.[51]

Inter-denominationalism and an explicit exclusion of confessional and party political matters from the union did not mean that either religion or politics were unimportant

---

[50] IZF, *Bergarbeiter Zeitung*, 28. 1. 1905; Ross, *Beleaguered Tower*, pp. 102, 108; Loth, *Katholiken im Kaiserreich*, pp. 247-77.

[51] Hue, *Bergarbeiter* ii. 615; StAB, 463, *Amt* Bochum II to KLB, 12. 3. 1895; Schneider, *Die Christlichen Gewerkschaften*, pp. 61, 65.

to the Gewerkverein. Indeed, where both Catholics and Protestants could unite was in hostility to the unpatriotic and anti-religious social democrats and—by extension—their apparent instrument, the Alter Verband. Until 1905 the Gewerkverein's statutes explicitly stated that by joining the union members declared themselves opponents of social democratic principles and actions. Although the two unions were willing from time to time to sink their differences and co-operate in a particular campaign, for most of the pre-war period they engaged in strong competition and relations between them were frequently bitter. Each suspected the other of seeking to dominate and each was accused of putting sectional and divisive political interests in front of the real interests of the miners. In the rhetoric which surrounded this power struggle, religion was one of the themes stressed by the Gewerkverein. In 1905, for instance, much was made of a comment said to have been made by Carl Legien, chairman of the general commission of the free trade unions, that 'our members are anti-religious because they are sensible people', and the alleged failure of Otto Hue and other Alter Verband leaders to reject such remarks.[52] The hostility and bitterness reached a new intensity during and after the abortive miners' strike of 1912.

Protestant workers' clubs

There was no Protestant tradition of social concern or activism comparable to that of the Catholics in the Ruhr. This reflected in part the position of the offical Protestant Church as an integral part of the political and social establishment in Germany and in part the fact that local employers were mainly Protestant. Just as the *Kulturkampf* highlighted the outsider status of the Catholics, so it tended to confirm the connections between the Protestant Church, patriotic politics, and employer resistance to the apparent attempts by Catholics to subvert workers in industry. Hostility towards the 'unpatriotic' and 'irreligious' social democrats was axiomatic in Church circles.

[52] STAM, RA I 82, *Gelsenkirchener Zeitung*, 26. 6. 1905. See also Schneider, *Die Christlichen Gewerkschaften*, p. 57; Erdmann, *Die christlichen Gewerkschaften*, p. 90.

Nevertheless it became clear that some Protestant response was needed in the face of the economic and social changes which swept the district in the later nineteenth century. The spur was the apparent success first of the Catholics and later of the social democrats in wooing the workers. In 1904 Friedrich König, the *Superintendent* of the Bochum area Synod, outlined the issues as he saw them:

How great are the tasks which the Church faces, due to the new configuration of social life in our time, the distance from the Church to which the anti-godly *Weltanschauung* has brought great numbers of our parishioners, the influx of great masses of people of both German and Masurian origin into our Synod's district; to say nothing of the struggle against the dominance of the Roman power in German life which has been forced upon us.

But the Church was responding to the challenge:

How manifold are the proclamations of the gospel in special services, childrens' services, bible studies, community classes during evangelizing campaigns, and so forth. This is a loyal effort to rally the susceptible members of our district, to prove the youth of both sexes and to unite the Protestant-Christian and patriotic forces of German life. What a labour of love for the imperilled, the sick, and the needy parishioners through the manifold exercise of the Church's social mission, through parish nurses, womens' clubs, housing assistance, and so on. It all demonstrates how the Church in its synodical organs has become conscious of its newly received obligations in the social sphere.[53]

Such activities were not enough to counter the threats to the Protestant Church. In the 1880s it was clear that the Catholic workers' clubs were exerting an appeal even to some Protestants and might in the end undermine their faith. It was to counter this that in 1882 Ludwig Fischer, a Protestant miner from Gelsenkirchen, went to his local pastor and suggested the formation of a rival Protestant workers' club. The pastor was sceptical but Fischer won support from a local teacher. In May 1882 the first Protestant Workers' Club (*evangelische Arbeiterverein*) was founded. The tone of the new organization was revealed in its statutes:

The Protestant Workers' Club is founded on the Protestant faith and has the aims:

[53] H. Rothert, *Kirchengeschichte des westfälisch-rheinischen Industriegebietes vom evangelischen Standpunkt* (Dortmund, 1926), p. 142.

a) of arousing and strengthening Protestant consciousness amongst the followers of the creed;

b) of achieving the moral uplift and general education of its members;

c) of ensuring and cultivating amicable relations between employers and employees;

d) of maintaining loyalty to Kaiser and *Reich*.[54]

The club prospered and more were founded. An association of Protestant clubs in the Rhineland and Westphalia was formed and in 1889 Dr Forster from Schalke, the association's chairman, explained the clubs' aims at their assembly in Witten; again the threat from the Catholics was prominent:

The workers' clubs have in the first place the aim of strengthening Protestant consciousness; secondly they serve to provide an effective barrier to Roman influence without, however, being intolerant of different beliefs; they also work for a harmonious relationship between employers and employees; they concern themselves too with the elucidation of social problems. . .[55]

The legalization of the SPD in 1890 created new fears for the Protestant Church. The Westphalian clergy were instructed by their provincial Synod to keep a close eye on events in their parishes and particularly any social democratic agitation. They were to visit parishioners in their homes, study social problems, develop their help for the sick and needy, and in general to use their influence to counter the threat to their charges. The laity had their duties too:

The members of the presbytery have a duty to support with all their ability, through personal participation and any other permissible support, the clubs and other activities of their parish established to fight unbelief and unpatriotic persuasions, particularly Protestant workers' clubs formed to promote Christian, patriotic, and socially harmonious views as well as Protestant mens' and youths' clubs. They are to offer their help in forming such clubs and similar ones to combat unbelief in those parishes where they do not yet exist.[56]

From combatting Catholicism the aim of the clubs thus swung in large part to the defeat of social democracy. Two months later a long statement directed against the social

[54] P. Göhre, *Die Evangelisch-Soziale Bewegung* (Leipzig, 1896), p. 110.

[55] STAM, *Oberpräsidium* 2828a, *Neue Preussische Zeitung*, 11. 7. 1889. See also Göhre, *Evangelisch-Soziale Bewegung*, p. 114.

[56] STAM, *Oberpräsidium* 2693 Bd. 2, *Rheinisch-Westfälische Zeitung*, 30. 9. 1890.

democrats (although not mentioning them explicitly) was read in all Protestant churches in Westphalia:

. . . a deeply rooted movement has taken hold of our people. Our parishes are affected by it and the struggle is carried right into family life. Many hearts have been disquieted and many consciences have been thrown into disorder. A deep cleft threatens to ruin our people. Amongst the lower orders dissatisfaction and complaints increase, amongst the better-off discomfort and impatience, amongst others perplexity; in many circles unrestrained pleasure-seeking and immorality have gained the upper hand. Brutality and indiscipline are openly prevalent. There is a shared guilt from which none are free. It has befallen us in accordance with the words: he who sows the wind will reap the whirlwind. For long enough unbelief has been toyed with and belief ridiculed and mocked and now the fruits are before all eyes. It is not our aim to discuss the matter in so far as it is a question of changing or re-ordering the economic conditions of the people's life. Rather, we welcome everything which removes poverty by peaceful means and which aims at achieving a better lot for the small men and the economically weak, in harmony with the noble efforts of our beloved Kaiser and king. But there is a dark force which wants to monopolize the reordering of these matters for itself—a force which wants to destroy everything which has been sacred to our fathers and to ourselves in Church, family and state; but this force is not able to replace them with anything better, and above all can not and does not wish to create anything other than a war of all against all and a desolate wilderness in place of our Christian and moral heritage, the ornament and honour of our German people. Under the pretence of wishing to improve the condition of the people they proclaim—at first secretly and covertly but later openly and fearlessly—the renunciation of the fatherland and the destruction of the sanctity of the family. That is the ungodly and bleak teaching of modern times.

We declare ourselves firmly against this spirit and its seductive powers and call on the Christian and moral force of our parishes. We maintain and testify to the truth that all situations and all mankind are under the power of the one God. If is God's will that rich and poor, the higher and the lower orders of society, should co-exist with each other; no power in the world can change this any more than the course of the sun in the heavens or death on earth can be altered . . .[57]

The Protestant workers' clubs, like their Catholic counterparts, were generally supervised by the minister. Finance often came from local firms: the Bochumer Verein was one company which gave regular donations to Protestant clubs around Bochum—grants to Catholic organizations were

[57] STAM, *Oberpräsidium* 2693 Bd. 2, *Neue Preussische Kreuz-Zeitung*, 29. 11. 1890.

rarer. Members met regularly for talks and discussions, and activities included Sunday outings and walks. Increasingly the clubs provided their members with insurance and friendly schemes and even co-op stores. Libraries were common. In the early 1890s a central building for the local clubs was established in Bochum with meeting-rooms and restaurant facilities. Some clubs built their own premises and in 1909 an office to give help and advice to members was opened in Herne. Cultural activities, often of a propagandistic nature, were held: in 1890 the Witten club put on a play entitled 'Luther and his times'.[58] Special youth clubs were also founded: the life of one in Wanne was described by the pastor:

The young persons' club in this area brings together young people between the ages of 14 and 20 on Sunday afternoons. It seeks to help them to a proper, Christian Sunday and to protect them from the dangerous life of the taverns which only too frequently ruin body and soul and from the wordly diversions and dissipations to which, unfortunately, only too many young people abandon themselves these days. It seeks to promote their spiritual, physical, and moral welfare. The meetings take place from 5 to 7 o'clock. For about the first hour the young people play games . . . talk, or read the magazines or books in the club's library. The club's affairs are then dealt with, instruction given on this or that matter, serious or comic stories are told or read out. Every meeting is closed with a song, a short reflection on a text, a prayer, and the blessing. A few times a year the club puts on a larger festivity in which music from the club's brass band, addresses, singing, and declamation alternate with each other . . .[59]

The Protestant clubs, in contrast to the 'papist' and 'ultramontane' Catholics and to the 'treacherous' social democrats, prided themselves on their patriotism, lack of which was seen as a crucial moral failing. Religious and patriotic talks and songs seem to have been almost

[58] Göhre, *Evangelisch-Soziale Bewegung*, .pp. 112-13; StAB, 444; StAB, *Magistratsbericht*, 1892/3, p. 36; BA, 18/68, *Louise Tiefbau Aufsichtsrat*, 6. 5. 1901; STAM, *Oberpräsidium* 2694 Bd. 2, *Siegener Volksblatt*, 18. 5. 1909; StAB, 479, *Bürgermeister* Witten to KLB, 6. 5. 1897; KA, 129 00 Nr. 18, 20, 23, 24. See also K. Saul, *Staat, Industrie, Arbeiterbewegung im Kaiserreich* (Düsseldorf, 1974), pp. 148 ff; BA, 14/119 *Zeche Friedrich der Grosse to Bergrevierbeamten* Herne, 5. 12. 1912.

[59] STAM, *Landratsamt* Gelsenkirchen 48, *Pfarrer* Haeseler to *Amt* Wanne, 16. 9. 1902.

interchangeable.[60] In Herne a Protestant committee for youth work was formed in 1914 with the aim:

of protecting our youth through appropriate measures from physical and moral dangers and of putting back on the right lines those who have already gone astray. It is the duty of our nation to assist in this area, in view of the moral and economic strength and its immense value lost in the flood swallowing up defenceless young men and girls if a life belt is not thrown them in time. A generation must be raised with sun in its eyes, steel in its sinews, pure minds and defiant hearts; a generation which honours God and the king and is German to the marrow.[61]

The Protestant clubs interpreted their commitment to industrial peace as a general support for the employers and an unwillingness to support strikes or trade union activities. In 1885 a Bochum Protestant Workers' and Citizens' Club even opposed Catholic agitation for legal controls on the length of the working day and Sunday work.[62] During the 1889 miners' strike the clubs called on their members to accept the employers' promises and return to work. They claimed that only around half of the 6,200 miners organized in the clubs at the time stopped work, a much lower proportion than amongst the miners generally.[63] Nevertheless, the ambiguity of the Protestant workers' clubs' position was soon evident: how could they credibly claim to speak for the workers' interests if they rejected all action against employers? Different Protestants answered this problem in different ways and divisions soon emerged within the movement. Pastor Neumann from Frankfurt became the spokesman for a more socially progressive Protestant workers' movement. The Ruhr clubs generally opposed his ideas but at the national conference in 1893 a compromise was reached between the supporters of Neumann and the conservatives.[64] Within the Ruhr itself divisions also appeared, despite the dominance of the conservatives. In 1894 38 Protestant workers' clubs and 19 miners' associations (*Knappenvereine*) joined with their

[60] STAM, *Landratsamt* Gelsenkirchen 48, *Amt* Bismarck to *Landrat* Gelsenkirchen, 30. 9. 1902.
[61] BA, 14/119, *Ev. Jugend-Ausschuss* Herne to *Gewerkschaft Friedrich der Grosse*, 20. 5. 1914.   [62] Tenfelde, *Sozialgeschichte*, p. 554.
[63] STAM, *Oberpräsidium* 2828 Bd. 4, *Westfälische Volkszeitung*, 18. 5. 1889; ibid., Bd. 3, *Landrat* Gelsenkirchen to RPA, 12. 5. 1889; ibid., *Oberpräsidium* 2828a, *Neue Preussische Zeitung* 11. 7. 1889.
[64] Brakelmann, *Soziale Frage*, pp. 188–91.

Catholic counterparts in the foundation of the Christian miners' union, the Gewerkverein.[65] The conservatives, in contrast, insisted that all trade union activity was unacceptable. By 1897, however, it was clear that the Essen, Elberfeld, and Rhineland clubs were ready to adapt a more progressive stance.

The main strength of the conservative wing of the Protestant workers' club movement lay with the Bochum and Gelsenkirchen clubs led by Hermann Franken, the chairman of the area association. Franken was said to be of working-class origins and to have become a factory owner in Schalke through his own efforts. He was a National Liberal in politics and was supported in the Bochum district by Rudolf Quandel, the editor of the main National Liberal paper the *Rheinisch-Westfälische Tageblatt*. The hardening line of the Bochum area was expressed by the Wattenscheid club, which declared in 1897 that its aims were chiefly 'Protestant and national and only third place social'.[66] In March 1898 the split went so far that the 'Bochumers' threatened to leave the Rhineland and Westphalia association; it was only the threat from the social democrats in the *Reichstag* election that year (elections in which Franken stood and won as National Liberal candidate in Bochum) that prevented a split. The 'Bochumers' were given a greater say in the association and more seats on its executive.[67]

This compromise did not end the dispute. In 1901 the split reappeared on the question of participation in trade unions. Once again the Bochum area under the leadership of Franken proved the staunchest opponent of change. There were demands that Neumann be expelled from the movement and some clubs threatened to disaffiliate if this was not done. In May 1902 at the clubs' national conference in Düsseldorf Neumann and Stöcker (another progressive) failed to be re-elected to the national executive. At this the Württemberg association disaffiliated. Quandel expressed his satisfaction with the outcome in a letter to a Bochum factory owner:

There is no doubt that the Protestant workers' clubs, which have made it their task to further the love of Kaiser and *Reich*, to strengthen

[65] Kalis, *Kirche und Religion*, p. 39; Göhre, *Evangelisch-Soziale Bewegung*, p. 122.
[66] StAB, 479, RPA to *Minister des Innern*, 9. 11. 1897.
[67] StAB, 479, RPA to *Minister des Innern*, 13. 4. 1898, 13. 11. 1898; STAM RA I 104, *Rheinisch-Westfälische Arbeiter Zeitung* 21. 5. 1897.

Protestant awareness and to preserve good relations between employers and employees, are of particular importance at this time when the working classes are being increasingly courted for endeavours which run directly counter to national and social harmony. In the turbid flood of anti-monarchical and revolutionary waves in which a large part of the German workers are caught today the Protestant workers' clubs have proved themselves a sure and immovable rock in the ocean, on which the shock of the anti-state and anti-law and order waves break in vain. In particular, the clubs of our area association have consistently shown that they take seriously the defence [of workers] against the false socialist spirit and the fostering of good relations between employers and employees, especially through their firm attitude towards the efforts of men like Pastor Neumann. They have earned the recognition of all loyal people.[68]

After this the national leadership did its best to stop further discussion of the trade union issue. The 'Bochumers'' mistrust was not, however, allayed and they temporarily seceded and formed their own Protestant Workers' Association (Evangelische Arbeiterbund). Although the breach was quickly healed they retained their separate identity.[69]

The strong anti-union line adopted by the Bochum area organizations was not shared by all organized Protestant workers in the locality. In 1899 discussions were held about the possibility of launching a Protestant miners' union: the main protagonist of the idea, a miner from Grumme named Fürkötter, was a former social democrat who had been imprisoned for lese-majesty. He was unable to muster sufficient support and the proposal died. A clearer test came six years later with the 1905 miners' strike in which the vast majority of miners participated. Franken and Quandel issued leaflets calling for the strike to be ended and there was a bitter newspaper war between Quandel and the Gewerkverein's paper, *Der Bergknappe*, in which Quandel was accused of trying to sabotage the strike. But Franken and Quandel were fighting a losing battle. The Protestant clubs did not oppose the stoppage as strongly as they had in 1889 and even expressed support for some of the strikers' demands.

[68] IZF, *Volksblatt*, 12. 9. 1902.
[69] StAB, 480, RPA to *Minister des Innern*, 15. 11. 1901, 24. 11. 1902, 8. 12. 1903, 20. 12. 1904; Brakelmann, *Soziale Frage*, p. 193. The Bochumer Verein gave some financial support to the Evangelische Arbeiterbund: KA, 129 00 Nr 23, *Verwaltungsrathssitzung*, 19. 10. 1904.

Many protestant clergy, despite their clear dislike for strikes, called for concessions from the Government and employers. After the strike many Protestant workers joined the Gewerkverein: a few tried without success to form new unions appealing to Protestants and National Liberals. The Government's reform proposals were welcomed by many Protestant workers' clubs. In April 1905 Franken, disillusioned at these developments, resigned.[70]

Under the new chairman, Pastor Bokamp from Bochum, the clubs took a more conciliatory line. In 1906 at a conference at Wattenscheid a new approach to the trade union issue was adopted, although against opposition from some members. The new resolution read:

1. Since the workers can never solve the labour question alone, the conference recognizes the trade union movement as justified when it is of a purely economic nature and seeks to further the common good in co-operation with other professional classes;
2. the conference therefore expects members of the Protestant workers' clubs, in accordance with their constitutional concern for a harmonious relationship between employers and employees, to avoid or leave such trade union organizations as are linked with social democracy and recommends them only to join such unions which are based on national and Christian principles, restrict themselves simply to the representation of professional interests and therefore refrain from any influence on the religious and political convictions and activity of their members;
3. the conference therefore makes it a duty of members of Protestant workers' clubs who are members of or who join the Christian Gewerkverein to ensure within this union that they avoid any link with the social democratic unions, since any such link directly contradicts the constitution of the Protestant workers' clubs as well as that of the Christian and national workers' organizations.[71]

Thus although Protestants were now permitted to defend their economic interest through trade unions and could even join Catholic-dominated organizations their hostility towards the socialists remained as explicit and strong as ever.

[70] G. Brakelmann, 'Evangelische Pfarrer im Konfliktfeld des Ruhrbergarbeiterstreiks von 1905', in Reulecke and Weber (ed.), *Fabrik, Familie, Feierabend*, pp. 297–314; StAB, 455, *Amt* Langendreer to KLB, 1. 2. 1905; StAB, 480, RPA to *Minister des Innern*, 22. 12. 1905; IZF, *Bergarbeiterzeitung* 8. 5. 1905; STAM, *Oberbergamt* Dortmund 1845, *Der Bergknappe*, 18. 2. 1905; Schneider, *Die Christlichen Gewerkschaften*, p. 64; Saul, *Staat, Industrie, Arbeiterbewegung*, p. 472 (note 158).
[71] STAM, RA I 98, *Polizei-Commissar* Bochum to RPA, 12. 11. 1906.

The Protestant workers' clubs strongly supported the Gewerkverein's refusal to join the miners' strike of 1912 and its appeal to the Government to defend miners who wished to work. The leaders of the Rhineland and Westphalia association issued a stern warning to their followers:

Social-democratic and anarcho-socialist agitators are trying to drive the Ruhr miners into a strike. At some pits the work force is already partially out. We urgently warn our members not to participate in the poorly justified and therefore hopeless strike. The workers' cause will only be harmed by such a stoppage. The German workers have no cause to enter a strike in favour of anti-German English industry or to satisfy the agitation needs of the Social Democratic Party . . .[72]

The opposition of the Protestant clubs to the social democrats was also expressed in elections. Ludwig Fischer, the founder of the original club in Gelsenkirchen, became an office-holder in the National Liberal party. In the 1893 *Reichstag* election he wanted to stand as candidate in Bochum but was eventually persuaded by the party to stand down in favour of Dr Haarmann, the mayor of Witten. The National Liberals agreed, however, in future to consult the leaders of the Protestant workers' clubs before selecting candidates.[73] In 1898 Hermann Franken himself stood for the party in the *Reichstag* election in Bochum and the clubs were active in his campaign. Pastor Goecker, addressing the Witten club, urged them to vote for Franken 'who was himself a worker, who did not have inherited wealth and who, basing himself on the Protestant faith, has a heart for the workers . . .'[75] Shortly before the poll the executive of the Bochum area Protestant workers' clubs issued an appeal:

The Protestant workers' clubs are not political. But their members, as individuals, must be made fully aware that every Protestant Christian and patriotic voter shares responsibility for the tremendous decision of election day. Protestant voters! You must not allow an unbelieving and unpatriotic social democrat nor an anti-Protestant ultramontane to secure the victory. The only candidate in the Bochum electoral district who comes into question for you and for us is Herr Hermann Franken

[72] STAM, *Oberbergamt* Dortmund 1856, *Rheinisch-Westfälische Zeitung*, 9. 3. 1912.
[73] Brakelmann, *Soziale Frage*, p. 193; IZF, *Rheinisch-Westfälische Arbeiter Zeitung*, 24. 5. 1893.
[74] Nettmann, *Witten in den Reichstagswahlen*, pp. 133–4.
[75] ibid. pp. 135–6.

from Schalke . . . Every man on board! Every Protestant worker must be an agitator! Try to encourage the lukewarm, to set right those led astray! Confront them seriously with the question, 'What has Fuchs, what has Lehmann achieved and what has Franken achieved? ' Anyone who answers this honestly will not find the decision difficult, he will vote on the 16th of June for Hermann Franken of Schalke![75]

At subsequent elections the clubs continued to support National Liberal candidates. In 1903, despite the internal difficulties of the movement, most of the clubs came out for the party. And in 1912 the party selected as candidate a miner, Heckmann, who was a member of the Protestant Workers' Association.[76] With the help of tactical Catholic voters Heckman was able to win back the Bochum seat from the social democrats who had won the two previous elections.

Although adopting a generally conservative political line, offering electoral support to the National Liberal party, and receiving financial subsidies from the employers, it would be wrong to see the Protestant clubs simply as the tool of business interests. Their relatively independent line during the 1905 miners' strike, the subsequent resignation of Franken and other industrialists and their support for the 'Christian' trade unions meant that the clubs were in significant opposition to the views of heavy industry in the Ruhr. This became even clearer in the last pe-war years when the employers sought to encourage the growth of 'yellow' company unions— organizations which were completely subservient to employer interests. The Protestant workers' clubs strongly opposed this trend. Within the National Liberal party itself they also played an independent role, pressing for more working-class candidates and even threatening on occasion to withdraw political support if their demands were not met. Like their Catholic counterparts, therefore, the Protestants walked an ambiguous and narrow path between the sometimes conflicting aims and aspirations of their political and financial patrons and those of their working-class members.[77] In the process they emerged as at least ambivalently authentic and independent spokesmen for an important section of the working class.

[76] StAB, 480, RPA to *Minister des Innern*, 8. 12. 1903; IZF, *Arbeiter Zeitung*, 2. 2. 1912.

[77] Saul, *Staat, Industrie, Arbeiterbewegung*, pp. 168–72, 472 (note 158), 485 (note 374).

The denominational clubs were generally successful in recruiting members although, like most organizations in the Ruhr, they suffered from the geographical mobility of many workers. In Altenbochum in 1911 the SPD branch had 280 male and 100 female members; those members came from neighbouring Laer and Querenburg as well as from Altenbochum itself. The Catholic miners' club had 180 members and two Church-sponsored Polish clubs had a total of 310 members. Two Protestant workers' clubs had 178 members between them.[78] There was thus no question in this mixed area of any one club predominating. The religious organizations showed no sign of losing their influence as the war approached; in 1913 the Langendreer *Amtmann* could report that in the previous year the local SPD branch had declined from 600 to 450 members and that the social democratic agitation had slackened and lost impetus; on the other hand 'there are strong Protestant and Catholic workers' clubs which have frequently held well attended meetings and have had a strong growth in membership.'[79] In 1901 there were reported to be 37 Protestant workers' clubs in the Bochum-Gelsenkirchen area; by 1909 (although the area may not have been exactly the same) the organization had 69 clubs and some 12,500 members—an increase at least sufficient to keep up with the growth of population.[80] Although the numerical evidence is patchy there is no doubt that the religious clubs continued to enjoy widespread support in the years before 1914.

Conclusions

Despite fears that industrial and urban development would lead to a decline in religious life and a loss of religious loyalties it is clear that the Churches and religiously tinged organizations continued to play an important role within the newly forming working class. Many workers did indeed cease to attend church and some even renounced any belief in Christian

[78] StAB, 482, *Amt* Bochum II to KLB, 18. 8. 1911; KLB to RPA, 25. 8. 1911.
[79] StAB, 482, *Amt* Harpen to KLB, 12. 8. 1913.
[80] StAB, 480, RPA to *Minister des Innern*, 15. 11. 1901; STAM, *Oberpräsidium* 2694 Bd. 2, *Siegener Volksblatt*, 18. 5. 1909.

dogma. But despite this the social role of religion remained of the first importance. In a largely new environment, with a limited physical and social infrastructure, religious organizations could offer not only a familiar language for the expression of important personal emotions and events but a framework for the establishment of social and community ties and even for the definition of social identity. The very fact that the district was denominationally mixed and that the constant movement of people threatened to alter existing local religious balances tended to reinforce the importance of religious labels as a primary social identifier. Such attitudes were confirmed and strengthened by the pervasive influence of religiously-orientated organizations which between them offered to meet not only the spiritual but also the educational, health, recreational, cultural, and even trade union needs of their members. Indeed, so far did some religious organizations go that concern was expressed that they were in danger of becoming secularized themselves in the process and of losing their original Christian purpose— a fear which ironically mirrored concern amongst social democrats that some of their activities might be losing their specifically socialist character.[81]

It is hard to measure the precise strength of the appeal of religious organizations to ordinary workers and much research remains to be done in this important field. The Catholic sub-culture was certainly more firmly and authentically based within the working class than its Protestant rival. Not only were Protestants generally less assiduous church attenders but they failed to develop an effective equivalent or rival to the Gewerkverein. Indeed, the Protestant working-class movement emerged largely as a response to the rival efforts of the Catholics and social democrats. As we shall see below, Protestant workers proved less well insulated against the rival appeal of social democracy than their Catholic colleagues. Nevertheless it is clear that even the Protestant

---

[81] Brepohl, *Industrievolk Ruhrgebiet*, p. 132; Pieper, *Lage der Bergarbeiter*, p. 238. For social democratic fears about the loss of socialist meaning in May Day celebrations, see chapter 6 below. The importance of denominational clubs in filling the social vacuum left by the withdrawal of the state from close involvement in the miners' lives has been stressed by Tenfelde in *Sozialgeschichte*, p. 362 and 'Mining Festivals in the Nineteenth Century'.

working-class organizations were able to achieve a significant degree of independence and support and that religiously-orientated organizations of both denominations did enjoy a widespread appeal throughout the pre-war period.

The political effect was doubly conservative. In the first place, the religious organizations almost all—though to differing degrees—encouraged traditional and conservative values and attitudes: commitment to social and industrial harmony, support for the emperor and fatherland, and bitter hostility towards social democracy. Second, they preserved and strengthened divisions within the working class. Religion did not prevent workers from experiencing social injustice and conflict. Indeed, efforts by the Churches to discourage participation in strikes, trade unionism, or nationalist politics achieved at best modest success. But it did mean that grievances and aspirations were frequently articulated within a particular religiously-orientated language, largely exclusive of other confessional groups and quite antithetical to the non-religious or even anti-religious language of social democracy. Social ties and loyalties were focused not on workers' clubs and workers' organizations as such but on Catholic or Protestant workers' organizations, with further subdivisions largely on ethnic lines. In later years some of the distrust between Catholics and Protestants was overcome —but largely as a result of their common hostility towards the social democrats. There was thus not one working-class sub-culture in the Ruhr but a number of rival ones, outwardly similar (notably in the love of clubs and associations which was common throughout the area) but characterized by a high degree of mutual incomprehension and suspicion. These divisions constituted a profound hindrance towards any attempt to create a united working-class sense of community or struggle for change.

The political importance of religious organizations was recognized by the state authorities, who classified their regular reports under the heading 'measures against social democracy'. The Arnsberg *Regierungs-Präsident*, whose administrative district included the eastern Ruhr, observed in 1895:

It is above all the patriotic and Christian associations such as the Protestant workers' and youth clubs, the Catholic workers' and youth clubs and the Catholic apprentices' clubs which offer the possibility of bringing the advance of social democracy to an effective halt. The monthly meetings with instructive lectures and all sorts of exhibitions revive in a gratifying manner the feeling for home and family, for fatherland and Church, and in many areas bear witness to the harmonious relations which exist between employer and employee. The glorious days of 1870/71 are celebrated by the clubs with widespread participation and it is to be expected that these festivities will be of lasting influence on many workers.[82]

Thirteen years later the Gelsenkirchen *Landrat* reported: 'There are Protestant and Catholic workers' clubs everywhere. As yet they have made themselves conspicuous politically by confronting the social democratic heresy and by seeking to guide their members to true citizenship. Most of them are led by priests'.[83] This official recognition of the political utility of religious organizations seems to extended widely within the adminstration: from the *Amtmann* in Langendreer who advocated the creation of a new Catholic parish there as a bastion against social democracy, to the Chancellor Bethmann Hollweg himself who interceded with the Vatican on behalf of the Christian trade unions on exactly the same grounds.[84]

---

[82] StAB, 479, RPA to *Minster des Innern*, 20. 10. 1895.
[83] STAM, RA I 100, K. *Landrat* Gelsenkirchen to RPA, 1. 9. 1908.
[84] Croon, 'Studien', p. 102; Ross, *Beleaguered Tower*, pp. 112–13.

4

Work in the Mines

Work dominated the miner's life. For one thing, it took up
most of his time and energy. Directly or indirectly, its
demands reached deep into his family life and his leisure
activities and concerns. Beyond its impact on individuals,
however, the shared experience of mine-work formed the
basis of that collective experience which gave miners their
special identity and consciousness. It thus provided the
possible basis on which social and cultural divisions might
be transcended in a common sense of solidarity and a common struggle for change. In this chapter we will consider
the characteristics of work in the mines. In subsequent
chapters we will examine the actions which grew out of that
experience.

Jobs at the mine

Most miners followed the same career pattern. Although
boys left school at the age of fourteen, they were forbidden
by law to work below ground until the age of sixteen, and
thus for their first two years had to be employed at the
surface. Here they booked trucks as they came up from the
pit, noted the face from which they came, helped to empty
them, to sort the coal from 'dirt' or stone, and to load the
coal into railway wagons. They did the lamp-cleaning and
general odd jobs. Because the amount of such work was
limited, many school-leavers first sought factory work and
only applied to the pits when they became eligible to work
underground: this led to complaints from the mine companies that they were losing young workers, including miners'
sons, who found mine-work unacceptable after a taste of
factory work.[1]

At sixteen the youth went underground. Here he did such

[1] Münz, *Lage der Bergarbeiter*, p. 29; BA, 18/22.

jobs as manning the main gates at the shaft, controlling loaded trucks on inclines and when they arrived at the shaft (*Bremser*), and handling the pit ponies (*Pferdejunge*). At eighteen he could become a haulier (*Schlepper*), responsible for transporting the trucks between the coal-face and the pit shaft. The haulier had a limited amount of assistance in this, mainly from pit ponies but to an increasing extent from machines. Ponies were first introduced into the pits in the 1850s, and in 1903 it was estimated that there were still around 8,000 in the region. The introduction of mechanical transport was slower in the Ruhr than in some other coalfields (e.g., in the Saar or in England) because there were more curves and bends, due to the relatively convoluted coal seams. Nevertheless, during the 1890s a number of mines introduced powered rope systems for pulling trucks over stretches of around 1,000 metres or more. Over shorter distances powered chutes (whereby the coal was shaken forward) and conveyor belts were tried in the last decade before the war, though with only limited success. But despite the use of ponies, and increasingly of machines, the haulier remained primarily dependent on his own physical strength, particularly in the narrower, steeper, and more contorted passages.[2]

After around two years as a haulier (and his period of military service) the young man became an apprentice hewer (*Lehrhauer*). Here he was supposed to learn the art of cutting coal and all the associated skills, working under the eye of an experienced older hewer. In addition to cutting coal and shovelling it into the trucks, the apprentice hewer was usually responsible for pushing the full trucks from the face to the point where they were collected by the hauliers, for maintaining the miners' tools and for ensuring an adequate supply of timber pit-props.[3]

It was only after this succession of jobs, and after at least a year as an apprentice hewer, that the young man normally

---

[2] Oberschuir, *Heranziehung*, pp. 19-25; Pieper, *Lage der Bergarbeiter*, p. 26; Schunder, *Tradition und Fortschritt*, pp. 96-101; B. L. Coombes, *These Poor Hands* (London, 1939), p. 135; W. Weber, 'Der Arbeitsplatz in einem expandierenden Wirtschaftszweig: Der Bergmann', in Reulecke and Weber (ed.), *Fabrik, Familie, Feierabend*, pp. 89-113; Brüggemeier, *Leben vor Ort*, pp. 92-136.

[3] Münz, *Lage der Bergarbeiter*, p. 30; Levenstein, *Aus der Tiefe*, pp. 47, 53-4.

became a full hewer. Hewers formed the largest single category of worker in the mine and were the men responsible for actually cutting and filling the coal. Until after the First World War they relied almost exclusively on the traditional tools of picks and explosives. Often in extremely cramped conditions, frequently crouching or lying down, the hewer hacked out or drilled into a section of the face, either to try to get the coal to fall from its own weight after the removal of temporary props or to place an explosive charge which would loosen it. To do this with maximum efficiency and minimum of physical labour required years of experience and particularly the ability to 'read' the inherently unpredictable coal seam. As one miner observed: 'In mining the character of the rock can change any moment. As you advance into the coal seam or across in the rock the conditions sometimes appear quite different from what were expected.'[4] Once the coal was loosened it had to be shovelled back and into the trucks for conveyance from the face. This too required physical contortions in a restricted space. As the face advanced, pit-props had to be put into position; eventually the exhausted area had to be safely abandoned, either by engineering a controlled roof-fall (in the traditional *streichende Pfeilerbau* mining technique) or by filling in the spaces with rock and rubble (in the *Strebbau mit Bergversatz* technique which had largely replaced it by the 1900s). No extra payment was made for these tasks.

The work was hard and unpleasant. One miner wrote:

The coal seam where I am employed at present has a 50° incline and a width of 11–15 inches. Here I work almost 7 hours without a break, either lying always on the same side with one shoulder resting on the down side and the other on the up side, or lying on my back where it is impossible to turn round, the feet resting on a thin wooden post since at 50° one cannot work without a foot-hold. Anyone can easily see that with such work—the pick constantly in the hand—one soon gets fatigued. The tiredness is worst when one gets up in the morning—then all the bones feel as though they are shattered.[5]

Another miner commented: 'when the shift ends I am no longer tired—I am a wreck.'[6] Heat, water, and dust added to the discomfort. Temperatures varied, but tended to rise

[4] Levenstein, *Arbeiterfrage*, p. 21.   [5] ibid., pp. 82–3.   [6] ibid., p. 84.

with the depth of the pit and the distance of the face from the ventilation shafts. Temperatures of over 30 degrees were not uncommon, and miners preferred to work in as few clothes as possible. Max Lotz, a hewer at the *Vereinigte Gladbeck* pit, reported that he and his colleagues worked merely in thin trousers—and would have worked naked if that were not forbidden. In the warmer parts of the pit the miners had to wring out their trousers several times each shift to remove the worst of the damp—each time it looked as though a bucket of water had been spilled. The presence of underground water was a further problem, soaking the miner and making the floor slippery and muddy. The damp was accentuated by the practice of spraying water to keep down the coal-dust. By shift-end men were often soaked.[7]

Other unpleasant features of mine-work included the constant dangers of accidents—to which we shall return later—and the need for unremitting vigilance against them; the dust in the air which hampered breathing and vision; the gloom in which the work had to be conducted—electric safety lamps were not in general use before the First World War, and the gas-light gave out only about half the light of a candle; and until the 1900s the almost complete absence of sanitary provision and clean drinking-water underground.[8]

There was little impact from machines on the hewer's work before 1914. Various cutting machines, mainly British and American, were tried. But they were large and unwieldy; many seams in the Ruhr were too steep and contorted for them and the coal was frequently too soft. The only significant advance was the adoption of the power hand-drill, held by the miner and powered by electricity or compressed air. It was first used for coal-cutting in Germany in 1906, but although it later became the miner's chief tool, as late as 1914 there were still fewer than 600 in use. Some miners disliked them because of the vibration which was thought to be harmful to health. Mechanization generally seems not to

[7] Levenstein, *Aus der Tiefe*, pp. 34, 57.

[8] One advantage of the gas lamp over the electric one was that its flame was affected by the presence of gas and thus gave warning of dangerous accumulations. C. Treptow, F. Wüst, and W. Borchers, *Bergbau und Hüttenwesen* (Leipzig, 1900), pp. 228–9; H. S. Jevons, *The British Coal Trade* (London, 1969 edition), p. 395.

have been welcomed by many miners—in part, no doubt,
due to fears that the resulting productivity increases would
simply mean reductions in wage rates. Pick, shovel, and
explosive retained their vital role and remained the hewer's
prime tools. Apart from them he relied on sheer physical
strength and dexterity.[9]

This had important implications for employers and miners
alike. Reliance on manual methods meant that despite the
high capital cost of sinking a pit and technical advances in
other areas of mine-work such as transport and ventilation
the industry remained substantially labour rather than
capital intensive. Between 1886 and 1913 miners' wages
in the Ruhr represented on average between 47 and 60
per cent of the value of production—a far higher proportion
than in the metal industry (in the Bochumer Verein in the
1880s the proportion stood at between 17 and 23 per cent
and in other metal firms the figures were comparable). This
helps to explain the coal-owners' acute sensitivity on wages
questions and their strong resistance, which we shall note
below, to any steps which might curtail their right to resolve
such issues autonomously. Reliance on manual methods
limited the scope for productivity improvements, and in fact
for a number of reasons productivity declined in the Ruhr
mines in the decades before 1914. Output could only be
expanded by the deployment of additional labour: hence the
need for massive immigration to the growing coal field. The
premium on physical strength and stamina rather than on
technical training meant that in the Ruhr, as in other mining
districts of Europe, it was relatively easy and advantageous
for employers to bring in young strong workers from outside
—even men with no previous knowledge of mining; and
conversely made it impossible for the miners to seek to
protect their status and conditions by imposing restrictions

[9] On the slow pace of mechanization of mine-work in Germany and Britain,
see A. J. Taylor, 'The Coal Industry', in D. H. Aldcroft (ed.), *The Development
of British Industry and Foreign Competition* (London, 1968), p. 56; R. Samuel,
'Mineral Workers', in Samuel (ed.), *Miners, Quarrymen and Saltworkers*, pp. 34–7;
R. Samuel, 'The Workshop of the World', in *History Workshop Journal* (Spring
1977), pp. 21–3; Schofer, *Formation of a modern labor force*, pp. 11–12; Weber,
'Der Arbeitsplatz', pp. 100–12; Schunder, *Tradition und Fortschritt*, p. 91; Oberschuir, *Heranziehung*, pp. 27–33; Pieper, *Lage der Bergarbeiter*, p. 150.

on access to the industry in the manner of workers in more highly skilled and technically advanced trades.[10]

Hewers worked in small teams, known as *Kameradschaften*. The size varied, reaching up to around twenty men although they were usually smaller and sometimes consisted of only two men. The predominance of small teams seems to have resulted in part from the lack of powered cutting machines, for until they were introduced in the 1920s there was relatively little incentive to organize the work around a few long faces rather than a larger number of small ones; certainly the 1920s did see a rapid change to long faces in the Ruhr mines.[11] Each *Kameradschaft* had a leader known as the *Ortsältester* who was appointed by the mine management. In the case of a two-man *Kameradschaft* the *Ortsältester* would be the hewer while his assistant would frequently be an apprentice hewer. The *Ortsältester* was responsible for safety and the effective conduct of the work and acted as spokesman for the *Kameradschaft* in dealings with management—particularly negotiations on piece-rates. Max Lotz described his role in the following terms:

As *Ortsältester* I am responsible for the conduct of work and for the division of labour at my face. Much depends on my authority over the workers assigned to me and I must let it be my aim to maintain the unity of my section and to direct them. The responsibility which I bear generally compels me to an opposing position to my work comrades. Small disputes therefore occur. . . . However, through the honest and tolerant way in which I exercise my authority I have won the respect of my comrades and they are especially pleased when

[10] HKB *Jahresberichte*; Koch, *Bergarbeiterbewegung*, p. 140; Weber, 'Der Arbeitsplatz', pp. 94, 100; Oberschuir, *Heranziehung*, p. 15. On British miners' inability to preserve their position in the face of the influx of unskilled outsiders, see R. Harrison, 'Introduction', pp. 4–6 and A. Campbell and F. Reid, 'The Independent Collier in Scotland', pp. 59–60 in Harrison (ed.), *Independent Collier*.

[11] Pieper, *Lage der Bergarbeiter*, p. 24; Münz, *Lage der Bergarbeiter*, p. 62; Schunder, *Tradition und Fortschritt*, p. 88; Weber, 'Der Arbeitsplatz', pp. 100–3. Tenfelde has suggested that changes in the organization of mine-work, even in the pre-war period, led to significant changes in the size and character of *Kameradschaften*. The available evidence suggests, however, the essential continuity in the character of mine-work until the major technical innovations and 'rationalization' of the 1920s. K. Tenfelde, 'Der bergmännische Arbeitsplatz während der Hochindustrialisierung', in Conze and Engelhardt (ed.), *Arbeiter im Industrialisierungsprozess*, pp. 283–335; Brüggemeier, *Leben vor Ort*, pp. 110–11.

I tell the overman and other mine officials the truth good and strong and defend our *Kameradschaft* against the officials' attacks. Therefore they see beyond the rather petty grumbles, which I have got used to, and I know very well that if I leave the work, perhaps to drink coffee or to do something else, they talk about me. . .[12]

A minority of hewers could advance to other jobs. Some became specialists, exclusively concerned with shot-firing, driving or maintaining the roadways, or similar jobs. Some rose to become pit deputy or overman (*Steiger*), a post of considerable social status in the district. Overmen supervised a number of faces and were responsible to management for achieving the desired output. Potential overmen did a two-year part-time training course at one of the twenty-five mining institutes in the area. It was even possible in theory for a miner to become a pit manager (*Betriebsführer*).[13] However, all these routes to advancement were only open to a minority. Most stayed as hewers until accident or failing strength forced them to leave underground work and perhaps return to the surface for the final years of their working life.

Not all mine workers followed this career pattern. Some learned particular skills which kept them at the surface, working with the machinery or in the brick-works which accompanied many pits. New immigrants to the area could become apprentice hewers immediately if they were strong and demand for labour was high.[14] Nevertheless, this broad experience was shared by most miners. Differences between them normally reflected differences in age and physical strength rather than more permanent divisions between trades or between the 'skilled' and the 'unskilled' which were common in other industries. The strength and dexterity of the good miner, which enabled him to earn well in his best years, declined with age and could not guarantee future high earnings. Nor could strength and skills be passed from father to son: it was impossible for an élite of workers to

[12] Levenstein, *Aus der Tiefe*, pp. 37–8.
[13] Münz, *Lage der Bergarbeiter*, p. 139. There can have been few, if any, of the completely illiterate and innumerate overmen who were found occasionally in the Durham pits. See D. Douglass, 'The Durham Pitman', in Samuel (ed.), *Miners, Quarrymen and Saltworkers*, p. 216.
[14] STAM, *Frankfurter Zeitung*, 11. 2. 1912.

maintain themselves and their sons as a permanent 'aristocracy' from which others could be excluded. This pattern
could and did create tensions between older, experienced
miners and youngsters who, through their greater physical
strength, could earn high wages: it was claimed in 1890 that
the young apprentice hewers had lost their traditional respect
for the older men with whom they worked and from whom
they were supposed to be learning their skills, and that their
only concern was to boost their earnings as much as possible.[15] But despite such frictions, the career structure meant
that the expectations and experience of work were broadly
common to the great majority of miners and thus provided
at least a potential basis for a common sense of identity,
interest, and solidarity.

How did miners themselves view their work? The evidence is fragmentary but does supply some clues. The drawbacks of mine-work—the gruelling physical demands, the
dangers, the harsh working conditions—were obvious.
Nevertheless, there were compensations. As Georg Werner
noted in 1912, the work made full use of a man's skill and
resource: 'The miner's activity has this beauty to it: it is not
routine work and with every action the intelligence can come
into play. There are constantly occasions, in drilling, placing
timbers, clearing falls, etc., where a good idea can save many
hours work. Such activity offers satisfaction. . .'[16] He might
have added that, unlike the factory worker, the miner was
largely his own master when it came to the detailed planning
and execution of his work; instead of being subject to the
minute-by-minute supervision of the factory foreman, the
hewer was one in a semi-autonomous group of colleagues. This
combination of knowledge (of the characteristics of coal,
rocks, timber, gas, etc.), physical dexterity and skill, and
reliance on independent judgement could give the experienced
miner a real sense of pride in his abilities and profession.
Franz Hoffeld, who had worked in a factory, at a blast

[15] StAB, 462, *Westfälische Volkszeitung*, 7. 5. 1890; see also StAB, 379,
Amt Hofstede to KLB, 31. 7. 1900; Brüggemeier, *Leben vor Ort*, p. 101.

[16] STAM, *Frankfurter Zeitung*, 11. 2. 1912. See also Levenstein, *Aus der
Tiefe*, p. 40; Lucas, *Arbeiterradikalismus*, p. 45; Stearns, *Lives of Labour*,
pp. 230–1; Campbell and Reid, 'Independent Collier in Scotland', pp. 57–61;
Brüggemeier, *Leben vor Ort*, p. 270.

furnace, and on building sites as well as in the mines, commented that despite all the drawbacks and dangers, 'the miner's life seems to me the most interesting and the most free.'[17]

Nevertheless, it would be wrong to exaggerate or romanticize these relative satisfactions. Hoffeld also described the miner's life as 'rough and brutal'.[18] Of 749 Ruhr miners who were asked, shortly before the First World War, whether they enjoyed their work, 171 said they did, 71 expressed indifference, and 507 said they did not. The sample was not random and the question was poorly worded but the drift of opinion was clear. Even those who said they enjoyed their work did so primarily because of the wages (92) or 'from habit' (42). One who recognized that there were interesting aspects of mine-work was in no doubt about the balance of his views:

My work gives me absolutely no pleasure—that is virtually impossible in mining. At least I have never met anyone who found pleasure in pit work. The work is done purely mechanically, under compulsion. One has to work if one does not wish to become a vagabond and nothing better would be found in other jobs. Now and then I am interested in new technical mining achievements, new working methods, new machines, and also in the sometimes strange rock formations.

An apprentice hewer put his feelings more bluntly: 'The work gives me no pleasure. I go to work as if to my death.'[19]

Health and safety

The young miner's figure of speech only too often became grisly reality. Mining was not the only dangerous industry: transport and foundry work were among the small number of occupations with comparable accident rates per employee. But the numbers involved in mining, the high proportion of fatalities amongst accident victims, the sheer scale of individual disasters and the unique horror of death deep below the ground together singled out mining as the most dangerous industry in contemporary Germany.[20]

[17] F. Hoffeld, *Bilder aus dem Bergmannsleben* (Dortmund, n.d.), p. 6.
[18] ibid., p. 14.   [19] Levenstein, *Arbeiterfrage*, pp. 54–5.
[20] M. Metzner, *Die soziale Fürsorge im Bergbau* (Jena, 1911), p. 67; Koch, *Bergarbeiterbewegung*, p. 145.

The most dramatic danger came from explosions. Fire-damp was one common cause. This was a mixture of methane and air which—in the right proportions—could explode with the slightest flame or spark. Firedamp was liable to accumulate in sheltered parts of the mine and its lack of smell increased the danger. The answer was to improve ventilation to prevent pockets from accumulating and to improve safety lamps to prevent open flames or sparks. The second major cause was coal-dust. Unfortunately, the very ventilation which discouraged the accumulation of firedamp helped to spread the dust around the pit. The main pre-ventive measure was to spray water over the coal trucks and over the work faces and passages underground. High under-ground temperatures added to the difficulty and expense of this. It increased the general discomfort of the miners, who had as a result to work in damp conditions, and contributed to the spread of disease.[21]

Firedamp and coal-dust accounted for most pit explosions. The effect depended on the particular circumstances, and might vary from the fairly innocuous to the mass tragedy. In November 1889 a coal-dust explosion at *Constantin der Grosse* killed fourteen miners and injured four. A fire-damp explosion at *Prinz von Preussen* in 1895 killed thirty-eight men. An explosion at *Carolinenglück* in 1898 resulted in the deaths of 116 men and many injuries: it was alleged that firedamp had been allowed to accumulate in the pit, and that there were inadequate sprinkling facili-ties. A firedamp explosion at *Friedlicher Nachbar* at two in the morning in April 1903 led to one death and four men injured. A firedamp explosion at *Lothringen* in 1912 killed 114 miners. These were just some of the explosions which occurred at mines near Bochum over the years. The worst Ruhr pit explosion took place at *Radbod* near Hamm (north-east of Dortmund) in November 1908: 348 men were killed and 21 injured in what was thought to be the worst industrial disaster which Germany had experienced. To appreciate the potential danger from explo-sions, however, it is worth recalling the disaster at Courrières

[21] Metzner, *Soziale Fürsorge*, pp. 78–9; Weber, 'Der Arbeitsplatz', pp. 109–11; Jevons, *British Coal Trade*, pp. 388–401.

in France in 1906, when a coal-dust explosion caused 1,100 deaths.[22]

Although dramatic and potentially catastrophic, explosions caused only a minority of accidents in the mines. Falls of rock and coal caused many more. They could occur at almost any time with serious consequences for anyone in the immediate vicinity. Prevention required comprehensive timbering of passages and work-faces. Particularly in the earlier years, however, this was commonly deficient: the policy was rather to put up timber supports only where a specific danger was thought to be present. A particularly dangerous moment followed shot-firing to loosen coal: the shot might have weakened the roof, but the miners returned to the face virtually blinded by dust and could not watch for tell-tale signs. At shift-end, when the men were tired and anxious to fill as many trucks as possible to boost their earnings, carelessness could increase the risks. Rock falls were thought to be responsible for 45 per cent of all serious accidents in the Ruhr in 1885/6 but to have fallen to around a third by 1901. This compared with around 10 per cent of accidents caused by explosions. The decline in the proportion of accidents caused by falls resulted partly from improved timbering and partly from the growing practice of filling in exhausted workings.[23]

Explosions and falls accounted for the bulk of accidents in the pits. Others were caused by any one of many factors: fire could break out; accidents could occur in the transit of coal and trucks around the pit and to the surface; as mechanization advanced an increasing number of accidents resulted from the use of machines and power tools.[24] The accident rate in German pits actually rose over the years. In 1886 the number of registered accidents stood at 65 per

[22] WWA, HKB *Jahresbericht*, 1889; StAB, *Magistratsbericht*, 1895/6, p. 48; IZF, *Deutsche Berg- und Hüttenarbeiter-Zeitung*, 26. 2. 1898; *Zeitschrift für das Bergbau-, Hütten- und Salinenwesen*, 1904; Hue, *Bergarbeiter* ii. 638, 652; R. G. Neville, 'The Courrières Colliery Disaster, 1906', in *Journal of Contemporary History* xiii. 1 (1978), pp. 33, 48; Metzner, *Soziale Fürsorge*, p. 80.

[23] Pieper, *Lage der Bergarbeiter*, p. 151; Metzner, *Soziale Fürsorge*, pp. 75–6; Koch, *Bergarbeiterbewegung*, pp. 82–3; Neville, 'Courrières Colliery Disaster', p. 49; Levenstein, *Aus der Tiefe*, p. 96.

[24] Münz, *Lage der Bergarbeiter*, p. 107; Imbusch, *Arbeitsverhältnis*, p. 130.

thousand insured mineworkers but the rate rose fairly
steadily to reach 100 per thousand workers in 1899 and 127
in 1906. The proportion of fatal accidents fell, from 2.55 per
thousand insured workers in 1886 to 1.79 in 1906. Nevertheless, the death-rate in German mines was worse than that in
other European countries: between 1897 and 1911 it
averaged 2.21 per thousand, appreciably worse than that for
France (1.52), the United Kingdom (1.32), Austria (1.28), and
Belgium (1.03), but better than the United States (3.31). Within Germany the Ruhr was the most dangerous mining district:
between 1891 and 1900 on average 2.73 per thousand miners
died there, compared to 2.6 in Upper Silesia, 2.23 in the
Aachen district, 1.8 in the Saar, and 1.47 in Lower Silesia.[25]
The picture in the Ruhr was thus very bleak, not just in
absolute terms but also by comparison with other coal-fields.

There were a number of reasons for this. One factor was the
wages system, which was designed to encourage the miners to
produce as much coal as possible but gave no specific payment
for ancillary tasks such as timbering. Another was the failure of
the Government inspectors to enforce effectively the legal
safety requirements on the mines. This was partly due to
insufficient numbers: they had to supervise health and safety
provisions and also other technical activities; many mines or
parts of mines very rarely saw an inspector. Personal contacts
between inspectors and managers were sometimes too close:
there was a recognized career progression from Government
service into private management. This was thought to encourage tip-offs of forthcoming inspections, enabling management
to ensure that things were in order before the inspector
arrived. Parts of the mine where conditions were unsatisfactory might even be closed up and the inspector informed
that they were no longer being worked. Finally, workers
might be reluctant to raise complaints with the inspectors,
for fear of subsequent victimization by management.[26]

---

[25] These rates were based on the total of all workers in the mining industry:
the rates for underground workers alone would be higher. In 1901–7 Upper Silesia
had a slightly worse record than the Ruhr. Metzner, *Soziale Fürsorge*, p. 70;
Münz, *Lage der Bergarbeiter*, p. 107; Imbusch, *Arbeitsverhältnis*, pp. 129–30;
Koch, *Bergarbeiterbewegung*, p. 82; Jevons, *British Coal Trade*, p. 374.

[26] Kirchhoff, *Sozialpolitik*, p. 127; Metzner, *Soziale Fürsorge*, p. 86; Pieper,
Lage der Bergarbeiter, pp. 87, 143.

Two major accidents led to improvements in the mines inspection service. The *Carolinenglück* disaster of 1898 was partly blamed on inadequate inspection of the pit, and in the following year the size of the inspectorate was increased. The Government considered, but finally rejected, a demand from the miners' unions for workers' safety inspectors. These already existed in some other countries, and in Germany itself they were introduced in Bavarian mines in 1900 and in the Saar in 1902. Eventually the *Radbod* disaster of 1908 led the Government to insist on their introduction in the Ruhr. The safety officer was elected by the men and had the right to inspect his part of the mine twice a month with the over-man and to make additional inspections at the request of either the management or workers' committee. The date and time of the inspection was left to him. He was paid by the mine, except for inspections made at the request of the workers' committee. In practice, however, the effectiveness of the new post was limited. It aroused little interest or enthusiasm and seems to have had very little impact.[27]

High turnover of labour and the influx of immigrants added to the risks. Many newcomers had no prior experience of mining work. Not surprisingly, they were liable to make mistakes and to fail to recognize danger signs. Foreigners and immigrants from the eastern provinces (many of them Polish speakers) were far more liable to injury than other miners: in 1905, for instance, 168 per thousand miners employed in the Ruhr were injured in accidents, but this concealed considerable differences between immigrants and others: the accident rate was 253 per thousand amongst foreigners, 195 per thousand amongst immigrants of German nationality (but mostly of Polish or Masurian ethnic origin) and only 144 per thousand amongst other Germans.[28]

In 1899 the Government introduced a requirement that workers should have a minimum knowledge of German, so

---

[27] Kirchhoff, *Sozialpolitik*, pp. 128–30, 170–3; IZF, *Deutsche Berg- und Hüttenarbeiter-Zeitung*, 12. 3. 1898; Brüggemeier, *Leben vor Ort*, pp. 119–20.

[28] Koch, *Bergarbeiterbewegung*, p. 82; Münz, *Lage der Bergarbeiter*, p. 102. The proportions were similar in other years. It was suggested by Georg Werner that the difference was largely due to the concentration of immigrants in the more dangerous jobs and pits: G. Werner *Unfälle und Erkrankungen im Ruhr-bergbau* (Essen, 1910?).

that they could understand colleagues and supervisors, before they could be employed in the mines; certain posts were only to be held by those who could read German. The Government did not, however, accept the suggestion that all notices be translated into the main foreign languages in use in the Ruhr. The attempt to enforce linguistic standards was bitterly resented by the Poles and other non-German speakers, who saw it as an attempt to discriminate against them by restricting their access to better jobs. The measure had little effect on the incidence of accidents. The problem was accentuated by the movement of miners within the Ruhr. Conditions frequently varied between mines and it took a certain time to learn the exact nature of the coal, the rock, the atmosphere, and all the other factors which could contribute to an accident in a new pit. An explosion in 1893 at *Kaiserstuhl*, near Dortmund, in which 60 men died was said to be due to the failure of a miner who had recently moved from *Hardenberg*, where the coal was firm, to reduce the amount of explosive used in accordance with the softer conditions at his new mine. The Bochum area mines inspectorate commented in 1897 that accident rates were highest at pits with a high labour turnover while relatively stable pits such as *Hannover* and *Hannibal* were less affected by accidents.[29]

Despite high accident rates, miners ran an even greater risk of having their livelihood interrupted by illness. In 1905, when the number of men injured in accidents stood at 168 per thousand men employed, the number who lost three or more days from work through illness stood at 473 per thousand. The Ruhr was not untypical of German mining districts in the high rate of illness. Miners were far more susceptible to disease than other workers: the level of injury and disease combined averaged only 390 per thousand for all German insured groups. Only the building industry had a comparable sickness rate.[30]

The high sickness rate in mining was in part a result of

[29] Kirchhoff, *Sozialpolitik*, p. 130; Münz, *Lage der Bergarbeiter*, p. 102; Pieper, *Lage der Bergarbeiter*, p. 141; StAB, 431, KLB to *Staatssekretär des Innern*, 22. 12. 1908. In Breslau, unlike the Ruhr, safety notices were posted in Polish: Wehler, 'Polen im Ruhrgebiet', p. 453.

[30] Koch, *Bergarbeiterbewegung*, p. 83; Münz, *Lage der Bergarbeiter*, p. 116; Metzner, *Soziale Fürsorge*, pp. 92–4.

the conditions in which many miners lived, including over-crowded accommodation. But many other workers lived in poor physical conditions: we must look to the particular conditions of work to explain the specific sickness rates. One underlying factor was simply the physically demanding nature of mine-work and the general effect which months and years of it had on strength and resistance to disease. Many miners were in a state of semi-permanent exhaustion, with only Sunday to recuperate. Overtime added to the problem. A second factor was the violent changes in tempera-ture to which they were subject. The temperature at the coal-face was usually high—frequently well over 20 degrees—and this contrasted sharply with the temperatures in the main roadways, at the bottom of the shaft, and outside. The problem was exacerbated by damp: clothes were soon damp or even soaked from sweat and water and in these the miner made his way back to the shaft at the end of the shift; here he sometimes had to wait before being winched to the surface. Ruhr miners did, however, have the advantage over their British comrades that most pits provided bathing facilities, so that they did not have to make their way home in dirty and damp pit clothes.

These factors explain the weak physical condition in which many miners had to meet infection and disease and the rheumatism and influenza which commonly afflicted them. Arthritis was encouraged by these factors and by the pressures of the hip caused by the position in which miners had to work. Laryngitis was also common. Amongst the diseases common amongst miners anthracosis, silicosis, other forms of pneumoconiosis, and emphysema affected the lungs and breathing organs. These diseases, sometimes reinforced by TB and referred to as 'black-spit', arose primarily from breathing dust underground. Coal-dust blackened the lungs and a man's spittle, but greater damage to the lungs was caused by the stone-dust which accompanied it. The miner suffered from coughing and gradually increasing difficulty with breathing. This limited his physical capacity and pre-vented strenuous work. In extreme cases breathing became virtually impossible, with death as the final result. Other common diseases—trachoma and nystagmus—affected the

eyes and could lead to blindness. Trachoma was easily passed
on, and in 1899 baths were banned from mines and had to
be replaced with showers.[31]

The most dramatic outbreak of disease came from the so-
called 'worm disease' (ancylostomiasis, or human hookworm)
whch swept the Ruhr pits in the early 1900s. The adult
worms lived in the human small intestine and laid eggs which
were passed in the faeces. The larvae first lived free in the
soil, but later penetrated human skin if this was available, or
were swallowed in water. The disease was prevalent in
tropical countries, requiring fairly high temperatures, considerable moisture, and poor sanitary conditions. It spread
first to Italy and then to Hungary, Belgium, France, and
finally Germany. Conditions in many mines were well suited
to the disease, combining moisture, warmth, and inadequate
sanitation with many semi-dressed men. It was only in
response to the epidemic of the early 1900s that the mines
began to take seriously the problem of underground sanitation: the traditional method was to provide a number of
wooden tubs, but the number was often quite inadequate
for the work-force; they were situated too far from the
work-face, and were infrequently emptied. The result was
that the men often made only limited use of them and preferred to find a quiet place near their work to relieve themselves. Another problem was the lack of drinking-water.
Miners usually took around three litres of diluted coffee with
them to drink, but in hot areas this was not always sufficient
and they resorted to the impure water used for damping
down dust.[32]

The symptoms of the 'worm disease' were described by
a contemporary: 'sallow and pale face, buzzing in the ears,
shortage of breath, dull eyes, pale or white inner sides of the
eyelids, swelling of the feet, diarrhoea and loss of appetite,
general tiredness, dilation of the heart, and finally a craving
for water.'[33] The symptoms usually took three to four weeks
to appear. Death was the result only in extreme cases.

[31] Münz, *Lage der Bergarbeiter*, pp. 119–21; Pieper, *Lage der Bergarbeiter*,
p. 153.

[32] WWA, K2 213; Münz, *Lage der Bergarbeiter*, p. 122.

[33] Pieper, *Lage der Bergarbeiter*, p. 155.

The first recorded case of the disease in the Ruhr area occurred in 1886 and there was a second in 1892. Between 1896 and 1899 there were around a hundred each year, in 1901 and 1902 between one and two thousand, and in 1903 no fewer than 29,374 cases (or over 11 per cent of the total work-force). This dramatic outbreak stimulated the authorities to undertake checks to determine how many men were affected by the disease (for it was possible to carry it without showing symptoms); checks at a number of pits showed that at some of them (*Graf Schwerin* and *Erin*) up to three-quarters of the workers were affected.[34]

The authorities took vigorous action: they insisted that no new miner could be taken on without a medical examination and large numbers of men were obliged to undergo 'cures' of one to two weeks. This caused great discontent amongst the miners, partly because carriers who did not themselves feel ill had to undergo the cure, partly because the cure could be unpleasant and sometimes had to be repeated, but mainly because of the cost. No compensation was given for the first three days of pay lost due to the cure, and for the rest the compensation only amounted to around a quarter of the normal wage. If the cure had to be repeated the family could get into serious financial difficulties. By the end of 1903, in fact, many mines were beginning to make a greater contribution to the medical costs and were providing their employees with compensation to bring their benefit up to average wage levels. This helped to reduce the discontent.[35]

Other measures were taken to improve sanitary conditions in the pits. The old wooden toilets were replaced with iron ones and attempts were made to increase their number, their accessibility, and the frequency with which they were emptied and cleaned. The Gelsenkirchener Bergwerks AG tried to encourage their miners to use the toilets at the surface before starting the shift. Attempts were made to provide the miners with clean drinking-water: at *Julius Philipp*, however, there were protests when the men were charged 10 pfennigs for a half-litre of water, deductable from

[34] WWA, K2 213; Koch, *Bergarbeiterbewegung*, p. 84.
[35] StAB, 464, *Polizei-Commissar* Bochum to RPA, 27. 7. 1903; StAB, 480, RPA to *Minister des Innern*, 8. 12. 1903.

wages. Nevertheless, the measures seem to have been effective: the number of cases fell from over 29,000 in 1903 to 5,000 in 1905. By 1906 the disease was effectively eliminated from all but a few pits.[36]

Accidents and disease were thus commonplace. Every day that a man entered the pit could prove to be his last; and even if he was not killed outright the injuries he was liable to suffer, the dust he breathed in, and the diseases to which he was subject combined to undermine his health and shorten his life. The average age of invalidity in Prussian mines dropped from over 53 years in the 1860s to under 47 in the 1900s. Miners were generally finished by their mid-forties —'at an age at which other groups of workers are virtually still at full strength'.[37] The miner suffered from pain, growing incapacity, and, ultimately, premature death. Almost as serious, however, was the impact of incapacity on his earnings. It was the loss of pay, rather than the insanitary conditions which caused the disease, which aroused most protest over the worm disease. Even a fairly minor injury or illness could have serious financial consequences for the miner's family, not just in an immediate loss of earnings, but over the succeeding years if the man was left to any significant degree weaker.

Miners were somewhat better provided with insurance cover than many other workers in Germany. The *Knappschaft*, the insurance organization for the mining industry in the area, dated from 1769, and even by the beginning of the twentieth century—by which time some social security provisions had been extended to other groups of workers—it still offered many facilities which compared favourably with those available to other workers: miners, for instance, were better able to get help with special assistance in case of particular need, cheap loans, help for schoolchildren, provision of washhouses, etc., than were other workers. Nevertheless, in their main social security provisions the miners were no longer the privileged group they had been early in the nineteenth century.

[36] WWA, K2 213; IZF, *Bergarbeiter Zeitung*, 13. 6. 1903; Koch, *Bergarbeiterbewegung*, p. 84; Münz, *Lage der Bergarbeiter*, p. 125.

[37] R. Schneider, *Die Entwicklung des niederrhein.-westfälischen Bergbaus und der Eisen-Industrie* (Bochum, 1899), p. 34; Metzner, *Soziale Fürsorge*, p. 97; Pieper, *Lage der Bergarbeiter*, pp. 15–16.

In theory at least the *Knappschaft* was financed and managed jointly by employers and workers. Both made financial contributions and both were represented on its board. In practice, however, the organization was dominated by the employers and was the focus of continuing complaints and disputes. Until 1908 three-quarters of the financial contributions came from the workers, whose representatives nevertheless only had half the seats on the board. In 1908 the employers' contributions were raised to match those of the workers. At the same time the indirect elections through which the workers' representatives (known as *Älteste*) were chosen were replaced by a more direct system with the aim of giving the miners a more effective voice. In practice, however, the employers seem to have continued to dominate the organization.

The *Knappschaft*'s main function was the provision of medical facilities and sickness and invalidity benefits. The benefit a man received depended on his contribution record but after 1908 stood at around half the level of average wages. This was probably sufficient to avoid extreme destitution but certainly not enough to prevent a severe drop in living standards for a man and his family if he was prevented from working for any length of time. It represented but a modest cushion against the threat of injury or sickness.[38] No such protection existed against the threat of unemployment.

Job security and hours of work

Until the 1860s the Ruhr miners had enjoyed considerable state protection against dismissal and unemployment. The liberal reforms of 1860 and 1865, however, introduced the concept of the work contract, freely entered into by employer and employee and terminable by either after just two weeks' notice.[39] This immediately made miners vulnerable to the loss of their job.

[38] Metzner, *Soziale Fürsorge*, pp. 110–17; Münz, *Lage der Bergarbeiter,* p. 127. Until the reforms of the 1850s the *Knappschaft* had been much more than an insurance organization and had fulfilled a range of social functions: Tenfelde, *Sozialgeschichte*, pp. 90–8, 282–91.

[39] W. Fischer, *Die Bedeutung der preussischen Bergrechtsreform (1851–1865) für den industriellen Ausbau des Ruhrgebiets* (Dortmund, 1961); Kirchhoff, *Sozialpolitik*, chapter 1; Tenfelde, *Sozialgeschichte*, pp. 262–3.

Fortunately for the miners, the long-term growth of the industry resulted in a sustained demand for labour. So long as expansion was maintained unemployment could only pose a relatively marginal problem, affecting individuals rather than large groups of workers. However, the long-term trend concealed cyclical fluctuations of varying severity and during these unemployment could become a real possibility. The worst depression was that of the 1870s and early 1880s when demand for industrial products and coal collapsed and with it the demand for labour. The number of Ruhr miners fell by 10,000 between 1875 and 1877. The problem was accentuated by continued immigration and poverty became more acute. The number of families dependent on poor relief in Bochum rose from 100 in 1874 to 328 in 1881.[40]

The depression gradually lifted and the mining industry resumed its rapid growth. Later cyclical downturns were nothing like so drastic or so prolonged and posed less of a threat to miners' jobs. Never after 1887 was there a fall in the total number of miners employed. The worst setbacks were in 1902, when the number of miners employed in the Ruhr showed no increase on the previous year, and 1913 when the increase consisted of only few hundred. Nevertheless, the continued influx of workers into the district meant that downturns did cause real concern about unemployment. Each one was marked by short-time working ('free shifts'), wage reductions, reduced recruitment, and some lay-offs. Mass unemployment, however, never reappeared before 1914.

The main reason was the sustained expansion of the industry. Downturns were relatively brief. Since the main problem facing management was to secure and retain a labour force sufficient to fully exploit the expanding market, they were reluctant to part with workers, even when in the short term they constituted a net cost to the company. The mines tended, therefore, to react to falls in coal demand by cutting back the number of shifts worked, ending overtime and re-deploying men from coal-cutting to maintenance and safety work. These measures, combined with cuts in wage

---

[40] StAB, HKB *Jahresberichte*; Koch, *Bergarbeiterbewegung*, p. 139; Hue, *Neutrale oder parteiische Gewerkschaften?*, p. 35.

rates, reduced labour costs without actually laying off men —and thus threatening the company's position when the slump ended. It was usually only after such methods had been tried that the mines turned to more drastic action. The Bochum Chamber of Commerce noted in 1913 that even if the recession of that year worsened they did not expect many redundancies:

The mines themselves have a considerable interest in maintaining the core work force [*Arbeiterstamm*] which they have brought together at considerable cost, even in bad times. The mines use times of poor demand to start more rock work [preparatory operations] or to put more manpower onto it, so that the men freed from coal production can be used here. In addition, they will try to maintain their operations at about the existing level by stockpiling coal and coke. Both methods have already been started here and there.[41]

There were complaints that the mines did not go far enough in arranging work to keep men employed through recessions. Heinrich Imbusch, a Catholic miners' leader, conceded that there were difficulties in stockpiling large amounts of coal; but he felt that there was considerably greater scope for concentrating preparatory work in periods of recession: 'During booms one could then employ virtually the entire work-force on coal production. A powerful boost in the production figures would naturally result. Some managements have already worked in this way. But there remains a great deal more that could be done in this direction.'[42]

A further factor limiting the impact of cyclical booms and slumps on the coal industry, and thus helping to preserve jobs during downswings, was the existence of the coal syndicate. This organization, set up in 1893 and including in its membership nearly all the Ruhr mining companies, exercised some control over the industry by imposing quotas on each company. This prevented the kind of extreme competition between mines which would have encouraged the less economic to sack large numbers of workers during recessions. In 1901 the Bochum *Landrat* noted that the

[41] WWA, K2 923, HKB to RPA, 27. 10. 1913. See also WWA, K2 857, HKB to RPA, 27. 9. 1902.
[42] Imbusch, *Arbeitsverhältnis*, pp. 75–6; see also Pieper, *Lage der Bergarbeiter*, p. 82.

effects of the recession were at least modified through this means:

The coal syndicate's sticking to its long-term agreement has had the beneficial consequence that the working class has not been hit too suddenly by the ending of the boom. There has been a quite gradual shake-out of labour in such a manner that at first the unharmonious and inefficient elements have been dismissed. The works which are concerned to preserve their skilled labour force have helped by introducing free shifts and short-time. Thus there is as yet no major shortage of work; redundancies on a large scale have not yet taken place, and are not expected in the near future.[43]

Not everyone agreed with this argument: Dr Pieper blamed much of the unemployment of 1902 on the syndicate's price-fixing, and claimed that if prices had fallen, output and employment would not have slumped so badly. Nevertheless Otto Hue, one of the leading social democrats and miners' leaders in the district, expressed public support for the moderating effect which the syndicate exerted on cyclical fluctuations.[44]

While pit managers generally tried to retain many workers during recessions they did not hesitate to dispense with those they felt to be 'unharmonious and inefficient'. These were often identified as union members and 'agitators'. The mines inspector for the Witten district commented in 1901: 'Here and there the economic recession is used by managements to rid their labour force of those who have become troublesome through agitation, or those notable for their unruliness.'[45] Men were sometimes encouraged to resign by a tightening of discipline: in 1901 at *Baaker Mulde* and *Präsident* fines and punishments were suddenly much more toughly enforced. The *Volksblatt* commented:

At many works regular free shifts have been introduced to avoid having to sack workers. Other managements resort to such objectionable methods as excessive wage cuts, harsh punishments, bad treatment of the men, etc., to encourage the workers to give notice themselves.

[43] STAM, RA I 1485, KLB to RPA, 19. 11. 1901.
[44] Pieper, *Lage der Bergarbeiter*, p. 83; StAB, 480, RPA to *Minister des Innern*, 8. 12. 1903; F. Mariaux, *Gedenkwort zum 100-jährigen Bestehen der Harpener Bergbau AG* (Dortmund, 1956), p. 218; Koch, *Bergarbeiterbewegung*, p. 78; see also StAB, *Magistratsbericht*, 1907, p. 30; Brüggemeier, *Leben vor Ort*, pp. 86-7.
[45] Pieper, *Lage der Bergarbeiter*, p. 89.

Thus at many works, especially mines, many workers leave of their own accord, despite the poor chance of finding work elsewhere.[46]

Unemployment thus remained a distinct possibility for individuals. There was also a certain amount of seasonal hiring and firing. Nevertheless, for the great majority of miners unemployment was a relatively remote problem. As one commentator noted in 1909: 'Thanks to the extraordinarily favourable development of the Ruhr mining industry one cannot speak of an insecurity in the Ruhr miner's existence in the last decades, or in the forseeable future; a fact which is not to be found in any other industry.'[47]

The converse of the sustained expansion of the industry and the demand for labour, however, was considerable pressure on the miners over hours of work. There were three main issues: the length of the normal shift, the number of such shifts worked, and the overtime on top of the ordinary shifts. All these issues were at their most acute during economic upswings.

The normal shift was usually eight hours long, enabling a three-shift day: the morning shift generally started at 6.00 a.m., the afternoon shift at 2.00 p.m., and the small night shift at 10.00 p.m. Most men worked on the morning or afternoon shifts, while the night shift was used primarily for preparatory and repair work. The eight-hour shift dated back to the eighteenth century and was one of the miners' most cherished heritages. Surface-workers and workers in other industries in the Ruhr normally had appreciably longer shifts: as late as 1905 the shifts in the metal industry in and around Bochum varied betwen ten and eleven and a half hours, though ten hours was becoming the norm. The miners' eight-hour shift was under challenge even before the economic liberalization of the 1860s, which enabled employers to determine the hours of work. Some employers did indeed lengthen the shift: in 1889 many pits had basic shifts of a little over eight hours, although others had slightly shorter ones. Nevertheless, eight hours did generally continue as the

[46] IZF, *Volksblatt*, 25. 7. 1901.
[47] Münz, *Lage der Bergarbeiter*, pp. 28-9; StAB, 462, *Zeche Julius Philipp* to KLB, 20. 8. 1890.

normal shift length; employers found short-time or overtime to be more flexible methods of reducing or increasing production.[48]

Nevertheless, the length of the basic shift was the cause of much controversy. As the mines expanded, becoming deeper and much longer underground, the question of exactly what the eight hours should cover became more and more contentious. Journey-time between the shaft and the actual workplace underground became longer, so that by the late 1880s it was taking up to an hour each way at some pits. Walking underground was physically tiring: the passages were often narrow with low roofs and timbers below which the miner had to duck. They could also be wet and slippery, and in the poor light it was difficult to keep an adequate watch for obstacles. The men commonly had to carry their tools and a timber prop. Thus any extension of journey-time was an addition to the physical toll of the miner's day. Larger numbers of men going in and out of the expanding pits could also mean bottlenecks and delays at the pit-head: Franz Hoffeld recalled how at one pit the men were supposed to be winched down between 5.30 and 6.00 a.m., but because of the numbers it was necessary to be in line by 5.00 a.m. to get to the face on time: lateness led to ill-treatment from the overman.[49] A further problem was that deeper pits with higher temperatures at the face meant that an eight-hour shift became physically more exhausting. The increasing size and depth of the mines thus meant that the working day—even with the same number of hours of actual work—tended to increase and become less supportable. The employers nevertheless argued that the eight-hour shift meant eight hours actually at the coal-face, while the miners claimed that it should represent eight hours underground, including journey-time.

The issue was most acute during economic upswings, when the employers were keen to maximize output. At such times the number of shifts worked also tended to rise. Hewers and hauliers worked on average 288 shifts during the recession

[48] WWA, K2 741; StAB, 442; Imbusch, *Arbeitsverhältnis*, p. 62; Hue, *Bergarbeiter*, ii. 151–6; Tenfelde, *Sozialgeschichte*, pp. 264–8.
[49] Hoffeld, *Bilder aus dem Bergannsleben*, p. 13.

year of 1902, but the number rose to 315 and 313 in the boom years of 1906 and 1907.[50] Closely associated with extra shifts was the practice of working overtime at the end of the normal shift. Normally this would take the form of an additional quarter shift (i.e., two hours) but it could consist of anything up to a full double shift. In theory overtime (which was not paid for at a higher rate) was purely voluntary and men had the right to refuse it; but in practice considerable pressure was exerted on them. Some men may have welcomed the chance to increase their earnings; but many disliked the system because of the physical exhaustion it entailed and because they considered that it tended to depress wages for the normal shift. At the inquiry following the 1889 strike there were complaints that at some pits it was not possible to earn a living wage without overtime: the *Neu Iserlohn* miners' spokesmen called for 'reasonable earnings *without* overtime'.[51] Management, however, normally regarded overtime as essential to maximize output during booms. Unfortunately, to provide full cover for overheads it was necessary to have as many men as possible staying on to work the additional shift; and to secure the greatest efficiency and facilitate the book-keeping it was desirable to keep existing teams of miners together rather than create new combinations. The management of *Unser Fritz* commented in 1889 that only 'general' overtime—i.e. overtime when all the men worked—was of any value.[52] A mines inspector reported in 1899:

Overtime shifts to secure greater production are best, both for the workers and for the mine, when they last two or four hours; this, however, is only possible when there is general participation, since otherwise the winding equipment which has to be kept running is too expensive. It is therefore vital that the labour force is willing to do the overtime, and that they are additionally satisfied with two or four hours. This is generally the case at the southern mines with an established and settled labour force; at the new northern pits with their corresponding labour force general participation is hard to achieve. The workers there are also more in favour of 8-hour overtime shifts, reasoning that if they

[50] Münz, *Lage der Bergarbeiter*, p. 55.
[51] StAB, 442; Münz, *Lage der Bergarbeiter*, p. 54; Pieper, *Lage der Bergarbeiter*, p. 53; StAB, 445, *Denkschrift über die Untersuchung*, p. 9.
[52] StAB, 442.

are to bear the unpleasantness of a long period of work at all, it must at least be as concentrated and as profitable as possible.[53]

To maximize overtime participation pressure was often put on miners. Sometimes they were required to register a day in advance with the overman if they did not want to work over- time; complaints about this from men at *Friedrich der Grosse* in 1889 drew the management response that it was necessary 'for the maintenance of order'. Men who had not registered by the time specified were sometimes prevented from leaving the pit until the overtime was completed: the 1889 enquiry heard complaints about this from men at a number of mines and at *Baaker Mulde* it was conceded that this was the practice: 'Agreed; done to achieve higher pro- duction'.[54] One incident at the *Vereinigte Wallfisch* pit in June 1889 illustrates the difficulties which could arise: the management issued a notice announcing that the next day's morning shift would continue for an additional two hours and that anyone not wanting to do this should register with the overman. Eight men registered and when the basic shift ended next day at 1 o'clock they, and a few others who had arrived at the shaft, were allowed out. But other men decided that the air was bad and that they had had enough and left their stalls too—apparently at their normal time. When they reached the shaft, however, they found that the winding of coal trucks had resumed and that they could not go to the surface until 3 o'clock; 'wet through with sweat', they had to wait at the draughty pit bottom for two hours. In a report on the incident the mines inspector commented that the management had been 'thoroughly correct' in its actions and had followed the 'general custom'.[55]

Such pressure persisted in later years. In 1899 men at *Präsident* were fined for failing to work overtime without having registered with the overman. In April 1900 three miners at *Vollmond* had their pay cut after leaving at the end of eight hours without permission.[56] In 1905, as the largest

---

[53] Pieper, *Lage der Bergarbeiter*, p. 50.
[54] StAB, 442; Tenfelde, *Sozialgeschichte*, p. 267.
[55] StAB, 439.
[56] Imbusch, *Arbeitsverhältnis*, p. 68; IZF, *Volksblatt*, 19. 4. 1900.

strike in the Ruhr was about to begin, one close observer reported:

It should not be denied that overtime shifts can sometimes be necessary; nor that individual workers themselves volunteer to do them from a desire for higher wages because of family concerns, to make up lost shifts or lost wages resulting from illness, fines, deductions etc., or for other reasons. In most cases, however, overtime is done because of direct or indirect pressure from the mine-owner or his officials, to utilize the favourable economic conditions or to make economies (by having a smaller workforce and burdening them with overtime), etc. One frequently reads in the miners' press: 'Those who refuse overtime get reduced wages and worse places of work'.[57]

At the height of the boom of 1906 and 1907, when labour was in demand and wages were high, many miners simply refused to work overtime: the Gelsenkirchener Bergwerks AG complained that this was a factor behind the coal shortage; in April 1907 a miners' meeting at *Shamrock III/IV* voted unanimously not to work any further overtime, and not to co-operate with any foreign workers who the management might bring in to work the extra shifts.[58]

Economic upswings were thus accompanied by pressure on the length of the working day, particularly through an increase in the number of shifts and an increase in overtime. Discontent mounted amongst miners who felt that they should be able to earn an adequate wage without having to spend longer than eight hours underground. Ironically, when booms were at their height and all the pits were working flat out production was sometimes disrupted by shortages of railway trucks to transport the coal, and men had to be sent home.[59] Such interruptions were, however, the exception: the crucial feature of booms was the mounting pressure on men to work longer and longer hours, and their growing resistance to it.

[57] L. Pieper, 'Die Gärung im Ruhrrevier', in *Soziale Praxis* (12. 1. 1905).
[58] *Glückauf*, 23. 3. 1907; STAM, *Landratsamt* Gelsenkirchen 40, *Polizei* Eickel report, 29. 4. 1907.
[59] StAB, HKB *Jahresberichte*, 1899, 1907; Münz, *Lage der Bergarbeiter*, pp. 56–7; Schofer, *Formation of a modern labor force*, p. 9.

Holidays and absenteeism

The normal working week in the pits was six days, and during booms when overtime was being worked the miners had little time to call their own. Nor did they have much relief from the pressure of work through official holidays. There were a number of religious and traditional local festivals which allowed a day off—although employers might try to arrange for work to continue if economic conditions were favourable —and there was a trend towards working on saints' days. Employers did allow men to take holidays: but there was no entitlement and no wages were paid. In 1907 the concept of the annual paid holiday was introduced into the Prussian state-owned mines, but there were few of these in the Ruhr and the idea was not imitated by the private mines. There were occasional suggestions that paid holidays be introduced —the workers' committee at *Dannenbaum II* requested it in 1909—but a survey in 1910 by the Bochum Chamber of Commerce revealed that the breweries were the only local industry which had introduced paid holidays for workers (although some industries did provide them for more senior employees) in any systematic way. Even in the brewing industry, however, it had been introduced against much opposition: the Schlegel Brauerei argued that other employers should resist the introduction of paid holidays as long as possible and that only workers who were 'industrious and work in the interests of the business' should receive them. The first private mine to introduce paid holidays for underground miners was *Amalie*, near Essen, in 1912: men over thirty who had worked for five years consecutively were given five days off a year with pay. But the custom of granting paid holidays only became at all widespread after the war.[60]

[60] Münz, *Lage der Bergarbeiter*, p. 58; BA, 18/85, *Arbeiterausschuss* meeting *Zeche* Dannenbaum II, 24. 8. 1909; WWA, K2 683; IGBE, A1 98, *Christliche Gewerkverein Geschäftsbericht*, 1911/12; Adelmann, *Soziale Betriebsverfassung*, p. 183; Tenfelde, *Sozialgeschichte*, p. 395. At least one instance of a mining company closing a traditional fair is recorded: Lucas, *Arbeiterradikalismus*, pp. 102-4. See also E. P. Thompson, 'Time, work-discipline and industrial capitalism'; J. Reulecke, 'Vom blauen Montag zum Arbeiterurlaub', in *Archiv für Sozialgeschichte*, (Bonn, 1976), pp. 205-48.

Miners therefore resorted to more informal ways of getting time off. Sickness might be pleaded. Since the doctors were appointed by the colliery rather than by the men themselves and since in any case there was no sickness benefit payable for the first days of illness there were limits to the effectiveness of this ploy. Nevertheless, greater willingness to sign on sick in borderline cases may partly explain the fact that dry and sunny periods saw the highest sickness rates and that August was the worst month for illness.[61]

It was generally simpler, however, just to stay away from work for a day or two. The penalty was greater as well, since in addition to the loss of wages an absentee could be fined if he missed a shift without permission. Nevertheless the habit of extending the weekend was common enough for the first day of the week to be popularly known as 'blue Monday', and pay-days (which occurred twice monthly) and public holidays were also generally followed by widespread absenteeism. Max Lotz observed that some men would not return to work until they had drunk away their earnings and denounced the 'violence, brutality, robbery and bloodshed' which characterized pay-days.[62]

Absenteeism of this sort took place at all times, whatever the state of trade. During recessions, when money was tight, the hours of work in any case reduced, and jobs under threat, absenteeism did not pose too great a problem, partly because the men did not stay away so much and partly because management welcomed it: it reduced production and could be used as an excuse to dispense with unwanted labour. But as the trade cycle improved the problem became more acute. Longer hours and better earnings made men physically more tired and under less pressure to earn every mark they could; the growing demand for labour also made them less afraid of losing their job. More men were therefore willing to trade in some of their better earning-power for additional leisure, or at least felt that any earnings lost at the beginning of the week could be recouped later on. It was consequently in boom years that most of the complaints

[61] Münz, *Lage der Bergarbeiter*, pp. 117–18.
[62] Levenstein, *Aus der Tiefe*, p. 62; Pieper, *Lage der Bergarbeiter*, p. 54; StAB, 445, *Denkschrift über die Untersuchung*, p. 13.

from employers were heard. In 1899 the Bochum Chamber of Commerce pointed out 'in the workers' interest' that the miners were not fully exploiting the boom, both by letting productivity drop and by staying away from work on Mondays and after pay-days: they claimed that this behaviour demonstrated 'the great economic immaturity of a substantial proportion of our working population'. The official *Zeitschrift für das Bergbau-, Hütten- und Salinenwesen* noted that in the boom years of 1906 and 1907 (and to some extent in 1908 too) the number of shifts missed through absenteeism rose, but that when the boom ended in 1909 and 1910 it fell. Absenteeism, of course, was a common feature of mining life, not just in Germany: in 'Ashton' in Yorkshire, for instance, it was normal in the 1940s for men to miss one or two shifts per fortnight, usually on Mondays. It is easy to understand why men should be reluctant to leave home for the pit. The custom also reflected the tendency of some (but by no means all) miners to live from hand to mouth on a very short-term basis: the uncertainties and dangers of the pit, combined with the changing economic conditions which meant that money could be flush at one moment but short the next, could induce a certain fatalism. The next month could look after itself.[63]

The wages system

Work in the pits was hard, unpleasant, and dangerous. The only significant reason for doing it was the pay. This was naturally one of the miners' central concerns.

Wages were calculated in different ways for various categories of workers. Those not directly involved in the actual cutting of coal—most of the surface-workers, pony-minders, hauliers, and specialists such as repair workers, explosive experts, etc.—were generally (though not always) paid on a time basis, at a set rate for each shift worked. The hewers themselves, in contrast, were paid in accordance with the actual amount of coal they produced. This was usually

---

[63] StAB, HKB *Jahresbericht*, 1899; *Zeitschrift für das Bergbau-, Hütten-, und Salinenwesen*, 1906–1910; Münz, *Lage der Bergarbeiter*; Dennis *et al.*, *Coal is our Life*, p. 185; Schofer, *Formation of a modern labor force*, pp. 131–6.

measured by the number of trucks of coal produced by the *Kameradschaft*. While shift-rates tended to remain stable for relatively long periods, the piece-rates—known as *Gedinge*— paid to the hewers were subject to monthly renegotiations between the manager or his representative and the *Ortsäl-tester*. 'If there is any significant change in the rock, seam, or other factor, either side may demand an immediate alteration or abolition of the rate' was how one set of mine rules put it; since the conditions of few seams remained constant for long this system produced a state of almost constant negotiation.[64]

The *Gedinge* system was a natural consequence of the conditions under which coal was cut. Payment on a time basis generally assumes either a reasonably effective system of supervision or else a pace of work determined primarily by factors outside the worker's control—e.g. the speed of machines—since otherwise there is little immediate incentive to maintain what management considers a reasonable intensity of work. In the Ruhr mines, however, mechanization of the coal-face before 1914 was limited while supervision was extremely difficult, due to the large number of scattered work-places. Overmen were able to visit each face perhaps only once or twice during a shift. This meant that to maintain output payment had to be by results. One mines inspector described piece-rates as 'encouraging activity without supervision and therefore, with our mining conditions, indispensable'.[65] That the rates had to be subject to constant renegotiation was the result of the geological nature of the coal-seams in the district; unlike many seams in England, which were said to be relatively constant in their steepness and in the quality of coal and thus allowed fairly long-lasting price agreements, the coal seams in the Ruhr tended to be convoluted and the coal could vary considerably in thickness and hardness. As a result the effort required to produce a given quantity of coal varied enormously. The solution adopted was to assess the difficulty of the work afresh each month or whenever conditions showed a significant

[64] StAB, 456, *Arbeitsordnung der Zeche Bruchstrasse*, paragraph 13; StAB, 464, *Gewerkschaft Constantin der Grosse* to KLB, 26. 4. 1906.
[65] Dr Herbig, 'Schwierigkeiten des Lohnwesens im Bergbau', in *Glückauf*, 28. 12. 1907, p. 1752.

change and to agree a rate in accordance with these new conditions.[66]

However, the system did create problems. One was that the hewers were simply paid for the coal they produced and although this was supposed to cover not merely coal-cutting but also the associated secondary tasks—such as timbering —no payments were made specifically for such jobs. This created an incentive to cut corners and take risks. As one miner put it: 'When working on piece-rates—or *Gedinge*— one is driven from two sides: first, by the mine officials through the threat of low wages, and secondly by one's mates to screw out the highest possible wage. Hence the numerous accidents.'[66]

The system also meant that there was almost continuous friction between management and men. Many miners disliked the system anyway, preferring hourly pay for the greater security and financial stability it provided.[68] Constant negotiation meant constant conflict. Every month negotiations took place to settle the rate. Usually the overman negotiated on behalf of the manager, although any agreement he reached might be only provisional until the manager had approved it himself. The *Ortsältester* of the morning shift negotiated for the men. The two sides' interests were clearly opposed: management wanted to keep wages down as far as possible and would therefore stress the favourable aspects of the forthcoming work; the men, on the other hand, highlighted the problems and argued that higher rates were needed if they were to earn a tolerable wage; to give their case credibility in the next month's negotiation they might limit their current output. Disputes also arose over the definition of the 'local normal daily wage' which was supposed to be paid if no agreement had been reached after a certain number of days.[69] In fact the bargaining might be a war of nerves, with the workers threatening to leave the mine and the management threatening to sack them if the

[66] Münz, *Lage der Bergarbeiter*, pp. 68–9; Metzner, *Soziale Fürsorge*, p. 52.

[67] Levenstein, *Arbeiterfrage*, p. 22.

[68] Two-thirds of Levenstein's sample of Ruhr miners preferred hourly wages, while only 13 per cent said that they preferred piece-work. ibid., p. 25.

[69] Herbig, 'Schwierigkeiten des Lohnwesens'; Hasslacher, 'Was ist unter "ortsüblicher Tagelohn" . . . zu verstehen?', in *Glückauf*, 19. 9. 1903.

other side did not accept their demands. At the inquiry at *Bruchstrasse* following the 1905 strike the miners' delegates complained that the mine officials were very hostile to the workers in wage discussions: 'if the rate on offer was not accepted they talked of notice or even immediate dismissal'.[70] In response to complaints about his behaviour an overman named Gailenbrugge observed that:

he had always had as his aim that the rate should be set so that a hewer would earn at least 5 marks. He normally negotiated for a lengthy time about the agreement, since the workers normally demanded two or three times as much at first. He had not been rude. He did remember an occasion in the autumn of the previous year when he certainly had dealt sharply with them, and when they had rejected an offer of 1.50 marks had shortly told them that they could pack their things and leave. The reason was that he had come across them having a long conversation and not working. He had often noticed at *Bruchstrasse* that the men often stopped work and chatted. This was particularly true at the start of the morning shift. They were only allowed to stop for refreshment once in the shift, and he had been enforcing this rule. . . [71]

There were similar complaints at other pits. At *Shamrock* an overman named Schmidt explained that when he offered a wage rate:

normally the men were at first not satisfied. After we had discussed the work the *Ortsältester* signed the agreement. There were cases virtually every day in my section when some of the men rejected the rate at first and would not sign. But it happened just as often that the men earned quite satisfactorily at the rate which they had at first rejected.[72]

The overmen in fact had only limited freedom to negotiate since they had to ensure that the total wage-bill for their section did not exceed the limits laid down by management. The system was a recipe for continuous friction. *Bergassessor* Herbig noted:

In daily inspections there is hardly ever not a small dispute in which the worker emphasizes the bad aspects of the current conditions of work while the mine official has to be concerned, in the interests of the employer, to check these problems for their true significance

---

[70] STAM, *Obergergamt* Dortmund 1735.
[71] ibid.
[72] StAB, 458, *Bergwerksgesellschaft Hibernia* to KLB, 22. 2. 1905.

and certainly not to overvalue them. This concern with the fixing of piece-rates thus intrudes daily into relations between officials and workers; and thus one of the main advantages which the piece-rate system has in other industries—namely that with an agreement this fundamental and therefore sharply disputed point is removed from debate, and that for as long as the agreement lasts there is a ceasefire —is lost. In mining the silent struggle over piece-rates never lets up.[73]

The miner's chief weapon in this 'silent struggle' was to threaten to resign and seek work elsewhere. The effectiveness of this threat depended in practice on the state of the trade cycle. During booms pits were keen to attract new labour so that finding a new job was not difficult; but during recessions the problems were greater and a miner who stuck out for a better deal was taking a significant risk. This mechanism helps to explain why both job-changing and wages rose during booms and fell in recessions. We find the process at work at *Shamrock III/IV* in December 1904: a hewer named Schulz was offered a reduced rate for the next month and rejected the offer: 'After this the overman was so constantly on my back that, after I had tried to find work at other mines but failed, I eventually signed the agreement.'[74] This willingness to look elsewhere for better pay naturally encouraged job-changing and meant that the freedom to move from one pit to another—a freedom which the employers were keen to curtail—was of the utmost importance to miners. Jakob Brodam, a miners' leader in Gelsenkirchen, was only one of many who denounced an attempt by employers in 1889 to restrict job-changing by refusing to take on men from other pits: 'This ban is preventing wages from rising, since it is no longer possible for the worker to leave one pit and seek work at another. Thus all competition is prevented.'[75] Fortunately for the miners, the right to move in search of work was guaranteed in the liberal

---

[73] Herbig, 'Schwierigkeiten des Lohnwesens'; STAM, *Frankfurter Zeitung*, 11. 12. 1912.

[74] StAB, 458, *Bergwerksgesellschaft Hibernia* to KLB, 22. 2. 1905. On the cyclical nature of job-changing see chapter 1.

[75] StAB, 461, *Rheinisch-Westfälische Zeitung*, 29. 10. 1889. Other miners' leaders, including Ludwig Schröder and Johannes Mohr, made the same point: cf. StAB, 462, *Rheinisch-Westfälische Zeitung*, 14. 12. 1889; *Amt* Herne to KLB, 16. 12. 1889.

reform laws of the 1860s and was underpinned by the sustained demand for labour: job-changing remained endemic in the Ruhr right up to the war. In 1910 one mine inspector commented on the experience of the previous fifteen years:

The freedom to change jobs was one of the workers' chief weapons in struggles with the mine owners, particularly in wage conflicts. Because of their freedom of movement the miners were not only in a position to take advantage of favourable wages at this or that mine, but could virtually compel higher shift- or piece-rates by entire *Kameradschaften* giving notice.[76]

It was hardly surprising that owners were willing to invest in company housing and other measures designed to reduce such mobility.

One result was that hewers' wages were very sensitive to cyclical fluctuations. During upswings they could exploit the general demand for labour and force pits into competitive wage-bidding but during recessions they had to accept what was offered. Since agreements lasted only a short time, wages responded quickly to changes in economic conditions. This was less true of workers paid by the shift: time-rates were relatively inflexible, since they were less frequently adjusted. The fluctuations in hewers' wages— both up and down—were therefore generally more marked than those of other mineworkers. In 1889, for instance, hewers' earnings in the Bochum area were reported to have risen by between 30 and 40 per cent, compared with 18 per cent for hauliers and 13 per cent for pony-minders. In the recession year of 1901, on the other hand, the average wages of hewers fell by 9 per cent, while those of other underground workers fell by 7 per cent and those of surface workers by only 4 per cent.[77] The relative stagnation of the wages of hauliers and other shift-paid workers during booms produced particular frustrations among them. In 1906 we hear of hauliers and repair workers being put onto piece-rates to enable them to join in the general prosperity;[78] as we shall

[76] Oberschuir, *Heranziehung*, p. 14; Brüggemeier, *Leben vor Ort*, p. 131.

[77] Hewers' wages in the Ruhr rose on average by 15.5 per cent between 1888 and 1889, while hauliers' etc. wages rose by 11.1 per cent and surface-workers' by 8.9 per cent. Koch, *Bergarbeiterbewegung*, pp. 17, 149; StAB, HKB *Jahresberichte*, 1889, 1901.

[78] StAB, 464, *Gewerkschaft Constantin der Grosse* to KLB, 26. 4. 1906.

see in the next chapter, these frustrations—particularly among the younger workers—were an important cause of strike action.

The pressure of market forces could create significant wage differentials between one pit and another. Locally adjacent pits tended to keep reasonably closely in step: as one newspaper reported in 1912 when several mines were considering raising wages, 'if appreciable wage increases are introduced at some mines, others—particularly neighbouring mines—will have to follow to prevent people leaving their employment.'[79] This did not prevent local differences but tended to ensure that they were generally short-lived. A more sustained differential, however, persisted between the wages paid by the older mines in the southern part of the Ruhr district and the newer ones to the north. The northern mines had to attract and retain a virtually brand-new labour force; and being bigger and deeper, with greater fixed capital investment, they could less well afford any loss of output. The result was that wages at the northern mines were generally higher—ranging on average between 970 and 1,348 marks a year between 1890 and 1900 compared with a range of between 923 and 1,296 marks a year at the more southerly mines in the same period.[80]

More objectionable to many miners, however, were wage variations within one mine itself. Hewers earned considerably more than surface- and other workers: at *Constantin II* in January 1890 hewers earned on average 4.66 marks per shift compared with only 2.32 marks for surface-workers; at *Bruchsï asse* the hewers earned 4.51 marks compared to 2.55 marks for surface-workers and the other mines showed similar differentials.[81] But there were also considerable variations between the earnings of hewers themselves, resulting partly from the differences in the physical conditions they faced, partly from the different terms they had been able to

[79] *Kölnische Zeitung*, 3. 2. 1912, quoted in H. Imbusch, *Bergarbeiterstreik im Ruhrgebiet 1912* (Köln, 1912), p. 15. In January 1890 the average wage of hewers at 26 pits around Bochum was 4.53 marks per shift; ten of the pits were paying on average more than five per cent above or below that rate, but only two—*Präsident* and *Hannover*—were paying more than ten per cent beyond the local average; figures from StAB, 461.

[80] WWA, K2 213, *Denkschrift betr. die Stillegung verschiedener Steinkohlen-zechen des Ruhr-Reviers*, p. 9.

[81] StAB, 461.

extract from the management, and partly from differing strength, skill, hours of work, and effort on the part of the men themselves. Table 10 shows the spread of hewers' earnings at one large mine (unnamed) in June of each year between 1900 and 1907 and demonstrates the wide range of hewers' earnings, despite the fact that in each year between 42 and 55 per cent of them were concentrated in one band of 50 pfennigs. The degree of bunching varied from year to year. The table also illustrates the general fall in earnings in 1902 and the astonishing rise in 1907 (the average earnings of hewers in the Ruhr as a whole rose by 12 per cent in 1907, from 1,664 marks in 1906 to 1,871 marks).[82] The spread of wages may have been even greater at other times and places: at *Bruchstrasse* in the final quarter of 1904 around 11 per cent of hewers were earning less than 4 marks per shift and another 11 per cent earned over 6 marks, while the distribution between these points was more even than that shown in Table 10. Similar spreads of earnings were found elsewhere.[83] Otto Hue commented: 'A small minority of the *Kameradschaften* achieve very much higher wages than the average. This forces the "average" up, but the wages of one and the same category of worker fluctuate per shift, often by several marks!'[84] The figures quoted suggest that the high earnings at the top were roughly balanced out by poor earnings at the bottom. Hue's comment does, however, point to the perceived reality behind the figures: that for any actual hewer the figures for 'average' wages had only a limited relevance, since the pay which he might expect to receive could easily be quite different.

These differentials related to men doing the same job. While they may partially have reflected differences in effort and physical strength they did not reflect fundamentally different skill, as factory differentials commonly did; and

[82] Koch, *Bergarbeiterbewegung*, p. 149.
[83] At *Bruchstrasse* 11 per cent earned under 4 marks; 17 per cent 4–4.50 marks; 25 per cent 4.50–5 marks; 23 per cent 5–5.50 marks; 13 per cent 5.50–6 marks; and 11 per cent over 6 marks; StAB, 455, *Königlich Preussische Staatsanzeiger* 8. 2. 1905. Cf. StAB 462, *Bergwerksgesellschaft Hibernia* to KLB, 15. 2. 1890; StAB 445, *Denkschrift über die Untersuchung*; Tenfelde, *Sozialgeschichte*, p. 298; Brüggemeier, *Leben vor Ort*, pp. 122, 167.
[84] Hue, *Bergarbeiter*, ii. 679.

TABLE 10
Hewers' earnings, June 1900–1907[a]

Year	Percentage of hewers earning:						
	>M4.00	M4.00 -4.50	M4.50 -5.00	M5.00 -5.50	M5.50 -6.00	M6.00 -6.50	M6.50+
1900	0.4	1.6	18.0	55.2	20.2	4.6	–
1901	0.4	2.9	19.3	54.6	19.7	3.1	–
1902	1.5	23.5	46.1	26.2	1.3	1.4	–
1903	1.5	12.9	27.1	42.8	13.5	1.6	0.6
1904	–	3.1	14.3	52.2	26.6	3.3	0.5
1905	–	4.0	22.1	52.4	20.4	1.1	–
1906	–	–	6.6	46.1	38.0	9.3	–
1907	–	–	–	–	0.4	50.3	49.3

[a]Münz, *Lage der Bergarbeiter*, p. 64.

they certainly did not reflect differing social status, as between the skilled and unskilled. In 1905, indeed, it was claimed by one union leader (a member of the Christlicher Gewerkverein) that the skilled and experienced native Westphalians were penalized, compared with recent immigrants from the east, since they were given the more difficult seams where the opportunities for high output were limited. Others, including Hue, suggested that 'miners' fate' and the personal whims of the overmen were the decisive factors in determining who earned badly or well.[85] Whatever the reasons, the wide spread of earnings for one and the same job was commonly felt to be unjust. At the 1905 official commission of inquiry at *Bruchstrasse* the miners' delegates complained, 'that some *Kameradschaften* who have worked hard and well earn poor wages, while in contrast others earn good wages. The difference is very marked and unjust, and there absolutely must be an equalization.' The commission agreed: in their conclusions they reported, 'the wage situation can not be regarded as unfavourable, although it must be conceded that it appears desirable that the management introduce some degree of equalization of the piece-rates of *Kameradschaften*.'[86]

[85] STAM, *Oberbergamt* Dortmund 1844, *Mitteilungen der Hauptstelle Deutscher Arbeitgeberverbände*, 25. 1. 1905; IZF, *Westfälische Freie Presse*, 29. 4. 1891; Hue, *Bergarbeiter*, ii. 679.
[86] StAB, 455, *Königlich Preussische Staatsanzeiger*, 8. 2. 1905.

Wage levels

Whatever the problems and conflicts caused by the methods of calculating miners' wages, contemporaries and historians have generally accepted that Ruhr mineworkers did at least relatively well in their actual levels of pay. Relatively high wages were necessary, of course, to attract new workers to the district—although it should be remembered that the industry aimed to attract men primarily from agriculture, other mining districts, and comparable low-skill work rather than from the highly-paid skilled industrial trades. Although challenged first by the Saar and later by the Aachen coal-fields, the Ruhr mines generally and on average paid higher wages than the other German coal-fields. Dr Jüngst of the employers' federation, the Verein für die bergbaulichen Interessen, claimed that the highest wages on the continent were paid in the Ruhr.[87] It was frequently argued that the question of wages did not justify industrial conflict and strikes: thus the Bochum Chamber of Commerce described the wage demands raised during the 1889 strike as 'quite unjustified' on the ground that even before the stoppage pay levels had been rising fast; and in 1890 the management of the *Hannibal* pit claimed 'that in no other industrial district do the colliers earn so much with shorter hours as they do in the Westphalian district'.[88] Historians have reinforced this picture: Crew has pointed out that miners' wages compared favourably not only with those of unskilled labourers but even with many skilled metal-workers, and concluded that the source of industrial conflict in the mining industry cannot be located in low earnings; discussing the causes of the 1905 miners' strike, Koch has commented that 'even less than in 1889 can one speak of an "economic state of distress" '.[89]

Nevertheless, we shall see in the next chapter that the level of wages was a perennial source of discontent and that substantial increases were frequently put forward as central

[87] Metzner, *Soziale Fürsorge*, pp. 11, 56.
[88] WWA, HKB *Jahresbericht*, 1888; StAB, 462, leaflet headed 'Zeche Hannibal', 15. 3. 1890.
[89] Crew, *Town in the Ruhr*, pp. 174–9; Koch, *Bergarbeiterbewegung*, p. 106.

strike demands. This suggests that there was a gap in the perception of the adequacy of miners' wages between employers
and other commentators on the one hand and many miners
on the other.

The level of miners' wages rose appreciably in cash terms
after the dark days of the depression of the 1870s and 1880s.
In 1879 the average level of hewers' earnings fell to 2.55
marks per shift; by 1882 it had reached three marks, by
1890 four marks, by 1900 five marks, and by 1907 six
marks.[90] It was this long-term rise in money wages which
enabled the Bochum county judge, Neukamp, to comment in
1889 'that one could never speak here of starvation wages;
that the miners have rather always earned wages which are
not just adequate but rise proportionately with the improvement of the industrial situation'.[91]

The judge was right to point to the close connection
between miners' wages and the state of the industry. We have
already noted the unusually high proportion of total mining
costs represented by wages. In these circumstances the
employers were only likely to contemplate increases when
the industry was prospering; when recession struck it was the
wage-bill which offered the most promising area for savings.
The labour-intensive nature of the industry thus made
miners' wages vulnerable to the vagaries of the coal market.
This worked to the long-term advantage of the Ruhr miners
in this period since the market for coal expanded rapidly;
but the long-term rise in output and wages was marked by
cyclical recessions, during which output, hours of work, and
wages were all cut back. Thus the six-marks-per-shift average
for hewers which had been reached during 1907 was not seen
again until 1912. This cyclical vulnerability was one source
of the gap between the perceptions of miners and others of
the true state of their wages: while an outsider might point to
the long-term improvement, the miner was more immediately
interested in the specific recent fluctuations which he had
seen in his pay packet. Since the figures for average wages
also concealed very considerable disparities, many individual
miners did not feel that they were benefiting particularly

[90] Koch, *Bergarbeiterbewegung*, pp. 17, 148-9.
[91] StAB, 441, *Zeitschrift für Bergrecht* (1889, Heft 4), pp. 513-14.

from the general prosperity about which they read in the newspapers.

A further problem was that the figures generally used for such calculations represented gross wages, not take-home pay. The miner had to pay for the tools, explosive, and lamp-oil that he used: in early 1898, when the average level of hewers' wages stood at 4.44 marks a shift, these deducations were thought to average some 18 pfennigs a shift; his contribution towards the *Knappschaft* averaged a further 16 pfennigs. In addition to these standard stoppages, he would find, if he lived in a company house, that his rent was taken from his wages; and if he had been granted credit at the company store any debts would be deducted too. Finally and perhaps most important were the fines which could be imposed for late arrival, missing a shift without adequate reason, poor work, or other misbehaviour such as drunkenness at work. These fines could be fairly substantial: at *Bruchstrasse* in 1905 a man could be fined half an average day's earnings.[92] Such deductions were, of course, to some extent subject to the decisions of the miner concerned; some, particularly cheap company housing, may actually have saved him otherwise necessary expenditure. Nevertheless, they did have the effect of reducing wage packets at the end of the month and emphasizing the gap in perception between the 'average' wages which were usually quoted and those which an individual actually received. Many miners distrusted official statistics—not least because they were based on the employers' returns. Ludwig Schröder, one of the miners' first leaders, declared in 1889: 'For me, and for the miners generally, the only proof lies in the wage books.'[93]

The role of overtime or short-time working was a further source of ambiguity and dispute over the interpretation of the movement of miners' wages. Annual earnings fluctuated more markedly—both up and down—than wages per shift, reflecting the importance of the number of shifts worked in settling miners' actual earnings. Thus between 1905 and 1907

---

[92] StAB, 463, RPA to KLB, 5. 3. 1898; StAB, 456, *Arbeitsordnung der Zeche Bruchstrasse*; Pieper, *Lage der Bergarbeiter*, p. 90; Fischer-Eckert, *Lage der Frauen*, p. 107.

[93] Pieper, *Lage der Bergarbeiter*, p. 76.

average wages per shift of all Ruhr mineworkers rose by 21 per cent while average annual earnings rose by 32 per cent; over the following two years the decline was by 8 and 14 per cent respectively.[94] However, there were frequent claims that these official figures understated the extent to which higher earnings during upswings reflected longer hours rather than higher rates, since many overtime shifts were never reported to the authorities. In 1899 the Bochum social democrat press complained that bourgeois papers were presenting a distorted account of miners' pay by assuming that around 25 shifts were being worked per month when the true figure was between 30 and 40; according to the social democrats, higher earnings resulted merely from these longer hours.[95] In its report for the same year the main miners' union commented:

It only needs ten overtime shifts, each at three marks, to be included with the normal shifts, and with 300 normal shifts in the year the wage rate will appear to have risen by ten pfennigs per shift—when in fact it has not risen by one pfennig! The more overtime shifts which are not separately calculated, the higher the 'normal wage' rises, but without the employer having to pay one jot more on his wages bill.[96]

It is impossible in the absence of systematic but non-official data to evaluate just how serious this problem was; nevertheless, it is clear that at least some of the increases in miners' earnings resulted—at least in the short term—from longer hours of work rather than an actual improvement in the rate for the job.

A final qualification to the rosy picture of miners' pay was presented by corresponding increases in prices, the effect of which was to reduce if not eliminate improvements. Information on real wages is patchy. Dr Lorenz Pieper tried to persuade a number of miners to record their expenditure in detail for a year; he failed, however, because the people were mistrustful and those who agreed to start did not keep their records going. Louise Fischer-Eckert had greater success with

[94] Koch, *Bergarbeiterbewegung*, pp. 149–50.
[95] IZF, *Volksblatt*, 5. 1. 1899. See also IZF, *Westfälische Arbeiter Zeitung*, 19. 1. 1889; Pieper, *Lage der Bergarbeiter*, p. 76.
[96] IGBE, A1 12, Bergarbeiter-Verband, *Jahresbericht*, 1899.

her studies of families in Hamborn and drew on the other available literature relating to Germany. Others made observations on the question from time to time. But there was no established index of the cost of living, particularly as it related to miners.[97]

Nevertheless, there are indications that when the cost of living is taken into account miners' wages were not particularly generous: indeed, for many they appear to have been distinctly inadequate. In 1878, during the depths of the depression, Louis Baare of the Bochumer Verein estimated that a worker's family needed some 800 marks a year as an absolute minimum. The average wage for hewers that year was 2.66 marks per shift, so that 301 shifts would have been needed to earn 800 marks: it is probable that few hewers worked so many shifts at that time; and the wages for other categories of mineworker were appreciably lower than those of hewers. In 1889 the mayor of Gelsenkirchen estimated that a worker's family with three children needed at least 1,067 marks: the average miner's income that year was 941 marks and even hewers averaged only 1,028 marks. It was variously calculated that a working-class family of four needed to spend about half its income on food, and one estimate based on this assumption and the cost of food in Germany as a whole concluded that such a family needed to earn annually at least 1,200 marks in the years 1881-9, 1,300 marks in 1890-1903, and 1,500 marks in 1904-9. The average earnings of hewers in the Ruhr reached these levels in only ten of the twenty-one years between 1889 and 1909, while the earnings of other categories of mineworker never reached them. Finally, in 1911 and 1912 the *Arbeitsmarkt-Correspondenz* published estimates of the cost of simply feeding a family of four in Germany, based on the rations of the marines and price data from 190 towns: between April 1911 and April 1912 it varied between 23.72 marks and 25.74 marks a week. The average miner's earnings in 1911 were 1,446 marks, and Fischer-Eckert estimated that rent for a four-room colony house (cheaper than

[97] Pieper, *Lage der Bergarbeiter*, p. 228; Fischer-Eckert, *Lage der Fauen*, chapter VI; Imbusch, *Arbeitsverhältnis*, p. 106; Münz, *Lage der Bergarbeiter*, p. 90.

a privately rented one) would take 192 marks, while rates, tax, and other unavoidable charges would require a further 66.60 marks. This left a disposable income of only 22.83 marks a week—below the level thought to be necessary merely to feed four people, let alone to clothe, clean, and generally supply them with all the necessities of life.[98]

Such estimates are useful in providing a broad indication of the general adequacy or otherwise of workers' earnings. They do not, however, do justice to the many and varied situations of the thousands of individual mineworkers and their families. As we have seen, the average figures concealed wide variations between individuals and fluctuations between the earnings of the same individual from one month to another. Just as important in determining standards of living, however, were differences in family circumstances. In her study of nearly five hundred workers' families in Hamborn, Fischer-Eckert found that the more children a family had the greater was the likelihood of serious poverty: not only were the actual costs higher but the mother found it increasingly difficult simply to cope with the crucial household tasks, including budgeting. The link between children and poverty and the strain which the fear of unwanted pregnancy could cause was expressed graphically by a 29-year-old Silesian miner: asked about his hopes and wishes, he replied:

My wish, and my wife's wish, is to have no more children. . . . [Herr Bebel] calls on women to emancipate themselves. But if only he knew how things are with most working-class women. Their entire thoughts and feelings are focused on the prevention of conception. One notes it everywhere in conversation. A missed menstruation date means at once there is great fear, since every working-class woman knows what another child means, more worry and want, because the pay does not increase. So for working-class women there is continuous fear, from one period to the next, since the contraceptives frequently don't work too.[99]

---

[98] Koch, *Bergarbeiterbewegung*, pp. 17–18, 148–50; Hue, *Bergarbeiter* ii. 241; Fischer-Eckert, *Lage der Frauen*, p. 106–10. See also D. Crew, *Industry and Community: the social history of a German town 1860–1914* (Ph.D. thesis, Cornell University, 1975), pp. 31–42; Tenfelde, *Sozialgeschichte*, pp. 307–21; Wolcke, *Entwicklung*, pp. 142–9; Schneider, *Die Christlichen Gewerkschaften*, p. 69; STAM, *Oberbergamt* Dortmund 1857, K. *Bergwerksdirektion* Recklinghausen to *Minister für Handel und Gewerbe*, 19. 2. 1912.

[99] Levenstein, *Arbeiterfrage*, p. 216.

The correlation between family size and financial strain was by no means peculiar to mineworkers: they shared the common feature of working-class life that earnings peaked in relatively young adulthood, well before family responsibilities and commitments were at their height. Where miners were particularly vulnerable was in their constant exposure to sudden and dramatic falls in earning power through injury and in their relatively short working life which meant that by their early forties, when families might still be young and growing, even the more skilled and lucky men were in physical and financial decline.[100]

Some families were able to supplement the father's income from other sources. Here too the stage of the family life cycle was important: while young children simply added to the family's costs, sons over school-leaving age could provide a second wage (provided, that is, they did not leave home). Many families, as we have seen, supplemented their income by lodgers. Some kept a pig, a goat, or some hens, and many grew their own vegetables. During a strike in spring 1891 one observer noted how the married miners busied themselves in their gardens, planting potatoes and beans.[101] In addition the companies commonly supplied potatoes and sometimes other food at low prices, sometimes from their own farms; and all miners were by custom entitled to cheap coal.[102] These practices helped to supplement miners' wages. On the other hand, as we saw in the first chapter, the opportunities for women to find paid jobs—in other settings one of the most important fall-backs for working-class families—were very limited in the Ruhr.

Other factors could have a dramatic impact on an individual family's standard of living. Illness or injury to either parent could be very serious. Conversely, savings could provide a fall-back. Some miners managed to accumulate considerable savings, but they were very much the exceptions.[103] The

---

[100] Fischer-Eckert, *Lage der Frauen*, pp. 82–95; Lucas, *Arbeiterradikalismus*, pp. 57–70. For this issue as it affected other German workers, see H. Schomerus, 'The Family Life-Cycle: a Study of Factory Workers in Nineteenth-century Württemberg', in Evans and Lee (ed.), *The German Family*, pp. 175–93.

[101] StAB, 447 *Kölnische Zeitung*, 23(?). 4. 1891.

[102] Münz, *Lage der Bergarbeiter*, pp. 94–5.

[103] The average size of miners' accounts in the Bochum town *Sparkasse* in

personal intelligence and skills of the parents—particularly
the wife—were extremely important when it came to running the household economically and managing on a tight
budget. These tasks were made no easier by the unpredictab-
ility of miners' earnings and the particular method of payment used in the Ruhr—an advance in the middle of the
month and the remainder paid at the end. Some miners tried
to keep a check on their wages by chalking up on a door at
home the number of hours and shifts they had worked
and how many trucks of coal they had produced; others
relied on their team leader to keep a tally.[104] The difficulties
which miners and their wives experienced with budgeting
were frequently noted, particularly by middle-class observers.
Dr Pieper commented:

It is a notorious fact that the Ruhr miner's household shows a striking
lack of economy, practical supervision, and a thrifty division of tasks.
One who has not seen it for himself would not believe the uneconomic,
ill-considered, and often virtually absurd manner in which goods and
food for a half or an entire month are purchased or borrowed and then
some—for instance meat, margarine, butter, etc.—allowed to spoil or
wasted too quickly. Failing to consider the period to the next pay-day,
they simply go ahead and buy freely. With weekly pay-days the miner
and his wife would become accustomed to better supervision of the
household necessities and manage the smaller sums more rationally.
Similarly, they would not borrow so readily and thus avoid dependence
on traders and shopkeepers.[105]

Running a miner's houshold on a tight budget was a demanding task, requiring a range of practical skills and experience
which some women simply did not possess. Many had little
or no previous experience of household management, or
perhaps even of living in a society where cash wages were
the prime means of support. The presence or lack of such
skills could mean the difference between modest comfort or
debt and poverty for the family concerned. The room for
manoeuvre was limited, and too many babies and too low

1895 was 1,190 marks—more than a year's average earnings. But only a small
minority of miners seem to have had an account at all, and the number 'decreased
rapidly between 1867 and 1895'. Crew, *Industry and Community*, p. 252; *Town
in the Ruhr*, pp. 95-6, 243.

    [104] Hoffeld, *Bilder aus dem Bergmannsleben*, p. 41; Levenstein, *Aus der Tiefe*,
p. 38.
    [105] Pieper, *Lage der Bergarbeiter*, p. 70.

wages could frustrate all but the most efficient household manager.[106]

Despite all the individual and family variations, however, it is possible to speak of a long-term improvement in the general level of miners' wages in the decades before 1914, even when price movements are taken into account. In part this was due to the low starting-point. In 1880 the Bochum town authorities reported that wages were 'at a level which enabled the worker merely to meet his immediate expenses. Illness or death in the family or temporary unemployment drove him—since there were no savings—to poor relief . . .'[107] From about 1880, however, money wages started to recover, and moved forward faster than food prices. From a low of 2.79 marks in 1879, hewers' wages rose to over 4.00 marks a shift in 1891—an increase of well over a third. Over the same period, despite the fact that 1891 was a year of particularly high food prices, only rye from amongst the basic foodstuffs rose by more: the price of rye at the Bochum market rose by over 50 per cent; bacon rose by 14 per cent, wheat by 8 per cent, and potatoes, beef, pork, and butter all rose by 5 per cent or less.[108] Between 1891 and 1893 wages fell, while food prices varied, mostly falling to some extent but some—pork, bacon, and butter—rising. After this set-back, the later 1890s saw a real improvement in average wages, relative to food prices.

The depression at the turn of the century brought a fall in the value of wages against food prices: between 1900 and 1903 annual earnings fell by almost 10 per cent, while wheat, potatoes, and beef rose in price, pork and butter remained steady, and rye fell slightly. Real wages rose again with the economic upswing, so that between 1903 and 1907 earnings rose by about a third while prices rose more moderately:

[106] Fischer-Eckert, *Lage der Frauen*, chapter V. See also Williamson, *Class, Culture and Community*, chapter 7.

[107] StAB, *Magistratsbericht* 1879/80, p. 23.

[108] Food prices from: Verein für die bergbaulichen Interessen, *Die Entwicklung des . . . Steinkohlenbergbaues* xii. 88-9; WWA, HKB *Jahresberichte*; Münz, *Lage der Bergarbeiter*, p. 91; Silbergleit, *Preussens Städte*, pp. 310-20. See also Tenfelde, *Sozialgeschichte*, pp. 307-21; Crew, *Industry and Community*, pp. 295-308; Wolcke, *Entwicklung*, pp. 147-9; STAM, *Oberbergamt* Dortmund 1857, K. *Bergwerksdirektion* Recklinghausen to *Minister für Handel und Gewerbe*, 19. 2. 1912; Brüggemeier, *Leben vor Ort*, p. 284.

grain (wheat and rye) by about 25 per cent, potatoes by nearly 20 per cent, meats by around 16 per cent, butter by 9 per cent, and bacon by 5 per cent.

This seems, however, to have been the end of the rise: average earnings declined by about 7 per cent between 1907 and 1911, while food prices continued to rise.[109] In their report for 1910 the Bochum Chamber of Commerce reported: 'The higher earnings of workers have certainly been partially cancelled out by the price rises for some necessities, particularly meat, so that the consumption power of the industrial worker can scarcely have increased'[110] In the winter of 1911-12 the town authorities established a special commission on prices, and the idea of taking over the distribution of vegetables was mooted. Eventually traders were persuaded to sell vegetables in bulk in a special cheap market and by the autumn of 1912 the price of many vegetables had fallen dramatically. The town authorities organized the purchase of cheap beef from Holland, only ending the service when prices appeared more reasonable in 1913.[111] What is clear from these unusual measures is that despite the improvements in real wages over the years the advance was neither massive nor irreversible. Writing shortly before the outbreak of war, Fischer-Eckert concluded that in over half of the Hamborn workers' families she had investigated 'the total family income did not cover the necessary expenditure.'[112] Uncertainty, tight margins, and in some circumstances real need continued to characterize the financial plight of many mining families right up to the war.

Social relations

Hard physical toil, serious danger, long hours, and fluctuating wages—these were central features of pit work and part of the normal experience of the rapidly growing army of miners in the Ruhr. Yet they do not tell the whole story.

[109] WWA, K2 816; StAB, *Märkischer Sprecher*, 8. 1. 1912.

[110] StAB, HKB *Jahresbericht*, 1910.

[111] StAB, HKB *Jahresbericht*, 1911/12; WWA, K2 816; StAB, *Märkischer Sprecher*, 8. 1. 1912; StAB, *Magistratsbericht*, 1912, p. 117; Brinkmann, *Bochum*, p. 223.

[112] Fischer-Eckert, *Lage der Frauen*, p. 127.

Mine-work was not an individual activity and its impact was not simply the sum of individual experiences. Rather, it was a social occupation with mutual support on one side and sharp conflict on the other at its very centre, day by day. It was this social dimension, even more than the hardships and dangers of the pit, which differentiated pit work from other hard manual jobs, gave miners a bond which distinguished them in their own eyes and in those of others from other occupational groups, and provided a special potential basis for solidarity.

For miners the social dimension of their work had four main reference points: their relationship, or non-relationship, with the men who owned or managed the mines and whose decisions ultimately determined their own conditions; their much more tangible relations with the mine officials who made the day-to-day decisions and whose impact on their lives was more obvious and immediate; their relations with other miners; and their sense of relative status *vis-à-vis* other manual occupations.

In the mid-nineteenth century the pits were generally small, with an average work-force of only 64 in 1850. In this situation it was easy for workers and employer to know each other personally. The tradition of the identifiable individual as head of the firm persisted: some companies, like Krupp, continued as family concerns; the majority, including the Harpener Bergbau AG and the Gelsenkirchener Bergwerks AG, were owned by shareholders but were often managed by very prominent individuals—in these cases Robert Muser and Emil Kirdorf—in a manner comparable to the private owners. As we have seen, many firms tried to build up a sense of company loyalty through the provision of housing and other social benefits for their employees.

Nevertheless, such policies could not obscure the fact that as the size of the mines increased it became less and less possible for any personal contact to take place between the individual miner and his employer. By 1890 the mines employed on average over seven hundred men, and the best that a pit manager could do was to visit each face once a month. Even this became impossible as the mines grew: by 1900 the average pit had 1,360 men and by 1913 2,360.

The increase affected long-established pits as well as the new, deep mines in the northern Ruhr. As the number of workers increased, there was a parallel concentration of ownership in fewer and fewer hands: in 1912 90 per cent of the Ruhr mines were reported to be owned by eleven companies; of 22 mines around Bochum no fewer than eight belonged to the Harpener Bergbau AG alone.[113]

The growing distance between mine-owners and managers and their employees did not reduce their interest in paternalist measures: indeed, as we have seen, there was growth in the provision of housing and other benefits in the pre-war years. The companies seem to have been trying to use such provisions in part to preserve a sense of company loyalty and to maintain paternalist control in a situation where these could no longer be sustained on a truly personal basis. It is difficult to guage their psychological impact and despite occasional company rhetoric it is hard to believe that many workers felt a particular glow of loyalty and personal appreciation when they thought of the directors and senior managers of their firms. During industrial disputes, however, the miners' hostility seems normally to have been directed against the junior mine officials, not the owners and directors.[114] This perhaps suggests that the gap between the miners and the coal-owners had grown so wide that the latter seemed beyond the ken of ordinary mineworkers.

If owners and senior managers seemed remote to many miners, this was certainly not true of the lower-level mine officials. The most important was the overman who exercised very considerable authority over the men (usually around fifty but sometimes more) under his direction. He was responsible for securing the required output of coal from his sector, for the formation of teams of miners (including the appointment of the team leader, the *Ortsältester*), for

[113] See chapter 1 above; StAB, 445, *Denkschrift über die Untersuchung*, p. 11; STAM, *Frankfurter Zeitung*, 11. 2. 1912; StAB, 465. Five mines to the south of Bochum which in 1864 employed on average 324 workers, in 1912 employed on average 1,850; Croon, 'Studien', p. 111.

[114] STAM, *Oberpräsidium* 2828 Bd. 4, K. *Landrat* Gelsenkirchen to *Oberpräsident* Münster, 18. 5. 1889; STAM, *Oberpräsidium* 2828a, *Dortmunder Zeitung*, 27. 7. 1889; STAM, *Oberbergamt* Dortmund 1844, *Mitteilungen der Hauptstelle Deutscher Arbeitgeberverbände*, 25. 1. 1905.

the allocation of work to teams, and for negotiating rates of pay (subject to ratification by senior management). He was responsible for the day-to-day supervision of work, for the regulation of overtime, and for the maintenance of discipline and safety-precautions. He was thus a powerful figure, the most important management representative in the ordinary miner's life. His importance was expressed in the miners' adage: *Der Kohlberg und der Steiger machen den Bergmann!*[115] His powers were greater, for instance, than those of his equivalents in Durham where under the cavilling system the miners generally formed their own teams, elected their own team leaders, and allocated work by lots. One who fell foul of overmen was the young August Schmidt— later to be a union leader—who stayed away from his work at the *Germania* pit near Dortmund on May Day 1906: he was promptly transferred to the night shift and to a coal-face where the scope for high earnings was limited, so that his pay fell from 6.50 to 4.75 marks; Schmidt left the pit.[116]

Overmen owed their position and their loyalty to management. A state official noted in 1907: 'The overmen have hitherto been the people on whom the mine-owners could depend unconditionally, particularly during strikes.'[117] Their reliability was due in part to the status which their position commanded and in part to their own dependence on senior management. Failure to meet management's demands, particularly output of coal, could mean a fall in their own income through lost premium payments (which represented a substantial proportion of their earnings) and ultimately through the loss of the job. There were modifications to the overman's position in the years before 1914: the growth in the size of the mines and the need for more sophisticated technical and financial control added to the number and layers of supervisory personnel and limited the scope for individual discretion by overmen—notably in fixing special financial deals with their men. A few overmen

[115] Pieper, *Lage der Bergarbeiter*, p. 67; Levenstein, *Arbeiterfrage*, p. 17; E. G. Spencer, 'Between Capital and Labor: Supervisory Personnel in Ruhr Heavy Industry', in *Journal of Social History* (1975); Brüggemeier, *Leben vor Ort*, p. 11.

[116] Douglass, 'The Durham Pitman', pp. 229–39; Schmidt, *Lang war der Weg*, p. 49.

[117] StAB, 481, RPA to *Minister des Innern*, 28. 11. 1907.

felt sufficiently distanced from senior management to form
their own union, despite the threat of instant dismissal if
their disloyalty were discovered. However, these changes
made little fundamental difference to ordinary mineworkers:
for them the overman remained the prime representative of
management and figure of authority at work.[118]

Relations between miners and overmen were often bad.
It was alleged that they enjoyed cutting wages and disliked
raising them. Miners were said to 'hate' overmen, and it was
claimed that some pits preferred former NCOs for certain
posts and that a parade-ground atmosphere prevailed. Indeed,
Heinrich Imbush maintained that conditions were even
worse: 'Apart from the fact that they took absolutely no
notice of the miners' feelings, some officials adopted a tone
which is not even used on the parade-ground. The miners
were often ridiculed, mocked, and insulted as they went
about their work, and even now and then [physically] mal-
treated.'[119] One Ruhr miner complained that the animals were
treated better in the pit than the workers.[120] More humane
treatment was a common demand during industrial disputes.

One practice which caused particular resentment was the
system by which trucks which contained too much rock or
were insufficiently full were completely discounted from
the *Kameradschaft*'s tally of output when it came to calculating their wages, despite the coal which they did in fact contain. This system—known as *Nullen*—was defended as
necessary to ensure that the miners sent up only coal to the
surface and did not ballast the trucks with rubble. The value
of the coal which the trucks did contain was commonly put
towards a social benefit fund, rather than taken as profit by

[118] STAM, *Frankfurter Zeitung*, 11. 2. 1912; Spencer, 'Between Capital and
Labor'; Schmidt, *Lang war der Weg*, pp. 68–70.

[119] H. Imbusch, *Arbeitsverhältnis und Arbeiterorganisation im deutschen
Bergbau* (Essen, 1908), pp. 126–7; *Rheinisch-Westfälische Zeitung*, 28. 6. 1889,
quoted in W. Köllmann and A. Gladen, *Der Bergarbeiterstreik von 1889 und
die Gründung des 'Alten Verbandes' in ausgewählten Dokumenten der Zeit*
(Bochum, 1969), pp. 196–7; Lucas, *Arbeiterradikalismus*, p. 271; Tenfelde,
Sozialgeschichte, pp. 253, 276 ff.; STAM, *Oberpräsidium* 2828a, *Dortmunder
Zeitung*, 27. 7. 1889, *Westfälische Volkszeitung*, 18. 6. 1889; STAM, RA I 82, *Dortmunder Zeitung*, 2. 2. 1903; STAM, *Oberbergamt* Dortmund 1849, K. *Bergwerksdirektion* Recklinghausen to *Minister für Handel und Gewerbe*, 27. 11. 1908.

[120] Levenstein, *Arbeiterfrage*, pp. 221–2.

the mine, and it is questionable whether the miners lost more overall under this system than under the suggested alternative of a system of fines. Nevertheless, the *Nullen* system caused bitter resentment between miners and officials and there were frequent demands for its abolition. One reason was the unfairness of a system which seemed to penalize teams working in poor seams where the coal and rock were harder to separate. More serious, however, was the arbitrary power which it gave to the mine officials: some stone was bound to get into many coal trucks, particularly if the men were under pressure to raise their output, and it was inevitable that trucks should lose some of their load in the long journey from the coal-face to the surface; the decision of the mine official to discount some trucks but not others often appeared, therefore, to be essentially arbitrary. It was a power which the management could use as harshly or as leniently as it chose—but in either case with immediate effects on the miners' pay packets. In 1904 the Essen police commissar described *Nullen* as 'very fashionable' and it was alleged that at a number of pits up to a quarter of some teams' output was being discounted.[121] In 1892 the miners were given the legal right to appoint a checkweighman who could watch over the actions of the official responsible for discounting trucks; but, unlike the parallel arrangements in England, the checkweighman had to be paid by the miners, and none seem to have been appointed. Following the miners' strike of 1905 *Nullen* was finally replaced by a system of fines, with the proviso that no worker should lose more than five marks a month; the truck was counted to the team's credit. Although such fines could bite just as hard into take-home pay and could be equally arbitrary in their incidence, the reform abolished a practice which had caused very considerable conflict and had become 'a symbol of arbitrariness and injustice'.[122]

[121] Koch, *Bergarbeiterbewegung*, p. 86; Hue, *Bergarbeiter* ii. 583-4; Kirchoff, *Sozialpolitik*, pp. 156-7; StAB, 455, *Denkschrift über die Untersuchung*, pp. 26-7; StAB, 456, report of a miners' meeting in Bochum 20. 1. 1905; STAM, RA I 95, *Polizei-Commissar* Gelsenkirchen to RPA, 31. 8. 1901.
[122] Kirchoff, *Sozialpolitik*, p. 157; Pieper, *Lage der Bergarbeiter*, pp. 97-8; Münz, *Lage der Bergarbeiter*, p. 79; IISG, *Volksblatt*, 16. 4. 1908. See also the poem, 'Etwas vom Nullen', by Heinrich Kämpchen, a militant miner and poet

The abolition of *Nullen* did not end friction between miners and overmen. Pressure to work overtime and the very nature of the pay bargaining system both led to constant negotiation and conflict. In addition to these major issues there were a multitude of more trivial questions which could lead to friction, mistrust, and a sense of grievance. In 1904 the Essen police commissar considered that relations between lower mine officials and men were good at very few pits and thought that poor relations were one of the most serious problems facing the industry.[123] Conflict was thus deep-rooted and endemic.

The obverse of the divide between ordinary miners and officials was a strengthened sense of common identity between miners themselves. As we have seen, most miners followed the same career pattern and held important parts of their experience and expectations of work in common. There were not the profound barriers—between skilled and unskilled, and between the various skilled trades themselves—which were found in the metal industry. There was therefore a good basis for a sense of what has been termed 'occupational community'.[124]

This was fostered by the conditions and organization of work underground. As the mines grew larger it became increasingly difficult for men to know the rest of their colleagues; but the mine's sub-organizations, the district (*Revier*) and above all the *Kameradschaft* provided each miner with a corps of colleagues who shared many of his interests and whom he could know personally. Apart from the work-face itself, most discussion and 'social' contact between miners seems to have occurred at the start and end of shifts, in the washhouse, or while waiting for the cage. Through such contacts news and views travelled rapidly round the mine. Members of the outgoing shift would bring those arriving for the next up to date as they met at the face, the shaft, or at the surface. At the heart of the mine as a social organization,

from Bochum, in W. Köpping (ed.), *Schwarze Solidarität* (Oberhausen, 1974), p. 12.

[123] Koch, *Bergarbeiterbewegung*, p. 86.
[124] Crew, *Town in the Ruhr*, pp. 186–94; Bulmer, 'Sociological Models of the Mining Community'.

however, lay the *Kameradschaft*. Its size varied from two men upwards, depending on the size and character of the face being worked. The members were entirely dependent on each other, both for physical safety, since a mistake by any one could cause a serious accident for all, and for their pay since this was based on the output of the entire team. Such mutual interdependence could only function smoothly when the members could trust one another. Surprisingly little is known about the social composition of Ruhr *Kameradschaften*, but it was not unknown for them to contain men of varying backgrounds and differing trade union loyalties. Nevertheless, it is likely that whenever possible fellow-countrymen, friends, and relatives worked together.[125] As has been noted with reference to Yorkshire miners: 'The team of colliers, with this system of mutual dependence, is the hub of the social structure of mining.'[126]

The sense of common identity within the *Kameradschaft* was fostered by the control which the members were able to exercise over at least some aspects of their work. With the overman only able to make intermittent inspections, responsibility for the pace of work, the precise methods of going about it, and the quantity of coal produced rested primarily with the members of the *Kameradschaft* and in particular the *Ortsältester*. They had to make a fine judgement, to ensure that they produced enough to give each member a reasonable wage without, on the other hand, producing so much that at the next re-negotiation the rate would be cut. The scope for choice was limited since the overman would aim to set a rate which obliged them to work intensively to achieve a good wage. Nevertheless, within limits each *Kameradschaft* did have real choices. The system thus fostered not only a sense of mutual responsibility and loyalty but also an ability to reach collectively acceptable decisions independently of views and pressures from outside.

Nevertheless, the *Kameradschaft*'s ability to promote close social relations and solidarity amongst miners generally should

---

[125] STAM, *Oberbergamt* Dortmund 1849, K. *Bergwerksdirektion* Recklinghausen to *Minister für Handel und Gewerbe*, 27. 11. 1908; Tenfelde, *Sozialgeschichte*, pp. 222–4; Klessmann, *Polnische Bergarbeiter im Ruhrgebiet*, p. 52; Brüggemeier, *Leben vor Ort*, p. 126.

[126] Dennis *et al.*, *Coal is our Life*, p. 45.

not be exaggerated. The team leader, the *Ortsältester*, was appointed by management and not elected by his comrades. Within the team tensions and conflicts could and did exist: Max Lotz, who was perhaps not typical, felt that his responsibilities as *Ortsältester* gave him a different outlook from his colleagues; and it is clear from some of his comments about them that, despite their close working relationship, he knew surprisingly little about their personal views. Friction could exist between older miners, anxious to do the job properly, and younger men impatient to boost their output and earnings as much as possible through their physical strength.[127] Moreover, except in a real emergency there was relatively little need or incentive for the mutual loyalties within a *Kameradschaft* to extend far to nonmembers. Sometimes overmen deliberately fostered rivalry and competition between teams, with rewards for higher output or by allocating attractive coal-faces to the team asking the lowest rate of pay.[128] In the last years before the war the *Kameradschaft* itself began to change as the first steps towards longwall methods of coal-getting were introduced. The effect was to increase the number of men working at one face and the level of direct supervison; and to reduce both their interdependence (each individual worked more separately and collective payment through *Gedinge* might be replaced by individually measured payments) and their collective autonomy at work. These structural changes do not seem to have been widespread before 1914. Nevertheless, they showed that there were countervailing factors which limited the extent to which mine-work automatically encouraged mutual loyalty and solidarity; and that social as well as technical structures in the mines were neither static nor to be taken for granted.[129]

Mine-work thus fostered sharp awareness of the social

[127] Levenstein, *Aus der Tiefe*, pp. 34–5, 37–8; StAB, 462, *Westfälische Volkszeitung*, 7. 5. 1890.

[128] Hue, *Bergarbeiter* ii. 162; D. F. Crew, 'Berufliche Lage und Protestverhalten Bochumer Bergleute und Metallarbeiter im ausgehenden 19. Jahrhundert', in Mommsen and Borsdorf (ed.), *Glück auf, Kameraden!*, p. 84.

[129] Tenfelde, 'Der bergmännische Arbeitsplatz', pp. 317–18; C. Jantke *et al.*, *Bergmann und Zeche: die sozialen Arbeitsverhältnisse einer Schachtanlage des nördlichen Ruhrgebiets in der Sicht der Bergleute* (Tübingen, 1953); Brüggemeier, *Leben vor Ort*, pp. 110–11.

distance and the inevitable conflict between ordinary mineworkers on one side and management—particularly the
overmen—on the other; and a sense of the common fate
and common interests binding miners themselves together,
focused primarily but not necessarily exclusively on the
Kameradschaft. But the social dimension of mine-work was
related not just to the internal dynamics of the mine. A further important element was the sense of mine-work as a distinct social occupation, different in nature and status from
other manual jobs.

The feeling that mine-work is a special occupation and that
miners are in some sense a 'race apart' has been widespread
in different societies and cultures. The very fact of working
deep below ground, the danger of death by burial, the
uniformly blackened faces, and the geographically distinct
mining communities are amongst the factors which have
helped to create this popular image. But a sense of separate-
ness implies a yardstick for comparison. In the case of the
Ruhr this was provided particularly by the metal and
engineering industry. Although Ruhr miners lived largely in
physically distinct villages or streets, few were far from some
plant or works of the booming metal industry and many
knew men who worked in it.[130] A point of comparison thus
lay at their doorstep.

There is little doubt that many miners felt that their
occupation suffered a relative decline during the second
half of the nineteenth century. The problem was not primarily financial: highly skilled metal workers had long
earned more than most miners and although miners' pay may
have fallen further behind during the depression years of
the 1870s and 1880s they seem to have increased somewhat
faster thereafter.[131] Rather, it was a perceived change in the
status of mine-work. Until the liberalization of the 1850s and
1860s mining had been a privileged and honoured calling,
distinguished from other manual occupations by a range of
special privileges such as membership of the *Knappschaft*

---

[130] Crew, *Town in the Ruhr*, pp. 191–3.
[131] Tenfelde, *Sozialgeschichte*, pp. 114–15, 340; Däbritz, *Bochumer Verein*,
Table 4; Crew, *Town in the Ruhr*, pp. 174–9; Lange, 'Wohnungsverhältnisse',
p. 98.

(which had fulfilled important social as well as insurance functions), exemption from military service, job security, direct management by royal officials, special uniforms, and celebrations. As Crew has observed:

To be a miner was not simply to earn a living digging coal, but to exercise moral qualities and responsibilities: 'The efforts of a miner', ran an ordinance of 1824, 'must be directed to the loyal execution of his exceptional calling, and through good moral conduct, orderliness, industriousness and obedience towards his superiors to the winning of respect for his estate.'[132]

This position changed drastically as legal privileges were abolished and the direct patronage of the state was in large measure withdrawn.

Associated with these changes was the transformation of the economic and social character of the industry, so that Ruhr miners ceased to be a small, select, and largely hereditary group and instead became a giant labour force, largely composed of newcomers to both the district and the job. In place of a protected, secure place of work the miner was compelled to compete in an economic environment characterized by uncertainty, fluctuation, and change; and from being the élite workers of the district, miners found this position going increasingly to highly prized skilled metalworkers. The mass influx of immigrants, often with cultural backgrounds despised by native Westphalians and Rhinelanders, demonstrated to all that mine-work was no longer in any sense an exclusive and socially respected profession.

By the end of the century there is no doubt that skilled metal-work was seen as a far superior and attractive occupation. The decline in status and 'proletarianization' of mine-work was a constant theme of miners' literature and publicity, so that although no working miners had any personal experience of the former conditions, many had at least a vague consciousness that their lot was worse than that of earlier generations. As a union diary put it:

'Schön ist's Bergmannsleben, herrlich ist sein Lohn!'——so runs an old colliers' song which is still sung in certain 'mining' circles today. In fact, compared with those of today's colliers, the working and living conditions of their forefathers were very favourable. The spirit which

[132] Crew, *Town in the Ruhr*, p. 181.

in those days ruled the treatment of colliers and forge-workers is most beautifully expressed in the old Thuringian mining regulation which said: 'Item, the colliers need much freedom since the free air makes them bold'. How different today! Today mine-work is much more dangerous and burdensome than in the time of the old mining regulations; but if the collier seeks freedom he is told he is a malcontent and has no discipline.
Previously the collier was a respected citizen with aristocratic privileges —today any employer's fool can insult him and even physically maltreat him. If he tries to defend himself he must often leave his job too—'because of his misdemeanour'. The worker is penalized for every trivial thing at work—but his tormentor suffers no penalty.[133]

The theme was reflected in the writings of both social democrat and Catholic miners' leaders. As Heinrich Imbusch put it: 'If the miners were formerly particularly highly respected, with the passage of time they became the least respected. Yes, even workers in other trades commonly thought they could look down upon them.'[134] In 1908 the Witten factory inspector reported that youngsters, even from mining families, who had once worked in a factory were very unwilling to return to pit work when opportunities there were open to them.[135] Fischer-Eckert noted:

In general the miners are less highly regarded socially than factory workers, because the mining profession attracts very many who only want temporary work or have a desperate need for work. The factory worker, on the other hand, must—particularly if he works at the smelter, the blast furnace, or in the rolling mill—deliver quality work, for which his years of training and apprenticeship have qualified him.[136]

The Bochumer Verein was heavily oversubscribed with would-be apprentices seeking careers in the metal industry; and while skilled metal-workers and artisans used their local knowledge and connections to try to ensure that their sons also achieved skilled status, miners used theirs to help their sons avoid mine-work altogether. Even the terminology changed to reflect the lowered social esteem: the prestigious

---

[133] IGBE, AI 71, *Notizkalender für Berg- und Hüttenarbeiter 1902*; IGBE AI 146, *Bergarbeiter! Aufgewacht und erkennet eure Macht!* (1911).
[134] Imbusch, *Arbeitsverhältnis*, p. 126. See also Hue, *Bergarbeiter* ii. 136.
[135] BA, 18/22, *Betriebs-Inspektor* Witten to *Bergwerksdirektor* Kleine, 19. 8. 1908.   [136] Fischer-Eckert, *Lage der Frauen*, p. 77.

Bergmann was gradually replaced with the common *Berg-arbeiter*.[137]

Miners have often shown themselves a historically aware profession, conscious of and knowledgeable about their links with earlier generations who toiled below the ground and who shared many of the same experiences. A sense of history has itself contributed to their collective development and to their struggles. It was symptomatic, for instance, that both Otto Hue of the Alter Verband and Heinrich Imbusch of the Gewerkverein should write massive works of miners' history. Despite the great discontinuities of the nineteenth century —radical changes in the economic and technical basis of the industry and the swamping of the old mining population by newcomers—a sense not just of present discontents but also of a lost past persisted amongst Ruhr miners. The feeling that mine-work was, at one and the same time, unique in its economic importance, its harshness, and its dangers and yet was losing status and respect—that it was in fact under-valued, both financially and in standing—gave an edge, a sense of moral bitterness, to many miners' natural discontent with their material lot. It was a moral dimension which few other trades could match.[138] In combination, the material and the psychological experience of mine-work offered an unusually potent basis not merely for discontent but for a sense of collective identity and perhaps for collective action.

[137] WWA, K2 669; *Lage der Bergarbeiter*, p. 14; Crew, *Industry and Community*, pp. 95–8; Fischer, *Bedeutung der preussischen Bergrechtsreform*, p. 23; Tenfelde, *Sozialgeschichte*, p. 339; Conze, 'Vom Pöbel zum Proletariat'.

[138] See Barrington Moore, *Injustice*; Douglass and Krieger, *A Miner's Life*.

5

Miners' Strikes

Working conditions in the mines clearly provided grounds for discontent and seeds of conflict between workers and employers. The historically interesting question, however, is not whether conflict occurred but whether it took forms and generated forces which gave it a wider significance. In particular, did the shared experience of work enable miners to transcend the divisions—ethnic, cultural, social, and denominational—between them? Did it produce a basis for mutual solidarity and united action by mineworkers? And if so, how firm a basis was it? Could it be translated into industrial strength and ultimately into political power? This chapter addresses the history of miners' strikes, the most direct and immediate form of collective action. The next considers the attempts to go further and establish, through organizations, more lasting forms of collective solidarity and strength.

Strikes and organizations were not the only expressions of discontent. We have mentioned above other common manifestations. One was simply to stay away from work, a practice particularly common after pay-days and weekends; although not providing any lasting change to conditions at work, it did offer some relief from them. Another was to leave the job and find work elsewhere—a practice fostered by the unsettled nature of much of the mining work-force, the close geographical proximity of many pits and the constant bargaining which was so central a feature of the wages system. Absenteeism and job-changing were widespread and endemic expressions of discontent and of a desire for something better. Both were more pronounced during economic upswings than recessions since men realized that they were then in a strong bargaining position and ran little risk of unemployment. In most cases, however, they were the actions of individuals. They did not necessarily imply solidarity with other workers and thus differed significantly from strikes and organizations which depended for success on a collective approach and a collective loyalty.

Strikes and the trade cycle

Until the liberalization of the 1850s and 1860s strikes were unknown in the Ruhr mines. Miners could and did express their collective wishes, through petitions and pleas to the royal mining authorities and ultimately to the Prussian king himself. Although this form of expression subsequently declined in importance echoes did persist. The last major attempt to secure improvements through petition came in 1889, during the great strike of that year, but the attempt was already anachronistic. Petitions had been based on an assumption that disputes would be resolved harmoniously by an impartial state anxious to protect traditional rights and status as much as to boost economic efficiency. With the withdrawal of the state from all but the most minimal direct involvement in the industry and the explicit replacement of tradition by market forces as the decisive guiding factor, a different approach to the resolution of disputes was needed. Strikes and the attempts at organization which sometimes followed them implied a recognition that conflicts of interest did exist between workers and employers and that workers needed to intervene actively in the market and create a force of their own.[1]

The first miners' strikes in the Ruhr occurred in the late 1850s and the 1860s. One in 1868 has been described as the first 'modern' strike.[2] The largest strike in these early years occurred in 1872, when up to 18,000 miners took part in a six-week stoppage. The onset of the depression inhibited strike activity until the major dispute of 1889. Virtually every pit was affected by that stoppage and by subsequent ones in 1905 and 1912. The 1889 and 1905 strikes were thought to be the largest single strikes in Europe to date.

[1] The history of pleas and petitions in the Ruhr mining industry has been traced in detail in Tenfelde, *Sozialgeschichte*. See also G. A. Ritter and K. Tenfelde, 'Der Durchbruch der Freien Gewerkschaften Deutschlands zur Massenbewegung im letzten Viertel des 19. Jahrhunderts', in H. O. Vetter (ed.), *Vom Sozialistengesetz zur Mitbestimmung* (Köln, 1975), pp. 63, 87.

[2] Tenfelde, *Sozialgeschichte*, p. 453.

There were in addition many smaller stoppages: some, such as those of 1899 and 1907, could affect a number of pits in one district; others were smaller and more localized, affecting anything from one to half a dozen mines and usually blowing over in a few days.

These strikes occurred mainly during economic upswings. 1868 and 1872 were both years of prosperity and although strikes did take place during the depression years they were isolated and relatively insignificant. From 1888, however, the economic climate improved and demand for coal and steel increased. The boom of 1888 to 1891 was accompanied by a quite unprecedented scale of labour unrest, with a major strike in the spring of three consecutive years and more limited ones and threats of strikes in the intervening periods. After 1891, however, the boom ended and with the exception of the strike of 1893 (which was untypical in that it was deliberately called and not 'spontaneous') industrial peace returned to the Ruhr coal-field for several years. The upswing of 1896 to 1901 was accompanied by several local strikes including an important one in 1899 which affected a number of mines around Herne. The end of this boom in 1902 led to reduced earnings and some lay-offs, but discontent was not expressed in work stoppages: at *Holland* in April 1902 union leaders successfully persuaded the men not to strike when changes in the shift arrangements were proposed; in May forty hauliers stopped work at *König Ludwig*, near Recklinghausen, but all except five were back at work in two days and the five were promptly sacked.[3] This seems to have been the extent of strike action in protest at what were significant cuts in the miners' standard of living.

The next boom, which lasted from 1903 to 1907, saw further strikes, including the largest pre-war strike in 1905. The end of the boom in 1908 meant reduced earnings, but once again there were virtually no strikes. In February 1908 union members in Hordel discussed striking against the wage cuts but nothing further was heard of it. In March when the management of the *General* pit in Weimar announced

[3] StAB, 480, RPA to *Minister des Innern*, 24. 11. 1902; StAB, 464, RPA to KLB 4, 7. 5. 1902.

a second wage cut in two months, thirty-nine hauliers immediately stopped work and the next day some sixty hauliers and pony-minders refused to work. Management refused to talk until they had returned to work. The older workers did not join the young strikers and the local union official called on them to resume their work. The day after the strike began they went back to work without any concessions and no one gave notice when the cuts were implemented the following month. Relations seem to have remained bad at the pit since there was a further stoppage that year—again without success—in protest at the excessive water levels in the mine and the effect on the workers' health. A similarly brief and futile stoppage by some hauliers occurred at *Präsident* on 20 March.[4]

These minor rumblings seem to have been the only attempts, in the Bochum area at least, to use the strike weapon against the cuts in living standards which followed the end of the boom. It was only with the improved economic conditions which began to return from 1910 that strikes appeared to be a serious possibility again. In that year discussions began between the miners' unions which led eventually to the 1912 strike.

The outbreak of strikes

Miners' strikes in the Ruhr—like strikes in other industries and other areas—thus occurred predominantly during the upswings of the trade cycle.[5] This was sometimes adduced as evidence of the unscrupulous cynicism of the strikers. The Bochum Chamber of Commerce called the 1889 wage demands 'completely unjustified' since in the previous year wages had risen by more than coal prices and the Arnsberg *Regierungs-Präsident* said that the strike 'was whipped up by

[4] StAB, 464, *Amt* Hordel to KLB, 5. 2. 1908, *Amt* Weitmar to KLB, 16, 18. 3. 1908; IISG, *Volksblatt*, 16, 17, 18, 20. 3. 1908; StAB, 454, *Amt* Weitmar to KLB, 8. 4. 1908; StAB, 431, *Amt* Weitmar to KLB, 19. 10. 1908.

[5] The main economic booms from 1888 onwards were accompanied by strike waves affecting other coal-fields and other industries in both Germany and Europe generally. See Ritter and Tenfelde, 'Durchbruch der Freien Gewerkschaften', pp. 84–5; Schofer, *Formation of a modern labor force*, pp. 156–8; D. Geary, *European Labour Protest 1848–1939* (London, 1981), p. 39; E. Shorter and C. Tilly, *Strikes in France 1830–1968* (Cambridge, 1974), chapter V.

socialist efforts aiming at the subversion of the existing order
in a manner calculated to endanger public peace and particularly the harmony between classes'.[6] Others saw the hand
of Catholic ultramontanes behind the stoppage, while Dr
Schulz, the Bochum deputy in the Prussian *Landtag*, claimed
that the inquiry which followed the strike had shown that
'need' was not the cause.[7] Later strikes, too, were sometimes
blamed on 'agitators'. The Gelsenkirchen (Protestant) Synod,
for example, described the 1905 strike as 'artificially fostered',
and at least one local state official thought that it had been
long planned in order to strengthen social democratic
influence.[8]

In reality, however, most miners' strikes broke out without
visible or significant planning. Prior to the 1889 strike, for
instance, the few miners' organizations which existed were
small in scale and did not seek to provoke confrontations.
The Catholic Johannes Fussangel's Rechtsschutzverein and
the more socialist orientated Glückauf societies (led by
Ludwig Schröder) concentrated on such things as insurance
provisions and avoided such emotive issues as wages, hours,
and conditions of work. In late 1888 and early 1889 industrial unrest affected a number of industries and localities
in Germany. Nevertheless, the first public discussion of
miners' wages was at a meeting of miners' delegates in
January 1889; and even then the issue was subordinated to
others such as improved medical facilities for miners and
their families and the establishment of a miners' newspaper
for the whole of Germany. The leaders seem to have deliberately avoided the subject of wages and although in March and
April wages, hours, and other immediate issues came to the
fore, the initiative seems to have come from below. Talk of
strike action to support wage demands was met by Schröder
with the argument that it was more important to build

[6] WWA, HKB *Jahresbericht*, 1888, p. 11; StAB, 436, RPA to HKB, 29. 5.
1889.

[7] StAB, 440, KLB to *Aemter*, 28. 5. 1889; speech, 13. 4. 1890, printed in *Der
Bergarbeiter-Ausstand des Jahres 1889 im preussischen Abgeordnetenhause*
(Essen. 1890); StAB, 441, *Die Post*, 1. 9. 1889.

[8] Brakelmann, 'Evangelische Pfarrer', p. 312; StAB, 455, *Amt* Weitmar to
KLB, 28. 1. 1905. See also StAB, HKB *Jahresbericht*, 1891/2, p. 20; StAB, 451,
Kölnische Zeitung, 1. 7. 1899; WWA, K2 199, HKB to *Minister für Handel und
Gewerbe*, 19. 3. 1912.

a strong organization: that would enable demands to be won without the need to actually strike.[9]

When stoppages none the less began in April and May 1889 they did so in a random and uncoordinated manner. The last days of April saw isolated and short strikes for higher wages at *Präsident* in Bochum and *Wilhelmine Victoria* near Gelsenkirchen. On 2 May there were short stoppages at *Friedrich Ernestine* and *Dahlbusch*; at *Consolidation* a red flag was raised—and rapidly removed by the police. On Friday 3 May the hauliers at *Hibernia* (near Gelsenkirchen) demanded a wage increase of 20 pfennigs a shift and hauliers and other young miners at *Rheinelbe und Alma* and other pits around the town joined in with similar demands. The *Hibernia* hauliers received no reply to their demand and decided not to work the next day; forty-five of their colleagues at *Rheinelbe und Alma* were sacked for raising the demand at all. In the evening large numbers of young workers gathered in Gelsenkirchen and when the police tried to clear an inn there was an angry reaction: a street battle developed and there were attacks on shops, window-breaking, and some shooting. Only at about 11 o'clock did the police manage to restore order.[10]

The riot marked the start of the general strike. The military were called in to restore order and this seems to have acted as a spur to the men—hewers as well as hauliers—to stop work at pit after pit. August Siegel, one of the miners' leaders in the Dortmund area, recalled: 'Early on Monday morning some of the pits in the Dortmund district were already occupied by the military. At the sight of the soliders the lads turned back; thus one mine after another came to a standstill.'[11]

As the strike spread there were fears amongst officials and observers of intimidation and violence. Some incidents were reported: at *Julius Philipp* it was said that miners were being threatened by outside strikers. The worst violence, however,

[9] Ritter and Tenfelde, 'Durchbruch der Freien Gewerkschaften', pp. 84–5; D. Fricke, *Die deutsche Arbeiterbewegung 1869–1890* (Leipzig, 1964), p. 311; IZF, *Westfälische Arbeiter-Zeitung*, 19. 1. 1889; IGBE, A. Siegel, *Mein Lebenskampf* (unpublished MS), p. 64.

[10] Köllmann and Gladen, *Bergarbeiterstreik*, p. 32; WWA, HKB *Jahresbericht*, 1888, p. 11; *Der Ausstand der niederrheinisch-westfälischen Bergleute im Mai 1889* (Styrum-Rheinland and Leipzig, 1889), pp. 4–5.

[11] Siegel, *Mein Lebenskampf*, pp. 65–6.

came from the soldiers: at *Graf Moltke* near Essen three men
were shot dead and seven were seriously wounded, one of
them dying later, after an attack on the pit and attempts at
sabotage. In Herne a man was shot dead by the police after
allegedly opening fire at them himself. Outside Bochum
a man was bayoneted to death after trying to bring in his
(miner) son who had apparently been involved in an attempted
attack on the *Herminenglück Liborius* pit. In the centre of
Bochum itself troops opened fire to disperse a crowd and
killed two innocent bystanders who were emerging from the
main station and wounded four more. Other incidents were
reported elsewhere.[12]
Despite these incidents there appears to have been little
intimidation. Strikers from one pit visited neighbouring
mines, but their appeals to those still working to join them
seem generally to have been accepted without any need for
threats. Most of the reports to the Bochum *Landrat* emphasized the peaceful nature of the strike. From Stockum
on 9 May came the telegram: 'This morning work stopped
at both shafts of *Neu Iserlohn, Siebenplaneten, Borussia*, and
Germania. So far peaceful but gendarmes wanted.'[13] The
semi-official *Norddeutsche Allgemeine Zeitung* conceded
that, with individual exceptions, the strikers 'had not left the
ways of legality'.[14] Nor was there any sign that specifically
socialist agitation played any significant part in spreading
the strike. Nevertheless, despite the lack of prior organization and leadership, within a few days the strike affected
every mine and involved an overwhelming majority of the
mineworkers. By 10 May around 81,000 of the 115,000
mineworkers in the Ruhr were on strike and at twelve pits
around Bochum it was estimated that only 200 of the 9,700
miners had not joined the stoppage. By 13 May over 90,000
miners were out.[15]

[12] StAB, 436, *Julius Philipp* to HKB, 9. 5. 1889; *Der Ausstand*, pp. 13–14;
STAM *Oberpräsidium* 2828 Bd. 2, *Oberbürgermeister* Bochum to *Oberpräsident*
Münster, 10, 11. 5. 1889.
   [13] StAB, 436, *Amt* Stockum to KLB, 9. 5. 1889; *Amt* Bochum I to KLB,
7. 5. 1889.
   [14] STAM, *Oberpräsidium* 2828 Bd. 3, *Norddeutsche Allgemeine Zeitung*,
11. 5. 1889.
   [15] Koch, *Bergarbeiterbewegung*, p. 139; Köllmann and Gladen, *Bergarbeiterstreik*, pp. 70–1.

It was only when the strike was in full swing that any evident leadership emerged. At each pit the strikers met and elected delegates. Their backgrounds illustrated the breadth of strike solidarity: of 105 delegates from the Bochum area, 49 were Protestant, 46 were Catholic, and the religion of 10 was unknown; 24 of them were national liberals, 32 were Centre party supporters, 14 were social democrats, one was a 'Christian socialist', and the politics of the remaining 34 was unknown.[16]

Central leadership was only established at a conference of strike delegates on 10 May when a central strike committee was elected. Even then, however, the power of the elected leaders remained limited. Johannes Fussangel and Lambert Lensing, the two radical Catholic newspaper editors, exercised considerable influence. Of the three delegates who went on 14 May to Berlin to intercede with the Kaiser himself only one, Fritz Bunte, was a member of the strike committee; and he was overshadowed in importance by Ludwig Schröder who had been active for many years in the Glückauf miners' association. The three delegates had no formal mandate from the strikers and consulted the old socialist Wilhelm Tölcke before agreeing to go at all.[17] The lack of organization thus put considerable influence in the hands of generally respected individuals rather than formally elected leaders.

Real power, however, lay not with 'leaders' of any description but with the strikers themselves. This became painfully apparent in the later stages of the strike. On 19 May a delegate conference held in Bochum decided, against the advice of the central strike committee, that the dispute should be ended on the basis of limited concessions in the employers' 'Essen Protocol', but many miners felt cheated and refused to return to work. The central strike committee then called for the stoppage to continue and at a further delegate conference on 24 May, apparently in spite of their own reservations, they supported the calls for further strike action. But by now many pits were already back at work and others continued to return. On 25 May the delegates from *Holland, Fröhliche*

[16] StAB, 440. The delegates in question are those from Bochum North and South, Herne, Langendreer, and Werne.

[17] Koch, *Bergarbeiterbewegung*, pp. 36–7; Siegel, *Mein Lebenskampf*, p. 70.

Morgensonne, Hannover, and *Marianne* issued a proclamation calling on the men to return to work since the employers were fulfilling their promises in the Essen Protocol 'in all significant points'.[18] Partly for these reasons and partly because of increased repression from the authorities the strike did indeed collapse in the next few days. The hesitancy and indecision of the leadership had merely reflected their lack of real authority over the miners.

The 1889 strike was thus primarily a non-organized, grassroots, 'spontaneous' affair in which leaders could play only a severely circumscribed role.[19] Later in the year a miners' union was formed, providing a lasting organizational and leadership structure. Nevertheless, subsequent mining strikes continued to show many of the same spontaneous characteristics and the initiative continued to lie in nearly every case not with 'leaders' but with the miners themselves. In January 1890 a list of demands was made to the employers by the union; but in the agitation which took place in the following weeks the men at individual pits felt free to put their own, often differing, demands. When a strike eventually broke out at the end of March it did so in a completely uncoordinated manner, affecting only a handful of pits. After spreading to some neighbouring mines around Gelsenkirchen and Bochum the strike collapsed.[20]

In 1891 the third important strike in as many years took a similar course. In February a list of demands was formulated by a central meeting of miners' delegates. But when in April a strike broke out it did so without any co-ordination or central direction and seriously embarrassed the miners' leaders. The management at *Eintracht Tiefbau* closed off one of the shafts to prevent the men from leaving work early. Sixty men stopped work in protest and the next day saw a complete cessation of work. Three strike delegates were elected and although the local government official agreed to talk with them, the mine management refused to recognize

[18] STAM, *Oberpräsidium* 2828 Bd. 6.

[19] See also Tenfelde, *Sozialgeschichte*, p. 584; A. Gladen, 'Die Streiks der Bergarbeiter im Ruhrgebiet in den Jahren 1889, 1905, und 1912', in J. Reulecke (ed.), *Arbeiterbewegung an Rhein und Ruhr* (Wuppertal, 1974), p. 127.

[20] StAB, 462; Verein für die bergbaulichen Interessen, *Entwicklung des . . . Steinkohlenbergbaues* xii. 237-8.

them or make any concessions. The strikers called on men at neighbouring pits to support them and on 21 April men from *Fröhliche Morgensonne, Centrum, Hasenwinkel,* and *Friedlicher Nachbar* came out.[21]

The miners' political and union leaders were unhappy with the spontaneous stoppage. The social democratic newspaper commented on 24 April, as the strike spread from pit to pit:

Coal barons and ultramontanes clearly have an interest in the outbreak of a strike: the former to prevent coal prices from falling, and the latter to destroy the miners' organization. We repeat our warning to the miners not to follow the siren voices of the ultramontanes and the provocation of the coal barons, because in present conditions any strike must be regarded as lost from the outset.[22]

But the next day they had to recognize their powerlessness: 'If the miners do not listen to well intentioned advice or if they are unable to control their bitterness any longer, then all right; let it run its course; we cannot prevent it.'[23] It was only the next day, 26 April, that a union delegate meeting gave official support to the strike.[24]

By 1891 the leading Catholic miners had left the original union—henceforward known as the Alter Verband—and had formed their own rival organization (named Glückauf). The district between Bochum and Essen where the strike started was predominantly Catholic and the Catholic union leaders had participated in the original February meeting. Nevertheless, despite the allegations from the social democrats that they were fomenting the stoppage, the Catholic leaders showed themselves equally unable to control the situation. Anton Fischer, the chairman of Glückauf, at first showed some sympathy for the stoppage but on 26 April issued a statement in the name of the union's executive urging the miners to stay at work:

We are *against* a strike, and therefore call on the Christian miners of the Rhineland-Westphalian coalfield *not* to stop work. . . . We believe that our demands are justified and can and must be implemented. We

[21] StAB, 463, *Kohle und Eisen*, 18. 2. 1891; StAB, 447, *Kölnische Zeitung*, 23. 4. 1891.

[22] IZF, *Westfälische Freie Presse*, 24. 4. 1891. See also edition of 9. 5. 1891.

[23] ibid., 25. 4. 1891.

[24] StAB, 447, *Extra-Blatt des Rheinisch-Westfälischen Tagesblatts*, 26. 4. 1891.

also know that the present unrest has been provoked by the indefensible behaviour of the *Eintracht Tiefbau* management and that it has been exacerbated by social democratic agitators—even though the *Alter Verband's* paper is now speaking against a strike to let others get hurt. We urgently call on the government to implement the reasonable wishes of the miners in the forthcoming reform of the mining law.[25]

Nevertheless the *Eintracht Tiefbau* strikers rejected this appeal and on 27 April Fischer himself stopped work at *Herkules*.[26]

The fears of the various miners' 'leaders' were in the event fulfilled: the strike reached its peak on 28 April when 18,000 men (or 13 per cent of the miners in the Ruhr at the time) from 45 pits were out, but this was rapidly followed by a large-scale return to work under threats of dismissal from the employers. The ending of the strike was followed by the sacking of strikers and delegates at many pits.[27] The events of late April 1891 had demonstrated again the spontaneous and undisciplined character of mining strikes and the difficulties which leaders of all political persuasions had in exercising real authority over them.

The next major strike, in January 1893, was unusual in that it was one of the few specifically called by the miners' union leaders. There had been some agitation in the preceding months on the issue of reform of the *Knappschaft* and the introduction of revised and codified work-rules at each mine. But the agitation had not looked likely to lead to a strike and it was only the outbreak of one in the Saar mines late in 1892 which made a Ruhr strike a serious possibility. Miners' meetings were held in Essen, Gelsenkirchen, and Dortmund on 6 January and there were calls for strike action to express solidarity. On Sunday 8 January a delegates' meeting in Bochum decided to strike immediately.[28]

This strike too, despite its 'official' character, failed to

[25] StAB, 447, *Extra-Blatt des Rheinisch-Westfälischen Volksfreund*, 26. 4. 1891.
[26] StAB, 447, *Extra-Blatt der Zeitung der Deutschen Bergleute*, 28. 4. 1891.
[27] Verein für die bergbaulichen Interessen, *Entwicklung des . . . Steinkohlenbergbaues* xii. 239; BA, 20/A 45, *Geschichte der Zeche Hannover*; IZF, *Westfälische Freie Presse*, 30. 4. 1891; StAB, 447.
[28] StAB, 448, RPA to KLB, 31. 12. 1892; STAM, *Oberpräsidium* 2694 Bd. 1, RPA to *Minister des Innern*, 8. 5. 1893; StAB, 448, *Extra-Blatt der Bochumer Zeitung*, 8. 1. 1893.

win adequate support and ended in complete defeat. On 13 January over 21,000 miners—about 14 per cent of the total number in the Ruhr—were out, but the following day the number had fallen to only 15,600 and by the end of the second week the stoppage was virtually over. The strike might indeed have ended even more quickly but for the attitude shown by both the employers and the Government: the former threatened that all workers who broke their contracts by staying away from work without due notice would be sacked or fined, while the latter imposed blanket bans on meetings (an act of doubtful legality) and arrested both central and local union leaders. While this intimidated some—the notice given to 200 men at *Hibernia* led to a large return to work there—it hardened the resistance of others.[29]

The 1893 strike marked the end of the wave of unrest which had affected the Ruhr mines in the years after 1888. The next few years saw only isolated stoppages at individual mines. The strikes at *Constantin* in 1896 and at *Holland* and *Osterfeld* in 1897 were local and unplanned affairs, soon over.[30] The next substantial strike occurred at the pits around Herne in 1899 and once again the pattern of unorganized and unplanned militancy was shown.

The 1899 strike was preceded by very little agitation. The social democrats had been campaigning against the Government's *Zuchthausvorlage*, an issue which played no part in the strike. Only a week before the strike broke out the Herne branch of the Alter Verband had made an excursion to the Ruhr river valley to enjoy the scenery amid 'singing and beer'.[31] On the other hand an improving coal market and higher output meant that a number of mines in the area were raising, or were considering raising, the wages of the hauliers and other young workers and this seems to have raised sensitivity on pay questions.

The strike was sparked off by a substantial increase in the *Knappschaft* contributions of young workers. On 22 June, the pay-day for the previous month, many hauliers found

[29] WWA, HKB *Jahresbericht*, 1892, p. 12; StAB, 448.

[30] STAM, RA I 74, KLB to RPA, 24. 4. 1896; StAB, 479, RPA to *Minister des Innern*, 9. 11. 1897.

[31] IZF, *Volksblatt*, 6. 6. 1899; StAB, 451, *General Anzeiger, Dortmund*, 5. 7. 1899.

that their wage increases were eliminated or that their take-home pay actually fell as a result. The new rates had actually been introduced in April, but as there were five Mondays in May they had a particularly significant impact on pay packets for that month. There was much grumbling and the next day over 60 hauliers and pony-minders at *von der Heydt* stayed away from work. The next day they were joined by around 30 workers at the neighbouring *Julia* pit.[32]

The strike lasted for a week and affected fewer than twenty pits, all around Herne. Even here the strike was far from complete: German miners seem generally to have stayed aloof, as did the hewers of both German and Polish nationality. Strikers at one pit would return to work even as colleagues nearby came out. Indeed, as an industrial conflict the whole strike was a fairly minor affair, demonstrating the particular strike-proneness of the young hauliers but also illustrating their difficulties in setting off a broadly based stoppage.

What gave the 1899 strike its importance at the time was the particular role of the Poles and the violence which accompanied it. Frustration had grown amongst Polish miners about their position in the Ruhr—e.g. over the compulsory use of German in the mines. The *Knappschaft* contribution issue may have been felt particularly strongly by Poles with little sense of commitment to and identity with the area and a greater interest in immediate cash than in longer-term insurance entitlement. The violence seems to have been precipitated by an ill-considered official decision not to allow a miners' meeting, at which the strike was to be discussed, to go ahead. This immediately inflamed opinion, removed any forum for considered discussion of aims and tactics and gave the conflict an anti-police character —soon reinforced when incidents led to arrests, further violence, and eventually the calling in of troops to maintain

---

[32] StAB, 451, *Rhein.-Westfälische Zeitung*, n.d., *Kölnische Zeitung*, 2(?). 7. 1899; *Glück Auf. Berg- und Hüttenmännische Wochenschrift*, 8. 7. 1899, p. 581. On the strike generally see K. Tenfelde, 'Die "Krawalle von Herne" im Jahre 1899', in *Internationale wissenschaftliche Korrespondenz zur Geschichte der deutschen Arbeiterbewegung* (März, 1979 Heft 1), pp. 71–104; Brüggemeier, *Leben vor Ort*, pp. 202–11; Klessmann, *Polnische Bergarbeiter im Ruhrgebiet*, pp. 75–9.

order. Police protection of non-strikers heightened passions and meant that attempts to stop men from working could produce devastating conflicts. In the worst of the incidents three people were shot dead by the police in the centre of Herne.[33]

The strike was opposed by all shades of political opinion. The leaders of the Alter Verband, the main miners' union, heard nothing of it until 24 June, two days after the dispute started. Ludwig Schröder tried to appeal for a return to work at the abortive public meeting in Herne on 25 June; prevented from making his appeal in person he issued it instead through the union's paper. The social democrats also called for an end to the strike: their Dortmund paper commented:

Organized workers would have recognized immediately that a rise in *Knappschaft* contributions was not to be dealt with by means of a strike since it is not within the power of the mines to implement changes in this matter. Organized workers would not have started a wage struggle so unprepared. Not so the Poles. Their poverty of speech and unschooled intellect show them no way out of their troubles other than the work stoppage and violence.[34]

The Bochum socialist paper took the same line:

Unorganized Polish miners, with only partial mastery of our language, imported by the employers and their agents in thousands, have created a strike situation. . . . Social Democracy has no advantage from the ill-considered actions of these unorganized people and we fully support the appeal of the leadership of the German Mineworkers' Union who *call urgently for the strikers to return to work.*[35]

Polish nationalist and Centre leaders also opposed the stoppage. The abortive meeting on 25 June was also to have heard an appeal from Szczotkowski, a leading nationalist. The nationalists were particularly concerned to avoid violence: 'In these cases only calm can bring the miners their hoped-for wage increases. Anything which might contribute to disturbing the peace should therefore be avoided and the best way to ensure this is to stay at home instead

[33] StAB, *Märkischer Sprecher*, 28. 6. 1899.
[34] STAM, *Landratsamt* Gelsenkirchen 53, *Rheinisch-Westfälische Arbeiter Zeitung*, 28. 6. 1899.
[35] IZF, *Volksblatt*, 29. 6. 1899; see also Lucas *Arbeiterradikalismus*, pp. 264–5.

of standing around curiously on the streets.'[36] Although they sympathized with some of the strikers' aims and bitterly rejected the hostile characterizations of the Poles in sections of the German press, the nationalists were embarrassed by the whole affair. The Centre party too was hostile and embarrassed: they usually counted on Polish votes in elections, yet there were reports that the Dortmund party was considering a programme for 'civilizing' the Poles; one Westphalian party leader was reported to have declared: 'Do me a favour, fellows, and don't greet me in Herne; I will be pleased to see you again when we have elections.'[37] Whether apocryphal or not, the story does suggest the discomfort of the Centre in the face of these actions by their actual or potential supporters.

The Herne strike caused unusual concern and controversy because of the prominence of the Poles and the violence of some incidents. Nevertheless, this should not blind us to the fact that in its unplanned and disorganized origin it was similar to the great majority of Ruhr miners' strikes. Above all it was the action of the miners themselves—or at least some of them—taken without the encouragement of their organizations and even against their advice.

The largest strike of all—that of 1905—showed the same characteristic. It started at *Bruchstrasse* at Langendreer, to the east of Bochum. Hugo Stinnes had recently bought the mine and his efforts to introduce a more dynamic management style soon produced conflicts. In August 1904 it was claimed that Knepper, his new manager, wanted to lengthen the shift. In November there were complaints that *Nullen* was being practised too vigorously and at a miners' meeting there were bitter complaints about fines, deductions, and general conditions. There was thus already an accumulation of discontent when on 1 December the management announced that because of construction work winding-time would take longer. At this the men refused to work and elected a negotiating commission, including Husemann, the Alter Verband's

---

[36] StAB, 450, *Wiarus Polski*, 1. 7. 1899. The nationalists issued a direct appeal for calm: H. Mönnich, *Aufbruch ins Revier, Aufbruch nach Europa, Hoesch 1871–1971* (Dortmund, 1971), p. 168.

[37] StAB, 451, *Kölnische Zeitung*, 4. 7. 1899.

Bochum area official. An appeal to the Royal Mines Office produced a ruling that a month's notice had to be given before the shift length could be extended. Even so, it was only with difficulty that Husemann and the commission persuaded a meeting of over 1,000 *Bruchstrasse* miners that the strike should be ended. They eventually agreed to return to work but kept the commission in readiness for any renewed attempt to lengthen the shift.[38]

The management soon made it clear that they intended to increase the winding-time from 1 February. The Christlicher Gewerkverein (as the Catholic miners' union was now known), the Polish miners' union (which had been founded in 1902), and Husemann for the Alter Verband assured the miners of support should it come to a strike, since longer winding-time would inevitably open the door to a general increase in working hours. On 7 January, after it had become clear that there was no possibility of agreement, the entire *Bruchstrasse* labour force stopped work.[39]

The unions now sought to limit the stoppage to *Bruchstrasse*. On the same day that the men there decided to strike Ludwig Schröder spoke in Baukau, urging the men at other pits to stay at work. Two days later he and other union leaders spoke in Werne:

All the movement's leaders, especially the union vice-chairman Schröder, did their best to restrain those present from striking so that the *Bruchstrasse* strike could be energetically prosecuted. In the end it was decided to work today. But when the decision was announced there were so many cries of 'We strike anyway' and 'We won't let ourselves be led any more up the garden path!' that it seemed quite possible that the strike will hit the Werne pits this morning.[40]

On 9 January the leaders of the four unions (the fourth was the small, liberal, Hirsch-Duncker union) met and issued a general appeal to the miners to stay at work. Nevertheless, the strike rapidly spread. On 11 January *Vollmond*, near *Bruchstrasse*, came out and the next day neighbouring pits —*Neu Iserlohn, Heinrich Gustav, Amalia,* and *Wallfisch*

---

[38] StAB, 456, *Amt* Lagendreer to KLB, 1. 12. 1904; IZF, *Bergarbeiter Zeitung,* 10, 17. 12. 1904.

[39] StAB, 456, *Amt* Langendreer to KLB, 27. 12. 1904, 7. 1. 1905; *Polizei-Kommissar* Dortmund to RPA, 1. 1. 1905.

[40] StAB, 456, *Amt* Langendreer to KLB, 9. 1. 1905.

—and others were affected. It was estimated that nearly a quarter of all the Ruhr miners were already out. A conference of delegates from throughout the Ruhr met in Essen on the same day, formulated a series of demands and appealed to those men still at work to remain there until the demands were answered. This appeal too fell on deaf ears. On 15 January, after the employers rejected the unions' demands, the strike was made official. It reached a peak on 19 January when nearly 196,000 men—78 per cent of all Ruhr miners and 87 per cent of below-ground workers —were out.[41]

The 1905 strike thus dramatically illustrated the tendency of Ruhr mining strikes to break out without official support and even against the advice of the 'leaders'. As Hermann Sachse, the Chairman of the Alter Verband, declared at the Essen conference on 12 January: 'If anyone has fought against a general strike with all their power, it is us.'[42] Other delegates claimed that there was no question of persuading the miners to stay at work. Graf, a delegate from Herne, gave a dramatic account of the difficulties he faced:

Comrades! I come from the Herne district and must explain here that if today's conference—and the comrades there have set their hopes on today's conference—if this conference now were to declare that we are not to continue the strike, that we want to try to bring the comrades to return to work, comrades, I would not go there and tell them that. I am quite certain of that. I would not be able to do it, I would be torn down from the platform. I have tried to keep the comrades at work, I have told them they will get not a pfennig support if they strike; but this has not bothered them at all. They simply said, 'It has gone on long enough'.[43]

The course of the strike is well known. The employers refused to negotiate with the unions' joint organizing committee, the 'Commission of Seven', so they appealed to the Government instead. There was widespread public sympathy with the strikers, encouraged by the absence of violence, and the Government favoured some concessions. On 27

[41] StAB, 456, *Amt* Langendreer and *Amt* Werne to KLB, 12. 1. 1905; Koch, *Bergarbeiterbewegung*, p. 90, 144; E. Jüngst, 'Der Ausstand der Ruhrbergarbeiter vom März 1912 in statistischer Darstellung', in *Glückauf*, 29. 6. 1912, p. 1044.

[42] StAB, 456.

[43] ibid.

January, to the indignation of the employers, the Government announced that it was willing to revise the mining laws,
limiting overtime and the length of the shift and providing
for compulsory workers' committees, the abolition of *Nullen*,
and limits on fines. These concessions and a subsequent
promise from the Government of further discussions if the
men returned to work, combined with the inability of the
unions to support so many thousands of men and their
families, led the Commission of Seven to recommend in early
February that the strike be ended. A delegate meeting on
9 February agreed by 165 votes to 5 and despite protests
from some who wanted to continue the strike the vast
majority of the miners returned to work the following week.
This time at least the union leaders were reasonably in tune
with the miners.[44]

The unofficial character of most miners' strikes and the
unions' reluctance to support them was demonstrated yet
again in May 1907. This was the height of the economic
boom and hauliers and other young workers in the Recklinghausen district came out in pursuit of higher shift-rates
of pay. The strike followed months of sporadic complaints
and short, isolated stoppages. Ultimately around 2,500
workers from 18 pits were involved. Because there were
no violent incidents and no particular nationalist overtones
the strike attracted much less public (and historical) attention
than the Herne strike eight years previously; but in other
respects there were strong similarities. Once again it was
limited to the young workers at a limited number of mines,
concerned with the particular pay problems of their group.
Despite a suggestion by the *Oberpräsident* in Münster that
the strike was deliberately planned, the available evidence

---

[44] On the history of the strike, see Koch, *Bergarbeiterbewegung*, Kirchhoff,
Sozialpolitik, Gladen, 'Streiks'. Some historians have misleadingly implied that
there was widespread resistance to the call to return to work: see D. Fricke, *Der
Ruhrbergarbeiterstreik von 1905* (Berlin-Ost, 1955); D. Groh, 'Intensification
of work and industrial conflict in Germany 1896–1914', in *Politics and Society*
viii (1978), p. 377. The resumption was called with effect from 10 February
and the proportion of Ruhr miners away from work fell from 75 per cent on
9 February to 35 per cent on Saturday 11 February, 13 per cent on Monday
13 February, and under 1 per cent on 16 February. Technical reasons accounted
for some of the delay which did occur. Jüngst, 'Der Ausstand der Ruhrbergarbeiter', p. 1044.

suggests the reverse.[45] Most of the strikers seem not to have been union members and the Alter Verband opposed it strongly. At a meeting after the strike had lasted a week, Wilhelm Waterkotte, the local union representative, declared:

In future such *putsches* must be avoided. An unorganized mass cannot achieve anything against the mine administration. Stoppages must not occur again without previous consultation with the organizations. Those who have now simply stopped work without any consideration must bear the consequences.[46]

The last major strike in the Ruhr coal-field before the war differed from most in that it was deliberately called by three of the four unions. The first suggestion that the unions should unite to prosecute a joint wage claim came from the Alter Verband in the autumn of 1910 but was rejected by the Gewerkverein. In October 1911 a joint meeting was held between all four unions at which Otto Hue for the Alter Verband argued that the spring of 1912 would provide good conditions for a wage demand, particularly since the English miners looked like striking then. The Gewerkverein again opposed the idea and with a *Reichstag* election imminent the matter was postponed. In February 1912 a further joint meeting was held at which the Gewerkverein again opposed any campaign on wages, at least until the employers had had a chance to implement the increases which they were promising for the next few months. The atmosphere was politically highly charged, since in the previous month's election the Centre party in the Ruhr had supported the National Liberals against the social democrats; as a result the SPD had lost the Duisburg and Bochum seats. The Alter Verband, supported by the Poles and the Hirsch-Duncker union, decided to go ahead anyway and sent demands first to the employers' federation and then to the individual mines: they called for wage increases, the eight-hour shift inclusive of journey-time, and other reforms. Meetings were held and leaflets issued in support of the demands—which, it was clear, would be rejected. The

---

[45] StAB, 454; IGBE, AI 19, Verband der Bergarbeiter Deutschlands, *Jahresbericht*, 1907/08.

[46] STAM, *Landratsamt* Gelsenkirchen 40, Eickel police report, 17. 5. 1907.

Gewerkverein again expressed its opposition to the campaign but on 7 March the other unions decided that a strike should be called for 11 March.[47]

The strike started well, with half the miners away from work on the first day and over 61 per cent on the third. Since the three striking unions' combined membership in the Ruhr was little more than a quarter of the mineworkers, it is clear that the strike call had mobilized many thousands of non-unionists and even perhaps a number of Gewerkverein members. The Gewerkverein, however, continued to oppose the strike, instructed its members to stay at work and even called on the Government to provide military protection for those wanting to work. The deep division between the striking unions and the Gewerkverein was reflected in conflicts amongst the miners themselves. Unlike 1905 there were numerous violent incidents between strikers and non-strikers—a fact which the employers and their sympathizers used to the maximum to win public support. A ministerial attempt to promote conciliation having been rejected by the three unions before the strike began, the Government with the Kaiser's personal support determined to confront and defeat the strikers: troops were introduced to protect non-strikers. With the miners themselves deeply divided (unlike 1889) this show of strength seems to have encouraged those who were reluctant to strike to return to work and to have discouraged the strikers. By the end of the first week only around half of the miners were still out and in the second week the strike ebbed from day to day. On 19 March a delegate conference of the three striking unions decided to call off the stoppage and by 22 March it was over.[48]

The 1912 stoppage—the third 'general' strike affecting mines throughout the Ruhr—was thus unusual in that it was deliberately planned. Only two pits, *Kaiserstuhl* and *Scharnhorst*, both in the Dortmund area, experienced unofficial stoppages before the official strike call was issued.[49] When

[47] Koch, *Bergarbeiterbewegung*, pp. 121 ff,; Gladen, 'Streiks', pp. 141 ff; Hue, *Bergarbeiter* ii. 690 ff; IGBE, AI 21, Verband Deutscher Bergarbeiter, *Jahresbericht*, 1911/12.

[48] WWA, K2 199, Verein für die bergbaulichen Interessen, *Ausschreitungen Streikender und Belästigungen von Arbeitswilligen im Ruhrrevier.*

[49] Hue, *Bergarbeiter* ii. 710.

the strike was called it started smoothly and uniformly, with over half the miners stopping work on the same day. All this was in complete contrast to 1889 and 1905, when first one mine and then another came out, in 1889 without any organization and in 1905 in clear defiance of the unions' wishes.

Despite contemporaries' fears and suspicions about secret conspiracies most miners' strikes were thus 'spontaneous' stoppages, initiated by the miners themselves without reference to or even against the advice of their theoretical leaders. This did not mean that they were mindless, nihilistic acts. On the contrary, as we shall see, they were based on real issues and reflected a rational view of the position and needs of those involved. It did mean, however, that mining strikes generally followed a pattern which prefigured the concepts of organized unionism and which to some extent conflicted with them. Strikes spread, for example, not through union circulars and calls for action but through groups of strikers touring from pit to pit and urging their colleagues to join them. More critically, it meant that 'leadership' was widely diffused; crucial strike decisions might be taken through utterly informal networks of particular groups of mineworkers, notably the hauliers; by the traditional pre-union forum of the mass meeting of the men of a particular pit; by the strike delegates elected by them; or by the union structures imposed on top. Most seriously, it could lead to fundamental conflicts about both aims and tactics —conflicts within the miners' movement which were far from resolved before the end of the war and which emerged with greater ferocity and more tragic results after it.

Strike demands

The demands made by strikers offer an important key to understanding the nature of strikes and the problems which underlay them. Such demands cannot necessarily be taken entirely at their face value as an accurate description of the strikers' concerns: they may have a formal or symbolic element which hints at rather than states an underlying grievance. Nevertheless, when the same issues repeatedly appear in different guises and when they can be explained by reference to external factors (such as the trade cycle) it seems fair to attach weight to them as providing a vital clue to the concerns which were uppermost in the participants' minds.[50]

Sometimes—for example at *Neu Iserlohn* in 1889—the miners stopped work first and only set about formulating demands later. In March 1890 men at *Dahlhauser Tiefbau* refused to work but did not explain what it was they wanted: they were told to go home if they would not work and it was only later that the local union official explained that the men were not satisfied with a planned wage rise from July and instead wanted an immediate increase. When the *Hannover* men joined the 1891 strike they also gave no reasons. Similarly in 1899 the *Kölnische Zeitung* reported:

> The Polish workers do not give any notice, they put no demands, they give no real reasons for their behaviour, they simply do not work and thus—basta! This is an example of the impudence and the dumb stupidity which accompanies all Polish affairs. . . . They do not know what they want.[51]

In 1905 the men at *Carl Friedrich Erbstollen* stopped work but at first gave no reasons other than solidarity with the *Bruchstrasse* men; their own demands were only formulated later.[52] This lack of articulation is not surprising in view of the sudden and unplanned nature of many strikes. Nevertheless, in virtually all strikes demands were eventually formulated—if not at the very beginning then after a short delay.

The 1889 strike started with calls for higher wages. At *Präsident* the men stopped work when a request for a 20 per cent pay increase was rejected; at *Franziska Tiefbau* a deputation of three hewers called for a 30 per cent increase and when it was refused the men declined to start work. As the

---

[50] Shorter and Tilly suggest that 'the poorest way of knowing what workers want in strikes is to go by what they say they want.' While correctly warning that strike demands need careful interpretation, this seems to go too far in dismissing valuable evidence. Shorter and Tilly, *Strikes in France*, p. 66.

[51] StAB, 451, *Kölnische Zeitung*, 2(?), 7. 1899; StAB, 436, *Neu Iserlohn* to KLB, 9. 5. 1889; StAB, 462, *Landrat* Hattingen to RPA, 1. 3. 1890; BA, 20/A45, *Geschichte der Zeche Hannover*.

[52] STAM, *Oberbergamt* Dortmund, *Bergrevier* Hattingen to *Oberbergamt*, 10. 1. 1905.

strike got underway more detailed demands were formulated. The Bochum *Landrat* reported that at most of the meetings the chief demands were for wage increases of 20 to 25 per cent and the eight-hour shift inclusive of winding-time; the other demands were 'relatively minor side-issues'.[53] At *Shamrock, Constantin,* and *Lothringen* there were demands for a general 20 per cent wage increase; at *Hannibal* only 15 per cent was called for; at *Hasenwinkel* too there were demands for higher pay and those who made them were sacked; at *Baaker Mulde* 20 per cent was demanded. The north Bochum *Amtmann* reported that the miners in his district were demanding the eight-hour shift inclusive of winding-time, wage increases of 15 per cent, and the delivery of timber (for props) to the coal-face; the *Hannover* men were also demanding a limit to overtime working. At a meeting of the *Hibernia* miners demands were made for a general 15 per cent pay increase with specified averages for the various grades of worker, the eight-hour shift inclusive of winding-time, the delivery of timber to the coal face, restrictions on fines and more information about them, specific dates for the fixing of piece-rate agreements, the abolition of overtime, and the abolition of Sunday work. At *Siebenplaneten* the demands were for higher wages, the inclusive eight-hour shift, abolition of overtime except in emergency, and a free truck of coal per month for every married miner. At virtually all the Gelsenkirchen meetings the demands were for '15 per cent increases of all wages and the eight-hour shift inclusive of winding-time'.[54]

Demands for higher wages and shorter hours thus dominated all other issues. When the three strikers' delegates had their audience with the Kaiser they particularly stressed the question of hours; Ludwig Schröder explained to him: 'We demand that we have inherited from our fathers, namely the eight-hour shift. We attach no importance to wage

[53] StAB, 436, KLB to RPA, 11. 5. 1889; ibid. *Präsident* to KLB, 7. 5. 1889, *Bürgermeister* Witten to KLB, 9. 5. 1889.
[54] STAM, *Oberpräsidium* 2828 Bd. 2, *Landrat* Gelsenkirchen to *Oberpräsident,* 9. 5. 1889; StAB, 442, complaints to commission of inquiry, summer 1889; StAB, 436, *Amt* Bochum 1 to KLB, 7. 5. 1889; *Der Ausstand der . . . Bergleute im Mai 1889,* pp. 20, 31.

increases.'[55] This statement contrasts sharply with the evident importance of the wages issue in precipitating the strike.

The issues which had been raised in 1889 reappeared again and again in later disputes. In January 1890 the newly formed miners' union sent a list of demands to the employers:

1. general wage increases of 50 per cent;
2. eight-hour shifts including winding-time: 'as long as the length of the shift is not exactly eight hours this will remain a constant source of dispute';
3. no overtime shifts except in case of emergency: 'the present practice of minor officials calling upon hauliers, officials, pony-minders, repair workers, etc. to work overtime shifts is a form of indirect pressure and leads to persistent conflicts';
4. abolition of *Kohlenabzüge*—a system whereby hewers were prevented from earning excessively high wages:
5. wages to be paid four times instead of twice a month.[56]

At the miners' meetings which preceded the strike of April 1890 these demands were frequently modified. Nevertheless, the basic issues remained. Wage increases were virtually always demanded in one form or another: at some pits the demand was for more for the lower paid while at others minimum wages for various categories of mineworker was the goal. The eight-hour shift was another common demand. The *Nullen* system was frequently criticized. The *Vollmond* men called for the delivery of timber to the coal-face, separate cages for men and ponies, the abolition of all fines, and permission to hold meetings on mine property, in addition to minimum wages for hewers. At some mines the position of the miners' delegates was raised: at *General, Constantin*, and perhaps other pits management was asked to recognize them as the miners' official representatives with the right to speak on their collective behalf.[57]

Discontent in late 1890 was still said to focus around the question of pay, hours of work, *Nullen*, and 'rough treatment of the workers by the mine officials'.[58] In February 1891 the local union chairman in Herne declared that demands should

[55] WWA, HKB, *Jahresbericht*, 1888, p. 14.

[56] StAB, 462.

[57] StAB, 462; StAB, 461, *Constantin* delegates to *Zeche Constantin der Grosse*, 23. 2. 1890.

[58] StAB, 461, RPA to KLB, 20. 11. 1890.

be put to the owners again with the emphasis on shorter hours and higher wages. Two weeks later a delegate meeting called for the eight-hour shift including winding-time, no overtime without the permission of workers' committees, abolition of restrictions on maximum earnings and the introduction of workers' regulation of *Nullen*, general wage increases, the reinstatement of sacked workers, no further sackings without the permission of workers' committees, and more workers' control of the *Knappschaft*. Here all the old demands reappeared, with the difference that, instead of stressing the role of the miners' delegates, workers' committees with permanent powers were now called for— a proposal first put forward by liberal parliamentarians during the 1889 strike. These demands seem to have formed the basis of most of the points raised by the strikers in April.[59]

The 1893 strike was called in solidarity with the Saar miners and much of the public discussion naturally turned around this issue. Even in this atypical strike, however, the old issues were not forgotten. Immediately after it began a list of demands were sent to the employers; they included

1. the eight-hour shift inclusive of winding-time;
2. 25 per cent wage increases;
3. repeal of the newly promulgated work-rules;
4. reinstatement of sacked workers and no new disciplinary measures;
5. recognition of workers' committees and free elections to them.[60]

Nothing seems to have come of these demands.

Wages were the dominant issue in several of the small strikes in the later 1890s. The strikes at *Constantin* in 1896 and *Holland* in 1897 were both on this issue.[61] The 1899 Herne strike, triggered by changes in *Knappschaft* contributions, was primarily about the (net) pay of the young hauliers. On the other hand, it was the question of the hours of work —the number of overtime shifts and the length of the

---

[59] StAB, 461, *Amt* Bochum 1 to KLB, 3. 2. 1891; StAB, 463, *Kohle und Eisen*, 18. 2. 1891; StAB, 447, *Extra-Blatt der Zeitung der deutschen Bergleute*, 28. 4. 1891; Kirchhoff, *Sozialpolitik*, pp. 61–3.

[60] StAB, 448, RPA to KLB, 6. 2. 1893.

[61] STAM, RA I 74, KLB to RPA, 24. 4. 1896; StAB, 479, RPA to *Minister des Innern*, 9. 11. 1897.

'normal' shift—which led to short strikes at *von der Heydt* and *Barillon* in June 1900 and almost to one at *Holland* in 1902.[62] Extension of the length of the 'normal' shift was also the issue in strikes at *Baaker Mulde* and *Oberhausen* in 1903 and precipitated the dispute at *Bruchstrasse* which led to the 1905 strike.[63]

The 1905 strike was the occasion for the re-emergence of the full list of demands. Even at *Bruchstrasse* the strikers called not only for the old shift lengths but also for minimum wage-levels, the creation of a workers' committee to negotiate and settle disputes, and better treatment of the men by mine officials. At many pits the miners presented long lists of demands: at *Shamrock* thirteen points were raised and at *Siebenplaneten* fifteen. The central delegate meeting on 12 January made fourteen demands.[64] The chief issues remained the same: the eight-hour shift inclusive of winding-time, the reduction or abolition of overtime, higher wages, the abolition of *Nullen*, and the creation of elected workers' committees and/or elected workers' representatives with some supervisory functions. The delegates at the meeting of 12 January called for recognition of the unions, although this demand was only repeated at some of the individual mines. Demands were also made for reform of the *Knappschaft*, household coal to be provided to miners at cost price, and longer notice on the evacuation of company housing. The miners' chief concerns emerge clearly: they wanted shorter hours and more pay and they were angered by the arbitrary use of power by the mine officials, most obviously in the practice of *Nullen*. The demands therefore called both for immediate reforms and for the creation of lasting channels through which the miners would be able to express their views and exercise some control over certain management practices.

Later strikes were fought over the same or similar issues.

---

[62] StAB, 453, KLB to RPA, 7. 6. 1900; StAB, 480, RPA to *Minister des Innern*, 24. 11. 1902.

[63] IGBE, AI 16, Verband der deutschen Bergleute, *Jahresbericht*, 1903.

[64] StAB, 456, *Amt* Langendreer to KLB, 7. 1. 1905; STAM, *Oberbergamt Dortmund 1843*, *Bergreviere* Witten and Herne to *Oberbergamt*, 13. 1. 1905; WWA, K2 213.

Rumblings in 1906 and the hauliers' strike of 1907 were over pay. In 1912 the final major strike before the outbreak of war saw a conventional list of demands: wages should be raised by 15 per cent and the shift—including winding-time—should not exceed eight hours; overtime should be allowed only in emergencies; in addition there should be reforms of the wage payment system and in the notice arrangements for company housing; workers' committees should exercise some control over fines; the *Knappschaft* should be reformed; new arbitration courts should be estab-listed to settle disputes; the labour exchange system needed reform; and non-alcoholic drinks should be provided at all pits.[65] Beyond the specific demands there was on this occasion an implicit call for union recognition.

We can distinguish three main issues behind the various demands raised during these strikes. One—not necessarily the most important—was pay. This might be expressed as a demand for an across-the-board increase or it might take the form of a demand for minimum earnings for specific categories of mineworkers; it might also take a more obscure form, such as the fairly frequent call for timber to be delivered to the coal-face—thus relieving hewers of a chore for which they received no extra payment and allowing them more time to cut coal and earn money. The second major issue in strike after strike related to the hours of work. This had two main expressions: one was the constantly repeated demand for the eight-hour shift inclusive of winding-time; the second was the abolition or severe restriction of over-time.[66] These issues could represent two sides of the same coin: higher pay could free miners from the need to work long hours and grant them a less constrained choice between maxi-mizing income or leisure.[67] Conversely, general restrictions on the hours of work might force up pay by improving the

[65] Hue, *Bergarbeiter* ii. 708.

[66] Stearns is clearly wrong to suggest: 'German miners rarely raised questions of hours of work in their strikes, although their working day was two hours longer than that in France and Britain. Their docility in this matter was due to the fact that over half of them were freshly in from the countryside.' P. N. Stearns, 'Adaptation to Industrialization: German Workers as a Test Case', in *Central European History* (1970), p. 310.

[67] See the discussion in Crew, *Town in the Ruhr*, pp. 208-9.

miners' position in the labour market and by making firms compete through higher output from the standard shift (which would require better incentives to the men) instead of by lengthening hours.

Demands for higher pay and shorter hours were generally clear-cut and explicit. The third main issue, less clearly defined but almost as commonly present, related to the miners' desire for changes in the manner in which the pits were run. This could take a number of forms. Most simply, it was expressed in the demand for more 'humane treatment' of the miners on the part of overmen and other pit officials. It was expressed too in the calls for the abolition of *Nullen*—a system which permitted too many arbitrary decisions by mine officials. Calls for reform of the systems of discipline and punishment also reflected resentment at the unfettered and often arbitrary power exercised by supervisory staff. Underlying these issues was a desire for what Barrington Moore has described as 'greater control over their situation at work and [for] decent human treatment by their supervisors'.[68] In some strikes it took a more far-reaching form with demands for permanent institutional reforms to enable miners to air grievances and have them settled through negotiation instead of depending on the whims of mine officials. Thus there were calls for elected miners to be given permanent responsibilities for checking on pit safety or on the working of the *Nullen* system. Sometimes the demands went further, with calls for the creation of workers' committees with whom managements would be obliged to consult or for the recognition of the trade unions. At a meeting in Langendreer during the 1905 strike, for instance, a social democrat speaker argued that the most important strike demand was not for better pay or for shorter hours but for the establishment of recognized, elected miners' representatives with the ability to keep in close touch with the miners themselves and with (unspecified) authority *vis-à-vis* the mine management: this would ensure that the other demands were fulfilled.[69] Such demands were always strongly resisted by the employers, who saw them as an infringement of the

---

[68] Barrington Moore, *Injustice*, p. 241.
[69] StAB, 455, *Amt* Langendreer to KLB, 1. 2. 1905.

rights of owners to manage their property. Nevertheless, despite the occasional rhetoric, the demands did not necessarily have very radical implications: as we shall see, the Government proved willing to compromise and make concessions in this area. The central demand was not for a change in the ownership of the pits but rather for a reform of management style—to replace a largely authoritarian system with one where blatantly arbitrary acts were prevented and where the miners had a continuing voice in the affairs of the mine.[70]

If these were the main issues underlying strikes, what was the mechanism which linked them to the actual outbreak of strike action? Why should such questions seem more pressing and stimulate action at some times but not others? In particular, why should strikes over such perennial questions tend to be concentrated, as we have seen, during the upswing of the trade cycle?

One important factor, of course, was simply the changing balance of industrial power during the different phases of the trade cycle. During recessions 'agitators' were liable to be dismissed with relatively limited prospects of finding work elsewhere—a factor reinforced at times by various forms of blacklisting (which was also more effective when employers were not competing for any available labour). Miners were well aware from the shortening of hours and the squeeze on earnings that recession put them in a vulnerable position. At such times work stoppages might even be welcomed by employers. Recessions were therefore generally marked by fewer strikes and a general tightening of belts. The start of an upswing saw the end of many of these constraints. The signs that the owners were beginning to need manpower just as much as, or even more than, the miners needed jobs were clear: men began to be hired rather than fired; hours were extended instead of cut; higher output rather than care and maintenance became management's goal; and both profits and wages began to rise. Higher profits and dividends were

---

[70] Schofer draws a distinction between 'modern' strike demands, focusing on economic issues and union recognition, and 'pre-modern' demands focusing on work rules. It is not clear that such a distinction is particularly helpful in considering the Ruhr. Schofer, *Formation of a modern labor force*, pp. 156–7.

reported in the local papers and signalled to the miners that better days had arrived.[71] In such an atmosphere the time seemed ripe to remedy long-standing grievances and to ensure that the miners too shared in the general improvement in fortunes; conversely, any worsening of conditions at such a time or any apparent exclusion of the miners from the general improvement in fortunes was likely to be deeply resented.

Yet in several ways the onset of boom did actually worsen the immediate conditions of work and add to the sources of friction between management and men. Hours of work were increased. Instead of free shifts, miners were subjected to various forms of pressure to extend the length of the 'normal' shift and to work overtime afterwards. Shifts of one-and-a-quarter, one-and-a-half, or even twice the normal length became common and although this may have been welcomed by some for the extra earnings which resulted, the drawbacks in terms of simple physical exhaustion were obvious. The fact that absenteeism also increased markedly during upswings shows that many miners were as interested in having reasonable time off as in earning every possible pfennig. Miners also began to wonder whether shorter hours would not provide the same higher earnings by forcing up the price of coal and by boosting efficiency. It is not hard to understand how issues of overtime and the hours of work formed a constant source of conflict during booms and played so prominent a part in the outbreak of strikes.

Miners naturally hoped and expected that higher demand for coal and rising profits would result in substantial improvements in wages. Here again, however, the onset of the boom could result in disappointment. As we saw in the last chapter, earnings did rise with the improved economic situation. But higher earnings resulted in part from longer hours of work rather than from improved basic rates; there might be a delay before wage rates themselves followed profits upwards; and rising retail prices eliminated some of the value of improvements.[72] The effect, therefore, was often to whet the miners' appetite for improvement rather than to satify it.

    [71] StAB, 441, *Die Post*, 1. 9. 1889; Gladen, 'Streiks', p. 119.
    [72] Tenfelde, *Sozialgeschichte*, pp. 303–5.

One feature of the wages system which played a particular role in precipitating disputes and strikes during economic upswings was the discrepancy which soon became apparent between hewers' pay and that of other mineworkers on fixed shift-rates. As we saw in the last chapter, hewers' earnings were fairly responsive to cyclical fluctuation through their monthly wage negotiations and their ability to move from one pit to another to exploit favourable economic circumstances. Workers on shift-rates, however, found it more difficult to secure increases since once rates were set there was no automatic mechanism for changing them. Job-changing by young shift-paid workers, hauliers, pony-minders, and others, also took place. But there were obstacles which limited the young miners' ability to use job-changing as a means of bidding up their pay. The very fact that they were paid on standard rates made it easier for neighbouring mines to ensure that they all offered the same rates of pay. In addition, the fact that hauliers were in effect serving an apprenticeship could act as a tie to their pit: if they moved they risked having to serve a full period as a haulier all over again at the new pit.[73]

This meant that the wages of hauliers and the other shift paid workers were less responsive to cyclical fluctuations than those of the hewers. While this worked to their advantage during recessions, when their earnings remained relatively buoyant, during booms they soon found that they were being left behind and had no comparable mechanism to secure improvements. This situation, combined no doubt with youthful impetuousness and the lack of family responsibilities, helps to explain why many of the strikes started amongst these young workers—and why several never spread beyond them.[74] Thus the sporadic stoppages in late April and early May 1889, which heralded the strike of that year, were all the actions of hauliers, pony-minders, and other young workers. At *Franziska Tiefbau* it was reported

[73] STAM, *Frankfurter Zeitung*, 11. 2. 1912.
[74] Tenfelde notes the important role of hauliers in many mining strikes after 1877 but describes their actions as 'apparently unmotivated'. Tenfelde, *Sozialgeschichte*, pp. 513–14. On the relative inflexibility of shift-rates compared with piece-rates, see chapter 4 above.

that 'the young workers were the first who stayed away from work, and the older ones then followed them'.[75] The Werne *Amtmann* also noted their weakness so long as they acted alone: 'The youthful elements made themselves very conspicuous in the first days of the strike, until they were pushed into the background by the older miners. An attempted strike by the young workers would be quite hopeless if they did not know that the older ones stood behind them.'[76] The *Amtmann* for north Bochum took a similar view:

The relatively few young people employed at the pits here were hardly in a position to create a strike of the extent and generality that did in fact take place. It is certainly true that the wages movement started amongst the young hauliers, pony-minders and the lowest paid and that an increase had to be given to these people early in March and April; but the strike itself had deeper causes and they are not to be found in the heads of these youths. On the other hand it is true that the young lads proved themselves particularly active as spokesmen and strike propagators once it had broken out while the older, more settled workers, particularly those with a family and their own home or a company house, were more restrained.[77]

The 1891 stoppage also seems to have started, at some pits at least, amongst the hauliers and pony-minders, with their older colleagues joining in only later.[78] On other occasions, however, the hewers declined to follow the youngsters' lead: in 1896, when hauliers at *Constantin* stopped work and demanded an increase in their shift-rates, some fathers ordered their sons to return to work and the pit manager was able to put hewers onto hauliers' work.[79] The 1899 'Herne strike' was also essentially the work of the younger workers, although this aspect was obscured by the attention given to the prominent role of the Poles. That strike occurred at a time when some but not all pits in the area had raised

[75] StAB, 441, *Bürgermeister* Witten to KLB, 30. 9. 1889.

[76] StAB, 441, *Amt* Werne to KLB, 26. 9. 1889.

[77] StAB, 441, *Amt* Bochum I to KLB, 24. 9. 1889.

[78] StAB, 447, *Gendarm* Rose to KLB, 23. 4. 1891.

[79] StAB, 463, *Amt* Bochum I to KLB, 24, 25. 4. 1896; STAM, *Regierung* Arnsberg I Nr. 74, KLB to RPA, 24. 4. 1896. In 1890 strike talk amongst young workers at *Prinz von Preussen* seems to have been quelled by the opposition of older workers. StAB, 462, *Polizei* Altenbochum to KLB, 5. 9. 1890.

their shift rates of pay and it was immediately followed by
further increases. 'On not one of the pits affected by the
strike have the hewers put any demands, only the young
hauliers and pony-minders whose wage is on average only
2.50 to 3.00 marks', reported one miner from the strike
district.[80] The *Kölnische Zeitung* recognized that the young
miners at least had a case:

It may be conceded that a wage of about 60 marks, which many
young Poles here earn in the month after deductions, often cannot
suffice for a satisfactory standard of living with today's high prices
for food and lodging. But our entire industry is not structured to provide young assistants with the same wages as older, experienced men.[81]

The Bochum *Landrat* tried to appeal to the strikers' families
to exercise a moderating influence: 'I urgently call on the
sensible older miners, particularly the German family heads
of those who have for no good reason stopped work, with me
to smooth the way back to order and to lead the imprudent
youth back to their duty through work and example.'[82]

A number of the smaller strikes were also primarily the
action of these young underground mineworkers: those at
von der Heydt and *Barillon* in 1900 and at *König Ludwig*
in 1902 are examples. One of the clearest expressions of the
particular frustrations felt by young workers on shift-rates
occurred during the boom years of 1905 to 1907. Once
again hewers' earnings ran ahead of those of other underground workers. November 1905 saw a two-day stoppage by
pony-minders at *von der Heydt*. In March 1906 the workers'
committee at *Constantin IV/V*, newly formed after the 1905
strike but officially barred from discussing wages, called none
the less for a general wage increase, particularly for the
shift-paid workers. The pit manager claimed that an across-
the-board increase was impossible but said that he would see
if hauliers could be put onto piece-rates 'so that with a corresponding production they could earn more than hitherto'.[83]
On 30 May hauliers at *von der Heydt* struck work for two

[80] StAB, 451, *General Anzeiger, Dortmund*, 5. 7. 1899.
[81] StAB, 451, *Kölnische Zeitung*, 2(?). 7. 1899.
[82] StAB, 451, *Märkischer Sprecher*, 28. 6. 1899.
[83] StAB, 464, *Constantin der Grosse* to KLB, 26. 4. 1906; StAB, 480, RPA
to *Minister des Innern*, 22. 12. 1905.

days and in August at Hordel 'a mass demonstration took place for an increase in the hauliers' wages, without disturbance or success.'[84] In October the workers' committee at *Mansfeld* expressed satisfaction with the current piece-rates at the pit but reported that there were many calls for pay increases for shift-workers; at *Franziska Tiefbau* in Witten nearly 70 hauliers and pony-minders—only one of them a union member—struck work for eight days to demand better pay.[85]

These rumblings came to a head in the following spring. In May 1907 hauliers at a number of pits came out on strike, first in the Recklinghausen area and then around Bochum and Gelsenkirchen. In all some 17 mines and around 2,500 workers were involved. The hewers, however, remained at work—sometimes undertaking the work of their striking colleagues—and, as we have seen, the unions vigorously opposed the strike. In the end it achieved little: at *Hannover* 25 strikers were sacked and although some mines gave pay increases others did not.[86] During the rest of 1907 shift wages continued to rise but still somewhat more slowly than hewers' earnings.

Improving economic conditions therefore provided real grounds for growing conflict. Both sides sought to benefit from the improved conditions and the growing friction was expressed not just in strikes but also in absenteeism and job-changing. Personal relations worsened and insults and abuse became more widespread. Thus the fact that conflict was worst when material conditions were in some respects improving did not mean—as some contemporaries suggested—that it had no justification in terms of the objective circumstances and needs of the workers; rather, it reflected the sharpening clash of aims and interests as power relationships and pressures shifted with the changing economic climate.

[84] StAB, 481, *Amt* Hordel to KLB, 31. 8. 1906; STAM, RA I 83 *Geschäftsbericht des Vorstandes des Gewerkvereins christlicher Bergarbeiter Deutschlands* (1905/6), p. 67.
[85] StAB, 464, *Mansfeld* to KLB, 29. 10. 1906; IZF, *Arbeiter Zeitung*, 11, 17. 10. 1906; IGBE, AI 18, Verband der Bergarbeiter Deutschlands, *Jahresbericht*, 1905/6, p. 105.
[86] StAB, 464, *Amt* Hordel to KLB, 11, 15. 5. 1907; IGBE, AI 19, Verband der Bergarbeiter Deutschlands, *Jahresbericht* 1907/8.

Responses to strikes

If strikes represented one of the chief ways in which miners voiced their concerns and aspirations about their work, were they also effective? Did they succeed in their aims and secure the changes and improvements which were demanded? Or were the frequent doubts of union leaders about their usefulness well-founded?

The strike—unlike absenteeism or job-changing—was by its nature a collective action. Success depended on the achievement of a broad degree of solidarity. Miners were not generally in the position of skilled workers in a technically advanced and interdependent work-place, where the action of even a limited number of strategically placed workers could have a serious impact on the entire plant. Miners' strength lay in numbers: to exert effective pressure on employers—particularly those in the Ruhr who owned several mines and had an effective employers' association —required the mobilization of very widespread support. To actually win a trial of strength might require this mobilization to be sustained for many weeks or even months.[87]

1889 and 1905 showed that the miners were capable of a high degree of strike solidarity. At the peak of both strikes around 80 per cent of all Ruhr mineworkers were out and the proportion of underground workers was even higher.[88] Social and ideological differences were ignored. Shared resentments and shared demands—based on the common experience of work—overcame the deep divisions which normally characterized the working class in the Ruhr. Nevertheless, this impressive unity should not blind us to the fact that these strikes were far from typical. Even in 1889 the peak of solidarity lasted only a few days and was succeeded by a drift back to work. In 1905, by contrast, around three-quarters of the Ruhr miners stayed out for three weeks until the strike was officially called off. Even in 1905, however, there was a perceptible drift back in the last week of the

[87] British mining strikes were often very protracted: the 1844 strike lasted 4 months and subsequent disputes in 1893 (4 months), 1912 (6 weeks), 1926 (7 months), and 1984/85 (almost a year) were also long drawn out.

[88] Koch, *Bergarbeiterbewegung*, pp. 142–3; WWA, K2 213.

strike and many feared that if the dispute lasted much longer the return to work was bound to increase. The decision to end the strike was overwhelmingly accepted. In 1912 there was a 60 per cent turnout but this lasted only three days before a major return to work began. Even this level of support was unusual: in 1891 13 per cent of Ruhr miners stopped work and in 1893 14 per cent. Other strikes won even less support. Strike after strike failed to spread beyond a relatively limited geographical district or to widen its basis of support beyond the hauliers who started so many of them. Extended and sustained solidarity was exceptional rather than normal in mining strikes.

There were several reasons for this. Sometimes the hewers' different interests and alternative remedies made them unwilling to stop work in support of the particular grievances and precipitate action of their younger colleagues: indeed, they sometimes took on the strikers' work. In 1899 suspicion between Germans and Poles played a part in limiting the spread of the strike. Political and denominational divisions were sometimes important—most notably in 1912. Threats of dismissal and reprisals by the employers, occasional shows of strength by the authorities, and the lack of fall-back resources of many miners undoubtedly weakened their will and ability to stick out.[89]

Most fundamental, however, was the sheer size and rapid growth of the coal-field and the labour force itself. In 1904 Otto Hue described the practical problems. He assumed that the Gewerkverein would oppose any general mining strike and that only around 150,000 of the 270,000 Ruhr miners would therefore take part. In such circumstances the employers could maintain some production and compensate for reduced output through higher prices; this would enable them to keep going for several months:

But a strike lasting several months would be impossible for the workers, simply because the resources are lacking. To support 150,000 men would require millions each week but the union's ready resources would scarcely suffice for one day. Nor could the rest of German labour provide such sums on top of their other obligations. During the

[89] Lucas highlights the growth in poverty amongst striking families in 1905: Lucas, *Arbeiterradikalismus*, p. 127.

Crimmitschau lock-out the German workers' spirit of sacrifice achieved great things. But there only 7,000 men were involved and the support of perhaps 150,000 men would be beyond their power. The end result would be a lost strike, an utterly destroyed organization and unending poverty for the workers.[90]

In the event, the 1905 strike was more successful than Hue anticipated, with approaching 200,000 men participating. This did not prove sufficient to force rapid concessions from the employers but it did mean that the practical problems of sustaining a protracted dispute were even greater. The first two to three weeks were relatively easy, since most miners were paid twice monthly and had some cash in hand. Strike pay was organized for union members, but the sums available were quite insufficient. This was an important factor behind the decision to call off the strike.

1905 thus demonstrated the practical difficulties of sustaining a strike on the scale and for the time necessary to inflict a defeat on the employers. Also important, however, was the weakness—relative to the scale of the challenge—of the social and psychological ties and loyalties necessary to form the basis for effective action. The mutual loyalties of the *Kameradschaft* might, if the conditions were right, extend to others in the same pit or even to men in neighbouring pits; but they did not necessarily extend to cover the entire region. The solidarity born of face-to-face relations and personal knowledge which could exist in a small mining village was hard to recreate in a coal-field which by 1912 employed approaching 400,000 men. The steady influx of newcomers and the constant movement within the district discouraged strong, settled, and broadly-based local connections and social bonds. Yet such local ties were essential to sustain whole families—not just the men themselves—through long periods of industrial action, without wages and for many with the threat of homelessness. Comparisons between long-established families and newcomers to the district are instructive. Many Germans feared that the immigrants were a disruptive force, whose rawness and lack of restraint fostered industrial conflict, strikes, and violence.

[90] StAB, 480, RPA to *Minister des Innern*, 20. 12. 1904. Crimmitschau was a celebrated dispute in the Saxon textile industry in 1903.

Such prejudices were certainly fostered by the 1899 strike
with the highly visible role played by young Poles. Yet if
anything immigrants seem to have been less willing to strike
than their colleagues. Tenfelde has noted that in the early
mining strikes solidarity was stronger in the traditional
mining districts than in the new and rapidly expanding pits
to the north: the newcomers, despite their undoubted
frustrations and discontents, were simply not attuned to this
form of action. Similarly, when the authorities inquired
into Polish involvement in the 1889 and 1905 strikes they
found that Poles had not played a particularly important role.
Thus rapid social change and the divisions within the working
class weakened rather than strengthened strike solidarity and
hindered sustained and successful mobilization.[91]

Success did not depend solely on the degree of support
mobilized among the miners. The reactions of others—the
mine-owners, the Government, and broader public opinion
—were also important. Sometimes the strikers won significant sympathy beyond the ranks of the working class. Small
traders who depended on them for business naturally welcomed higher wages and hoped for concessions and an early
resumption of work. In 1889 the *Westfälischer Merkur*
reported that most of the press was sympathetic to the
strikers: 'The latter have won respect through their prudence and orderliness.'[92] The *Bochumer Zeitung* reported:
'In bourgeois circles many hope that the miners' efforts
will have success and this sympathy will not diminish so
long as the strikers rigorously avoid any excesses.'[93] The
employers' intransigence was frequently criticized. In 1905
many bourgeois papers were critical of the mine-owners'
stance and at the University of Bonn a public strike fund was
launched which raised a million marks; Dr Fischer, the
Catholic Archbishop of Cologne who had formerly worked
in Essen, sent 1,000 marks to the Gewerkverein to help
needy families; even employers from other industries criticized
the Bergbau Verein. Even when there was little sympathy
with the strike itself, heavy-handed over-reaction by the

[91] Tenfelde, *Sozialgeschichte*, pp. 511–14; StAB, 441, 455.
[92] STAM, *Oberpräsidium* 2828 Bd. 3, *Westfälischer Merkur*, 13. 5. 1889.
[93] STAM, *Oberpräsidium* 2828 Bd. 2, *Bochumer Zeitung*, 11. 5. 1889.

authorities could arouse middle-class protest. In 1893 the widespread arrests of local activists were severely criticized:

The bitterness which one finds among the workers about this is beginning to reach bourgeois circles. It is openly said that without the intervention of the gendarmes the strike would probably have suffered a significant decline today; but that it has in fact remained steady and that if the current methods persist it will continue for several more days at this level.[94]

The Government too showed occasional sympathy with the striking miners and impatience with the intransigence of the mine-owners. Official attitudes towards miners' strikes were often uncertain and ambiguous. At times the Government's overriding concern seems to have been to defend the existing social order against the apparent threat from strikers; this could involve branding them as dupes of socialist agitation, vigorous police action to hinder strike organization and to protect strike-breakers, the provision of gendarmes and even troops to maintain 'order', exemplary justice for activists, and general endorsement of employers' positions. At other times the Government aimed to preserve social harmony and to prevent extreme political polarization by presenting itself as fair-minded and impartial, concerned to defend the legitimate interests of every subject. This standpoint could lead it to seek to mediate and even to defend the rights of individual workers against the excesses of the employers.[95]

The Government showed both faces in its response to miners' strikes in the Ruhr. In 1889 the miners made it clear that they still looked to the state for remedies to their grievances. The Gelsenkirchen *Landrat* reported from his conversations that the strikers retained great trust in royal officials and had clear expectations of help from above.[96]

---

[94] StAB, 448, *Frankfurter Zeitung*, 13. 1. 1893; Koch, *Bergarbeiterbewegung*, p. 92; E. G. Spencer, 'Employer Response to Unionism: Ruhr Coal Industrialists before 1914', in *The Journal of Modern History* XLVIII, iii (1976), p. 400; IZF, *Bergarbeiter Zeitung*, 28. 1. 1905.

[95] See K. Saul, 'Zwischen Repression und Integration. Staat, Gewerkschaften und Arbeitskampf im kaiserlichen Deutschland 1884–1914', in K. Tenfelde and H. Volkmann (ed.), *Streik. Zur Geschichte des Arbeitskampfes in Deutschland während der Industrialisierung* (München, 1981), pp. 209–36.

[96] STAM, *Oberpräsidium* 2828 Bd. 4, *Landrat* Gelsenkirchen to *Oberpräsident* Münster, 18. 5. 1889.

Strike meetings often ended with a cheer for the Kaiser. This trust was not entirely misplaced: the Kaiser received a delegation of strikers and the Government tried to persuade the employers to make concessions. They refused, and the final stages of the strike were marked by more repressive behaviour by the Government authorities: strike meetings were banned and the central strike committee was arrested. Nevertheless the strike was followed by a (much criticized) official inquiry and eventually by some legal reforms. In 1890 arbitration courts were introduced. The *Novella* of 1892 obliged each mine to produce a proper set of work-rules and specified some of their contents: the length of the working day, the wages system, the disciplinary system, and the method of resolving disputes had all to be laid down. Certain limits were placed on what was allowed: a worker could not be dismissed without notice if the management had known the ground for dismissal for over a week; money from fines and deductions had to be used for the workers' benefit; and the employers were forbidden to mark a worker's papers with comments on his behaviour. The views of the miners on the draft work-rules of their pit were to be considered by Government mine officials with the aim of achieving agreement. These reforms by no means gave the miners what they had demanded: but their disappointment was matched by the outrage of the employers who saw them as a fundamental attack on their right to manage their property and to make agreements with workers as equals in a free market.[97]

The 1905 strike also saw Government attempts to conciliate and the offer of purely Government concessions. In early February the strike leaders were able to claim that the strike was 'a wonderful success' because of the promise of legislation.[98] In July a reform of the mining law abolished the *Nullen* system, limited the journey-time which could be added to the basic shift, restricted overtime, and created a system of workers' committees. Once again there was

[97] Kirchhoff, *Sozialpolitik*; Tenfelde, *Sozialgeschichte*, pp. 128–9; Saul, 'Zwischen Repression und Integration'.

[98] StAB, 455, flysheet of the Siebener-Kommission. Otto Hue was reported to have observed that the concessions were more valuable than a 20 per cent wage increase. *The Times*, 31. 1. 1905.

disappointment among many miners about the extent of the concessions and their sometimes ambiguous character: the new committees, for instance, were circumscribed in what they could discuss and there were severe limits on the eligibility of miners to stand or vote for them. Nevertheless, they did represent tangible concessions which were strongly resented by the employers.[99]

The Government thus showed itself sometimes willing to conciliate and to back this up with legislative concessions. Even in 1912, when it took a hard line, conciliatory noises were made before the strike began. In effect this policy marked a recognition of the inadequacy of complete reliance on the free working of the market economy and a limited return to the older tradition of close state involvement in the industry. Indeed, on more than one occasion the Government actively considered re-nationalizing at least part of the Ruhr coal industry—a policy which aroused the wrath of the coal-owners but which won quite wide support across the political spectrum.[100]

However, the Government's concern was not primarily to secure justice for striking miners. What it wanted was a stable and reliable industry, able and willing at all times to meet essential national requirements—particularly those of the strategic industries such as railways, shipping, and steel. While the apparent unreasonableness of the employers was sometimes blamed for jeopardizing this aim, the Government also showed generally little sympathy for disruptive workers. State authorities often reacted to strikes with tough action designed to contain and break the stoppage. In several strikes troops and gendarmes were brought in and there were many violent incidents. A clash at the *Moltke* pit at Gladbeck in 1889 ended with two persons shot dead by troops; as noted

[99] Workers' committees already existed in other sectors of German industry. They had been considered briefly during the 1889 strike, with the proposal coming not from the strikers but from a left-liberal *Reichstag* deputy. Although at first boycotted by the largest miners' union in protest at the restrictions on who could initially participate, the committees seem generally to have played a mediating role, reducing rather than increasing conflict and tension in the industry. Kirchhoff, *Sozialpolitik*, chapter 9; Spencer, 'Employer Response to Unionism'.

[100] Kirchhoff, *Sozialpolitik*, chapter 8; Medalen, 'State Monopoly Capitalism in Germany: the Hibernia Affair'.

above, two innocent bystanders were killed and four wounded when troops opened fire in the centre of Bochum to disperse a crowd during the same strike.[101] Most violence occurred when the miners were divided, since in such circumstances confrontations were likely to occur between strikers and non-strikers (and their respective families) and the police and troops were given clear orders to protect non-strikers as they went to and from the mines. The best-supported strike of all, that of 1905, was thus generally free of violence: although police reinforcements were brought in from Berlin and elsewhere no troops were needed and the Westphalian authorities reported that the strikers had respected the advice of their leaders to avoid violence and had 'generally acted with calm and prudence'.[102] Conversely, the 1899 and 1912 strikes—which aroused strong and conflicting passions amongst the miners themselves—were particularly violent. Many cases of violent intimidation of non-strikers were reported, particularly by the employers. The worst clashes tended to occur at shift changes. Crowds of strikers, sometimes with their wives, would then gather at the pit gate to berate those who stayed at work and to try to stop the next shift from going down. The police tried to defend the non-strikers from the wrath of the crowd and with passions high ugly incidents could easily ensue. One such at the *Shamrock* pit at Herne in 1899 was described by a barber who lived opposite:

The gendarmes drove apart the people who were standing by the pit gates and laid about both the strikers and also passers-by who had done nothing and who had previously been kept away. Most of those hit were not armed with sticks and so on at all. . . . One man who came by a field path was fearfully beaten with a bare sabre by a gendarme. The man was unarmed. He did not resist. He just kept his hands over his head so that it would not get hit too. A second gendarme came over and they both worked him over together. People were terribly beaten

---

[101] STAM, *Oberpräsidium* 2828 Bd. 1, *Landrat* Recklinghausen to *Oberpräsident*, 8. 5. 1889.

[102] StAB, 480, RPA to *Minister des Innern*, 22. 12. 1905. Significantly one of the few occasions during the strike when the police had to resort to firearms (albeit blanks) occurred when divisions emerged about the wisdom of calling off the strike. StAB, 455, *Landrat* Gelsenkirchen to *Polizeiverwaltungen*, 11. 2. 1905.

by the gendarmes, particularly by the long fence which runs from the *Shamrock* pit to Herne.[103]

Tough police action was not the only form of state action against strikes and strikers. Meetings were banned and strike leaders arrested, sometimes on very flimsy pretexts. The justice meted out by the courts seemed sometimes far from impartial. Where the miners were disunited the authorities did what they could to encourage those against the strike: in 1912 local police and officials were instructed to protect men distributing an anti-strike leaflet of the Gewerkverein, even when police permission for the distribution had not been granted.[104] Nevertheless, despite such actions, the Government's frequent response when faced with a serious stoppage —or even the prospect of one—was to look for grounds for compromise; and if the strike seemed likely to last the Government was ultimately willing to grant some concessions, if necessary against the wishes of the employers.[105]

The ultimate willingness of the Government to compromise contrasted sharply with the approach adopted by the employers. In strike after strike they refused to negotiate, insisting that the work contract was a private affair between the individual worker and his employer. In 1889 Dr Hammacher, chairman of the employers' association, did offer concessions, largely at the Kaiser's prompting. But these provoked bitter criticism amongst the employers and were

---

[103] StAB, 451, *Rheinisch-Westfälische Zeitung*, 25. 11. 1899. For reports of intimidation and violence during the 1912 strike see WWA, K2 199, Verein für die bergbaulichen Interessen im Oberbergamtsbezirk Dortmund, *Ausschreitungen Streikender und Belästigungen von Arbeitswilligen im Ruhrrevier* (1912); Saul, *Staat, Industrie, Arbeiterbewegung*, pp. 275–82.

[104] StAB, 459, RPA circular, 7. 3. 1912. The most famous abuse of justice to affect the Ruhr miners was the false conviction for perjury of Ludwig Schröder and others in 1895; but strike leaders, union activists, and social democrats were always at risk of prosecution for trivial offences and disproportionate punishments. See A. Hall, *Scandal, Sensation and Social Democracy: the SPD Press and Wilhelmine Germany 1890–1914* (Cambridge, 1977), pp. 79–83; K. Koszyk, *Anfänge und frühe Entwicklung der sozialdemokratischen Presse im Ruhrgebiet (1875–1908)* (Dortmund, 1953), pp. 166–7.

[105] Tenfelde's statement that 'for the miners the state stood—in contrast to earlier decades—on the side of the class enemy' is too one-sided. K. Tenfelde, 'Probleme der Organisation von Arbeitern und Unternehmern in Ruhrbergbau 1890-1918', in H. Mommsen (ed.), *Arbeiterbewegung und industrieller Wandel* (Wuppertal, 1980), p. 54.

subsequently withdrawn. Thomas Sattelmacher, a director
of the *Louise Tiefbau* company, wrote later:

Although the strike is now ended I cannot believe that the whole movement is finished. I very much fear that the indulgence shown at the
executive level will have the worst possible consequences. We here have
always taken the position that although we will gladly grant the justified wishes of the workers, so long as these do not hinder or impair
the progress of the business, we must nonetheless remain masters of our
own works; we would remain the masters of nothing if we had submitted ourselves to the bewitching Protocol of Dr Hammacher.[106]

In 1890 Hammacher was replaced as chairman by Jencke,
the general director of Krupp, a change which marked
a strengthened determination by the coal companies to make
no further easy concessions either to workers or to the
Government.[107]

It is hard to point to any real concessions from the
employers to striking miners. In 1889, as we have seen,
initial concessions were subsequently watered down or withdrawn. In 1905 the employers refused all negotiations and
made no concessions: the strike was called off on promised
reforms from the Government alone. The Bochum Chamber of
Commerce concluded that the miners had suffered 'a defeat
on the economic front' but had secured 'an undoubted success
in the field of state legal action, the chief significance of
which is political'.[108] In 1912 there were no negotiations
between strikers and employers and no concessions. Even
in the smaller and less critical strikes the employers generally
maintained an intransigent stance. At no time before the
war did the Ruhr mine-owners recognize the trade unions as
having the right to speak for and negotiate on behalf of their
employees and—unlike some other industries—no collective agreements were made.[109]

---

[106] BA, 18/65, Sattelmacher to Neumann, 5. 6. 1889.
[107] Kealey, 'Kampfstrategien der Unternehmerschaft'.
[108] StAB, *Magistratsbericht*, 1905, p. 16; Koch, *Bergarbeiterbewegung*,
pp. 94–5; Gladen, 'Streiks', pp. 138–9.
[109] See K. Schönhoven, 'Arbeitskonflikte in Konjunktur und Rezession.
Gewerkschaftliche Streikpolitik und Streikverhalten der Arbeiterschaft vor 1914',
in Tenfelde and Volkmann (ed.), *Streik*, pp. 177–93. There are some indications
that following the 1905 strike the mine-owners did briefly toy with the idea of
adopting a less intransigent policy; but nothing came of this. See H. Volkmann,
'Organisation und Konflikt. Gewerkschaften, Arbeitgeberverbände und die

The one area in which it could be argued that the employers did make concessions was over wages. Strikes were sometimes followed by wage rises, even if the increases did not match those demanded. The 1889 official inquiry found increases of up to 20 per cent. It is possible that the strike affected the timing but it is doubtful that it did much more. Wages were rising anyway and continued to do so well after the strike; there is no doubt that they would have risen even without it. The same was true both of the relatively successfully 1905 strike and the disastrous failure of 1912. Some of the hauliers' strikes were also followed by wage increases: this happened at *Constantin* in 1896 and the 1899 Herne strike was also followed by higher rates for hauliers, at pits both affected and unaffected by the stoppage. Here again the strikes occurred at a time when wages were rising anyway and probably affected little but the timing. The 1907 hauliers' strike ended in defeat: at *Hannover* twenty-five strikers were sacked and others were fined for breaking their contracts; some mines raised wages but others did not, and while rates generally continued to rise for the rest of the year they did so no faster than before and still more slowly than hewers' earnings.[110] Thus even the pay increases which sometimes followed strikes cannot generally be counted as strike gains. Of far greater importance was the general economic situation, with rising demand for coal enabling the employers to pay more for labour and the general labour shortage at such times requiring them to do so. The primacy of economic factors in setting the level of wages was clearly shown when booms ended and earnings fell again—irrespective of the impact of any earlier strikes.

The employers were thus not interested in conciliation and concessions to end strikes; instead, they aimed to undermine and defeat them. The economic and social organizations which bound together the coal industry facilitated the necessary co-operation. Nevertheless, new bodies were formed

Entwicklung des Arbeitskonflikts im späten Kaiserreich', in Conze and Engelhardt (ed.), *Arbeiter im Industrialisierungsprozess*, pp. 427–31.

[110] StAB, 442; Koch, *Bergarbeiterbewegung*, pp. 148–50; StAB, 463, *Amt* Bochum I to KLB, 25. 4. 1896; StAB, 464, *Amt* Hordel to KLB, 11, 15. 5. 1907; StAB, 450.

with the specific aim of strengthening the employers' hand in industrial disputes and the labour market generally. In 1890 a 'Strike Insurance Union' was set up to compensate companies involved in stoppages. It attracted many members but its effect seems to have been primarily psychological: by 1908 it had paid out a mere 700,000 marks. The 1905 strike and the expansion of the trade unions led to calls for a stronger employers' organization and in 1908 the Zechen-Verband was formed. Its aims were to defend common interests in labour questions and to provide compensation to those affected by labour disputes. The new organization was closely linked to the long-established Bergbau Verein. It promptly organized a new system of black lists so that miners who had been involved in a strike or who left their former pit without proper notice should not be taken on at any member's mine for three to six months. The system aimed to curb individual job-changing as well as strike action and was roundly condemned by miners and their spokesmen. Some local state officials also thought it went too far: at the *General* mine in Weitmar some miners stopped work without notice to protest about the amount of water in the workings and its effect both on the work itself and on their health. They found themselves blacked at neighbouring pits and had to seek work on building sites. The local government official expressed concern about the effect on the families, fearing that it would lead to an increased burden of poor relief: 'It must be understood that such categorical measures go too far and are liable to damage the well-being of the community.' Instead, he called for regulations to permit such action only where 'the miners obstinately refuse to work, although their health is in no way endangered by it'.[111] But his advice was ignored. His superior, the Bochum *Landrat*, reported to Berlin: 'The measure is used only against the unstable elements; it aims to introduce a certain order which is not only to the advantage of the mines but also to that of the community.'[112] In the *Reichstag*, the Government defended the system against its critics.

---

[111] StAB, 431, *Amt* Weitmar to KLB, 19. 10. 1908; Schunder, *Tradition und Fortschritt*, pp. 154–6.
[112] StAB, 431, KLB to *Staatssekretär des Innern*, 22. 12. 1908.

Nor did the Zechen-Verband stop there. In 1910 they introduced a new labour exchange system under their direct control. Member firms undertook to hire labour exclusively through the exchanges and workers were issued with certificates when they started and ceased work with a company. This made it easier to control the labour market and particularly to blacklist miners who left their pit without having served their proper notice. Once again the system aroused strong opposition particularly from the miners' unions who accepted the need for labour exchanges but wanted them run jointly by employers and unions. If the employers hoped that the system would enable them to contain job-changing generally, they were disappointed: in the final years before 1914 labour mobility in the industry rose significantly, much of it consisting of men coming new to the industry or leaving it entirely and thus remaining outside the new system. However, it did give them a stronger hand in imposing sanctions on individuals, particularly those involved in strikes.[113]

At pit level too the employers sought to strengthen their authority, to keep at least some work going, and to impose sanctions on the more prominent strikers. They could generally be sure of reliable support from the lower mine officials and *Steiger*.[114] They and other trusted men were often enrolled as mine protection forces during strikes, issued with black-and-white armbands with police insignia and armed with revolvers. Their role was to supplement the ordinary police by providing physical protection to mine buildings and equipment. They were supposed to operate within the mine compound and under the control of local government officials. Such forces were in existence in some parts of the Ruhr by the 1893 strike and with the positive encouragement of government officials were subsequently extended throughout the district. Not all the companies agreed to set up such security forces: the Harpener Bergbau AG was the most important firm to refuse and as late as 1910 the Arnsbeg *Regierungs-Präsident* was urging local officials secretly to encourage firms still without forces to set them up.

[113] Schunder, *Tradition und Fortschritt*, pp. 156–7; Koch, *Bergarbeiterbewegung*, p. 24.
[114] StAB, 481, RPA to *Minister des Innern*, 28. 11. 1907.

Nevertheless, by the 1900s most mines had some such force consisting of anything from two to around thirty men.[115]

That mine officials could be used in earnest during violent encounters with strikers was demonstrated during the 1899 strike in Herne. In one incident at the *Friedrich der Grosse* pit, when a crowd of strikers refused to leave the pit yard and instead threw stones, the handful of gendarmes authorized mine officials to be armed with sabres and used them to help clear the area. In the evening there were worse incidents following an apparent attempt to sabotage the pit's winding gear and the refusal of a crowd to disperse. Stones were thrown and shots fired. This time the police and mine officials responded with revolvers as well as sabres. The local government official was surprised that no one was seriously hurt.[116] The 1905 strike was less violent but the Arnsberg *Regierungs-Präsident* still felt obliged to issue a warning circular to local officials:

It has come to my knowledge that members of the mine protection forces have behaved provocatively towards workers or have become involved in violence without any need at all. I insist that care be taken that the mine protection forces apply the greatest restraint in their behaviour towards the strikers. The mine protection forces are only appointed for the immediate defence of the pits and to repulse a direct attack on those wishing to work and have to leave all further control functions, including the removal and reporting of strike pickets, exclusively to the gendarmes and police officials.[117]

More important than physical force, however, were the economic sanctions which the employers could bring to bear. It was not generally possible to break strikes by importing blacklegs on a large scale: the sheer size of the Ruhr labour force made this impracticable in large strikes, while small ones ones were generally over before such an operation could be mounted. Nevertheless, the employers did their best to keep their works open, to put what pressure they could on

---

[115] StAB, 448, 449. In 1905 it was reported that although Harpen did not have an official *Zechenschutzwehr* the company none the less armed its officials. StAB, 455, *Amt* Bochum II to KLB, 24. 2. 1905.

[116] StAB, 450, *Amt* Baukau to KLB, 11. 7. 1899.

[117] StAB, 455, RPA to KLB, 24. 1. 1905. In 1912 the mine forces were also active: Saul, *Staat, Industrie, Arbeiterbewegung*, p. 273.

their more vulnerable employees and to ensure that those willing to work had the maximum protection against the anger of the strikers. In the 1889 strike the Bochumer Verein used former miners employed in the steelworks to reopen their *Maria Anna* mine. Pressure was also put on strikers living in company housing. Prompted by Baare, the company's general director, the *Maria Anna* manager talked to the family heads living in the Eppendorf colony, offering military protection if they returned and stressing that decisions on pay increases would be made on an individual basis. A majority of the colony dwellers were soon back at work, several days before other strikers.[118] Similar pressure was exerted at other pits: at *Mansfeld* the strike lasted until 21 May but most of the colony dwellers had returned to work by 17 May. One local official noted the restraint of the older miners, 'particularly those with a family of their own or a company house'.[119]

The employers did not always need to issue overt threats to drive home the possible consequences of striking. Sometimes, however, they were very explicit. In 1891 the *Vollmond* management issued a notice indicating the date by which they expected everyone to be back at work; those who failed to do so would be deemed to have broken their contract and no longer to work for the company; those who lived in company housing would have to evacuate it. To back this up a mine official went down to the colony to explain in person what would happen.[120] In 1905 thirteen miners from *Louise Tiefbau* were sent a similar notice:

Since you have voluntarily stayed away from work for three consecutive shifts, we dismiss you from our employment under the power given us in paragraph 3 of the work-rules. Your name is deleted from the work list. Since you are no longer employed by us, in accordance with paragraph 2 of the lease agreement we dissolve the lease agreement of . . . and instruct you to evacuate the dwelling . . . within 3 days

---

[118] Ex-miners from the steelworks were used again in the 1891 strike. KA, 398 00 Nr. 1, Baare-Heiderich correspondence, May 1889; KA 126 00 Nr. 2, *General-Versammlung*, 28. 10. 1891; Däbritz, *Bochumer Verein*, p. 210.

[119] StAB, 442; StAB, 441, *Amt* Bochum Nord to KLB, 24. 9. 1889.

[120] StAB, 447, *Zeche Vollmond* to KLB, 28. 4. 1891.

from the 16th inclusive, if you have not by then made another work
contract with us in accordance with the work-rules.[121]

Similar threats were issued to miners at *Hannibal* and *Hannover*, while at *Friedlicher Nachbar* the mine manager aimed
to undermine the strike by persuading colony dwellers back
to work. The strike leaders felt it necessary to issue a proclamation assuring the strikers that 'the communal, county,
provincial, and state officials will not allow you to be
dumped on the street'—an explicit recognition that the
employers' hard line was subject to the moderating influence
of the state.[122] In 1912 there were similar pressures: at
Teutoburgia, near Castrop, the pit manager told the (non-
striking) workers' committee that strikers from the colony
would have to leave their homes after the strike was over; at
Bergmannsglück eighteen strikers who were regarded as
'agitators and ringleaders' were told to leave their company
homes; in addition overmen were used to maintain production, both by taking on production work themselves
and by escorting non-strikers to and from their homes at
the start and the end of shifts.[123]

The employers' threats were partly bluff: they could not
afford to lose large numbers of workers, particularly during
booms when they generally suffered from a shortage of
labour. Nor were they always effective: a statistical analysis
after the 1912 strike found no general correlation between
the proportion of miners living in company housing and the
level of support for the strike.[124] But this did not stop them
from implementing their threats on a selective basis. Virtually
every strike was followed by the sacking of 'agitators'—
which generally meant anyone who had played a prominent
part in the stoppage. The 1889 strike was followed by the
widespread dismissal of strike delegates. At *Karl Friedrich*

[121] BA, 18/71, 12. 1. 1905.

[122] STAM, *Oberbergamt* Dortmund 1844, *Siebener Kommission* strike notice,
29. 1. 1905; STAM, *Oberbergamt* Dortmund 1846, *Bergrevier* Nord Bochum to
Oberbergamt, 7. 2. 1905; STAM, *Oberbergamt* Dortmund 1843, *Bergrevier*
Hattingen to *Oberbergamt*, 10. 2. 1905.

[123] STAM, *Oberbergamt* Dortmund 1859, *Gewerkschaft* Teutoburgia to
Bergrevier Dortmund III, 14. 3. 1912; STAM, *Oberbergamt* Dortmund 1857,
Berginspektion Buer to *Bergwerksdirektion* Recklinghausen, 16. 3. 1912.

[124] Jüngst, 'Der Ausstand der Ruhrbergarbeiter'.

in Weitmar the two delegates, Bauer and Walter, were sacked in July. Walter had worked at the pit for thirty years and had an exemplary work record. He was a Catholic, not a social democrat, and had been elected delegate because he had the general respect of his comrades. Bauer was a more active politician and made himself unpopular with the management by his vigorous presentation of the miners' complaints to the commission of inquiry which followed the strike. Nevertheless, he had taken a generally moderate position: before the strike he had spoken against a stoppage and had apparently risked being beaten up as a result; at the commission of inquiry he had argued that reforms such as the introduction of workers' committees would lead to better social relations in the pits and to fewer strikes and had called not for higher wages all round but for the reform of anomalies in the wages system which enabled some to earn excessively while others were inadequately paid.[125] One of the *Hannover* delegates recounted his experience:

In spite of the fact that I had taken some holiday from the pit H. where I was employed, I was summoned at 11.30 p.m. in the night of 30 May by registered letter to start work early the next morning. I naturally did not start at the time indicated since I was not prepared and when one has not worked for some time there is a lot to do before everything is arranged, and in addition I thought the pit management would have the sense not seriously to summon a man to work with such short notice. But I was mistaken. When I arrived at the mine in the morning the manager Kracht told me I should return at five in the afternoon and collect my papers . . . Later, when I tried to collect my wages, not only was I not paid for the two shifts I had worked in which I had earned 7 marks but I was told that I owed them 8 marks. Long live Humanity! Long live the *Hannover* management![126]

The sackings were reinforced by a system of blacklisting, so that once dismissed a man found it difficult or impossible to find work elsewhere. Once again the employers' attitude was appreciably tougher than that of the Government. In October the Arnsberg *Regierungs-Präsident* issued a circular to local officials, noting:

---

[125] STAM, *Oberpräsidium* 2828a, *Frankfurter Zeitung*, 23. 7. 1889, *West-fälische Volkszeitung*, 8. 7. 1889; StAB, 440, *Amt* Bochum II to KLB, 6. 6. 1889.
[126] IZF, *Westfälische Arbeiter-Zeitung* 10. 7. 1889.

An agreement has been made between the mine managements of the Ruhr coal district that no miner who has been dismissed from a pit in this district or has resigned will be taken on at another mine. This rigorous measure can only be strongly regretted, since on the one hand it represents a quite unjustified restriction on the right of free movement of labour and on the other it plays a very important part in sharpening the social differences between employers and employees. In view of the discontent still prevailing amongst the miners it will be officials' task to draw serious attention to this agreement at every opportunity in the leading circles of the mining industry.[127]

Strike after strike was followed by sackings of activists. The 1890 strike was followed, it was claimed, by over 600 sackings. In 1891 the delegates at *Siebenplaneten* were sacked as soon as the men returned to work. The *Hannover* management dismissed 50 miners permanently and laid off a further 236 for a month. 70 of these men lived in company housing. Altogether some 288 miners were permanently sacked from nineteen pits in the Bochum area and a further 247 were temporarily laid off, although apart from the *Hannover* men only 8 lived in company housing; *Constantin* gave two sacked company tenants four weeks to get out of their homes. A number of strike leaders were also arrested but usually had to be released for lack of evidence; others were eventually charged with 'incitement', 'threatening behaviour', and the like.[128] The 1893 strike saw a particularly tough policy by the employers: the Bergbau Verein urged its members to make full use of their powers to sack and fine workers who broke their contracts and not to take on men dismissed from other pits. After the strike around 800 men were sacked.[129]

The 1905 strike was also followed by sackings. At twelve pits in the north Bochum district 59 men were sacked permanently and a further 321 laid off for periods of between

[127] StAB, 462, RPA circular, 19. 10. 1889. In November the employers' association warned members to be more careful with black lists and in December, faced with Government pressure and the possibility of further strikes, the black list was ended. StAB, 462, *Westfälische Volkszeitung*, 5. 12. 1889, RPA to KLB, 9. 12. 1889; StAB, *Märkischer Sprecher*, 9. 12. 1889; B. Aumann, *Die Bergarbeiterbewegung im rheinisch-westfälischen Industriegebiet* (Diss., Bochum, 1973), p. 38.
[128] StAB, 461, Verband zur Währung und Förderung bergmännischer Interessen to *Ministerium für offentliche Arbeiten*, Berlin, 22. 4. 1890; IZF, *Westfälische Freie Presse*, 30. 4. 1891; StAB, 447.
[129] StAB, 448; Brüggemeier, *Leben vor Ort*, p. 196.

a day and a month. Similar dismissals took place at many other mines. Some men were initially allowed to return to work but dismissed later for their behaviour towards non-strikers or pit officials. The sackings were not on a mass scale: the demand for coal and labour precluded that. But they were significant and emphasized the uncowed and uncompromising attitude of the employers, even after this most successful of miners' strikes. In 1912 the strikers were again treated as contract-breakers: around 156,000 men were fined the equivalent of six shifts' wages for participating in the stoppage.[130]

Contrasts

Ruhr miners showed themselves willing, on occasion, to engage the employers in the biggest strikes yet seen in Germany and in a number of less dramatic ones as well. Not surprisingly, their militancy impressed both contemporaries and historians. Rosa Luxemburg wrote with relish of the 'violent eruptions', the 'mass strikes of typical, elemental character' which in her view characterized industrial relations in the industry.[131] The strikes were rooted in the daily experience of pit work: harsh conditions, cumulative discontents, frustrated aspirations, and multiple points of friction with mine officials. Most broke out with little or no prior organization or leadership: several, indeed, were against the explicit advice of the men's ostensible leaders. Typically, they occurred during economic upswings when the points of conflict were accentuated, expectations were disappointed (including particularly the expectations of the young hauliers) and the balance of power swung more in the men's direction. Thus the major upturns were each accompanied by a growth in the general level of labour unrest: job-changing, absenteeism, small and short-lived strikes as well as the 'general' strikes of 1889, 1905, and 1912 which have attracted most historical attention. To a significant extent, therefore, the shared experience of work

[130] StAB, 455; STAM, *Oberbergamt* Dortmund 1845, *Bergrevier* Nord Bochum to *Oberbergamt*, 27. 2. 1905, *Bergrevier* Wattenscheid to *Oberbergamt*, 1. 3. 1905; IZF, *Bergarbeiter Zeitung*, 22. 4. 1905; Adelmann, *Soziale Betriebsverfassung*, p. 169.
[131] Luxemburg, *Mass Strike*, p. 56.

was able to transcend the social and cultural divisions amongst miners.

The militancy of the miners has been accentuated and highlighted by the contrast with the passivity of workers in the second major Ruhr industry, metals and engineering. Although here too conditions were frequently harsh, the grievances of individuals and of particular groups never coalesced into a broadly based strike movement. Such stoppages as did occur were generally brief and almost always limited to members of a particular trade in a single firm— usually one of the smaller companies in the engineering wing of the industry rather than the giant steel plants. Indeed, the Bochumer Verein experienced not a single strike in its steel-making and engineering works during the entire pre-war period.

A number of factors have been adduced to explain the relative quiescence of the metal-workers. The main cause, highlighted by Crew and Domansky-Davidsohn, was the divisions driven between the workers within the industry. The gulf between skilled and unskilled was deep, but was matched by further divisions—in type of work, payment systems, earnings, titles, and status—between one skill and another and even between different groups of the unskilled. Even those doing the same job might receive markedly different rewards according to their individual performance, their entitlement to seniority-based increments, and perhaps bonuses for effort, punctuality, and the like. These differences could produce marked conflicts of interest between workers within a single plant. The fragmentation of the labour force in the metal industry was illustrated by the fact that in 1910 it was possible to distinguish no fewer than 60 distinct occupational groups in the blast-furnaces and 94 in the metal-works of the Ruhr—even though in practice most were composed of little-skilled and fairly interchangeable workers. While the workers were thus divided the employers were well-organized, both through the size of the major individual firms and through their organizations. The result was a highly fragmented work-force, with individuals and groups divided from each other in their interests and aspirations and all conscious of their

dependence on their employer and of their vulnerability
to his displeasure.[132]

The metal-workers also lacked the sense of a different
and better past which helped the miners to focus and articul-
ate their discontents. This resulted from the relative newness
of the metal industry and the pace of change within it. Rapid
changes in technology and working practices accentuated
further the divisions within the work-force (as some skills
rose in importance while others declined) and inhibited the
growth of a sense of continuity, common traditions, and
shared interests amongst the workers.[133]

It was therefore much more difficult to unite metal-
workers than miners behind a common set of demands and
to express them through strike action. Only in the smaller
firms were industrial disputes more frequent but even they
tended to be rare and limited affairs, usually restricted to
a particular trade. It is likely that in this sector, where the
employers were less strong, skilled men were more able
to move from one firm to another and exploit their
market value on a craft basis. However, the results varied.
In 1897 26 moulders struck work at Munscheid in Gelsen-
kitchen: their demands were rejected, 7 were sacked and only
19 were able to return. On the other hand, when the polishers
at Mummenhof & Stegemann struck in 1900, they were able on
two occasions to win concessions from the company. A strike
in 1903 by 90 wire-drawers at the Westfälische Drahtwerke
ended with the firm recruiting and training new workers as
replacements and only taking back 14 of the original strikers.[134]

---

[132] Crew, *Town in the Ruhr*, chapter 5; E. Domansky-Davidsohn, 'Der Grossbetrieb als Organisationsproblem des Deutschen Metallarbeiter-Verbandes vor dem
Ersten Weltkrieg', in Mommsen (ed.), *Arbeiterbewegung und industrieller Wandel*,
pp. 95–116; Arbeitgeberverband für den Bezirk der nordwestlichen Gruppe des
Vereins Deutscher Eisen- und Stahlindustrieller, *25 Jahre Arbeitnordwest
1904–1929* (Berlin, 1929), pp. 13–59; D. F. Crew, 'Berufliche Lage und Protestverhalten Bochumer Bergleute und Metallarbeiter im ausgehenden 19. Jahrhundert',
in Mommsen and Borsdorf (ed.), *Glück auf, Kameraden!* pp. 71–88; D. F. Crew,
'Steel, Sabotage and Socialism; the Strike at the Dortmund "Union" Steel Works
in 1911', in Evans (ed.), *The German Working Class*, pp. 108–41.

[133] Barrington Moore, *Injustice*, pp. 272–3.

[134] STAM, RA I Nr. 74, reports March 1897; IZF, *Volksblatt*, 20, 27. 5. 1900,
7. 11. 1900; StAB, 454, *Amt* Werne to KLB, 30. 9. 1903–15. 1. 1904. Some
further strikes in the Bochum area (the list is not exhaustive) are mentioned in
Crew, *Town in the Ruhr*, p. 162.

Even in the smaller firms, therefore, strikes were risky, if not impossible, and most men steered well clear of them through-out the pre-war years.

But although clearly more militant than metal-workers, the miners' strike-proneness and above all the effectiveness of their actions should not be exaggerated. Considering the size of the industry and the potential for conflict within it, it might be argued that strikes were surprisingly infrequent. Job-changing certainly seems to have been a far more com-mon response to dissatisfaction.[135] The miners' militancy looks less impressive when compared not with the metal-workers but with workers in the building industry. The latter have received less attention, both at the time and since, but seem to have been just as industrially militant as the miners—perhaps more so in relation to their numbers—and certainly to have been more successful. Building was a largely seasonal industry in which struggles between employers and workers were regular events in the spring and summer months. The division of the industry between many employers, most of them small, the limited duration of the building season, the mobility of the workers, and their ability to find alternative work while disputes continued, all enabled them to isolate employers and force them to grant concessions. Unlike the miners, building workers operated on a craft basis—joiners, carpenters, builders etc.— gaining thereby an economic strength even in relatively small numbers and developing a sense of pride and skill in their trade over and above any more general sense of identity as building workers. Unlike many skilled metal-workers they operated in a reasonably free market, able to move between employers without incurring serious risks to their future employability and earnings. Most industrial disputes were conducted on a craft basis, with the other trades watch-ing closely and subsequently seeking to emulate for them-selves any gains made by others. In the 1900s the employers tried to protect themselves against these effective tactics by organizing and increasingly by taking the initiative them-selves. Look-outs and strikes were sometimes prolonged— that of 1905 lasted 12 weeks—but as neither side wished

[135] See chapter 1, Table 4, above.

to lose the entire season, compromise was the usual end result. The 1905 struggle ended with a regional agreement; five years later another months-long dispute was concluded with national level arbitration. The building workers rarely achieved their demands in full, but were able to obtain worthwhile concessions in the areas of wages and hours and won the principles of trade union recognition, collective bargaining, and collective agreements.[136]

Miners' strikes, in contrast, rarely achieved tangible success. Despite the fact that without mass support they were virtually doomed to defeat, on only three occasions were they supported by over half the mineworkers. Only in 1905 was strike solidarity sustained at peak levels for more than a brief period. Most strikes remained limited to one locality or to a particular category of mineworker—normally the young hauliers. The solidarity which was sometimes shown was therefore insufficiently strong, extensive, and sustained to be rendered truly effective. The mine-owners were never compelled to make significant concessions and usually demonstrated their unbowed state by sacking and fining strikers after the stoppage was over. Those gains which were made were essentially political concessions, granted by the state not wrested from the employers.

[136] STAM, RA I 74–79; StAB, 454; WWA, K2 1003; StAB, 482, *Amt* Weitmar to KLB, 8. 8. 1910. See also I. Fischer, 'Maurer- und Textilarbeiterstreiks in Augsburg 1899–1914', in Tenfelde and Volkmann (ed.), *Streik*, pp. 74–90; Saul, *Staat, Industrie, Arbeiterbewegung*, p. 61; Volkmann, 'Organisation und Konflikt', pp. 432–4.

6

Trades Unions and Politics

Strikes were not the only form of collective action. In this chapter we consider attempts to create other means of influence and power, through the organized labour movement. This took two main forms, the trade unions and a distinctively worker-orientated political movement, the social democratic party (SPD). Both need to be seen against the social and industrial background outlined in the previous chapters: for this background—the social divisions within the working class, the pressures and conflicts of the workplace, and the experience of strikes—defined both the context in which labour organizations appeared and the central issues and problems which they faced.

The crucial distinction between the labour movement and other forms of action such as job-changing or strikes was the role of organization. Organization as such was nothing new to the miners. From at least the mid-nineteenth century they had expressed their concerns in a structured manner through pit meetings, the election of delegates, regional conferences, and the like. But these were essentially limited and *ad hoc* measures, designed to meet an immediate need but no more. With the creation of unions and parties the aim went further, to provide lasting means through which workers' aspirations could be expressed and their interests defended. For some, the goal was widened to include the transformation of society itself. The establishment of these forms of organization therefore involved a longer-term view. More fundamentally, it involved an attempt to create new forms of workers' power. This was particularly important in the Ruhr where industrial militancy, unplanned and uncoordinated, was manifestly unable to win success.

Organization was an attempt to compensate for this weakness. The very word was constantly invoked. The Bochum SPD paper declared in 1901: 'Only by solid and united action, through the organization, can the worker's situation be remedied. Long live the organization.'[1] The emphasis was not accidental, nor merely the result of an unduly bureaucratic mentality. It was a reflection of the very purpose of the labour movement. Organization, it was hoped, would create a firmer and more resilient basis for unity and solidarity and establish a degree of working-class power which industrial militancy alone had proved unable to deliver. Indeed, in 1899 Otto Hue—echoing Ludwig Schröder ten years before—expressed the hope that a powerful organization would render strikes, which he described as a 'two-edged sword', completely unnecessary.[2] The stress on organization can thus be seen as a response to the persistent industrial weakness of Ruhr workers and an attempt to find a way of overcoming it.

Miners' unions

It was often the experience of strikes which provided the spur to organize. Thus the first attempts to unionize Ruhr miners—short-lived initiatives in 1868, 1872, and 1877—each followed a significant wave of strike action. These early unions sought to build on existing discontent and militancy but to give them a more lasting and well-established form. However, the aim was far from easy to achieve. Apart from the 'external' problems faced by the unions, including hostile employers and Government, violent economic cyclical fluctuations, and (particularly from the mid-1870s) a depressed labour market, they were faced from the start with the political and denominational divisions amongst the miners themselves. Despite efforts to overcome them through carefully-worded constitutions and balanced executives the divisions persisted; indeed, the last of these early union organizations was effectively doomed from

---

[1] IZF, *Volksblatt*, 22. 5. 1901. See also StAB, 481, *Amt* Weitmar to KLB, 31. 9. 1906; Tenfelde, 'Probleme der Organisation', pp. 44–7; Lützenkirchen, *Sozialdemokratische Verein*, p. 40. In 1896 Carl Legien, head of the (free) trade union Generalkommission, declared to the SPD party congress, 'The organization is everything.' J. A. Moses, *Trade Unionism in Germany from Bismarck to Hitler, 1869–1933* (London, 1982), i. 133.

[2] Fritsch, *Revisionismus*, p. 68; Siegel, *Mein Lebenskampf*, p. 64.

birth by the inability of socialists and even radical Catholics to work together.[3]

The first lasting miners' union was founded in 1889. The unplanned, poorly co-ordinated, and ultimately unsuccessful strike of that year was followed in August by the foundation of the Verband zur Wahrung und Förderung der Bergmänn-ischen Interessen im Rheinland und Westfalen. Reflecting the non-sectarian solidarity of the strike its first statute affirmed: 'Religion and politics are completely excluded in every respect.' It was supported by social democrats (notably Ludwig Schröder) and Catholics (most prominently, the editor Johannes Fussangel). Branches sprang up rapidly and by March 1890 it was estimated that in the villages around Bochum alone there were 26 branches with around 5,000 members.[4]

Unity, however, was short-lived. The union supported the strike of April 1890 but its disastrous failure led to recriminations. Fussangel blamed the 'complete defeat' on the union leadership: in a newspaper article he argued that the chief hope of success lay not in strikes but rather in gain-ing the support of the middle classes and the Government; it was precisely this which the leadership had lost through their inflexible 'demands'. Fussangel and his mainly Catholic supporters left the union and in May 1890 founded their own rival organization.[5] The division was not to be healed until after the Second World War.

The Alter Verband, as the original union was henceforth known, was not at first unduly harmed by this split. In September it was re-formed on a national basis as the Verband der deutschen Bergleute with a national paper the *Deutsche Bergarbeiterzeitung*. Membership continued to rise.[6] However, its underlying position was gradually weaken-ing. Apart from the split with the 'Christians', the repeated failure of the strikes of the early 1890s undermined its

[3] Tenfelde, *Sozialgeschichte*, pp. 437–522.

[4] StAB, 461; Koch, *Bergarbeiterbewegung*, pp. 48–9.

[5] StAB, 462, *Westfälische Volkszeitung*, 12. 4. 1890; Koch, *Bergarbeiter-bewegung*, p. 54.

[6] Membership in the Ruhr was estimated to have risen from around 27,000 in the autumn of 1890 to around 36,000 in the late 1891 and early 1892; but the figures cannot be regarded as reliable. StAB, 461.

credibility and effectiveness. Strikes were usually followed
by the sacking of local delegates. Some left the area entirely:
Johannes Mohr, an important figure in Herne and Werne,
went to the Saar; August Siegel, one of the three delegates to the Kaiser in 1889, fled in 1892 to England to escape
forthcoming court cases. Some sacked delegates—including
Lohmann in Witten and Bauer in Weitmar—stayed in their
neighbourhood as small traders or in some other job but were
inevitably more distanced from the miners.

More serious than individual harassment, however, was the
changing economic situation. 1890 saw the beginning of
a fall in industrial demand, a decline which began to affect
the Ruhr in 1891. As always, the metal industry felt the
changing economic situation first and by July 1891 men
were being laid off in the Witten engineering works. Demand
for coal began to fall off in August 1891 and by November
and December many pits were beginning to cut back on shifts
and to lay off men. In the first four months of 1892 it was
estimated that nearly four thousand miners were laid off
from Ruhr pits and that a further five thousand left voluntarily and were not replaced. At the same time wages began
to fall, from an average of 3.57 marks per shift in the third
quarter of 1891 to only 3.23 marks a year later. Demand for
coal remained weak (a factor which led to the founding of
the coal syndicate in February 1893) and the price was not
stabilized until the end of 1893. By that time average wages
had fallen to 3.15 marks, having been even lower earlier
in the year.[7]

The end of the boom marked the end not only of the
period of intense and semi-continuous industrial unrest in
the pits but also of union expansion. Between March and
June 1892 the reported membership of the Alter Verband in
the Ruhr fell from about 37,000 to under 26,000; the rival
'Christian' union also lost members and finance and had to
be dissolved in the summer of 1892. The disastrous official
strike of January 1893 accelerated the trend: Alter Verband
membership was reported to be down to around 15,000 by

[7] StAB, 463; Witten police to KLB, 24. 7. 1891; StAB, *Magistratsbericht*,
1891/2 pp. 14, 16; *Glückauf*, 20. 4. 1892; WWA, HKB *Jahresbericht*, 1893;
Koch, *Bergarbeiterbewegung*, p. 148.

the end of March 1893 and continued sharply downwards until there were fewer than four thousand in 1896.[8] By the beginning of 1894 the Langendreer branch—with a former membership of over 500—had ceased to hold meetings; at Werne the local branch had closed down; the Bärendorf branch still met, but it was always the same small group of eight to ten members; the Weitmar branch had ceased to hold meetings. In 1894 the union co-operative—which had had over thirty stores, nearly 3,000 members, and a substantial profit in the previous year—went bankrupt, leaving a heavy financial loss.[9] In Weitmar some people were said to be preserving their union membership merely in the hope of having a claim on the assets when it was eventually dissolved. The re-founding in the autumn of the 'Christian' miners' union—now named the Gewerkverein christlicher Bergarbeiter—posed a new threat. Otto Hue described the position vividly:

At the beginning of 1895 the *Alter Verband* was on the verge of death, a wreck, abandoned by the majority of those who had greeted the proud ship at its launch. It is a fact that even the least despondent leaders reckoned with a gradual dissolution. Opponents joyfully proclaimed that the hated Alter Verband was as good as gone.[10]

In February several of the union's leaders, including Ludwig Schröder who had led the 1889 delegation to the Kaiser and was its most respected figure, were arrested and sentenced to up to five years prison for perjury.[11]

This proved to be the union's low point and it was able to recover and grow during the following years. One factor was the emergence of a new generation of organisers. The most significant figure was Otto Hue, a former metal-worker who

---

[8] StAB, 461; Koch, *Bergarbeiterbewegung*, p. 55. Many members stayed on the books long after they had ceased active membership or to pay subscriptions: the collapse was almost certainly complete by 1893 and 1894; StAB, 461, *Oberbürgermeister* Bochum to RPA, 4. 7. 1891.

[9] Hue, *Neutrale oder parteiische Gewerkschaften?*, p. 75; STAM, *Oberpräsidium* 2694 Bd. 1, RPA to *Minister des Innern*, 8. 5. 1893; STAM, RA I 92, *Oberbürgermeister* Bochum to RPA, 31. 8. 1894; StAB, 461, *Aemte* Werne, Weitmar, and Langendreer to KLB, 21, 29, 30. 1. 1894.

[10] Hue, *Neutrale oder parteiische Gewerkschaften?*, p. 76.

[11] In 1911 it was finally established that they had been wrongly convicted. Hall, *Scandal, Sensation and Social Democracy*, pp. 78-83.

became editor of the union paper in 1894 at the age of 25. Hue rapidly became a prominent spokesman and policy maker: few could match his intellectual ability and energy which enabled him, in addition to his editorial duties, to travel and speak widely, to publish substantial works of history and theory, and to work actively in the SPD as well as the union movement. By 1905 the Arnsberg *Regierungs-Präsident* could comment: 'Hue is with Legien one of the most gifted union leaders and writers, both as an organizer and as an agitator. Even his political opponents in the Ruhr district have repeatedly recognized this.'[12]

Hue saw it as the function of a trade union to further the specific occupational interests of its members. It thus had fundamentally different objectives from political parties, which aimed at much broader changes. The two activities need not conflict with one another: Hue was himself an active SPD member and declared 'I am far from being merely a trade unionist [*ein Nurgewerkschaftler*]; I expect no more from the trade union than it can give. Therefore I also involve myself actively in party political propaganda.'[13] However, he argued that the particular importance of the trade unions was sometimes ignored and that many social democrats exaggerated the gains which could be expected from the ballot box alone. The power of the ruling classes was based ultimately on their economic strength and this would only be overcome when the workers created their own counter-vailing economic power:

The capitalists are today the masters of the state, because they rule over the economic power. Would I therefore be so terribly wrong if I maintained that if the Moloch is to be struck to its heart this will only happen when the economic power of Capital is opposed with that of the Proletariat—the trade union organization? [14]

He rejected the argument of some socialists that the trade unions could achieve nothing and that advance could only come from political action stimulated by the progressive impoverishment of the workers.

Hue thus maintained the importance and independent

---

[12] StAB, 480, RPA to *Minister des Innern*, 22. 12. 1905.
[13] Hue, *Neutrale oder parteiische Gewerkschaften?*, p. 142.
[14] ibid., p. 148.

validity of the trade unions. By joining the organization *en masse* and by following collective decisions the workers could create a weapon capable of confronting the employers and wresting improvements from them. To achieve this, however, unity was essential. A trade union could not be strong until it encompassed all, or at least the great majority, of the relevant workers. The search for unity was thus the major problem faced by a trade union, particularly in a district with such deep divisions as the Ruhr. Hue argued that the union must therefore avoid any involvement with divisive questions such as religion and politics: strict political and denominational neutrality was the only basis on which effective organizational solidarity could be built.

He also argued that hard-won organizational advance should not be jeopardized by premature and ill-judged industrial conflict. The years from 1889 to 1893 had shown that although unions had emerged in the aftermath of strikes a policy based simply on industrial militancy could neither succeed nor sustain the union in the face of disappointed hopes and expectations. The potential benefits of organization would not be realized until most miners were members and until then partial strikes, doomed to defeat, would only set back what was already achieved. In 1897 a miners' meeting addressed by Hue and Heinrich Möller, the Alter Verband chairman, decided not to strike since 'the only effect would be to harm the organization which is in the process of expansion'.[15] In 1903, when strike talk was again in the air, Hue told a mass meeting in Essen:

I am in principle no opponent of strikes. The strike is a weapon without which an organization cannot succeed. Even the German Printers' Union, which has the best reputation, could do no other than turn to the strike and, if it was necessary, set to with a strong hand if agreement could not be reached through peaceful means. . . . But how is it today with [our] organization? Consider that of the 60,000 union members around 40–42,000 live in the Ruhr; but there are 250,000 miners living here, of whom over 180,000 work underground. Of these some 40,000 belong to the union, or less than 25 per cent! From this the question arises, are these 25 per cent able to ignore the 75 per cent who are unorganized? That is impossible. The union leaders

[15] StAB, 463, *Polizei Bochum* to KLB, 28. 3. 1897.

are therefore not at present in a position to speak of strikes. We have the duty of warning against ill-considered steps.[16]

The advent of a new generation of leaders with a more cautious approach to strike action coincided with an improved economic situation. Membership recovered and started to grow rapidly, particularly between 1900 and 1905 when it rose from 13,000 to nearly 79,000. The 1905 strike led to a considerable influx of members, despite the union's original opposition to the stoppage. But in the next few years the union failed to grow and after 1910 started actually to decline. Table 11 shows that taken in relation to the total number of mineworkers in the Ruhr 1905 marked a membership peak which was never repeated. Although the Alter Verband managed to keep over a fifth of Ruhr miners in its ranks for some years thereafter, from 1912—the year of its major and disastrous strike initiative—even this level was not maintaned. The union thus suffered a double failure: in the first place it never managed, or even came near, to uniting the majority of miners behind it; secondly, what success it had achieved by 1905 was gradually eroded thereafter. If the near collapse of the mid-1890s was overcome, the broader hopes of the new leaders remained far from realization.

There were many reasons why the Alter Verband did not achieve more success. One important factor was the continued rivalry between miners of different denominational, political, and national outlooks. Despite the claims of Hue and others that the union was strictly non-political, there was much evidence to support the claims of opponents that it was a predominantly social democratic organization. Many of the union's leaders were avowed social democrats. Duing the 1903 election the executive argued that while, in their union capacity, they did not support any one party, union members were bound to consider the parties' views on issues crucial to the union, particularly the franchise,

---

[16] Fritsch, *Revisionismus*, pp. 66-7. See also StAB, 479, *Amt* Bochum II to KLB, 5. 11. 1899. On the general stress on organization and discipline within the German trade union movement following defeats in the early 1890s see Ritter and Tenfelde, 'Durchbruch der Freien Gewerkschaften', pp. 88 ff.

TABLE 11

Alter Verband membership in the Ruhr, 1894–1913[a]

Year	Alter Verband members	Mineworkers in Ruhr	Alter Verband members as per cent of Ruhr mineworkers
1894	5,158	152,650	3.4
1895	4,153	154,702	2.7
1896	3,938	161,870	2.4
1897	12,149	176,102	6.9
1898	17,974	191,847	9.4
1899	18,606	205,106	9.1
1900	12,945	226,902	5.7
1901	23,044	243,926	9.4
1902	32,832	243,963	13.5
1903	48,132	255,992	18.8
1904	56,153	270,259	20.8
1905	78,862	267,798	29.4
1906	78,879	278,719	28.3
1907	77,713	303,089	25.6
1908	80,143	334,733	23.9
1909	76,869	340,567	22.6
1910	76,418 (80,378)	345,136	22.7 (23.3)
1911	75,025	352,555	21.3
1912	69,648	393,879	17.7
1913	62,487	394,569	15.8

[a]Fritsch, *Revisionismus*, p. 111; Klessmann, 'Klassensolidarität', p. 154; Koch, *Bergarbeiterbewegung*, p. 139; Hue, *Bergarbeiter* ii. 616; StAB, 480, RPA to *Minister des Innern*, 22. 12. 1905. Fritsch and Klessmann quote differing figures for 1910. A number of historians have exaggerated the level of unionization by comparing national union membership figures with the number of miners in the Ruhr: see Kirchhoff, *Sozialpolitik*, p. 168; W. Köllmann, 'Die Geschichte der Bergarbeiterschaft', in W. Först (ed.), *Ruhrgebiet und Neues Land* (Köln, 1968), p. 92; Gladen, 'Streiks', p. 141; Spencer, 'Employer Response to Unionism', p. 399; Barrington Moore, *Injustice*, p. 255; Adelmann, *Soziale Betriebsverfassung*, p. 118.

freedom of assembly and association, and the tariffs. Neither the conservative parties nor the Centre could measure up to what was required. Without mentioning the party by name, the clear inference was that union members should vote for the SPD. On the eve of the poll the *Bergarbeiterzeitung* claimed that only the SPD was campaigning on a programme which accorded with the workers' and the union's interests.

A Gelsenkirchen police officer probably only partially exaggerated when he commented afterwards:

All the union's officers, all the *Bergarbeiterzeitung*'s distributors, all the union's local chairmen, secretaries, and treasurers are [SPD] agitators. ... Never before has the social democratic character of the union and the social democratic tendencies of its main work been so clearly revealed as in this year's *Reichstag* election.[17]

This was not an isolated occurrence. In 1905 the union declared that 'every miner must be just as energetically active in politics as in the union. Only trade union and political organization and agitation can free the working class from the degrading chains of capitalist exploitation.'[18] In 1907 *Bergarbeiterzeitung* denounced Germany's colonies and taxes: 'Such a taxation system cries to heaven. This system is maintained with the support of all parties with the single exception of the social democrats!'[19] Prominent union leaders stood as SPD candidates in elections throughout this period: Peter Recktenwald, a union delegate from Hordel in 1890, was 'known as a notorious agitator for the social democratic party'; the chairman of the Laer branch in the same year, a miner named Richter, declared in a public meeting that he was a social democrat.[20] Ludwig Schröder stood as SPD *Reichstag* candidate in Essen in 1893 and 1898. Johann Meyer, another founder member and the union's first treasurer, stood in Recklinghausen. Heinrich Möller, the union's chairman in the later 1890s, and his successor Hermann Sachse were both SPD *Reichstag* deputies, although not for Ruhr constituencies. Otto Hue was SPD *Reichstag* deputy for Bochum from 1903 to 1912. Friedrich Husemann, an important figure in the Bochum area (he was the chief union negotiator with the *Bruchstrasse* men prior to the 1905 strike) stood as SPD candidate in Bochum for the Prussian *Landtag* in 1908 and for the *Reichstag* seat of Hamm-Soest in 1912. Franz Pokorny, the leading Alter Verband figure in Gelsenkirchen, was SPD candidate in Recklinghausen in 1912. The degree of

[17] STAM, RA I 96, *Polizei* Gelsenkirchen to RPA, 17. 8. 1903; IZF, *Deutsche Bergarbeiterzeitung* 25. 5. 1903, 13. 6. 1903.
[18] StAB, 480, RPA to *Minister des Innern*, 22. 12. 1905.
[19] IZF, *Deutsche Bergarbeiterzeitung*, 5. 1. 1907; ibid., 12. 1. 1907.
[20] StAB, 462, *Amt* Bochum I to KLB, 22. 9. 1890; *Polizei* Laer to KLB, 10. 2. 1890.

overlap between union and party made claims of political neutrality hard to justify before a sometimes sceptical public.

The widespread suspicion of social democracy, frequently fostered by religious organizations, therefore rubbed off onto the Alter Verband. Social democrats were commonly held to be hostile towards religion, property, the state, and even the family, and for many devout or patriotic working-class people there could be no question of joining an organization which was clearly identified with them. Others felt that social democratic influence made the union too militant and liable to seek confrontation for political ends instead of giving top priority to the improvement of miners' conditions: such critics could point to the union's support for the disastrous strikes of the early 1890s and 1912.

That hostility to social democracy rather than indifference to trade unionism itself was the stumbling-block for many was demonstrated by the growth of the rival 'Christian' Gewerkverein. As we have seen, this union carried forward a long tradition in the Ruhr of radical Catholic activism in support of miners' interests. The union was founded in 1894 and seems to have rivalled the Alter Verband in terms of membership in the Ruhr until the mid-1900s. By 1910, however, the Gewerkverein could claim only around 33,000 Ruhr members compared to over 80,000 in the Alter Verband: two years later the gap had narrowed again, with the former rising to around 40,000 members in the district while the latter had declined to under 70,000.[21] Although in second place the Gewerkverein thus established itself as an important and viable organization. Generally it adopted a less militant posture than its larger rival, placing greater stress on the need for good relations between employers and workers and on the importance of legislative action as the means to improve workers' conditions. Nevertheless these sentiments aroused no reciprocal response on the side of the employers and the

[21] Klessmann, 'Klassensolidarität', p. 154; Schneider, *Die Christlichen Gewerkschaften*, p. 65. Comprehensive membership figures for the Gewerkverein in the Ruhr do not appear to exist and some of the available figures are inconsistent. See, for example, the report of the union's 1905 congress in STAM, RA I 82, *Gelsenkirchener Zeitung*, 26. 6. 1905.

Gewerkverein proved willing to voice miners' demands and to support them if necessary in strike action. The Arnsberg *Regierungs-Präsident* even commented in 1900 that the Gewerkverein 'scarcely knows how to hide its socialist character'.[22] Its appeal was thus based in part on its credentials as a true miners' union. In addition, however, it distinguished itself sharply from the Alter Verband. Characteristic of the tone of the debate was an appeal by the Christian unions to Protestant workers in 1907:

You have recognized the need for organization! . . . Which organization must you, male and female workers, now join? There is no question for you, as Protestant and patriotic workers, of the free (social democratic) unions. You could not possibly belong to a union which cavalierly hurls your highest ideals in the dust, which instead of pursuing practical work for today pursues frivolous class struggle and revolutionary games. Indeed, the free (social democratic) unions represent least of all the trade union ideal which can be contemplated by sensible-minded workers. The activities of the social democratic (free) unions will always be directed by the 'highest social democratic party clique'. First in every action come the fantasy plans of the social democrats, only in second place the welfare of the workers! . . . The free trade unions are the mortal enemies of Christianity and of every national sentiment. They are based on the materialist philosphy and have thereby created an unbridgeable gulf between themselves and the Christian and nationally-minded workers.[23]

Although the split between the Alter Verband and the Gewerkverein was the most fundamental division within the union movement, it was not the only one. The liberal Hirsch-Duncker union movement had established a miners' section in 1883 and this union maintained a small presence in the Ruhr: by 1912 there were around 2,000 members in the district.[24] Although politically moderate—the Hirsch-Duncker unions were modelled on the supposedly

---

[22] StAB, 479, RPA to *Minister des Innern*, 24. 11. 1900; Schneider, *Die Christlichen Gewerkschaften*, p. 68. For the union's preference for legal rather than strike action, see StAB, 463, *Amt* Bochum II to KLB, 29. 3. 1897; ibid. *Amt* Weitmar to KLB, 30. 3. 1897.

[23] STAM, RA I 99, *Unsere Stellung zur Gewerkschaftsfrage!? Ein offenes und ernstgemeintes Wort an die evangelische und nationale Arbeiterschaft.*

[24] Koch, *Bergarbeiterbewegung*, p. 122; Fritsch, *Revisionismus*, p. 109; Adelmann, *Soziale Betriebsverfassung*, p. 115; J. Tampke, *The Ruhr and Revolution. The Revolutionary Movement in the Rhenish-Westphalian Region 1912-1919* (London, 1979), p. 171.

non-political British trade unions—this union was willing to
support militant action and joined in both the 1905 and
1912 strikes. More important, however, was the creation
in 1902 of a separate union for Poles. This reflected not
just the growing sense of national identity amongst Poles in
the Ruhr but also specific discontent with the 'German'
unions. Both of the main unions had Polish members in the
1890s, and although reliable figures are not available it is
likely that most joined the Gewerkverein. Neither union,
however, seems to have taken sufficiently seriously the
special concerns of Polish miners. The Alter Verband had
a particularly difficult task since its socialist reputation
formed a barrier to many of the strongly Catholic Poles.
The union did, however, launch a Polish-language paper in
1897. The Gewerkverein, by contrast, was more complacent
and did not launch an equivalent paper until 1903.

The rapid influx of Polish immigrants and the growth of
nationalist sentiment among them provided the backdrop
to the growing tension between German and Polish trade
unionists. Many Germans argued that mass immigration
caused lower wages and higher accident rates. Particular
resentment was caused by claims that newcomers were put
onto easy coal-faces offering high earnings while the more
experienced natives were given the more difficult seams
where the scope for high output and wages was low. In 1898
the Gewerkverein created much bitterness when it con-
temptuously rejected Polish calls for increased representation
in the *Knappschaft* elections and for a printed Polish transla-
tion of *Knappschaft* regulations. Both unions lost more
support in 1899: at the start of the year they welcomed as
a useful safety measure a police regulation which banned
anyone who could not understand German orders from
working underground and anyone unable to read and speak
German from promotion to supervisory functions; most
Poles, however, saw the measure as a piece of overt discrimination. Shortly after, relations became even more
strained during the 'Polish' strike in Herne and the violent
incidents which accompanied it. Despite union attempts to
play down the ethnic factor in the dispute and to promote
a peaceful resolution, many Poles felt betrayed and isolated

while the German press was full of criticism of the 'uncivilized' Poles. The Polish nationalist paper *Wiarus Polski* denounced the 'socialist' Alter Verband and claimed that socialists 'are enemies of the Polish workers and would be happy if the Poles were prevented from working'.[25]

The Zjednoczenie Zawodowe Polskie (ZZP), as the Polish union was called, was finally launched in 1902 as a clearly nationalist organization, stressing its national character as much as its specific trade union functions. Although dominated by miners membership was open to any Pole. Its constitution reflected that of the Gewerkverein, explicitly stressing the importance of 'Christian teaching' and the need to avoid 'any agitation in the spirit of social democracy'. Nevertheless, the union did not shrink from participation in the 1905 strike and in later years proved willing to co-operate with the Alter Verband, even in the 1912 strike which the Gewerkverein opposed. Its combination of overt national appeal and a willingness to adopt a forceful industrial line won it substantial backing amongst the Poles: although both of the main unions retained a minority of Polish members, by 1912 over 30,000 Ruhr miners were members of the ZZP compared to around 40,000 in the Gewerkverein and approaching 70,000 in the Alter Verband.[26] The Poles had thus emerged as a distinct but powerful third force.

The hope of achieving a non-political and non-denominational trade union in which miners of all background could unite to pursue their common interests thus remained unrealized. Instead, four separate unions appeared, each reflecting a distinct political standpoint. This did not necessarily mean that united trade union action was impossible. On occasion—for example in the *Knappschaft* elections of 1899 and 1900—the Alter Verband and the Gewerkverein

[25] Klessmann, 'Klassensolidarität', p. 160.

[26] Klessmann, *Polnische Bergarbeiter*, pp. 110–25; Klessmann, 'Klassensolidarität', p. 154; R. C. Murphy, 'Polnische Bergarbeiter im Ruhrgebiet: Das Beispiel Bottrop', in Mommsen and Borsdorf (ed.) *Glück auf. Kameraden!*, pp. 89–108. The ZZP's success is illustrated by the almost incredible admission by the Gewerkverein in 1906 that they had very few Polish-speaking members in Herne and Castrop and no one capable of public speaking in Polish; hence they were unable to mount any effective agitation amongst the large numbers of Poles there. STAM, RA I 83, *Geschäftsbericht des Vorstandes des Gewerkvereins christlicher Bergarbeiter*, 1905/6, p. 70.

were able to agree on joint action. But August Brust, the first chairman of the Gewerkverein, was unwilling to maintain this policy so that until 1905 co-operation between the two main unions was the exception rather than the norm. In 1905 all four unions joined together to form a joint committee— the 'Commission of Seven'—to direct the strike which had broken out in the first place against their wishes. The strike and its aftermath saw a considerable growth in union membership and a return to inter-union rivalry. Nevertheless, the Commission continued in existence for some years. The replacement of Brust as chairman of the Gewerkverein in 1904 had made co-operation somewhat easier. However, the proposal from the Alter Verband in 1910 that the four unions pursue a joint wage claim—an initiative which eventually led to the 1912 strike—was rejected by the Gewerkverein: the eventual strike was supported by the 'Dreibund' of Alter Verband, ZZP, and Hirsch-Duncker but was bitterly opposed by the Gewerkverein. Although the strike failure was followed by some calls for the creation of a single united miners' union, the bitterness of the strike effectively removed any possibility of serious co-operation in the remaining two years before the outbreak of war.

Perhaps more serious than the divisions between organizations was the fact that most miners were not members of any union. The available figures do not permit precise estimates of the level of unionization in the Ruhr. However, from the evidence which is available it appears that combined union membership in 1902 was around 66,000—or 27 per cent of Ruhr miners; in 1910 the figure stood at around 140,000 or 41 per cent and in 1912 at 142,000 or 36 per cent. Amongst underground miners the proportion was higher but even here the level of unionization seems never to have stood at much above half.[27]

This naturally weakened the unions' authority. It would be misleading, however, to conclude that the miners were divided into two permanent camps of members and non-members with the latter implacably hostile to union appeals and aspirations. The membership figures concealed a high level of turnover. In Linden the free union had 5,750 members

[27] See Table 11 above; Hue, *Bergarbeiter* ii. 720; BA, 18/9.

in 1908 and 5,960 two years later; but this apparent stability concealed a turnover of 1,900 members—around a third— over the same period. The district organizers described some of the reasons:

This turnover takes place mainly at Stinnes' mines. The reason lies clearly in the fact that at these pits there is no payment for the secondary jobs: repair and maintenance work is included in the piece-rates. When therefore a *Kameradschaft* sees that a seam is bad and that they can earn nothing from it they naturally look for other work. The turnover is worst in the housing colony of the *Friedlicher Nachbar* pit. Our local officials can run a house-to-house agitation each month and they will gain from five to twenty new members each time; but when they return a fortnight later to collect the subscriptions, they only find half the new members; the others are already gone.[28]

The Gewerkverein faced the same problems:

Our successes were undermined by the frequent loss of members as a result of the high turnover of jobs and homes. Transferring members very often fail to register properly, so that the delivery of the union's paper and the collection of contributions are interrupted. In this way we lose many members.[29]

The situation was thus volatile, with many miners passing through unions but failing to maintain a lasting involvement. Such occasional support was undependable and reduced the scope for effective control by the unions. Hue described the 'colossal membership turnover'—which was a problem faced by many German unions—as 'the greatest evil in a trade union life' and considered that ex-members generally had a discouraging effect on other miners.[30] The problem reflected the fact that many Ruhr workers saw their stay as temporary, even short-term: they aimed to earn as much as possible as

[28] IGBE, AI 20, Verband der Bergarbeiter Deutschlands, *Jahresbericht*, 1909/10, p. 162; Lucas, *Arbeiterradikalismus*, pp. 250–1.

[29] IGBE, AI 97, *Geschäftsbericht des Vorstandes des Gewerkvereins christlicher Bergarbeiter*, 1909/10, p. 130.

[30] IZF, *Deutsche Berg- und Hüttenarbeiter Zeitung*, 28. 5. 1898; StAB, 482, KLB to RPA, 27. 8. 1912; Crew, *Town in the Ruhr*, p. 217. On the importance of membership instability to the unions generally and its contribution to the stress on strong organization and central leadership see K. Schönhoven, *Expansion und Konzentration. Studien zur Entwicklung der Freien Gewerkschaften im Wilhelminischen Deutschland* (Stuttgart, 1980), pp. 150 ff; Langewiesche, 'Wanderungsbewegungen', pp. 38–40; Niethammer and Brüggemeier, 'Wie wohnten Arbeiter im Kaiserreich?', p. 134.

quickly as possible and then to move on. If the pay or conditions at one particular pit were unattractive, the simplest
remedy was to move elsewhere. Trade unions had relatively
little to offer such men or to hold their loyalty if they did
once join. Instead, trade unionism implied a financial sacrifice, the possibility of discrimination by employers, and
a psychological longer-term commitment to and identification with the industry, the area, and other workers.[31]

The main practical benefit of union membership was the
prospect of financial help in the event of sickness, unemployment, strike, or death. Benefits were generally payable only
after an initial period and varied according to the length of
membership. Union members were also entitled to legal
support in certain circumstances. The importance of such
benefits was shown in 1905 when hope of strike pay was an
important factor behind the sudden growth in union
membership. However, improved benefits and larger numbers
of potential recipients meant that dues had to be raised substantially and this in turn led to a drop in recruitment.

In normal times local union activities seem to have focused
on the regular union meetings, the newspaper, and the continuing effort to win new members. Branch meetings were
generally held monthly. It was sometimes difficult to find
a suitable local room, since pressure was put on landlords to
refuse facilities. Meetings seem often to have been dull and
poorly attended. One Witten miner complained in 1899:

The union's life suffers from the fact that as a rule there is little
more at the members' meetings than the collection of dues. At the
most some little question will now and then be dealt with. There
are very seldom talks which would contribute to the illumination
and further education of our colleagues. In a word, the proper spirit
is missing from the meetings. The result is that most of the members
stay away from the meetings and the union movement suffers greatly as
a result.[32]

---

[31] Schönhoven, *Expansion und Konzentration*, p. 88. Women sometimes
sought to discourage their husbands from union membership. Fischer-Eckert,
Lage der Frauen, pp. 44-5, 83-5, 134; for American experience of first-generation
suspicion of trade unionism see Gutman, *Work, Culture and Society*, pp. 29-32.

[32] IZF, *Volksblatt*, 19. 5. 1899; IGBE, AI 146, *Bergarbeiter! Aufgewacht
und erkennet eure Macht!*, 1911; Hue, *Bergarbeiter* ii. 612-16; Pieper, *Lage
der Bergarbeiter*, p. 190.

The most important means of communication to members was the weekly newspaper, and maintaining its distribution was one of the prime local activities. In addition, there were occasional house-to-house leafletting campaigns to recruit new members. To organize the work at local level there was a branch structure: by 1910 the Alter Verband envisaged six local office-holders whose main job, apart from maintaining local agitation and winning new members, was to be available to the members and maintain communications between them and the union's executive. Filling these posts was sometimes difficult, particularly when activists were sacked in the aftermath of strikes. In 1906 in the Recklinghausen area local branch officials were having to deliver the union paper themselves. Occasional social events were arranged for union members and their families. Some Gewerkverein branches organized evening classes and discussions and formed their own libraries. Alter Verband members, like other 'free' trade unionists, were entitled to use the Bochum Trades Council library and other services. The Bochum Alter Verband branch held well-attended festivities for members in the Querenburg woods in 1909 and in the town itself in 1910. Nevertheless, the union felt obliged sternly to remind members that 'the union is certainly no social club and social events should not take place too often'.[33]

The unions were able to achieve some success in the elections for miners' representatives on various official industry organizations. Elections took place for seats on the *Knappschaft* and (from 1894) the *Gewerbegericht* —a conciliation service established by the Government in the aftermath of the 1889 strike. After 1905 elected workers' committees with restricted powers were set up at each mine. Following the *Radbod* disaster elected safety-officers were introduced. Apart from the long-established *Knappschaft* the very existence of these posts and the platforms which they could offer to the unions was due to Government

---

[33] IGBE, AI 140, *Instruktion*, 1910; IGBE, AI 18 and 20, Verband der Bergarbeiter Deutschlands, *Jahresberichte*, 1905/6, p. 108, 1909/10, p. 166; STAM, RA I 96, *Polizei-Commissar* Bochum to RPA, 10. 10. 1904.

intervention and legislation, usually against the wishes of the employers. Union candidates generally did well in elections. In *Gewerbegericht* elections in 1906 the union candidates won almost 27,000 votes compared with 300 for employers' candidates; in 1910, 299 *Knappschaft* mandates were won by Alter Verband candidates, 83 by the Gewerkverein, 29 by the ZZP, 3 by the Hirsch-Dunker union and only four by non-unionists; in elections for safety-officers in the same year the Alter Verband candidates won 806 out of 935 posts and only 17 went to non-unionists; in 1912, despite the strike defeat and the growth of the 'yellow' company unions, the Alter Verband won over half of the 1,003 safety-officer posts while yellow unionists won 33 and non-unionists 96 posts; in elections in the same year to the workers' committees only 89 out of 569 seats failed to go to the three leading unions.[34]

These elections offered the unions a focus for activity and their success gave them a certain legitimacy as spokesmen for the miners. But the practical effect was limited: none of these posts were of more than marginal importance, particularly on the central issues of wages, hours of work, and the general conditions of employment, and winning them constituted no real challenge to the power of the employers. The elections seem generally to have aroused relatively modest interest: in elections for safety-officers in 1910 around 45 per cent of those entitled to vote did so and two years later the turnout fell to around 40 per cent.

In the main struggle with the employers, however, the unions had no comparable success. Early attempts by strike delegates in 1889 and the early 1890s to win recognition as miners' spokesmen were unsuccessful and the employers refused to recognize or negotiate with the unions—including the non-socialist unions—right up to the military and

---

[34] IGBE, AI 20, Verband der Bergarbeiter Deutschlands, *Jahresbericht*, 1909/10, p. 165; STAM, *Oberpräsidium* 2694 Bd. 2, RPA to *Minister des Innern*, 16. 10. 1910; STAM, RA I 98, *Polizei Commissar* Bochum to RPA, 12. 11. 1906; STAM, *Oberbergamt* Dortmund 1852, 'Zusammenfassung der . . . Neuwahlen von Sicherheitsmännern und Ausschussmitgliedern August 1912'; Koch, *Bergarbeiterbewegung*, p. 128; Hue, *Bergarbeiter* ii. 650; Klessmann, *Polnische Bergarbeiter*, p. 284. Some of the figures quoted by Klessmann differ slightly from those quoted but the discrepancies are minor.

political collapse of 1918. Instead, they did their best to hinder union activities. Attempts were made to exclude union literature and activities from company property, including housing colonies. Prominent unionists were subject to harassment and even the sack. Friedrich Ebbert, a Catholic and Alter Verband activist in Laer, claimed in 1901 that when he became a delegate at *Dannenbaum I* he had been placed under constant pressure by the management until eventually he left. At his new pit, *Prinz von Preussen*, he was given an extremely poor coal-face—so that again he left the mine. After a lengthy period of unemployment he found work at *Caroline* and remained undisturbed until he made a speech which was seen as partly responsible for some unrest at the mine: he was promptly sacked. He could now find no job in Laer and intended to move to seek work elsewhere. In 1905 August Schmidt, at the time Alter Verband branch chairman at the *Borussia* pit, was sacked for arranging a public meeting at which Otto Hue had called for the prosecution of the mine management following an accident in which 39 miners died.[35]

The final years before the war saw an important new initiative by Ruhr employers designed to strengthen company loyalty and to weaken the appeal of the trade unions: the creation of so-called 'yellow' unions. These were company organizations, generally founded on the initiative of the employer and given substantial financial support by the company. They were generally pledged to foster good industrial relations and to oppose other trade unions. They offered tangible benefits in the form of sickness and similar insurance, social events, and the opportunity—which it was claimed that many miners valued—to mix socially on occasion with the company's senior managers and employers. The movement was originated in the Ruhr by Krupp and began to spread to the mining industry on a significant scale in the aftermath of the 1912 strike. From 7 unions and 131 members in the industry in 1911 the movement grew to 93 unions and over 21,000 members (or around 5 per cent of Ruhr mineworkers) in early 1914. The independent trade

[35] StAB, 463, *Amt* Bochum II to KLB, 18. 8. 1901; Schmidt, *Lang war der Weg*, p. 47; Pieper, *Lage der Bergarbeiter*, p. 205.

unions had to view this growth with concern. In some ways it was the Gewerkverein and the confessional workers' clubs which were most directly threatened since their political outlook was closer to that of the yellow unions and their members were more likely to be drawn away. But the yellow unions formed a direct threat to the very principles of independent trade unionism and were bitterly opposed by all the existing unions. In 1914 the SPD commented:

Although hitherto the foundries and the factories formed the successful recruiting ground for the yellow unions, we should not ignore the fact that the yellow movement is also constantly gaining ground amongst the miners. The yellow movement is above all a serious danger to the further development of the trade union and political movement in the industrial area of the Rhineland and Westphalia where such great masses of uncommitted poeple are gathered together. The employers encourage this movement with every conceivable means in order to make use of it as a defence force in economic and political struggles.[36]

Ironically, one effect of the growth of the yellow unions was to provide the independent unions with an issue on which they could unite; but this was not to become an important factor until the later years of the war.

The unions did not disguise their failure to form an effective counterweight to the power of the employers. In 1911 the Alter Verband contrasted the organizational strength of the employers with the weak and divided miners:

'Unity is strength!' Things would stand well with the German miners if they had understood the meaning of this inscription half as well as the German mine-owners. The great power which is bestowed on the capitalists simply through their property does not satisfy the mine-owners. They want more, they want to be the unrestrained rulers over all with whom they come into contact. Therefore they created *Zechenverbände* and *Bergbauvereine* to crush the workers, established syndicates and marketing associations to abuse the consuming masses. Total freedom to exploit, maintenance of the power of mining capital over the mineworkers, suppression of wages, and higher prices for their products—that is the programme of the employers' associations in the mining industry. And unfortunately it must be conceded that in recent

---

[36] IZF, *Arbeiter Zeitung*, 10, 11. 7. 1914; K. J. Mattheier, 'Werkvereine und wirtschaftsfriedlich-nationale (gelbe) Arbeiterbewegung im Ruhrgebiet', in Reulecke (ed.), *Arbeiterbewegung*, pp. 173–204; Koch, *Bergarbeiterbewegung*, pp. 117–18; Saul, *Staat, Industrie, Arbeiterbewegung*, pp. 168–86.

years the mine-owners have achieved great success through their organizations.[37]

The unions, in contrast, had achieved little. Heinrich Imbusch of the Gewerkverein claimed that the unions had had a positive impact on the level of wages but did not offer supporting evidence; otherwise he had to concede that because so many miners stood outside their ranks the unions lacked the strength necessary for success.[38] In 1914, in a leaflet circulated to Bochum members, the Alter Verband conceded their weakness on the central issues of pay and hours:

On matters of pay the owners play fast and loose with the miners. They pinch and press down wages as they will. If the economic situation is good they let wages rise, but by so little and so slowly that the increase is barely noticeable. But when difficulties, contraction of demand, and similar problems arise—then what was granted in spoonfuls is quickly taken away again with shovels. Nor is it much different with the hours of work! What happened to the eight-hour shift in the last two years? If all the overtime shifts were taken into account, many men would be seen to have been working, a 12- to 15-hour shift . . .[39]

This situation contrasted sharply, it was claimed, with that in building, timber, transport, and other industries where the employers had reached agreements with the unions. It certainly provided a sorry epitaph to almost twenty-five years of continuous union activity in the Ruhr coal industry.

Might the unions, and the Alter Verband in particular, have achieved greater success with a different policy? Would a less cautious, less 'bureaucratic' approach to industrial relations have encouraged activity and commitment and contributed to a greater awareness amongst the miners of the need for unity and collective solidarity in the face of the employers? There was certainly something mechanistic and rigid in the union's persistent stress on the need to secure organizational solidarity before industrial action should be attempted. On several occasions miners showed themselves more willing to strike than the union leaders; and 1889 and 1905 in particular showed that the relationship between industrial action and

[37] IGBE, AI 21, Verband der Bergarbeiter Deutschlands, *Jahresbericht*, 1911/12.   [38] Imbusch, *Arbeitsverhältnis* p. 100.

[39] STAM, RA I 1476, *Verband der Bergarbeiter Deutschlands Bezirkskommission an die Mitglieder im Bezirk Bochum 1914*; Lucas, *Arbeiterradikalismus*, p. 251.

organizational growth could be more dynamic, with the experience of industrial struggle itself producing a stronger and more united trade union movement. Although the unions' caution cannot very usefully be attributed to 'bureaucracy'—since the policy was established well before any significant bureaucracy existed—there was at times a significant difference in perception between the leadership and many of the miners.[40] But we cannot conclude from this that a different approach would have been more successful. The miners' strike militancy, however strong at moments like 1889 and 1905, was essentially sporadic and unpredictable. In the pre-war years it never developed into a sustained critique of the leadership's policies. Even the 1889 and 1905 strikes failed to achieve victories for the miners and the repeated strikes of the early 1890s ended in defeats, the sacking of activists, the collapse of one union, and the near-destruction of the other. It was in response to this experience above all else that the more cautious approach of subsequent years evolved. The merits of such a policy seemed to be confirmed in 1912 by the collapse of the one major strike positively encouraged by the Alter Verband and two of the other three unions. If Hue and other union leaders were open to the accusation of placing undue weight on the simple fact of organization, critics who wanted a more militant policy overlooked the real dangers of defeat, increased suffering for individual miners and perhaps even the collapse of the entire movement.

Politics

The trade unions represented one attempt to secure, through organization, advances for the miners collectively which as individuals they were too weak to achieve. But even

[40] Groh has criticized the Alter Verband's 'fundamentally hesitant and passive policy of wait and see'. Fritsch has argued that the union's 'revisionism' was due to bureaucracy. However, the main lines of union policy were established during the 1890s; in 1898 the union employed only four office staff and even in 1914 the number of staff at head-office reached only 19 while the total number of 'officials' stood at 94—a fairly normal number in relation to the size of the union. Groh, 'Intensification of work', p. 378; Fritsch, *Revisionismus*, pp. 19–20; IGBE, AI 10 and 22, Verband der Bergarbeiter Deutschlands, *Jahresberichte*, 1897/8 and 1913/14; Schönhoven, *Expansion und Konzentration*, p. 229. See also Guttsman, *German Social Democratic Party*, chapter 6.

those who laid greatest stress on the importance of a strong, independent, and politically neutral trade union movement recognized the need for a parallel political struggle. Thus it was Otto Hue who, in the aftermath of the 1905 strike, proposed a motion to the Alter Verband's conference calling for more active political agitation:

The general meeting also calls on the comrades to draw the lesson from the general strike that trade unionism alone [*eine Nur-gewerkschaft-lerei*] is wrong and that therefore every miner must be just as active in party politics as in the trade union. Only trade union and political organization and agitation can free the workers from the degrading chains of capitalist exploitation.[41]

The party which claimed above all to speak for workers *qua* workers and to represent their political interests was the SPD. As a leaflet circulated in Bochum in 1901 put it, this was the only party:

. . . which at all times stands guard, unafraid, for the rights and welfare of the people. . . . She alone represents the interests of the working people; she alone seeks to create a society in which there are no more masters and servants, no class domination, no exploitation, no obscurantism, no bloody horrors of war.[42]

Yet despite these claims, despite the active support of many leading Alter Verband figures, despite even the comment of Friedrich Engels that the miners belonged 'potentially and necessarily' to social democracy, the SPD faced an uphill struggle in the Ruhr.[43] The forces against it were strong and well entrenched. The National Liberal party (and its predecessors) had the support of most employers and of the Protestant denominational organizations; political Catholicism, on the other hand, was expressed through the Centre party. These parties, both bitterly opposed to social democracy, dominated politics in the eastern Ruhr throughout the 1870s and 1880s. Social democracy, by contrast, was weak: socialist candidates stood in *Reichstag* elections in Bochum in 1874, 1877, and 1878, but won only between one and five per cent of the poll.[44]

---

[41] StAB, 480, RPA to *Minister des Innern*, 22. 12. 1905.

[42] StAB, 479, *Männer und Frauen des Arbeitenden Volkes!* (1901).

[43] Quoted in Wehler, 'Polen im Ruhrgebiet', p. 451.

[44] Nettmann, *Witten in den Reichstagswahlen*, p. 163. Election figures in the following section are based on this source. See also Table 12.

The anti-socialist legislation of 1878 prompted new measures against socialist sympathizers. At the Government's prompting, the Bochum Chamber of Commerce circularized local firms:

The undersigned Chamber of Commerce has noted with great satisfaction that the management of the great industrial concerns of the Gelsenkirchen district and some individual employers in and around Bochum have determined to act strongly against the excesses of social democracy; and that they have resolved to threaten with dismissal those workers who continue to support it through subscription to socialist journals, attendance at socialist meetings and clubs, and through financial contributions. As the representatives of the general interest of trade and industry in the Bochum district we regard it as our duty to give explicit support to these measures against social democracy and to urge all employers in our area to follow suit promptly.[45]

In Bochum there was no SPD candidate in the *Reichstag* elections of 1881 and 1884. In 1887 a candidate stood but won only 2 per cent of the vote.

Just as the 1889 strike marked the effective birth of the miners' union movement so it gave a great boost to the SPD. Many social democrats had played an active part in the strike and had won credibility as miners' spokesmen. In the *Reichstag* election of February 1890, with the anti-socialist law still in force, prominent miners' leaders including Schröder, Siegel, and Meyer stood as SPD candidates. The National Liberals, in contrast, were identified as the employers' party: during the strike Berger, the relatively progressive National Liberal representative for Bochum in the Prussian *Landtag*, had declared: '. . . as far as I am concerned, I stand before your High Court today as counsel for the defendant, the mine owners'.[46] The National Liberal candidate in Bochum, Hermann Müllensiefen, was a factory-owner. In the ballot the SPD for the first time won a significant proportion of the vote: nearly 15 per cent in Bochum. The run-off between Centre and National Liberals saw a narrow Centre party victory.

A by-election in Bochum later in the same year, following the resignation of the Centre victor through ill-health, allowed

---

[45] WWA, K2 1076, HKB to employers, 16. 6. 1878; *Handelsministerium* Berlin to HKB 13. 6. 1878.

[46] Nettmann, *Witten in den Reichstagswahlen*, p. 107.

the newly legalized SPD to consolidate its advance. August Bebel came to speak and 6,000 heard him denounce the German *Reich* as a class state because it laid all the burdens on the poor; he criticized food taxes and described the National Liberal party as 'the party *par excellence* of capitalism, of the money bag'.[47] The SPD share of the vote rose to 20 per cent but this time the National Liberals were able to defeat the Centre in the run-off.

The next *Reichstag* election took place in 1893 at a time of economic depression and in the aftermath of the failed strike of that year. The SPD candidate in Bochum, as in previous elections, was Gustav Lehmann, a former joiner and party activist in Düsseldorf and since 1890 working in Dortmund as a party editor and branch chairman. In his speeches he concentrated on national issues such as the tariffs and the need for social legislation to protect the workers. But the social democrat press reminded the voters of the events of the previous January:

It was the National Liberals who drove you to strike, who scornfully rejected your just demands or did not even answer them at all since they regard themselves as too superior to mix with the plebs, or the 'mob' as they call you. It was National Liberals who summoned gendarmes and the military, even though you had only made use of a legally guaranteed right; it was National Liberals who demanded that the ring-leaders be thrown in jail without any legal process, in disregard of the law; National Liberals threw thousands of fathers onto the street, giving them a lesson in hunger! Did this happen to criminals? No, they were honest, honourable working men who turned to the final, desperate, but fully legal weapon in order to secure a larger slice of bread and to help their brothers in the Saar. And National Liberals threw them onto the street, unconcerned with their plight because these workers dared to question the idol of National Liberalism, the money bag! Workers! Give this insolence the answer it deserves tomorrow.[48]

SPD support rose from 20.2 per cent to 29.6 per cent. This was not enough to push the Centre into third place and in the run-off the Centre defeated the National Liberals.

In less than four years the SPD had thus grown from a small minority party to a serious challenger, with almost

[47] IZF, *Westfälische Freie Presse*, 13. 12. 1890.
[48] IZF, *Rheinisch-Westfälische Arbeiter Zeitung*, 14. 6. 1893.

a third of the vote in the first round and a real chance of reaching the run-off. In large part this was a reflection of the perennial industrial conflict of those years and the party's ability to project itself as a spokesman of the workers. Already, however, the SPD in the Bochum district was nearing its peak. In the remaining twenty years and four elections before the outbreak of war the party made relatively little progress. In 1898, indeed, its share of the vote fell to 26.7 per cent, despite fears that the Government planned to curtail the rights of assembly and association and even to abolish universal suffrage for *Reichstag* elections. In 1903 Otto Hue was adopted as the party's candidate in Bochum: his popularity played an important part in the growth of the SPD share to 35.5 per cent. The appearance of a separate Polish nationalist party in this election took votes from the Centre party and relegated them to third place. In the run-off Hue for the SPD narrowly defeated the National Liberal candidate and for the first time Bochum sent a social democrat to the *Reichstag*.

In 1907 the SPD's success was repeated although their vote in the first round fell to 32.8 per cent. The final pre-war *Reichstag* election in 1912 saw the party's share rise again to 36.9 per cent; but an electoral pact between the National Liberals and the Centre ensured that in the run-off Centre votes were put behind the National Liberal candidate who therefore won comfortably. Despite the growth of SPD votes in the first round the seat was thus lost.

Despite the fact that the SPD held the *Reichstag* seat for Bochum from 1903 to 1912 the party's fundamental position had therefore improved relatively little since 1893. It continued to win only around a third of the first ballot—the best measure of its underlying appeal The appearance of the the Polish nationalists from 1903 weakened the Centre party and virtually ensured that the SPD would reach the run-off: but its fortunes at that stage depended on how Centre and Polish supporters then cast their votes.[49] In 1903 and 1907

---

[49] If the Centre and Polish voters had combined in the first ballot, they would have beaten the National Liberals into third place in 1903 and 1912 and the SPD in 1907. So at least two of these elections would have ended with different results.

the Centre gaves its supporters a free choice while the Poles supported the SPD; but the vulnerability of the social democrat position was amply demonstrated in 1912 when the Centre threw its weight behind the National Liberals, who therefore won the run-off. The same happened in Duisburg. The results of Bochum *Reichstag* elections are summarised in Table 12.

The SPD's failure to win more than around a third of the popular vote was not limited to Bochum. In the *Regierungs-Bezirk* Arnsberg, which included Dortmund and Bochum, the party won 22 per cent of the vote in 1898, 30 per cent in 1903 and 1907, and 34 per cent in 1912; in *Regierungs-Bezirk* Düsseldorf, which covered the western Ruhr, the SPD vote was 22 per cent in 1898, 32 per cent in 1903, 30 per cent in 1907, and 34.5 per cent in 1912.[50] The underlying trend was upwards: but even in this heavily working-class region the SPD was still far from achieving majority support.

Party membership represented another index of the SPD's appeal. It is virtually impossible to calculate the party's membership before 1906 since only then was a firm organizational structure established with an agreed geographical area (the *Reichstagswahlkreis* or electoral district) and clear criteria for party membership. The newly formed party organization for the Bochum *Reichstagswahlkreis* in January 1906 had 1,500 members, but within months this had grown to 2,552. Helped by a change in the law in 1908 which permitted women to join, membership continued to grow until 1910 when it reached a peak of 6,763. Thereafter it fluctuated below this level, with a low of 5,820 in 1913 and a recovery to 6,598 in the following year. These were disappointingly low figures: in 1912 almost 162,000 men (but no women) were eligible to vote in the Bochum *Reichstagswahlkreis* and only 3 per cent were SPD party members. The ratio of party membership to party voters was also poor: in 1907 there were 11 party members for every 100 SPD voters in Bochum compared with 15 in Dortmund and a national figure of 16.5. In 1912 there were 12 members for every

[50] K. Koszyk, 'Die sozialdemokratische Arbeiterbewegung 1890 bis 1914', in Reulecke (ed.), *Arbeiterbewegung*, p. 150.

TABLE 12
Bochum *Reichstag* election results, 1884–1912[a]

Election	National Liberals		Centre		Polish Nationalists		SPD		Others	
	Total	%	Total	%	Total	%	Total	%	Total	%
1884[c]	25,715[b]	54.2	21,522	45.8						
1887[c]	31,761[b]	59.4	20,580	38.5			1,160	2.1		
1890	18,639	33.2	21,889[b]	39.0			8,388	14.9	7,204	12.9
	28,824	49.1	29,869[b]	50.4						
1890[d]	18,939	39.1	18,131	37.5			9,770	20.2	1,534	3.2
	27,304[b]	51.5	25,641	48.5						
1893	25,447	38.5	20,351	30.8			19,585	29.6	737	1.1
	32,567	48.6	34,444[b]	51.4						
1898	31,623	37.6	30,029	35.7			22,379	26.7		
	46,838[b]	54.2	39,600	45.8						
1903	33,403	30.4	31,267	28.2	6,500	5.9	39,125	35.5		
	49,300	49.6					50,063[b]	50.4		
1907	41,538	33.7	34,208	27.7	7,333	5.8	40,356	32.8		
	57,818	49.2					59,738[b]	50.8		
1912	43,257	29.8	37,650	26.0	10,630	7.3	53,333	36.9		
	78,833[b]	54.8					64,934	45.2		

[a] Nettmann, *Witten in den Reichstagswahlen*, p. 168.

[b] indicates the winner.

[c] The 1884 and 1887 contests were settled by majority support for one party in the first ballot; all subsequent elections had to go to a run-off between the two most successful parties in the first round.

[d] A by-election occurred in 1890 following the resignation of the existing deputy.

100 SPD voters in Bochum, again much lower than the figure of 19 in Dortmund and 22.8 nationally.[51]

Little hard information is available about the social composition of the SPD. Denominationally, the party proved more successful in appealing to Protestants than to Catholics. In the 1903 election it was estimated that around 70 per cent of SPD voters in the Bochum *Reichstagswahlkreis* were Protestant and only 30 per cent Catholic. The only available occupational breakdown of party members relates to the Dortmund town branch in 1906. Not surprisingly, this showed that the SPD was overwhelmingly a working-class organization: 85 per cent of the Dortmund members were industrial workers and most of those in other occupational categories were either employees of the labour movement itself or were former workers who had turned to small-scale shopkeeping or similar trades, often as a result of their trade union or political activities. Outside the town the proportion of manual workers was almost certainly even higher. The most numerous occupational group was the building workers who comprised 34 per cent of the members; they were followed by miners (15 per cent), metal-workers (14 per cent), and timber workers (13 per cent). Building, mining, and timber workers were over-represented in comparison with their numbers in the town generally while metal-workers were slightly under-represented; foundry workers, who comprised 14 per cent of the Dortmund labour force, were almost completely absent from the party. Outside the town itself, however, it appears that building workers may have been less ready to join the party: in the pit villages miners almost certainly predominated. The only available evidence for the Bochum area relates to the party's local 'leaders and agitators', as identified by local government officials. Taking lists compiled in 1891, 1902, and 1906 together, we find that no less than 79 per cent of those named were Protestants and 71 per cent were miners. Cumulative records for the three localities of Weitmar, Herne, and Harpen between 1896 and 1912 named 124 SPD 'leaders

[51] IZF, *Arbeiter Zeitung*, 19. 11. 1907, 3. 10. 1911, 4. 7. 1914. The 1912 ratio of party members to SPD voters is swelled by the admission of women members who remained disenfranchised.

and agitators' of whom 92 were miners (and several others ex-miners), 91 were Protestant, 26 Catholic, and the religion of 7 was unknown or unaccounted for (including one who was specifically recorded as having 'no religion').[52] Overall, the impression is of a party dominated occupationally by miners and denominationally by Protestants, with a more varied occupational base only in the larger centres and a more balanced religious composition only where Catholics were particularly numerous.

Nor did the entry of women to full party membership after 1908 greatly alter the balance. Everywhere they remained in a minority, although the size of the minority varied inversely with the total size of the local party: thus in Dortmund, the largest of the three party organizations in the eastern Ruhr, women formed around 19 per cent of the party's membership between 1910 and 1914; in the smaller Bochum party around 22 per cent of members were women, while in Recklinghausen—with 4,439 members in 1914 compared with 6,598 in Bochum and 9,802 in Dortmund—around 32 per cent of the members were women. We do not know enough about the internal life of these parties to account for the varying level of female membership although it may be that women found the smaller organizations less intimidating and more welcoming towards potential new members. The lack of female employment opportunities meant, however, that the influx of women did not signify the introduction of a new occupational group. As the party noted in 1914: 'Many female workers are employed before their marriage in offices and shops and a few also in factories; however, only a tiny proportion of the girls in employment are organized. It is almost exclusively workers' wives who join our organization.'[53]

The Ruhr was an overwhelmingly working-class society and the SPD stood openly as the workers' party. As Gustav Lehmann declared in 1898:'Only the social democrats strive to improve the position of the workers; it is therefore also

[52] Lützenkirchen, *Sozialdemokratische Verein*, pp. 123–5; STAM, RA I 96, *Polizei Commissar* Gelsenkirchen to RPA, 17. 8. 1903; STAM, *Oberpräsidium* 2693 Bd. 2, RPA, 16. 2. 1891; StAB, 479, 480, 483, 484, 'Führer und Agitatoren der socialdemokratischen Partei'.

[53] IZF, *Arbeiter Zeitung*, 30. 6. 1914.

the duty of every worker to give his vote to social democrat candidates.'[54] Yet these hopes were only partially realized and many workers failed to heed the call. On the eve of war the SPD leaders for the eastern Ruhr summed up their failure:

It is deeply sad that our powerful industrial district, where one pit lies right by the next, where one foundry and one factory borders on another, where the land is covered with thousands of chimneys and where a working class numbering hundreds of thousands slaves and wears itself down for miserly wages in these enormous work places, sends to Parliament men who are either the direct representatives of Capital or are 'workers' representatives' like Giesbarts and Brust [Centre] and not true representatives of the workers, social democrats. The mass of the people here are still very unenlightened and politically backward. They stand aside from the struggles for justice and freedom fought by the class-conscious proletariat.[55]

There were several factors behind the social democrats' failure to win the support they expected. Like the trade unions, they suffered from the high geographical mobility of people in the district. Max König, the party's organizer for the eastern Ruhr, saw the 'enormous fluctuation' as one of the main obstacles to recruitment.[56] Local branches could be badly affected when leading figures in the locality moved elsewhere. The departure of Louis Jäger in 1909 was a severe blow to the party in Weitmar:

One can see a standstill, if not even a step backwards, in the social democrat movement. Since the area organizer Louis Jäger left here for Gelsenkirchen some three months ago there have been no public political meetings at Schröder's inn. Jäger was the heart of the agitation and a fluent speaker. He knew how to attract the working masses and was a zealous propagandist for his party.[57]

Two years later no one had stepped into his shoes in Weitmar: 'There are no good speakers who can attract the working masses; as a result the social democratic movement was not conspicuous.'[58] This was not an isolated instance: of the 124 SPD 'leaders and agitators' identified in Weitmar, Herne, and

---

[54] *Wittener Tageblatt*, 6. 6. 1898, quoted in Nettmann, *Witten in den Reichstagswahlen*, p. 134.
[55] IZF, *Arbeiter Zeitung*, 11. 7. 1914.
[56] IZF, *Arbeiter Zeitung*, 13. 12. 1909.
[57] StAB, 481, *Amt* Weitmar to KLB, 13. 8. 1909.
[58] StAB, 482, *Amt* Weitmar to KLB, 14. 8. 1911.

Harpen over the period 1896 to 1912, half were active in their locality for only one or two years; only 15 were reported to have been active for more than 6 years. The result was a lack of continuity. In Herne in 1899, for instance, there were four main activists: of these, three had only moved to Herne in the previous year and the other actually lived in Bochum; one of the three, a Catholic joiner named Ludwig Kostrop, having moved from Essen to Herne in October 1898, moved on to Recklinghausen in March 1899.[59]

High turnover was also common amongst ordinary members. Table 13 illustrates the scale of the problem. The overall membership figures concealed an unstable and volatile situation, with large membership gains and losses even in years when the total showed little change. Party membership, like union membership, was not a closed world where a person, having joined, was likely to stay indefinitely. Many did, of course, but large numbers joined for a time and then left or let their membership lapse. The turnover demonstrated the party's difficulties not simply in winning new support but in maintaining the commitment of existing members. In 1914 König had to report that there had been the equivalent of a complete turnover of party members in the eastern Ruhr over the previous three years.[60]

The party also suffered from harassment which restricted its ability to organize and agitate effectively. Employers, police, and local government officials all actively sought to obstruct the social democrats by a variety of means including the rigorous application of the law. Dealing with enquiries and correspondence from the police was a routine activity for the party's secretariat and any apparent failure to comply with a legal requirement, however trivial, could lead to prosecution before generally unsympathetic courts. In 1902 two members of the Bochum party executive were fined ten marks for failing to de-register a member within three days of his death. Five years later the party secretary

---

[59] StAB, 479, *Amt* Herne to KLB, 20. 3. 1899.
[60] ibid. See also D. Fricke, *Die deutsche Arbeiterbewegung 1869 bis 1914. Ein Handbuch über ihre Organisation und Tätigkeit im Klassenkampf* (Berlin-Ost, 1976), pp. 246–9.

TABLE 13

SPD members, *Reichstagswahlkreis* Bochum, 1910-1914[a]

Year	Total membership	New members: Total % of all members		Leavers: Total % of all members	
1910	6,763	2,215	33	1,242	18
1911	6,325	2,560	41	2,998	47
1912	6,368	2,298	36	2,255	35
1913	5,820	1,106	19	1,654	28
1914	6,598	2,525	38	1,747	26

[a]Calculated from figures in IZF, *Arbeiter Zeitung* 4. 7. 1914.

was acquitted of the same offence, but only on appeal and only on the grounds that responsibility rested with the party representatives in the localities.[61] Party journalists were repeatedly fined and imprisoned for 'defamatory' and 'libellous' articles; within a month of becoming editor of the recently-founded Bochum SPD paper, the *Volksblatt*, in 1899, Paul Wolf received three fines of between 50 and 200 marks and two prison sentences of two and six weeks; two years later he received a nine months' sentence. Apart from the personal strains such repeated penalties imposed on the journalists themselves, the court cases and fines represented a significant financial burden on the party.[62] Other forms of activism were also subject to official intervention and restriction. Mass marches and demonstrations required prior police permission, which was seldom granted, and were very rare events. Any unauthorized demonstration was likely to be swiftly broken up by the police: this happened on May Day in Gelsenkirchen in 1892 when between 150 and 200 people attempted to march through the town.[63]

Public meetings were also restricted. They too had to be registered and normally had a police presence. Meetings which contravened any law or regulation—e.g. by the use of

[61] IZF, *Volksblatt*, 3. 7. 1902. *Arbeiter Zeitung*, 19, 21. 11. 1907.

[62] Koszyk, *Anfänge und frühe Entwicklung*, pp. 166-7; STAM, RA I 95, *Polizei-Commissar* Bochum to RPA, 23. 10. 1899, *Stadt* Bochum to RPA, 2. 10. 1901.

[63] STAM, *Oberpräsidium* 2693 Bd. 3, RPA to *Oberpräsident* Westfalen, 4. 5. 1892.

Polish or through 'libellous' statements—could be stopped at once and the offenders arrested and charged. Even more serious, both for the party and for the 'free' unions, was the shortage of rooms for meetings. They were usually held at inns but landlords were often put under pressure by the police, e.g. by threatening to impose a ban on the sale of drink during any SPD meeting, and sometimes by other customers not to let their rooms to unionists or social democrats. The police aim seems normally to have been harassment rather than to prevent all SPD meetings, since that might have led to underground agitation which was more difficult to watch and control. Despite attempts to combat the pressure through boycotts of offending landlords and the cultivation of friendly ones, the shortage of meeting-rooms was a serious and lasting problem for the party. In 1901 the lack of rooms in Langendreer resulted in members arranging informal and unregistered discussions instead: the organizers were fined for attempting to evade the law. In 1907 the party estimated that there were only around 20 inns in the whole *Reichstagswahlkreis* (including Bochum, Gelsenkirchen, Witten and Herne as well as the smaller surrounding villages) available to the party; only two or three of these were suitable for large meetings. During elections it was sometimes impossible for the party to hold any meetings at all in some localities.[64]

In the Ruhr as elsewhere the SPD also suffered from the attacks of its opponents and from their lurid accounts of its aims and policies. Allegations that the party was unpatriotic and that it wished to confiscate all private property must have done it some damage amongst the more naïve voters, although how much it is impossible to say. The greatest obstacle, however, was posed by the strong links between the social and cultural life of the district, religion, and politics. As we saw above, the party's stance on religion was ambiguous, with an emphasis on the private and non-political nature of religious belief combined with support for a 'materialist' view of man and society and occasional anti-Church campaigns. It was faced, however, with influential

[64] STAM, RA I 95, *Polizei-Commissar* Bochum to RPA, 30. 8. 1900, 2. 10. 1901; IISG, *Volksblatt*, 2. 12. 1907.

working-class 'sub-cultures' characterized by strong denominational commitments and fiercely antagonistic attitudes towards 'atheistic' socialism. Pastors and priests openly spoke against social democracy and the resources of the denominational workers' organizations were thrown behind the Centre and National Liberal parties. In this conflict the SPD was confronting more than a set of abstract ideas and beliefs about religion. Many workers' very sense of cultural identity had a strong denominational element and religious loyalties and organizations played a large role in the community and social life of the district. The SPD could and did rival the Churches with its own plethora of clubs (singing, cultural, sporting, etc.), its newspapers, its educational activities, and its social life, but it remained only one among a number of rival sub-cultures. Moreover, by appealing more successfully to Protestants than to Catholics the suspicions of the latter were reinforced. This situation was particularly serious in a district where Catholics were—just—in a majority amongst workers.

These problems were even greater when the SPD tried to appeal to the Polish minority. Here a very Polish Catholicism and an anti-German nationalism were combined with a rhetoric which left little room for 'atheistic', 'German' social democracy. In the 1890s most Poles seem to have supported the Centre party but growing tensions led to Polish Nationalist candidates standing in 1903 for the first time in the *Reichstag* elections in the Ruhr. Nationalist sentiments were reinforced by subsequent discriminatory actions, such as the legislative changes of 1904 and 1908 which prevented Poles from purchasing smallholdings in the east and gave legal force to the ban (already sometimes invoked in practice) on the use of the Polish language in public meetings. In Bochum the Polish nationalists' share of the vote rose from under 6 per cent in 1903 and 1907 to over 7 per cent in 1912. The efforts of the SPD to win Polish support therefore had only limited success. In 1908 a Polish Secretary for the Ruhr district was appointed; shortly before the 1912 elections, however, he resigned his post and went abroad—apparently depressed at his lack of success. He was not replaced. Even the purely Polish social democratic party (PPS), which operated in the Ruhr from 1898 independently of the SPD, failed to win significant support.[65]

The failure of the SPD to win more than minority electoral support did not mean, however, that class was unimportant in the political life of the district. The Centre and National Liberal parties were themselves increasingly faced with the need to respond to workers' concerns and aspirations in order to maintain their electoral appeal. The history of these parties in the Ruhr has barely begun to be studied. However, as we have seen, there was a strong tradition of Catholic social concern: the Protestantism of most employers helped the Centre party to appeal to workers and voice their aspirations even though elsewhere in Germany, including the mining districts of Silesia, Catholicism was also the religion of the employers. However, the party hierarchy remained ambivalent so that divisions appeared: in 1877 an unofficial workers' candidate stood against the party's nominee in a *Reichstag* election in Essen and won. In the 1881 *Reichstag* by-election in Bochum the party's aristocratic candidate, Freiherr von Schorlemer-Alst, felt obliged to appeal directly to the class interests of the workers:

Workers! Show at the election on 8 November that you wish to be treated in a Christian manner . . . that when the assertion is made that wages have generally risen by 15 per cent you also want to see something of this 15 per cent. At the large factories and mines you have experienced nothing of better wages; when you have earned something more you have had to work longer for it and sweat more while those who now flatter you and try to win you for Dr Löwe [Progressive] quietly pocket the biggest return.[66]

Von Schorlemer won and in the next year made a vigorous and widely reported attack in the *Reichstag* on the mine-owners. He sharply criticized the pressure on miners to work overtime, deductions from wages, fines, and the wage statistics which, he maintained, failed to make proper allowance for overtime and for officials' salaries. The speech caused much

---

[65] IZF, *Arbeiter Zeitung*, 30. 6. 1914; Wehler, 'Polen im Ruhrgebiet', p. 452; Klessmann, *Polnische Bergarbeiter im Ruhrgebiet*, pp. 89–91, 125–8.

[66] G. Zehnter, 'Sie vertraten Bochum im Reichstag', in *Ruhr-Nachrichten*, 12, 13. 8. 1961.

controversy and was roundly criticized by the employers' spokesmen but strengthened the claim of the Centre party to be a true champion of the miners' interests.[67]

Little more was heard from von Schorlemer in the following years, although Catholics and Centre supporters such as Lambert Lensing (editor of *Tremonia* in Dortmund) and Johannes Fussangel were active in the miners' movement in the Ruhr. Conflict on class lines within the party reappeared in the aftermath of the 1889 strike. The selection of a candidate for Bochum in February 1890 proved difficult. Walter, a Gelsenkirchen party delegate, commented: 'One must fear that if a miner is not nominated as candidate many miners will go with the social democrats on 20 February'; Bauer, a prominent figure during the strike in Weitmar and subsequently sacked from *Karl Friedrich*, criticized von Schorlemer's support for grain tariffs and commented: 'A large estate owner can never qualify as a miners' representative.'[68] A meeting in Bochum attended by 3,000 people nominated a miner as candidate; but five days later, after von Schorlemer had avoided questions about his attitude to the miners' movement because of influenza, a meeting of party delegates none the less readopted him as candidate for Bochum. Subsequently von Schorlemer explained: 'I will always intercede for the workers with the aim of achieving harmony between employers and employees on the basis of legal regulation of workers' representation, of their rights, and of workers' protection measures such as the arbitration courts and conciliation offices.'[69] This declaration encapsulated the Centre's party's approach to the social question: the aim was to achieve fair treatment for workers and involved concessions from both sides. The mechanism, however, was harmonious agreement, supported if necessary by legislation, rather than conflict and struggle. The party was particularly proud of its support for legal measures to protect workers. It was a policy of class conciliation, not class conflict. Despite the growth in the SPD vote the Centre won, confirming the Elberfeld

[67] Kirchhoff, *Sozialpolitik*, p. 33; Tenfelde, *Sozialgeschichte*, p. 534; H. O. Hemmer, 'Die Bergarbeiterbewegung im Ruhrgebiet unter dem Sozialistengesetz', in Reulecke (ed.), *Arbeiterbewegung*, p. 103.

[68] StAB, *Märkischer Sprecher*, 4. 2. 1890.

[69] ibid., 7, 12. 2. 1890.

social democratic press' description of the town as 'black Bochum'.[70]

Following von Schorlemer's early resignation through ill-health, the new candidate in the December 1890 by-election was a former mayor of Gelsenkirchen, Wilhelm Vattmann. He had assisted von Schorlemer with his controversial 1882 speech and had been disciplined for it. But despite his sympathy with the miners' cause the main thrust of party policy continued to be the need for harmony, not conflict, between the classes. Vattmann himself had maintained in 1882 that it was only at a minority of pits that conditions were bad. In 1890 he was presented as a man who could speak not just for the miners but for all social groups:

As mayor of Gelsenkirchen he knows the needs of every rank and every occupational group; he knows where the artisan's shoe pinches, the problems of the countryman, what is necessary for the protection of our homeland's industry; and he knows especially how things are for the working class and what is possible and necessary to improve their social situation. The Centre party's election committee could therefore not have found another man able to offer better guarantees that he will not represent a single class or a single calling in the *Reichstag* but rather will represent the community and every single individual.[71]

The Centre party was thus subject to tension between the party establishment, who stressed the ultimate aim of harmonious social relations, and the radicals, including many active in the Christian trade unions, who wanted less equivocal support for workers' interests. In 1893 the original candidate for Bochum was compelled to withdraw in the face of protests that he was a factory-owner. In 1903 the party put forward a miner as their candidate and in 1907 the Centre throughout the Ruhr adopted worker-orientated candidates. The party's appeal was deep-rooted and fairly steady, despite political vacillations and support for food tariffs. Although the Centre vote fell from nearly 36 per cent in 1898 to only 28 per cent in 1903 this was largely due to the appearance of a Polish nationalist candidate. The 1907 and 1912 elections saw a fairly steady Centre vote

---

[70] Koszyk, *Anfänge und frühe Entwicklung*, p. 48.
[71] *Tremonia* Nr. 284, quoted in IZF, *Westfälische Freie Presse*, 13. 12. 1890; Kirchhoff, *Sozialpolitik*, pp. 34–5.

(28 and 26 per cent respectively) while if the Poles are taken into account the electoral appeal of 'political Catholicism' was effectively stable at 36 per cent (1898), 34 per cent (1903), and 33 per cent (1907 and 1912).

If both the SPD and the Centre parties could claim to represent workers' interests and were able to win substantial working-class support, was there a basis for co-operation between them against the National Liberals—described by the SPD in 1900 as 'the party of smokestack *Junkers*, coal barons, and iron kings. Main representative of large Capital and serving its interests'? The prospects were not good: in the same publication the SPD described the Centre as 'the most mendacious, hypocritical, untrustworthy of all bourgeois parties'; the party was accused of manipulating the religious feelings of Catholic workers but of betraying their economic interests through its support for the Government's taxation and naval policy; the Centre was 'the worst and most dangerous enemy of the workers because it impedes them in common struggles to improve their conditions. The victory of social democracy in the [Ruhr] industrial region depends on the destruction of the Centre.'[72] The run-offs of *Reichstag* elections, when supporters of parties knocked out in the first round had to choose between the two front runners or abstain, provided the test of whether such sentiments would prevail over a common interest in defeating the National Liberals.

In the 1893 and 1898 elections the SPD in Bochum was eliminated in the first round and its supporters were faced with a choice between the Centre and the National Liberals in the run-off. In 1893 the SPD denounced both candidates as 'the representatives of two reactionary parties' and urged their members to abstain.[73] Very few heeded the advice: the run-off saw an increased total vote, with former SPD voters voting by two to one for the Centre. In 1898, however, despite support in the run-off for the Centre by Franz Pokorny, a leading social democrat and miners' spokesman in Gelsenkirchen, around two-thirds of SPD voters in the first round supported the National Liberals in the second: in part,

---

[72] StAB, 479, *Westfälischer Volks–Kalender* (1900).
[73] IZF, *Rheinisch-Westfälische Arbeiter Zeitung*, 21. 6. 1893.

perhaps, a reflection of the reduced level of industrial conflict and the improved economic climate since the early
1890s; but also, no doubt, the result of the strong appeal to
Protestant sentiment which the National Liberals made on
this occasion.

The 1903 election was the first in which the Centre failed
to reach the run-off, largely because of the appearance of
a separate Polish candidate. In this and subsequent elections
Centre supporters and Polish nationalists were compelled to
choose between the SPD and the National Liberals in the run-
off. In 1903 the Poles came out in support of Hue but the
Centre advised its supporters not to vote for the SPD. The
SPD was able to exploit the fact that Hermann Franken—
the National Liberal candidate—was a strong Protestant
to appeal to the Catholic voters: a poem on this theme by
Fussangel was circulated as a campaign broadsheet by the
SPD. Nevertheless, in the vote almost a third of former
Centre and Polish voters abstained, the same proportion
voted SPD, while over 40 per cent voted for the National
Liberal candidate. Despite this, the increase in the SPD
vote was enough to give them a narrow first victory in
Bochum.[74] In the 1907 run-off the Poles again supported the
SPD, while the Centre gave their members a free choice.
This time approaching half of their first-round voters sup-
ported the SPD, under 40 per cent voted for the National
Liberals and only 14 per cent abstained. Once again the SPD
finished as winner with the help of these votes.

The social democrats tried to develop this trend further in
the run-off of the Prussian *Landtag* election of 1908. This
time, because of the three-class voting system, the SPD was
in third place and had to decide what to do in the run-off.
In Bochum the party gave its support to the Centre who
accordingly won. The decision was criticized by some within
the SPD, particularly in Essen, who maintained that elsewhere the Centre had failed to support SPD candidates

[74] STAM, RA I 96, *Extra–Abzug*, 25. 6. 1903; IZF, *Volksblatt*, 15. 10. 1927.
After the election Hue claimed: 'In the run-off the predominantly Catholic places
in the northern half of the district gave us the victory. The Catholic workers
came over to social democracy *en masse*.' This assertion is not borne out by the
voting statistics. StAB, 480, RPA to *Minister des Innern*, 8. 12. 1903; STAM,
Landratsamt Gelsenkirchen 40.

and that the Centre rather than the National Liberals now constituted the main opposition to the SPD in the Ruhr. The Bochum party replied that the Centre had done all they could for the social democrats and that they were clearly the lesser of two evils. The Bochum party secretary defended the decision:

No one thinks that the Centre is more reliable than the National Liberals; the aim was rather to oust the capitalists' party from their dominant position in the Ruhr and secondly to take from the Centre any weapon for agitation against us. We were fighting honourably for a better franchise and could not therefore allow an outspoken opponent of the franchise to have the mandate.[75]

There were thus some signs of *rapprochement* between the SPD and supporters of the Centre and Polish Nationalists. The politicians were in part building on the solidarity shown in the 1905 strike and continued on an organizational level subsequently by the 'Commission of Seven' which represented all four miners' unions. However, again like the inter-union co-operation, these attempts to work together collapsed in disarray in the final years before the war. This was largely a consequence of the tactical rightwards shift in the Centre's national position after 1909 and their alliance with the Conservatives. As a result they were bitterly criticized for supporting the tariffs which were held to be responsible for rising food prices in 1911 and 1912. Hue published a leaflet in December 1911 attacking the Centre sharply for its support for tariffs: only the rich industrialists and the better-off farmers benefited from them, he argued, not the small peasants in whose name the Centre sometimes claimed to speak and certainly not the workers. The *Bergarbeiter Zeitung* also denounced 'the clerical and conservative taxers'.[76]

[75] STAM, RA I 100, *Volksblatt*, 25, 26. 8. 1908; IISG, *Volksblatt*, 18, 20, 22. 6. 1908. The position of the Essen SPD reflected the Centre's dominance there. In Bochum local elections the anti-SPD alliance of Centre and National Liberals broke apart in 1908, mainly due to a split in Liberal ranks, and the Centre won a rare complete victory in the third class. Crew, *Town in the Ruhr*, p. 138.
[76] IGBE, *Deutsche Bergarbeiter Zeitung*, 6. 1. 1912; StAB, O. Hue, *Die Verteuerung der Lebensmittel und ihre Ursachen* (Bochum, 1911).

The 1912 run-off was again fought between the SPD and National Liberals. This time the Centre came out in full support of the National Liberals. The announcement of a pact between the two parties in which Centre candidates would be supported in Essen and, less formally, in Düsseldorf while National Liberal candidates would receive joint support in Duisburg and Bochum was enthusiastically welcomed at a Bochum meeting of 1,000 Centre activists. Leading Centre figures appeared on National Liberal platforms: at one meeting the Bochum Centre candidate, Professor Weskamp, denounced social democracy as 'the common enemy' and described the SPD as a revolutionary party, opposed to both Fatherland and God.[77] The *Bergknappe*, organ of the Gewerkverein, attacked Hue:

> Down with the social democracy . . . especially in the Bochum constituency! As is well known, Otto Hue is standing there in the run-off —the most spiteful and dishonourable opponent of our movement. His attacks on us are well known. For almost two decades he had fought, mistrusted, and abused our movement. At first it was for him a 'still-born child'. Then he accused it of being an ultramontane foundation, an employers' gang, a company union. For years the union's members were abused as company unionists in Hue's paper, the *Bergarbeiter Zeitung*, in the most malicious manner. Even when the 1905 strike had palpably and clearly proved that such descriptions were unjustified and untrue, they did not cease. . . . What must now be done is to throw back at this enemy of our movement the malicious smears and his damage to the workers. That is the honourable course for every Christian unionist. No-one must stay away from the poll! Everyone must be an agitator against our enemy!
>
> > Down with every social democrat!
> > But above all, down with Hue![78]

Both the party establishment and the union wing thus combined in a virulent campaign against the social democrats. The Poles were advised this time to abstain. Worse was to come on the eve of the poll, when rumours spread that the socialists had scrawled 'Vote Hue' slogans and had left human excrement in the main Catholic church in Bochum, one much used by Poles. A later SPD inquiry found no evidence that

[77] StAB, *Märkischer Sprecher*, 20, 22. 1. 1912.
[78] Quoted in IGBE, *Deutsche Bergarbeiter Zeitung*, 27. 1. 1912.

the party was responsible for what was most probably an attempt to discredit the social democrats.[79]

In the run-off Centre and Polish voters divided by three to one in favour of the National Liberals with very few abstentions—by far the most clear-cut decisions on one side that they had yet taken. The 1912 election thus marked the complete destruction of hopes of non-sectarian class unity between social democrats, Centre supporters, and Polish Nationalists. Sectarianism and hostility to social democracy had triumphed. And the stage had been set for the even more bitter destruction of working-class unity in the miners' strike which broke out two months later and which left a lasting legacy of division and hatred.[80]

One reason for the failure to achieve a common political front between the SPD, the Centre, and the Polish Nationalists on the basis of common working-class interests was the fact that they were not the only parties which enjoyed significant working-class support. Even the National Liberals —'the party *par excellence* of capitalism, of the money bag' as Bebel described it—succeeded in winning many workers' votes. That the party was dominated by industrial interests was not in doubt. In Bochum the party had particularly close links with the Bochumer Verein. Louis Baare himself sat as a National Liberal in the Prussian *Landtag*; for years the firm subsidized the *Rheinisch-Westfälische Tageblatt*; and the party itself received a regular income from the firm —1,000 marks a year during the early 1900s, of which half was for the local party and half for the regional organization —in addition to substantial *ad hoc* grants to help with election expenses. 5,000 marks were donated for the 1903 election and 9,000 marks in 1907. Local officialdom was also generally pro-National Liberal.[81] Some of the party's success

[79] StAB, *Märkischer Sprecher*, 17. 1. 1912; IZF, *Arbeiter Zeitung*, 29. 1. 1912.

[80] The SPD attributed its poor showing in the 1913 *Landtag* elections in large measure to the legacy of the strike: 'The great number of workers who through ignorance or malice did not join the 1912 strike are no longer voters for us. They have been led to the Centre, through the *Gewerkverein*, or to the National Liberals through the yellow unions.' IZF, *Arbeiter Zeitung*, 10. 7. 1914. The Centre-National Liberal pact was maintained in local elections: StAB, 482, *Amt* Langendreer to KLB, 12. 8. 1913.

[81] Däbritz, *Bochumer Verein*, p. 164; KA, 12900 Nr. 15, *Verwaltungsraths-sitzungen*, 22. 11. 1887, 28. 7. 1890; KA, 12900 Nr. 22, *Verwaltungsrathssitzungen*,

in winning working class votes was due to an extension of this political support into more or less overt pressure. Allegations of the misuse of economic power for political ends were common. In 1882 the Centre party accused Bochum employers of distributing National Liberal election propaganda and encouraging mine officials to ensure that workers under their supervision voted the right way; those who did not were liable to be sacked. In local elections in 1889 and 1890 the Bochumer Verein was accused of pressuring its workers to vote National Liberal, with time off to attend the party's meetings, circulation of leaflets to employees, and foremen present at the polling stations. In 1898 at least one pit manager was involved in distributing the party's propaganda and it was claimed that Hermann Franken, the party's factory-owning candidate, had sacked workers who expressed anti-National Liberal sentiments. In 1907 the SPD alleged that in Baukau a dozen *Steiger* attended the polling station all day to maintain pressure on the men, and that workers at *Friedrich der Grosse* who opposed the company's approved candidate were liable to be sacked. In the *Landtag* election in 1908 an overman at the same pit was said to have repeatedly told the miners that they should vote for those who provided their bread. In Hamborn the 1913 *Landtag* election was known as the '*Schnapps-*election': miners from *Deutscher Kaiser* were marched by their foremen to the polling booths where they were met by company managers who dispensed *Schnapps* and urged them to vote National Liberal.[82]

It is impossible to judge how widespread such practices were or how effective in actually influencing votes. Few of the allegations were substantiated in detail. What the reports do suggest, however, is a climate of pressure in which employees might reasonably fear that failure to support the approved candidate would be seen as a sign of disloyalty

20. 1. 1900, 29. 3. 1900, 27. 6. 1903; KA, 12900 Nr. 24, *Verwaltungsraths-sitzung*, 26. 10. 1907; STAM, RA I 100, *Polizei-Commissar* Bochum to RPA, 10. 9. 1908.

[82] Kirchhoff, *Sozialpolitik*, p. 34; IZF, *Westfälische Arbeiter Zeitung*, 20. 3. 1889; StAB, 461, *Westfälische Volkszeitung*, 25. 11. 1890; IZF, *Rheinisch-Westfälische Arbeiter Zeitung*, 14, 24. 6. 1898; IISG, *Volksbatt*, 18, 27. 11. 1907, 23. 6. 1908; Lucas, *Arbeiterradikalismus*, p. 136.

and might lead to reprisals. But the National Liberals did not rely on such crude pressures alone; they offered more positive attractions, appealing to workers' patriotism, Protestantism, and loyalty to employer and firm. Company loyalty, as we have seen, was actively encouraged, particularly in the metal industry, and may explain why workers in the large engineering companies and the glass industry were thought to be particularly reluctant to support the social democrats: it was claimed that only around ten per cent of Bochumer Verein workers voted SPD in 1903.[83] In later years these sentiments were reinforced by the growth of the 'yellow' unions. Patriotic feeling was fostered by, amongst others, the veterans' associations. Many workers were proud to join these organizations after their military service and paraded through the town with bands, flags, and uniforms on national days. Social democratic views were naturally bitterly opposed by the veterans' associations and even members of the 'free' trade unions were liable to find themselves barred from membership. The Bochum *Landrat* described these organizations as 'an appropriate means for the struggle against social democracy' while his colleague in Riemke and Hordel identified the Veterans' Association, the Artillery Association, the People's Library, and the Patriotic Womens' Association as particularly important.[84] Patriotic and anti-socialist activities—the two in fact went hand in hand—were actively supported by local employers. When Admiral Paschen spoke in Witten on the navy at the height of the political debate about its future, workers from the local steel plant were given time off to attend. The Bochumer Verein, like other local firms, donated funds to the pro-navy Flottenverein as well as to the nationalist Alldeutscher Verband and the Abwehrorganisation gegen die Sozialdemokratie designed to confront social democracy.[85] Such

[83] STAM, RA I 96, *Polizei-Commissar* Bochum to RPA, 10. 10. 1904; STAM, RA I 97, K. *Landrat* Witten to RPA, 14. 9. 1905, *Stadt* Bochum to RPA, 27. 9. 1905.
[84] STAM, RA I 100, KLB to RPA, 1. 9. 1908; StAB, 481, *Amt* Hordel to KLB, 19. 8. 1909; Crew, *Industry and Community*, pp. 135-7; Tenfelde, *Sozial-Feschichte*, p. 351; Tenfelde, 'Mining Festivals', p. 393.
[85] IZF, *Volksblatt*, 6. 2. 1900; KA, 12900 Nr. 20, *Verwaltungsrathssitzung*, 25. 6. 1898; KA, 12900 Nr. 23, *Verwaltungsrathssitzung*, 19. 10. 1904; KA, 12900 Nr. 24, *Verwaltungsrathssitzungen*, 26. 2. 1910, 25. 1. 1913.

bodies provided, in effect, an underpinning to the political base of the National Liberal party. The Masurian immigrants, who like the Poles had their own clubs and their own distinctive sub-culture, but who in contrast to the Poles identified strongly with the German state, were a further important bastion of the party: a special party paper was published for them and local party officers cultivated their support. Perhaps most important were the Protestant workers' clubs, discussed above, which provided a relatively independent working-class basis for the party's political appeal as well as forming an important source of organizational strength. Thus after 1907 the party secretary for the Bochum constituency was a former office-holder in the Protestant working-class movement.[86] Through such organizations the National Liberals were able to speak directly to many workers' basic loyalties and to their sense of community.

The National Liberals showed themselves at least partially independent of narrow employer interests and able to appeal directly to workers' concerns. In the 1891 Bochum by-election Hermann Müllensiefen, National Liberal candidate and the owner of a glass factory, declared:

I bring my full sympathy to all efforts to improve the workers' lot—this is self-evident.

I agree with the miners' desire that the 8-hour shift should include winding-time, both in and out of the pit. I myself have for thirty years allowed our glass vessel makers to work only six hours since they work in rooms which cannot be adequately ventilated . . . I agree with the miners' desire that higher wages should be paid for overtime and that no one-sided pressure to work overtime should be exerted on the worker.

I agree with the miners' wish that those workers who were dismissed as a result of the miners' organizational efforts should be reinstated . . . When I have an opportunity to put in a word on behalf of these miners' concerns I will do so . . . [87]

---

[86] Saul, *Staat, Industrie, Arbeiterbewung*, p. 473 (note 159); Wehler, 'Polen im Ruhrgebiet', p. 560. Enquiries in 1908 suggested that in the Bochum area the Masurians had not been particularly prominent either politically or in industrial action and that while some supported the SPD and the Alter Verband 'by far the greatest proportion of the Masurians living here belong to the National Liberal Party'. StAB, 481, *Amt* Bochum II to KLB, 19. 2. 1908.

[87] StAB, *Märkischer Sprecher*, 7. 1. 1891.

This statement—which had little in common with the policies and practices of the (mainly National Liberal) mine-owners—seems to have had some effect and Müllensiefen won the election comfortably. However, he spoke only once in the *Reichstag* and his 'elucidation' had no impact on the miners' conditions of work.

Internal conflicts within the party appeared in the 1893 election, when the leaders of the Protestant workers' clubs threatened to put up their own candidate—Anton Fischer, a former miner—in opposition to the official party candidate. They were only dissuaded with a promise that in future the clubs would be consulted before candidates were selected. Dr Haarman, mayor of Witten and *Reichstag* deputy for Bochum from 1884 to 1890, was reselected. His campaign was based on appeals to patriotism: at stake was 'the security of the country, both internally and externally'; the *Bochumer Tageblatt* accused the social democrats of being in receipt of French funds and of wanting to hand back Alsace-Lorraine.[88] This appeal was insufficient, however, to defeat the Centre in the run-off.

Protestantism and patriotism continued as the main themes of most National Liberal campaigns. In the pre-war years the party improved its organization and its publicity while the growth of the 'yellow' unions offered a new forum in which its political as well as industrial policies were propagated amongst workers.[89] They were particularly important in helping the National Liberals to success in the 1913 *Landtag* election. Some National Liberals, however, distanced themselves from these company organizations, fearing that too close an association with the employers would reduce the party's independence and undermine its credibility with working-class voters: they therefore endorsed the criticism of the yellow unions voiced by the Protestant workers' clubs as well as by the independent trade unions. For the same reason the party rejected calls to establish National Liberal workers' clubs, fearing that they would become simply the

---

[88] IZF, *Rheinisch-Westfälische Arbeiter Zeitung*, 18, 24. 5. 1893; *Märkischer Sprecher*, 12. 6. 1893, quoted in Zehnter, 'Sie Vertraten Bochum', in *Ruhr-Nachrichten*, 26. 8. 1961; IZF, *Rheinisch-Westfälische Arbeiter Zeitung*, 8. 6. 1893.
[89] IZF, *Arbeiter Zeitung*, 11. 7. 1914.

mouthpiece of the large employers. Conversely, the Protestant workers' clubs continued to argue within the party for the adoption of working-class candidates.[90] In the 1912 *Reichstag* election the party chose as candidate in Bochum a working miner, Karl Heckmann, who was also a member of his Protestant workers'club and a critic of the yellow unions. The SPD claimed that Heckmann had blacklegged in 1905 but this was vigorously denied. Heckmann argued that the tariffs were the basis of German prosperity and that more armaments were necessary, not fewer as the social democrats maintained. With the support of the Centre, he defeated Hue in the run-off.

Class was thus just one issue amongst others in elections. All the parties were able to mount a credible appeal to at least some sections of the working class. The Centre and the National Liberals—though ironically not the SPD—even put up miners as candidates. Despite all attempts to overcome it, denominational loyalty remained a crucial political factor and politics from 1893 onwards remained locked in a somewhat sterile three-way division between social democrats, Centre, and National Liberals, with the Polish Nationalists weakening the Centre from 1903 onwards.

It is against this background that the cautious political stance of the SPD in Bochum and more generally in the Ruhr needs to be seen. It has long been recognized that the reformist approach adopted by the SPD nationally for most of the pre-war period—and beyond—owed more to the caution of ordinary union and party supporters than to the work of 'revisionist' intellectuals such as Eduard Bernstein. Nowhere was this more true than in the Ruhr. In 1899 the party's regional conference rejected any attempt to 'dilute' party principles along revisionist lines. In 1903, the year in which the revisionists were condemned at the Dresden party congress, the Bochum party roundly declared that there could be no basis for revisionism in the district: 'In view of the brutal and coarse struggle against the labour movement in the Ruhr, any of our party comrades who could be

[90] Saul, *Staat, Industrie, Arbeiterbewegung*, pp. 168–77; IZF, *Arbeiter Zeitung*, 10. 7. 1914.

a revisionist would not have understood the ABC of class consciousness.'[91]

Nevertheless, despite the reluctance to adopt overt revisionism, the SPD in Bochum and the Ruhr stood generally on the right wing of the party in its political views and showed itself cautious and non-provocative in its actions. In part this reflected the power of the trade unions, especially the Alter Verband, within the party. As we have seen, several leading Alter Verband figures stood as SPD candidates in elections. Theodor Bömelburg, the building workers' union leader, represented Dortmund in the *Reichstag*. At a lower level union influence was also strong. Peter Meis, a prominent miners' leader in Gelsenkirchen, played a leading role within the Bochum SPD in the early 1900s, becoming *Kreisvertrauensmann* (the key organizational post in the pre-1906 structure); Georg Wihsmann, who worked for the Alter Verband and its newspaper, was Bochum party chairman in 1906; he was succeeded by Fritz Husemann, a rising figure within the union who in 1908 stood as SPD candidate in the *Landtag* election in Bochum and in 1912 stood in the *Reichstag* election in Hamm-Soest. Even those who made their way primarily through the party were often active within the union movement. Paul Wolf, a wood-worker by trade, and Max König, a metal-worker, in 1899 ran the *Volksblatt* and were described by the Bochum police commissioner as 'the most unrelenting agitators in the constituency'.[92] Both went on to play leading roles within the SPD, holding posts as party journalists, office-holders, organizers, and as delegates to congresses. König became regional party organizer and in 1912 *Reichstag* deputy for the nearby constituency of Hagen-Schwelm. Yet both also served as local labour secretaries—posts set up by the unions rather than the party to provide practical help to

---

[91] StAB, 480, RPA to *Minister des Innern*, 8. 12. 1903; STAM, RA I 95 and 96, *Polizei-kommissar* Bochum to RPA, 1. 10. 1899 and 15. 10. 1903. See also G. Fülberth, 'Zur Genese des Revisionismus in der deutschen Sozialdemokratie vor 1914', in *Das Argument* (März 1971), pp. 1–21; H. J. Steinberg, *Sozialismus und deutsche Sozialdemokratie* (Bonn, 1972), pp. 124–5. Tampke misleadingly suggests that the Bochum party was revisionist: Tampke, *Ruhr and Revolution*, p. 24.

[92] Koszyk, *Anfänge und frühe Entwicklung*, p. 112.

workers with legal, insurance, and similar problems; and in 1904 Wolf combined the chairmanship of the Bochum SPD with that of the town's Trades Council.

The trade union experience of so many prominent local party figures helped ensure that the SPD adopted a hard-headed, practical approach and showed relatively little interest in the theories and debates of the party intellectuals, whether of right or left. Thus in reporting on the Dresden party congress at which revisionism had been the main topic under debate, Hue denounced the 'personal' quarrelling which in his view—and that of the Bochum party which accepted his report—had limited the time for 'important practical debates'. In 1905, during a further bout of ideological in-fighting within the national party, the Bochum branch adopted unanimously a resolution denouncing 'the unending squabblings' of a group of party writers who threatened to turn the forthcoming Jena congress into an 'arena for personal literary battles'.[93] In practice such views favoured the right. Hue's own sympathies were with the revisionists and he declined to join in the general condemnation of their views at Dresden. On international affairs he declared himself a supporter of national defence and even of a progressive colonial policy. In 1907 he voiced scepticism about the optimistic but vague anti-militarism of the Stuttgart Congress of the Second International: 'Militarism is an international phenonemon. It will not be swept from the world so quickly . . . One ought not to deceive oneself about the significance of national feeling.'[94] In 1908 he defended the social democrats in the southern German states who voted in support of their *Land* governments' budgets and had been roundly condemned by the left. He could even adopt an overtly nationalist tone; in 1903, when appealing to miners in Stockum not to embark on an ill-considered strike, he declared: 'We do not want a strike; we have the duty of saying to all miners—we must not see ourselves simply as miners but also as citizens of the state. As such we should

[93] StAB, 480, RPA to *Minister des Innern*, 8. 12. 1903; STAM, RA I 97, *Polizei-Commissar* Bochum to RPA, 1. 10. 1905.

[94] IZF, *Arbeiter Zeitung*, 16. 12. 1907, 30. 10. 1911; STAM, RA I 95, *Polizei-Commissar* Bochum to RPA, 30. 8. 1900.

not embark on anything which will bring harm to the state.'[95]

Hue was unusually outspoken and seems at times to have made a point of challenging the orthodoxies of the left. Within the Bochum party there was intermittent criticism of his views, especially around the turn of the century when he was emerging as the dominant figure within the Alter Verband. The critics particularly opposed his policy of political neutrality for the trade unions, arguing that the Alter Verband should instead show positive support for social democracy and seek to guide trade unionists into the party; they also called for a more militant and aggressive industrial policy—even at the risk of defeats at the hands of the employers. However, in Bochum the criticism remained muted. Hue was generally able to carry the local party with him, even when there was a clear undercurrent of concern about his more overtly right-wing opinions. His critics never coalesced around a particular issue or leader and never mounted a major challenge. Most party members seem to have shared, or at least accepted without explicit criticism, Hue's general stress on the need for cautious and non-radical policies and tactics. The characteristic party tone was expressed by the *Westfälische Freie Presse* just after the party's legalization in 1890. The paper explained that the party had 'never' used the term 'revolution' in a sense implying the use of force: the party's principle was 'revolutionary', aiming at fundamental changes in the state and society. And these changes should be achieved not through a "violent overthrow" but rather through organic development. We know that one cannot change society overnight or through arbitrarily mounted acts of force.'[96] Party rhetoric was often studiously vague about ultimate aims and how they were to be achieved, preferring to concentrate on specific issues, such as the iniquity of the food tariffs, or to lapse into generalized and unchallenging formulas. Thus the *Westfälischer Volks-Kalender*, published by the SPD in 1900, described the party

[95] STAM, RA I 96, *Polizei* Gelsenkirchen to RPA, 17. 8. 1903. See also a speech by Hue in 1899 quoted in Fritsch, *Revisionismus*, p. 68.

[96] IZF, *Westfälische Freie Presse*, 25. 11. 1890; IZF, *Volksblatt*, 28. 1. 1899; STAM, RA 1 95, *Polizei-kommissar* Bochum to RPA, 30. 8. 1900; 2. 10. 1901; ibid., *Stadt* Bochum to RPA, 31. 8. 1900.

and the unions as the twin halves of the labour movement the aim of which was 'to obviate the pernicious effects of capitalist production through legislative measures for the protection of the workers; above all to raise the working class as such to a higher moral, social, and political level'—hardly a call to the barricades. Otherwise the party concentrated on its own organizational growth: as Max König put it in 1905, 'here in the black Ruhr district our task is above all to strengthen our position by widening our organization and by winning new supporters'.[97]

Political radicalism, in contrast, seems generally to have been a weak and localized force in the Ruhr. The most significant radical figure was Konrad Haenisch, editor of the Dortmund party paper. His critique of the policies of the Alter Verband and its supporters within the SPD reached a head during the miners' strike of 1905, when the union leadership was calling for restraint in party propaganda in order to avoid offence to the Catholic and other non-socialist miners and to preserve the widest possible strike unity across political boundaries. Haenisch, on the other hand, felt that the mobilization achieved in the strike should be used as a basis for socialist advance. In the *Leipziger Volkszeitung* he argued that the strike had offered an opportunity to mobilize 'the masses' for the party and in particular to smash the anti-socialist Catholic organizations; only lack of leadership had prevented this. Karl Kautsky, the SPD's most respected theoretician, gave some support to this view when he argued in *Neue Zeit* that the strike had been a defeat and that the unions should take a broader, more political view of their actions. Hue rejected such criticisms, maintaining that they betrayed an ignorance of the true conditions in the Ruhr: 'There is no question of an individualist radicalism among us here in the Ruhr, because we are not the masters of the situation. The personal inclinations and the views of the individual play no role here, because we have to deal with facts which take precedence over the speculations of individuals.'[98]

[97] StAB, 479, *Westfälische Volks-Kalender* (1900); Lützenkirchen, *Sozialdemokratische Verein*, p. 40.

[98] IZF, *Arbeiter Zeitung*, 13, 14, 15, 11. 1905; Koch, *Bergarbeiterbewegung*, pp. 101–4; *Aufsätze über den Streik der Bergarbeiter im Ruhrgebiet* (1905), p. 50.

The main 'fact' which Hue claimed his critics ignored was the power of the employers, which made caution imperative and meant that industrial action could not be undertaken lightly. That year he ostentatiously declined to attend the party congress at Jena, where he knew he would be strongly criticized, on the pretext that he had to campaign in a by-election in Essen. Paul Wolf went instead and tried—against frequent interruptions from Rosa Luxemburg and Konrad Haenisch—to defend the *Bergarbeiter Zeitung*. The tone of the dispute is illustrated by an unsigned article in the *Bergarbeiter Zeitung* after the congress:

Frau Rosa Luxemburg accused us at Jena of advising her to go to Russia to struggle with the workers against the knout-regime instead of writing 'revolutionary' articles from health resorts. The *Bergarbeiter Zeitung* did indeed write that, and rightly so. The Russian workers are bleeding but great revolutionary theoreticians, who play superficially with bloody revolution in their speeches and writings, stay far from the fire. In Jena too Frau Rosa Luxemburg and those who think like her made speeches which dealt with blood and revolution. Sensible people tell themselves, 'Dogs which bark loudly don't bite' . . . [99]

Despite—or perhaps because of—the experience of the 1905 miners' strike, the radicals' call for the political mass strike found little echo in the district. In Dortmund Haenisch was opposed by the most prominent figures in both the unions and party, including Bömelburg and König. Indeed, so isolated did he feel that before the year was out he left for the more congenial atmosphere of the *Leipziger Volkszeitung*. A year later he returned and under his editorship the *Arbeiter Zeitung* became one of the more radical papers in Germany. Yet the shallowness of this was demonstrated in 1910 when Georg Beyer, one of the editors, left the paper. Haenisch once again found himself without support: 'At the moment I am completely isolated on the paper', he wrote, and three months later he again resigned. The paper promptly ceased to display its former radicalism, and in 1912 was even listed by the *Bremer Bürgerzeitung* as one of the party's revisionist papers.[100]

[99] IZF, *Bergarbeiter Zeitung*, 7. 10. 1905; STAM, RA I 97, *Polizei-Commisar* Bochum to RPA, 1. 10. 1905; StAB, 480, RPA to *Minister des Innern*, 22. 12. 1905; Nettl, *Rosa Luxemburg* (1969 edition), p. 206. Luxemburg did indeed return to Russia shortly afterwards.
[100] Lützenkirchen, *Sozialdemokratische Verein*, pp. 38-40, 76-84.

Haenisch claimed that he was always given full support when he addressed working miners in the area; and it has been argued that the defeats which he and the radicals suffered in Dortmund were due largely to the machinations of conservative party and union functionaries.[101] The radicals were unable to demonstrate, however, that they actually enjoyed the support of most party members or ordinary workers. Their sporadic attempts to organize opposition to the party and union leaderships achieved little success. In Brackel, outside Dortmund, the local SPD branch formed a radical stronghold for some years but no other local branches—certainly none in or around Bochum—achieved a parallel reputation. Local government officials considered that few workers had much interest in the more political and ideological aspects of the SPD's policies. The Hattingen *Landrat* commented in 1898:

I remain strongly of the view that a large proportion of those who have cast social democratic votes are not really committed social democrats, and certainly not so far as the monarchy and religion are concerned. They want to improve their material situation and see in social democracy, which is not niggardly with promises, the party which will bring them nearer their goals. One could describe such people accurately as economic social democrats.[102]

In such circumstances it proved hard to translate the latent discontent and sporadic strike militancy of the Ruhr miners into a broader, politically radical movement. This was clearly shown in the years after 1905 when a recognizable anarcho-socialist movement appeared, fuelled in part by frustrations amongst some miners with the conservative policies of both Alter Verband and SPD. In 1907 Ferdinand Kampmann, who lived in Brackel and was local chairman of an anarcho-socialist miners' association opposed to the Alter Verband, came to work at *Bruchstrasse*, the Langendreer pit where the 1905 strike had originated. He was regarded as one of the most hard-working and conscientious men. He fought

---

[101] Lützenkirchen, *Sozialdemokratische Verein.*

[102] STAM, RA I 94, *Landrat* Hattingen to RPA, 17. 8. 1898. When the Kaiser visited Dortmund in the following year he was well received and was assured 'that the many social democratic voters have long been not true socialists but citizens loyal to their Empire and King'. StAB, 479, RPA to *Minister des Innern*, 27. 11. 1899.

a sustained campaign against the Alter Verband, worked on May Day when some social democrats stayed away, and distributed anarchist publications. He had little success: in 1909 bad relations with his colleagues forced him to leave the pit. In 1910 a small group of anarchists—around ten in all—met regularly in neighbouring Werne. Local groups of the anarcho-socialist 'Free Miners' Association' were reported in Brackel, Dortmund and Berghofen; the organization was said to have around 450 members in the Ruhr as a whole, 250 of them former Alter Verband members. A 'Free Association for All Trades' was reported in Gelsenkirchen. This, however, was the movement's peak. A year later it had disappeared from Werne, although a branch of the Free Miners' Association with around twelve members was in existence in Langendreer. This branch too was shortlived: by 1913 it had closed down, apparently under the combined influence of the 1912 strike defeat and the high wages which were being paid in the district.[103]

These isolated and short-lived campaigns were the only reported attempts to create more radical organizations in the Bochum area in opposition to the policies of the Alter Verband and the SPD. Despite the occasional willingness of miners to ignore their leaders' advice when it came to industrial conflict, few were actively interested in a systematic political opposition. The prime interest of the miners in the immediate issues of the workplace was illustrated by their continued greater interest in union than party matters. Party membership never matched union membership. As the Arnsberg *Regierungs-Präsident* commented in 1901: 'The focus of the labour movement in the industrial district is without question the trade unions. The workers demonstrate greater interest in the economic daily questions than in the implementation of political theories. Social democracy knows well how to adapt to the given situation . . . Without doubt the party

[103] One factor behind the decline of the radical movement after 1910 was the more militant policy shown by the Alter Verband in the two years leading up to the 1912 strike. K. Tenfelde, 'Linksradikale Strömungen in der Ruhrbergarbeiterschaft 1905 bis 1919', in Mommsen and Borsdorf (ed.), *Glück auf, Kameraden!* pp. 199–223; Lucas, *Arbeiterradikalismus*, pp. 133–4, 162–4; StAB, 481 and 482; STAM, *Oberpräsidium* 2694 Bd. 2, RPA to *Minister des Innern*, 26. 10. 1910.

owes a large part of its success in elections to this work in the trade unions'.[104]

The general agreement between union and party on the need for a non-radical approach was clearly shown in their attitude to May Day, one of the touchstones on the left–right divide within the national party. Nor surprisingly, Otto Hue adopted a cool attitude towards the international day of labour. In a personal article on the subject in 1904 he commented: 'No one—not me either!—is completely against May Day. But since it should be a powerful demonstration for workers' protection and peace between peoples, strong mass participation must be possible.' May Day should therefore be celebrated on the first Sunday in May, when all workers could participate; mass strikes on 1 May were 'impossible' to carry out.[105] Although the article was criticized by the executive of the Alter Verband, Heinrich Sachse, the union chairman, agreed that strikes were not possible:

Certainly strike action on May Day has never been adopted by any union meeting, nor by any area or pit meeting. I too have never called for the general cessation of work on 1 May at any miners' meeting, because we were hitherto always too weak in the face of powerful mining capital. But on the other hand I, and other comrades, have argued for 14 years that those comrades on the night shift should participate in large numbers in the day-time meetings on 1 May and that those who have day shifts should participate in the evening meetings and festivities. I have not heard that we miners and foundry workers have been severely criticized at party congresses etc. where May Day is discussed and resolutions passed because we do not stop work on 1 May. Such criticism would have to be resolutely rejected. Because the mining capitalists have virtually always dismissed and

---

[104] StAB, 480, RPA to *Minister des Innern*, 15. 11. 1901. The primacy of the trade unions distinguished the SPD in the Ruhr from neighbouring Düsseldorf, where trade unionism was relatively muted and where the party itself was largely an instrument of outsiders, operating within a predominantly Catholic working class. The relative detachment of the party from close involvement in day-to-day industrial concerns gave it the freedom to operate with relatively few constraints in the sphere of pure politics. This in turn allowed Düsseldorf social democrats to espouse political goals and tactics of a more fundamentalist, radical nature than those of their Ruhr comrades. At the same time, it limited their scope for achieving results. Nolan, *Social democracy and society*.

[105] IZF, *Bergarbeiter Zeitung*, 12. 11. 1904.

disciplined comrades who stayed away on 1 May . . . Some will certainly claim that the 'possibility' [of striking] does exist for the miners and foundry workers. I say, no, not yet![106]

The Bochum SPD branch shared the general scepticism about May Day and submitted a resolution to the Bremen party congress calling for May Day to be celebrated on the first Sunday in the month.[107]

In practice no one seems to have regarded a mass strike on May Day as a serious possibility. In 1905 an SPD meeting in Langendreer decided, apparently without demur, that although meetings would be held on 1 May, a Monday, the main events would be held on the Sunday since the miners' strike 'has shown us how sharply the pit managements punish absence from work'.[108] The Bochum party debated the question again in 1907. Wetzker, editor of the *Volksblatt*, had told the national party congress in Essen that until he came to the Ruhr (he had previously worked on the *Vorwärts*) he had been a keen supporter of work stoppages on May Day but that his experience in the Ruhr had made him change his mind; the miners and the foundry workers would not support such strikes and in the Bochum constituency, which had around 42,000 SPD voters, only around one thousand participated in the May Day events. In a heated party meeting in Bochum, Sachse and Herzig maintained that support for May Day activities was higher than this; but no one claimed that significant work stoppages took place. One party member commented: 'The Dortmund and Essen delegates had exaggerated to an unbelievable extent. In this district the participation had remained pitiful. They should have had the courage to recognize the truth and simply end something which could not be carried through.' Franz Pokorny, the Gelsenkirchen miners' leader, suggested that 'the demonstrations could be just as effective on a Sunday as today's work stoppage—which is no work stoppage'.[109]

[106] IZF, *Bergarbeiter Zeitung*, 3. 12. 1904. On the general debate on May Day at the national and international level see Schorske, *German Social Democracy*, pp. 91-7; J. Joll, *The Second International 1889-1914* (London, 1974 edition), pp. 48-54.

[107] STAM, RA I 96, *Polizei-Commissar* Bochum to RPA, 10. 10. 1904.

[108] StAB, 480, *Amt* Lagendreer to KLB, 6. 3. 1905.

[109] StAB, 481, RPA to *Minister des Innern*, 28. 11. 1907; IISG, *Volksblatt*, 3. 10. 1907.

With both union and party opposed to strike action on
May Day it is not surprising that only one significant
stoppage is reported in the Bochum district throughout this
period. This occurred in 1909 when 150 men stopped work
at *Bruchstrasse*. In the main, however, May Day was celebrated
as a politically-coloured day out, enjoyed by those whose
shift permitted. Participation was far higher, therefore, when
May Day fell on a Sunday as in 1904 and 1910. Apart from
the speeches and resolutions it was a chance to enjoy a walk
through the neighbouring countryside in early summer. In
the morning groups would gather at various assembly points;
after passing the official resolutions they would walk from
one village to another, distributing the party paper and leaflets and stopping for refreshments along the way. Women
and children frequently joined in, making it a family occasion, and there was usually singing, dancing, and games. Many
of the groups would only be distinguished from ordinary
ramblers by their red insignia (ties and flowers), a police
presence, and their socialist literature. The police insisted
that the groups remain small and sometimes forced the red
insignia to be removed. The pettiest misdemeanour was likely
to end in arrest. In the evening further meetings were held,
particularly for those on the day shift, at which there was
a mixture of political speech-making and social enjoyment.
So great was the social element, indeed, that the party
became increasingly concerned that the day was losing its
political significance altogether. Despite efforts to overcome
this by centralizing more of the events and encouraging wider
popular involvement the party had to concede in 1914
'that May Day is constantly losing more and more of its
original character as a day of struggle'.[110]
Other areas of party life showed the same non-radical
and even non-political character. Like the Churches and
other organizations, the SPD sponsored a wide range of social
activities, including choirs (fourteen in the Bochum area
alone in 1907) and cycling and athletic clubs. The latter

[110] IZF, *Arbeiter Zeitung*, 30. 6. 1914; StAB, 482, *Polizei-Präsident* Bochum
to RPA, 30. 5. 1916. See also Hickey, *Class conflict and class consciousness*,
pp. 361–2; P. Friedemann, 'Feste und Feiern im rheinisch-westfälischen Industriegebiet 1890 bis 1914', in Huck (ed.), *Sozialgeschichte der Freizeit*, pp. 161–85.

were aimed particularly at young people who until 1907 were prevented by law from joining political associations. How 'political' these clubs were it is hard to say, but the impression is that they were primarily recreational. This was certainly true of the bowling club formed by Hue, Sachse, and other leading figures in Bochum in 1906: with tongue in cheek they called themselves the 'Klub der Königstreuen' and under this name were able to obtain the use of one of the town's better bowling alleys. Since most leisure activities had to take place on Sundays the social democratic clubs were in direct competition with the Catholic, Protestant, Polish, and other clubs, as well as less overtly political bodies such as the private drinking clubs which proliferated (in part due to the shortage of proper inns). Some of these private organizations may themselves have had a social democratic character, depending on the members. The penumbra of socialist leisure organizations certainly helped to to consolidate the party's advance by providing its members with a cultural environment which supported and reinforced their political convictions and to some extent isolated them from rival groups. Bearing in mind the turnover of members, however, relatively few workers can have spent long in a narrowly social democratic social setting. Perhaps the main effect of the growth of competing, ideologically-characterized recreational sub-cultures was to reinforce and consolidate the political divisions within the working class, reducing the likelihood that they could be readily overcome either by the social democrats or anyone else.[111]

In practice the party's main activity, apart from trying to build its organizational base, was fighting *Reichstag* elections—a task with a clear focus in which all shades of opinion could join enthusiastically. The party set new

[111] STAM, RA I 98, *Oberbürgermeister* Bochum to RPA, 29. 9. 1906; IZF, *Arbeiter Zeitung*, 29. 6. 1914. See also Brüggemeier and Niethammer, 'Schlafgänger, Schnapskasinos und schwerindustrielle Kolonie', and K. Tenfelde, 'Bergmännisches Vereinswesen im Ruhrgebiet während der Industrialisierung', in Reulecke and Weber (ed.), *Fabrik, Familie, Feierabend*; Friedemann, 'Feste und Feiern'. For the wider debate about the role of recreational organizations within German social democracy, see the special issue on workers' culture of *Journal of Contemporary History* xiii (1978); Eley and Nield, 'Why does social history ignore politics?'; Evans, 'The Sociological Interpretation of German Labour History'.

standards of electioneering activity which the others were
then compelled to match. Of particular significance, therefore, as the one issue outside elections which did generate
a substantial level of political activity and even signs of
uncharacteristic militancy. This was the campaign for the
reform of the three-class franchise for the Prussian *Landtag*,
an electoral system which ensured that the wealthy and
privileged maintained effective control over that important
legislative body. The issue came to the fore in the aftermath
of the 1905 miners' strike, when the original Government proposals for the reform of the mining law were watered down by
the *Landtag*. A miners' slogan read: 'In the *Landtag* we get
stones instead of bread!' Otto Hue declared at a party meeting:
'German policy is made not in the *Reichstag* but in the Prussian
Landtag. That is not just the case today, but has always been
so', and he called for increased agitation on the issue.[112]

Many meetings on the franchise question were held in
1907 and 1908, during the run-up to the *Landtag* election
of 1908. Some were so popular that people had to be turned
away. After one meeting in January 1908 a small street
demonstration took place in Bochum, against the wishes
of the party leadership; only around one hundred demon-
strators took part and it was quickly broken up by the police
with three arrests; this was the first reported unauthorized
political street demonstration in Bochum. The franchise
campaign was more subdued in 1909 but picked up in early
1910. Meetings—and in Hordel a torch-lit procession—were
held in January 1910 and mass meetings in February attracted
around 5,000 people in Bochum and 3,000 in Gelsenkirchen.
These meetings were followed by planned street demonstrations—the first in either town. The demonstrations passed
off without incident but in Dortmund there was conflict
with the police and a demonstration was broken up. The
Bochum police warned the SPD that in future any unauthorized demonstrations would be stopped. In March many more
protest meetings were held and on 10 April the largest mass
meetings of the entire pre-war period: some 15,000 were
estimated to have gathered at Bochum's main meeting hall,
the Schützenhof, and were addressed from three platforms.

[112] IZF, *Arbeiter Zeitung*, 16. 12. 1907.

In Dortmund over 20,000 heard Karl Liebknecht and others. This marked the climax of the campaign. Open-air meetings on the issue in October 1912 were not well attended and in 1914 the party expressed disappointment at the lack of enthusiasm amongst 'the masses' on the issue.[113]

The Prussian franchise campaign was the only significant instance of large-scale party mobilization outside *Reichstag* elections and the only occasion on which the SPD resorted to such provocative tactics as the street demonstration and the really large mass meeting. Despite the impetus given by the role of the *Landtag* in the aftermath of the 1905 miners' strike, the agitation in the Ruhr was but part of a wider national campaign, marked by massive popular support. This did not prevent bitter arguments within the party between those who wished to push the movement further, to employ the mass strike and to create a truly revolutionary confrontation with the existing order, and those who preferred to seek a broader parliamentary alliance designed to achieve this specific goal. Many of the party leaders found themselves caught between the competing currents and unable to take any decisive stand. On the issue itself, however, all could unite. Indeed, despite the obstacles to its achievement in the Wilhelmine state, reform of the Prussian franchise was fundamentally a liberal, 'reformist' demand on which the most right-wing social democrat—and even non-socialist liberals—could agitate with as much conviction as the radicals. Mass mobilization on this issue did not therefore represent a fundamental conflict with the party's generally moderate and pragmatic policies. The arguments were about wider goals and about methods and here the Bochum SPD showed again its characteristic conservatism: at the party's last pre-war general meeting a call for the use of the political mass strike on the issue was decisively rejected.[114]

[113] STAM, RA I 100, *Volksblatt*, 25, 26. 8. 1908; STAM, Bochum *Landratsamt* 178, *Amt* Hordel to KLB, 17. 1. 1910; IZF, *Arbeiter Zeitung*, 3, 4, 6, 9. 10. 1911; 10. 7. 1914.

[114] The mass strike call was rejected by 42 votes to 29. StAB, 482, *Polizei-Präsident* Bochum to RPA, 2. 7. 1914. On the Prussian franchise issue generally see Groh, *Negative Integration und Revolutionärer Attentismus*, pp. 128-60, 476-502; Schorske, *German Social Democracy*, pp. 171-87; Barrington Moore, *Injustice*, pp. 224-5.

Conclusions

Miners have long been noted for their solidarity and militancy. Writing in the 1920s, G. D. H. Cole observed:

The miner not only works in the pit, he lives in the pit village, and all his immediate interests are concentrated at one point. The town factory worker, on the other hand, lives often far from his place of work and mingles with workers of other callings. The townsman's experience produces perhaps a broader outlook, and a quicker response to social stimuli coming from without; but the miners' intense solidarity and loyalty to their unions is undoubtedly the result of conditions under which they work and live . . . Their isolation ministers to their self-sufficiency and loyalty one to another.[1]

In many ways the Ruhr might seem to have offered particularly favourable conditions under which such solidarity might grow. Not only was it one of the largest and most important coal-fields in Europe but it was a place where contrasts between the classes were strikingly obvious. On the one hand, the biggest and most advanced concentration of capitalist industry in Germany and perhaps in Europe: in terms of capital investment, technological innovation, growth rates, and structural rationalization, heavy industry in the Ruhr was in the forefront of economic progress. On the other, the most heavily proletarian social structure in Germany, with huge conglomerations of workers living and working in conditions which by any standard were harsh and raw.

Ruhr miners had much in common. Pit work varied little in essence from one mine to another and most miners carried out similar tasks. Differences between men at work were generally the result of varying ages or personal circumstances such as individual health or strength rather than the expression of lasting, structural divisions between 'skilled' and 'unskilled' or between the vast range of trades and

---

[1] Quoted in W. H. Scott *et al., Coal and Conflict: a study of industrial relations at collieries* (Liverpool, 1963), p. 25.

specializations which proliferated in the metal industry. Shared dangers, mutual reliance underground, the co-operative work ethos essential within the *Kameradschaft*, and the routine experience of conflict with pit officials reinforced the sense of shared interests and common identity. Although few had any personal experience of it, memories of the pre-liberalization regime, when miners had enjoyed high social status and had received special privileges and protection from the state, were still evoked and gave both a sense of moral anger that their collective position had been devalued and concrete illustrations of how perhaps it might again be improved.

Mine-work offered many grounds for conflict. The work was hard, dangerous, and unpleasant. Accidents and sickness were common. Discipline was harsh and the actions of pit officials seemed often arbitrary and demeaning to the men. It was better paid than some other jobs and earnings were higher in the Ruhr than in many other parts of Germany. Nevertheless for many miners, particularly those with large families and those whose strength was undermined through sickness or injury, earnings were barely adequate. Moreover, earnings were unstable and unpredictable, varying with the coal-face and the changing economic climate. Hours of work also fluctuated: booms created pressure to work longer and longer hours while recessions meant short time, lay-offs, and reduced earnings. In general, economic upswings led to heightened tensions as both employers and workers sought to capitalize on the improved conditions and as the balance of power shifted with the growth in demand for labour.

Not surprisingly, therefore, Ruhr miners engaged from time to time in militant industrial action and proved themselves capable of impressive demonstrations of solidarity. The strikes of 1889 and 1905 were primarily 'spontaneous', rank-and-file affairs and won overwhelming support. In the aftermath of the 1905 strike Rosa Luxemburg described miners' disputes as 'mass strikes of typical, elemental character' which demonstrated that 'the antagonism between labour and capital is too sharp and violent to allow of its crumbling away in the form of quiet, systematic, partial trade union struggles'.[2] 1912 saw a further major strike and

² Luxemburg, *The mass strike*, p. 56.

economic upturns were generally accompanied by bursts of smaller disputes as miners sought to improve their pay, limit the hours underground, and restrict the arbitrary and capricious acts of pit officials. The special circumstances of the hauliers and other younger mineworkers—their relatively rigid pay system, their youth, and their lack of commitments —meant that they were frequently in the van of such actions.

Solidarity could also find organizational expression: occupational associations enjoyed a long history in the region and miners' trade unions were amongst the earliest and most important in the union movement in Germany. Sometimes it took more overtly political forms: miners were prominent in the political life of the district and there were close relations between working-class union and political movements. The miners' militancy was further highlighted by the contrast with the metal-workers in the same district: despite the undoubted harshness of their conditions they rarely struck work, never undertook a major industrial dispute, and proved reluctant to join trade unions. This contrast has led historians to stress the factors which bound miners together, giving them a sense of 'collective identity' and creating an 'occupational community', expressed above all in collective, militant action.[3]

Yet despite this, the persistent theme of the present study has been the fundamental importance of the divisions within the working class in the Ruhr. These were the product of several factors. The massive influx of workers to the Ruhr, combined with high migration within the district, meant that throughout the pre-war period the working class was rapidly growing and changing. Coming from many different backgrounds, with varying cultural traditions and speaking several languages and dialects, the new workers often had little in common. Divisions were perpetuated by such features as company housing, frequently allocated on an ethnic basis and isolated even from the homes of fellow-workers, and the important role of denominational ties and organizations within the social and community life of the district. Religion did not stop workers from experiencing

[3] Crew, *Town in the Ruhr*, pp. 176–94; Barrington Moore, *Injustice*, p. 257.

social injustice or from participating in industrial and political conflict: but many workers did so within a linguistic and social framework which isolated them from other confessional groups and particularly from the 'atheistic' social democrats. Loyalties for many remained focused on particular groups, often defined in terms of ethnic origins or religious allegiance, and not on a broader concept of the workers at large.

Even at the work-place division and lack of solidarity was often crucial. This was particularly obvious in the metal industry where the multiple barriers between companies, plants, skills, trades, and even between individuals on the same task (through the use of techniques such as individually-tailored bonus systems) meant that broadly based conflict never occurred. Even within the mining industry, however, the signs of disunity were often apparent. Collective action was not the only or the most popular way of seeking relief or improvements. Much more common, and equally responsive to fluctuating economic conditions, were the more individualist methods of job-changing or simply absenteeism. Even when strikes did occur they normally failed to generate much support. Often they remained limited to the young hauliers who started them; hewers, who had less need to strike because they could improve their earnings through the regular bargaining system and the threat to move elsewhere, frequently failed to support them and sometimes even undertook their work. Most strikes remained limited to a particular locality. Even the solidarity of the three 'general' strikes of 1889, 1905, and 1912 was limited: although at their peak they all involved a large majority of mineworkers, in no case was it possible to sustain general support for a protracted period; the best performance was in 1905 when around three-quarters of the mineworkers stayed out for about three weeks; but even then it was widely recognized that once back-pay was exhausted a significant drift back to work was inevitable.

Disunity was also endemic in the trade union and political life of the district. The attempt to organize was itself a recognition that industrial militancy alone was unable to achieve the goals which the miners sought. Yet every attempt to establish a united organizational structure foundered on the insuperable rivalries of religion, politics, and ethnic suspicion. Not one but four miners' unions emerged and not one but four political parties managed to lay claim to the workers' votes. Co-operation on the basis of common interests was the exception rather than the norm. Certainly in the final years before 1914 co-operation between the two main wings of the organized working class, the social democrats and the Centre, and their respective union organizations, was a shattered hope.

What was the significance of this stress on the fluid, unstable, and divided character of working-class society and politics, in contrast to those factors which fostered co-operation and solidarity? Perhaps three main features emerge of broad significance for the history of labour in Germany.

In the first place, it serves to remind us that the 'working class' in Germany, even as late as 1914, was new, raw, unstable, and still in the very throes of creation. It was certainly not a mature and developed entity with well-established industrial and social structures and behaviour patterns. Industrial demands were changing; geographical mobility was high; social networks were being rapidly altered in new settings; 'communities' were often in the very process of construction. This perspective, while hardly novel, is sometimes lost when the prime focus rests as it so often does on the history of the SPD, which by 1914 had achieved an apparently impressive degree of maturity and solidity.

Secondly, this emphasis may help to redress the balance away from a sometimes one-sided emphasis on the causes and manifestations of social conflict and towards a greater concern with the results. For however impressive the militancy and solidarity sometimes shown by the Ruhr miners, it was never sufficient to actually defeat the employers. Militancy alone did not mean power. Indeed, it is hard to point to any significant concession extracted from the employers by miners' industrial action in this period. In this perspective the contrast between the miners and metal-workers is perhaps less significant than has sometimes been assumed: both were industrially weak, with the difference that most metal-workers recognized this and avoided confrontations while the miners from time to time risked—and duly lost —the gamble of strike action. Conversely, the as yet relatively unexplored contrast with building workers, who were able to achieve real successes through industrial action, may offer more fruitful lines of enquiry.

Thirdly, it may contribute towards a better understanding of the German labour movement itself. The emphasis on organization and the cautious, non-radical policies and tactics which accompanied it can be seen—in the Ruhr at least— largely as a response to the realities of an unsettled, divided working class and the experience of industrial weakness. It was the failure of strikes which led to the first efforts to organize and it was the experience of repeated defeats, above all in the disastrous years of the early 1890s when strike after strike ended in failure and the recently-formed unions were virtually destroyed, which impressed the leadership with the need to avoid conflicts which they were bound to lose. The appeal of unionism lay largely in the hope that it offered a more promising means of establishing effective workers' power than such strikes. From the beginning, therefore, there was an in-built tension between the characteristic strike behaviour of Ruhr miners and the concept of organization. The former typically consisted of unplanned, spontaneous stoppages, often led by relatively small groups of young miners and frequently never spreading much wider. The latter depended for success on the ability not merely to call out the vast majority of mineworkers but to sustain them in a protracted struggle: only this—or the credible threat that it could be achieved—was likely to sway the employers. To achieve it, however, required a co-ordinated and disciplined approach, a stress on organizational development, financial strength and the husbanding of resources until a particularly favourable opportunity occurred.

The politics of the labour movement are also most appropriately seen in this social context. Recognition that the miners remained deeply divided along social, religious, ethnic, and political lines led the Alter Verband to stress its ostensible political and religious neutrality. None the less, there was a substantial overlap between the union and the

SPD and the party was heavily influenced by the union's pragmatism, caution, and impatience with the remote disputations of party theorists. Not that the weakness of political radicalism within the SPD was due merely to the hostility of union and party leaders: in the Ruhr it was never a strong or widely supported cause in the pre-war period. The bitter experience of the mass strikes which did take place made it inconceivable to most members that, for example, strike action should be attempted on May Day or in support of other social democratic political objectives to which many workers were clearly opposed. Rather than pursue actions or ideological objectives which threatened merely to reinforce the existing divisions within the working class and to highlight again their lack of industrial strength, the party's main concern was to utilize the one political avenue which offered some prospect of success, the ballot.

More generally, the very culture of the labour movement can perhaps be seen as a response to the prevailing social realities of working-class life. The stress on discipline and deliberation can be seen as a reaction to the tendency towards precipitate and disastrous action. The attempt to create a distinct social democratic 'sub-culture' of social and cultural organizations was perhaps an implicit recognition that a cohesive, established working-class culture and community did not in fact already exist. The avoidance of controversial subjects like religion, and even aspects of politics themselves, reflected the divisions which existed amongst the workers on such issues. Above all, the stress on organization as such reflected the unstable and unsettled nature of so much working-class life and experience, the mobility of many workers, and the lack of lasting commitment even by many ostensible supporters—as evidenced by the rapid membership turnover. The labour movement was not so much building on a strong and cohesive working-class community and culture as trying to create one.

The fact that the policies of the labour movement can be seen in large measure as a response to the social characteristics of the area did not mean that the hopes of the leaders were realized in practice. Neither the Alter Verband nor the SPD succeeded in overcoming the divisions within the working class. The Gewerkverein and the Centre party retained the allegiance of many Catholic workers while disaffected Poles turned not to the social democrats but to nationalist organizations. Even the National Liberal party, the main political vehicle of the Ruhr employers, continued to appeal successfully to numbers of workers. Just as serious was the fact that most miners remained outside any organization at all while many of those who did join soon left again. The divided, unstable, and mobile character of the working class thus made organizational strength an attractive goal but rendered its achievement hard.

The result was that the organized labour movement, like miners' wild-cat strikes before it, failed to develop into an effective working-class power capable of seriously challenging that of the employers. This was demonstrated only too clearly in the twin defeats of 1912 when the miners' third mass strike ended disastrously within days and the SPD lost two *Reichstag* seats in the Ruhr. Up to 1914 the employers remained virtually as strong as ever.

Might a more radical approach by the labour movement have proved more successful? By the late 1900s the union itself had recognized that a policy of simply avoiding and restraining strikes until general unionization was achieved could not be sustained. The outbreak of the 1905 strike showed that the miners were not willing to forgo this weapon indefinitely. Nevertheless, it remains doubtful whether a more militant union policy would have achieved lasting success. The repeated failure of the strikes of the early 1890s had contributed to the union collapse which followed and showed the danger of simple reliance on industrial militancy; even the 1905 strike could not be sustained for the prolonged period necessary to seriously threaten the economic power of the employers; when finally three of the four miners' unions did combine in an aggressive strike in 1912 the result was an unmitigated disaster, followed by a fall in membership, serious demoralization, and a growth in 'yellow' unionism.

The inability of workers in the Ruhr, one of the main industrial centres of Germany and Europe, to mount an effective challenge to their employers signified a serious weakness at the very basis of the labour movement in Germany. It indicated that the autonomous power base of the labour movement and its scope for successful action was limited, particularly in the industrial and economic sphere. This weakness, which was by no means restricted to the Ruhr, may help us to understand the German labour movement's continuing overriding concern with and dependence on the sphere of pure politics. In some parts of the movement this took the form of an explicit denial that industrially-based, economically-orientated trade union action could ever achieve worthwhile results without a prior wholesale transformation of the political order in Germany. However, even for the reformists who dominated the movement, the hope of political concessions offered a possible way forward. It was significant, therefore, that despite the Wilhelmine state's antipathy to the labour movement, the few tangible concessions won by the miners came not from the employers but from the Government. Despite their clear limitations, concessions such as statutory limits on the working day, the establishment of workers' committees and workers' safety-officers— imposed against the wishes of the otherwise unbowed employers—suggested that the state might serve as a counter-weight, able to help the labour movement compensate for its own lack of industrial strength. It was a potential way forward from the impasse of powerlessness which was to become more explicit and important during the war and especially after it.

In a longer-term perspective it is possible to see a heavy dependence on politically-won concessions and legally-defined rights as a lasting characteristic of German labour —in contrast to the shop-floor power and non-statutory 'custom and practice' which has been the prime strength of labour in Britain. It is a characteristic which has enabled the German labour movement to secure major gains for its members when political circumstances have proved favourable, but which has also left it dangerously vulnerable to the vicissitudes of political change. The inability even of the miners to convert unparalleled militancy into effective industrial power was one element in this vulnerability and therefore of long-term significance not just for the industry but for the general direction of labour in Germany.

Postscript

The news of war on 25 July 1914 left the people on the streets of Bochum quiet and chastened. Five days later, several thousand marched through the town singing patriotic and soldiers' songs and ended with cheers for the Kaiser and for the town. The social democrats fell in with the national mood. The Bochum *Volksblatt* regarded it as 'self-evident' that its readers would fulfil their military duty and would accept the necessities of war—including the banning of party meetings. Overt opposition was rare: one protest meeting in Bochum, a man arrested in Gelsenkirchen for delivering 'inflammatory speeches' and a Polish nationalist arrested in Gerthe after signs of anti-German feeling among some Poles there.[4]

The war meant major changes. Around 100,000 miners were called up, creating serious labour shortages which eventually had to be filled with juveniles, prisoners, and labour from the occupied countries. Political authority and, increasingly, economic power henceforth lay in military hands. Working and social conditions worsened, with increased pressures at work, reduced attention to safety, and serious food shortages, especially in later years of the war.[5]

For the labour movement war offered an unprecedented opportunity to break out of the powerlessness which had hitherto rendered it so ineffective. The unions supported the 'Burgfrieden'—the cessation of internal conflict declared at the outbreak of war and intended to last for the duration. The Alter Verband, like other unions, did its best to maintain industrial harmony and to avoid strikes. In return, the unions were granted a degree of recognition and influence which they had never previously enjoyed. At the national level this was most clearly expressed in the Auxiliary Service Law of 1916, a measure which introduced some direction into the labour market but, more importantly for the unions, institutionalized a tripartite structure of Government,

---

[4] IZF, *Volksblatt*, 1, 8. 8. 1914; StAB, 482, *Amt* Harpen to KLB, 12. 8. 1914, *Polizei-Präsident* Bochum to RPA, 30. 5. 1916; StAB, *Märkischer Sprecher*, 27, 31. 7. 1914. SPD party meetings were soon resumed.

[5] Tampke, *Ruhr and Revolution*, chapter 3.

employer, and employee representation in important areas of economic life. In particular—and modelled to some extent on the committee structure introduced into the mining industry after the 1905 strike—an extensive system of arbitration and other committees was established, in which union nominees enjoyed equal status with those of the employers. Throughout the war, however, the Ruhr employers maintained their hostility to the unions, refusing to recognize them, opposing the Auxiliary Service Law in draft, and doing their best to minimize its impact in practice even after it was passed. Like the concessions which had followed the 1889 and 1905 strikes, the unions' gains were due primarily to the interventions of the state. While the Wilhelmine state, and particularly its military arm which was now the decisive influence, had little inherent sympathy for the unions, it was seized of the need to maintain coal output and avoid disputes which might disrupt war production. The result was that in the Ruhr as in the nation more generally the military found itself playing a mediating role, increasingly intervening in industry and persuading the employers to accept concessions which, left to their own devices, they would not have contemplated.[6]

The war thus made explicit the tripartite character of industrial relations in the Ruhr, a feature which had been present before 1914 but which had been less overt than the more obvious direct conflicts between employers and workers and the sometimes heavy-handed Government interventions on the side of the former. It meant an increased level of state control and a shift in the balance of power in favour of the unions. However, the fact that their improved position had not been won in battle with the employers but rested primarily on the Government's tactical concern with the maintenance of coal production meant that the unions were loath to jeopardize it by conflicting

[6] I. Marssolek, 'Sozialdemokratie und Revolution im östlichen Ruhrgebiet', in R. Rürup (ed.), *Arbeiter- und Soldatenräte im rheinisch-westfälischen Industriegebiet* (Wuppertal, 1975), p. 242; G. D. Feldman, *Army, Industry and Labor in Germany 1914–1918* (Princeton, 1966), pp. 134–5; Tampke, *Ruhr and Revolution*, pp. 52–3; J. Kocka, *Klassengesellschaft im Krieg* (Göttingen, 1978 edition), pp. 114–18; H. Mommsen, *Bergarbeiter: Ausstellung zur Geschichte der organisierten Bergarbeiterbewegung in Deutschland* (Bochum, 1969).

too seriously with the state authorities. Despite growing criticism of rising prices, inadequate food supplies, and mounting industrial profits, the miners' unions generally sustained their policy of industrial peace. The ground was thus prepared for the post-war period, when a far more sympathetic Government and a range of quite unparalleled concessions from the employers (union recognition, abandonment of the 'yellow' unions, introduction of the 8-hour day) created a yet stronger position for the unions—a position which they were even less willing to endanger by pursuing policies which, in their eyes, threatened to produce chaos and unleash a wholly unpredictable situation in which all the gains might again be lost.

The new-found legitimacy of the trade unions extended also to the SPD. Otto Hue told a meeting in 1915 that 'the war has not originated with Germany: it was imposed on her' and maintained that 'both [the party's] living and dead leaders had always said that they would intervene for their fatherland and reach for their weapons if a threat came to the frontiers'. It was necessary, however, to secure 'a peace which would not mean permanent enmity for us with other countries' and he criticized the food situation and the profits which the Junkers were making. The war had changed the position of the party: 'Before the war the social democrats were accused of being "*vaterlandslose Gesellen*" and insurgents. But they wanted to stop such imputations after the war and insist on equal consideration with the other parties.'[7] The local party in Bochum concentrated on maintaining its structure and organization, encouraging the authorities to make proper provision for widows, the wounded, and ordinary workers, and preparing for the eventual demobilization: 'When the war comes to an end the party organization will face difficult tasks. Comrades returning home from the field will certainly not want to face a ruined organization and to have to help rebuild what they left in good condition.'[8]

It is not surprising that when the SPD eventually split the Bochum party came out firmly in support of the orthodox

[7] StAB, 482, *Polizei* Gerthe to KLB, 8. 11. 1915.
[8] StAB, 482, *Polizei* Bochum to RPA, 30. 5. 1916.

majority. At the party's 1916 general meeting Haase's action was denounced as 'irresponsible' and Liebknecht was described as a 'wild brain' of no political significance. Speakers claimed that the radical minority had virtually no support in the area: a Gelsenkirchen speaker maintained that there at least nine-tenths of the party members supported the majority. The 'policy of 4 August' was approved as the only one which represented the interests of the working class.[9]

The labour movement in the eastern Ruhr thus found during the war a way out of the impasse of the final pre-war years, acquired a new legitimacy, and carried further its pre-war commitment to the avoidance of industrial conflict and to political moderation. After the revolution of 1918 these policies were even more firmly espoused as the SPD itself became the governing party and as a whole series of fundamental and long-standing union demands were at last granted.

This, however, was only one side of the story. The other was the continuance and sharpening of the old pattern of conflict and unrest in the Ruhr pits. Industrial unrest was limited during the first two years of the war but as prices and profits rose, food shortages became more serious, and the pressure of work increased, it became more common. In autumn 1916 the first significant wartime miners' strikes broke out and in the following years they became more and more frequent. Like earlier strikes they concentrated on immediate issues of survival and the work-place: the food shortages naturally focused attention on questions of food supplies and wages. Only in the last months of the war were more political demands (peace and, on occasion, democracy) raised, as it became increasingly clear that these were the prerequisites for any other improvements.[10] The political changes of November 1918 did not—despite their great importance for the unions and the SPD—in themselves

---

[9] StAB, 482, *Polizei* Bochum to RPA, 30. 5. 1916. In 1917 the newly formed USPD was unanimously rejected by the party leaders in the eastern Ruhr. See J. Reulecke, 'Der erste Weltkrieg und die Arbeiterbewegung im rheinisch-westfälischen Industriegebiet', in Reulecke (ed.), *Arbeiterbewegung*, p. 227.

[10] Feldman, *Army, Industry and Labor*, p. 326; Marssolek, 'Sozialdemokratie und Revolution'. p. 300.

meet the concerns and aspirations of the miners and 1919 saw a further wave of major strikes.[11]

The similarity of post-war strikes with earlier ones was obvious. The Alter Verband and the SPD were unable to exercise effective control over their outbreak: but neither were the independent socialists, the communists, or the newly-powerful syndicalists. 'Leaders' and organizations of all kinds were obliged to follow what were essentially spontaneous and unplanned stoppages and were often driven to adopt progressively more extreme demands to preserve credibility.[12] The forms taken by the strikes were reminiscent of earlier stoppages.[13] The tendency of pre-war strikes to be limited to particular pits or districts was also maintained: it was not until April 1919 that an overwhelming majority of miners joined in a united stoppage. Finally, the demands raised by the strikers continued to be for better pay, shorter hours, and the introduction of a less arbitrary, more humane, and more participatory regime in the pits themselves. Political aims were of peripheral importance: even the demand for the 'socialization' of the mines, which was a major issue in early 1919, was not raised until two months after the revolution and one of its chief merits was its vagueness and the lack of concern shown even by its supporters about the fundamental questions of ownership, socialization was generally seen as a means of ensuring that the pits were run in a manner more responsive to the wishes and concerns of the miners. When workers' councils were elected, their prime concern was to remove unpopular mine officials: after this few of them seem to have had clear aims.[14]

[11] These strikes have been discussed extensively. See particularly P. von Oertzen, 'Die grossen Streiks der Ruhrbergarbeiterschaft im Frühjahr 1919', in E. Kolb (ed.), *Vom Kaiserreich zur Weimarer Republik* (Köln, 1972); H. Mommsen, 'Die Bergarbeiterbewegung an der Ruhr 1918–1933', in Reulecke (ed.), *Arbeiterbewegung*; Lucas, *Arbeiterradikalismus*; Tampke, *Ruhr and Revolution*; Brüggemeier, *Leben vor Ort.*

[12] Thus the demand for the 8-hour day was replaced by demands for 7 and 6 hours.

[13] Lucas stresses the importance of the forms of action as much as of the specific strike demands. Lucas, *Arbeiterradikalismus*, p. 84.

[14] On the lack of clarity and precision behind the concept see J. Tampke, 'The rise and fall of the Essen model', in *Internationale wissenschaftliche*

Despite the great changes which affected the Ruhr after 1914, there were thus important elements of continuity. On the one hand a careful, cautious, and conservative union and political leadership saw its tactics apparently vindicated as major concessions, which had still seemed exceedingly remote in 1914, were granted and as the state itself fell into their hands. On the other, the practical effect of these ostensibly dramatic gains was limited and was certainly insufficient to remove the causes of discontent amongst the miners and conflict within the pits. Indeed, the harsh experience of wartime, and revived but unfulfilled expectations released by peace and revolution, led to a resurgence of conflict on a pattern reminiscent of pre-war years. The result was a growing polarization within the labour movement itself. Again, this was not a new phenomenon but one which had been evident on several occasions before 1914. This time, however, it was deeper and more tragic, culminating in 1919 and 1920 not only in major divisions and regroupings within the trade union and political movements but in military confrontation between the armed forces of the SPD-dominated Government on one side and striking miners on the other.

But perhaps the most ominous element of continuity was in the continued underlying powerlessness of the labour movement. It remained critically dependent on the vagaries of national politics. Just as the few concessions won before 1914 had been the fruit of state intervention, so the wartime gains, and even the more far-reaching advances of 1918 and 1919, were primarily the result of Government concessions and a tactical retreat by the employers in the face of political collapse. The power of the employers was dented but not broken by the revolution. On the other hand, although the lines of division changed and the manifestations of industrial and political weakness altered after 1918, the miners remained critically divided and lacking in dependable and effective industrial and political strength. What they

Korrespondenz zur Geschichte der deutschen Arbeiterbewegung (Juni 1977, Heft 2); Tampke, *Ruhr and Revolution*, chapter 8; Mommsen, 'Bergarbeiterbewegung', p. 292; Lucas, *Arbeiterradikalismus*, pp. 177, 185-8.

had gained could be seen—particularly in retrospect—
as the fruits of a particular political conjuncture. As they
—and other German workers—were to learn in the following years, what politics could give, politics could take away
again.

Bibliography

Archival Sources

Contemporary manuscript and newspaper sources have been used at the following archives:

Archiv der Industriegewerkschaft Bergbau und Energie, Bochum
Friedrich Krupp Hüttenwerke AG Werksarchiv, Bochum
Institut für Zeitungsforschung, Dortmund
Internationaal Instituut voor sociale Geschedenis, Amsterdam
Staatsarchiv, Münster
Stadtarchiv, Bochum
Westfälisches Wirtschaftsarchiv, Dortmund

For full details of the specific archival sources used see S. H. F. Hickey, *Class conflict and class consciousness: the emergence of the working class in the Eastern Ruhr 1870-1914* (Oxford, D.Phil. thesis, 1978), pp. 393-8.

Annual Reports

Bericht des Magistrats zu Bochum (1861-1913)
Geschäftsbericht des Gewerkvereins christlicher Bergarbeiter Deutchlands (1907-1912)
Kassenbericht des Verbandes der deutscher Berg- und Hüttenarbeiter (1891-1897)
Jahresbericht des Verbandes deutscher Bergarbeiter (1897-1918)
Jahresbericht der Handelskammer zu Bochum (1857-1913)

Statistical Series

Statistik des deutschen Reiches (Berlin)
Statistisches Jahrbuch deutscher Städte (Breslau)
Statistisches Jahrbuch für den Preussischen Staat (Berlin)

Contemporary Books, Articles, Printed Documents etc.

Adelmann, G. (ed.), *Quellensammlung zur Geschichte der sozialen Betriebsverfassung Ruhrindustrie*, 2 Bde. (Bonn, 1960).
Die Arbeitsverhältnisse im Steinkohlenbergbau 1912-1926 (Berlin, 1928).
Aufsätze über den Streik der Bergarbeiter im Ruhrgebiet (1905).
Der Ausstand der niederrheinisch-westfälischen Bergleute im Mai 1889 (Styrum-Rheinland and Leipzig, 1889).

Der Bergarbeiter-Ausstand des Jahres 1889 im preussischen Abgeord-netenhause (Essen, 1890).

Bochumer Verein, *Bericht über die Jubel-Feier des Bochumer Vereins* (Bochum, 1894).

Denkschrift über die Untersuchung der Arbeiter- und Betriebs-Verhält-nisse in den Steinkohlen-Bezirken (Berlin, 1890).

Ehrenberg, R., and H. Racine, *Krupp'sche Arbeiter-Familien* (Jena, 1912).

Erdmann, A., *Die christlichen Gewerkschaften* (Stuttgart, 1914).

Festschrift zur Feier des 50-jährigen Besehens des Vereins für die Bergbaulichen Interessen im Oberbergamtsbezirk Dortmund in Essen (Essen, 1908).

Fischer-Eckert, L., *Die wirtschaftliche und soziale Lage der Frauen in dem modernen Industrieort Hamborn im Rheinland* (Hagen, 1913).

Fuchs, C. J. *Zur Wohnungsfrage* (Leipzig, 1904).

Gainsborough Commission, *Life and Labour in Germany* (London, 1906).

Glückauf. Berg- und Hüttenmännische Zeitschrift (Essen).

Göhre, P., *Die Evangelisch-Soziale Bewegung* (Leipzig, 1896).

Hasslacher, 'Was ist unter "ortsüblicher Tagelohn" . . . zu verstehen?' in *Glückauf. Berg- und Hüttenmännische Zeitschrift* (19. 9. 1903).

Herbig, 'Schwierigkeiten des Lohnwesens im Bergbau' in *Glückauf, Berg- und Hüttenmännische Zeitschrift* (28. 12. 1907).

Hoffeld, F., *Bilder aus dem Bergmannsleben* (Dortmund, n.d.).

Hue, O., *Die Bergarbeiter*, 2 Bde. (Stuttgart, 1910 and 1913).

Hue, O., *Neutrale oder parteiische Gewerkschaften?* (Bochum, 1900).

Hue, O., *Die Verteuerung der Lebensmittel und ihre Ursachen* (Bochum, 1911).

Hundt, R., *Bergarbeiter-Wohnungen im Ruhrrevier* (Berlin, 1902).

Hüsgen, E., *Ludwig Windthorst* (Köln, 1907).

Imbusch, H., *Arbeitsverhältnis und Arbeiterorganisation im deutschen Bergbau* (Essen, 1908).

Imbusch, H., *Bergarbeiterstreik im Ruhrgebiet 1912* (Köln, 1912).

25 Jahre Bergwerksgesellschaft Hibernia: Festschrift aus Anlass des 25–jährigen Bestehens der Bergwerksgellschaft Hibernia 1873–1898 (Düsseldorf, 1898).

Jansson, W., *Die Zustände im deutschen Fabrikwohnungswesen* (Berlin, 1910).

Jevons, H. S., *The British Coal Trade* (London, 1969 edition).

Jüngst, E., 'Der Ausstand der Ruhrbergarbeiter vom März 1912 in statistischer Darstellung', in *Glückauf. Berg- und Hüttenmännische Zeitschrift* (29. 6. 1912).

Kessler, G., *Die deutschen Arbeitergeber-Verbände* (Leipzig, 1907).

Knipping, F., *Zur Bochumer Eingemeindungsfrage* (Bochum, 1917).

Köllmann W., and A. Gladen (ed.), *Der Bergarbeiterstreik von 1889 und die Gründung des 'Alten Verbandes' in ausgewählten Doku-menten der Zeit* (Bochum, 1969).

Köpping W. (ed.), *Schwarze Solidarität* (Oberhausen, 1974).

Lange, C., 'Die Wohnungsverhältnisse der ärmeren Volkslassen in

Bochum', in *Schriften des Vereins für Socialpolitik* Bd. xxx (Leipzig, 1886).

Levenstein, A., *Die Arbeiterfrage* (München, 1913).

Levenstein, A., *Aus der Tiefe; Arbeiterbriefe* (Berlin, 1909).

Luxemburg, R., *The mass strike, the political party and the trade unions* (London, n.d.).

Luxemburg, R., *Socialism and the Churches* (London, 1972 edition).

Metzner, M., *Die soziale Fürsorge im Bergbau* (Jena, 1911).

Michels, R., *Political Parties* (New York, 1959 edition).

Münz, H., *Die Lage der Bergarbeiter im Ruhrrevier* (Essen, 1909).

Oberschuir, E., *Die Heranziehung und Sesshaftmachung von Bergarbeitern im Ruhrkohlenbecken* (Düsseldorf, 1910).

Pieper, L., 'Die Gärung im Ruhrrevier', in *Soziale Praxis* (12. 1. 1905).

Pieper, L., *Die Lage der Bergarbeiter im Ruhrgebiet* (Stuttgart and Berlin, 1903).

Pieper, P., *Kirchliche Statistik Deutschlands* (Freiburg, 1899).

Schneider, R., *Die Entwicklung des niederrheinisch-westfälischen Bergbaus und der Eisen-Industrie* (Bochum, 1899).

Seippel, M., *Bochum Einst und Jetzt* (Bochum, 1901).

Silbergleit, H., *Preussens Städte* (Berlin, 1908).

Spring, *Wohlfahrtseinrichtungen im Kreise Hörde* (Hörde, 1897).

Treptow, C., F. Wüst, and W. Borchers, *Bergbau und Hüttenwesen* (Leipzig, 1900).

Verband der Bergarbeiter Deutschlands, *Bergarbeiter! Aufgewacht und erkennet eure Macht!* (Bochum, 1911).

Verband der Bergarbeiter Deutschlands, *Bergbaulicher Verein und Arbeitswilligenschutz* (Bochum, 1912).

Verband der Bergarbeiter Deutschlands, *Instruktion für Mitglieder der Bezirksleitungen und Ortsverwaltungen* (Bochum, 1910).

Verband der Bergarbeiter Deutschlands, *Kalender für Bergarbeiter 1913* (Bochum, 1912).

Verband der Bergarbeiter Deutschlands, *Notizkalender für Berg- und Hüttenarbeiter 1902* (Bochum, 1901).

Verein für die bergbaulichen Interessen im Oberbergamtsbezirk Dortmund (ed.), *Die Entwicklung des Niederrheinisch-Westfälischen Steinkohlen-Bergbaues* Bd. xii (Berlin, 1904).

Vorstand der Gesellschaft für Soziale Reform (ed.), *Aufsätze über den Streik der Bergarbeiter im Ruhrgebiet* (Jena, 1905).

Werner, G., *Unfälle und Erkankungen im Ruhrbergbau* (Essen, 1910?).

Westfälischer Verein zur Förderung des Kleinwohnungswesens, *Ergebnisse der Wohnungsaufnahme in westfälischen Städten vom 1 Dez. 1905*, 2 Bde. (Münster, 1907 and 1909).

Wiebe, G., *Die Handelskammer zu Bochum 1856–1906* (Bochum, 1906).

Zeitschrift für das Bergbau-, Hütten- und Salinenwesen im Preussischen Staate (Berlin).

Zur Feier des 25-Jährigen Bestehens der Gelsenkirchener Bergswerks AG 1873–1898 (Düsseldorf, n.d.).

Secondary Books and Articles

Adelmann, G., *Die soziale Betriebsverfassung des Ruhrbergbaues vom Anfang des 19. Jahrhunderts bis 1914* (Bonn, 1962).

Anderson, M., *Approaches to the History of the Western Family 1500-1914* (London, 1980).

Anderson, P., *Arguments within English Marxism* (London, 1980).

Bacmeister, W., *Louis Baare. Ein westfälischer Wirtschaftsführer aus der Bismarckzeit* (Essen, 1937).

Bacmeister, W., *Gustav Knepper. Das Lebensbild eines grossen Bergmanns* (Essen, 1950).

Baudis, D., and H. Nussbaum, *Wirtschaft und Staat in Deutschland vom Ende des 19. Jahrhunderts bis 1918/19* (Berlin-Ost, 1978).

Bergwerks-Gesellschaft Hibernia 1873-1923 (n.p., n.d.).

Blackbourn, D., *Class, Religion and Local Politics in Wilhelmine Germany. The Centre Party in Württemberg before 1914* (New Haven and London, 1980).

Blackbourn, D., 'The problem of democratisation: German Catholics and the role of the Centre Party', in R. J. Evans (ed.), *Society and Politics in Wilhelmine Germany* (London, 1978).

Bock, H. M., *Geschichte des 'linken Radikalismus' in Deutschland. Ein Versuch* (Frankfurt, 1976).

Brack, R., *Deutscher Episkopat und Gewerkschaftsstreit 1900-1914* (Köln and Wien, 1976).

Brakelmann, G., *Die soziale Frage des 19. Jahrhunderts* (Witten, 1962).

Brakelmann, G., 'Evangelische Pfarrer im Konfliktfeld des Ruhrbergarbeiterstreiks von 1905', in J. Reulecke and W. Weber (ed.), *Fabrik, Familie, Feierabend. Beiträge zur Sozialgeschichte des Alltags im Industriezeitalter* (Wuppertal, 1978).

Brakelmann, G., *Kirche, soziale Frage und Sozialismus. Kirchenleitungen und Synoden über soziale Frage und Sozialismus 1871-1914* (Gütersloh, 1977).

Brandt, H. J., 'Kirchliches Vereinswesen und Freizeitgestaltung in einer Arbeitergemeinde 1872-1933: Das Beispiel Schalke', in G. Huck (ed.), *Sozialgeschichte der Freizeit* (Wuppertal, 1982).

W. Brepohl, *Der Aufbau des Ruhrvolkes im Zuge der Ost-West Wanderung* (Recklinghausen, 1948).

Brepohl, W., *Industrievolk Ruhrgebiet* (Tübingen, 1957).

Brinkmann, W., *Bochum. Aus der Geschichte einer Grossstadt des Reviers* (Bochum, 1968 edition).

Brüggemeier, F. J., *Leben vor Ort. Ruhrbergleute und Ruhrbergbau 1889-1919* (München, 1983).

Brüggemeier, F. J., 'Ruhr miners and their historians', in R. Samuel (ed.), *People's History and Socialist Theory* (London, 1981).

Brüggemeier, F. J., ' "Volle Kost voll". Die Wohnungsverhältnisse der Bergleute an der Ruhr um die Jahrhundertwende', in H. Mommsen and U. Borsdorf (ed.), *Glück auf, Kameraden! Die Bergarbeiter und ihre Organisationen in Deutschland* (Köln, 1979).

Bulmer, M. I. A., 'Sociological Models of the Mining Community' in *Sociological Review* xxiii (1975).

Burgdörfer, F., 'Migration across the frontiers of Germany', in W. F. Willcox (ed.), *International Migrations* (New York, 1929).

Burgess, K., *The Origins of British Industrial Relations* (London, 1975).

Campbell, A., and F. Reid, 'The Independent Collier in Scotland', in R. Harrison (ed.), *Independent Collier. The Coal Miner as Archetypal Proletarian Reconsidered* (Hassocks, 1978).

Coleman, T., *Passage to America* (London, 1974 edition).

Conze, W., 'Vom Pöbel zum Proletariat', in H. U. Wehler (ed.), *Moderne deutsche Sozialgeschichte* (Köln, 1970).

Conze, W., and U. Engelhardt (ed.), *Arbeiter im Industrialisierungsprozess. Herkunft, Lage und Verhalten* (Stuttgart, 1979).

Coombes, B. L., *These poor hands*, (London, 1939).

Costas, I., *Auswirkungen der Konzentration des Kapitals auf die Arbeiterklasse in Deutschland, 1880-1914* (Frankfurt a. M. and New York, 1981).

Crew, D. F., 'Berufliche Lage und Protestverhalten Bochumer Bergleute und Metallarbeiter im ausgehenden 19. Jahrhundert', in H. Mommsen and U. Borsdorf (ed.), *Glück auf, Kameraden! Die Bergarbeiter und ihre Organisationen in Deutschland* (Köln, 1979).

Crew, D. F., 'Definitions of Modernity: Social Mobility in a German Town, 1880-1901', in *Journal of Social History* (Fall, 1973).

Crew, D. F., 'Soziale Schichtung und Mobilität in Deutschland im 19. und 20. Jahrhundert', in *Geschichte und Gesellschaft* (Heft 1, 1975).

Crew, D. F., 'Steel, Sabotage and Socialism: the Strike at the Dortmund "Union" Steel Works in 1911', in R. J. Evans (ed.), *The German Working Class 1888-1933* (London, 1982).

Crew, D. F., *Town in the Ruhr. A Social History of Bochum 1860-1914* (New York, 1979).

Croon, H., 'Die Einwirkungen der Industrialisierung auf die gesellschaftliche Schichtung der Bevölkerung im rheinisch-westfälischen Industriegebiet', in *Rheinische Vierteljahrsblätter* (1955).

Croon, H., 'Die Stadtvertretungen in Krefeld und Bochum im 19. Jahrhundert' in R. Dietrich and G. Oestreich (ed.), *Forschungen zu Staat und Verfassung: Festgabe für Fritz Hartung* (Berlin, 1958).

Croon, H., 'Studien zur Sozial- und Siedlungsgeschichte der Stadt Bochum' in P. Busch, H. Croon, and C. Hahne (ed.), *Bochum und das mittlere Ruhrgebiet* (Paderborn, 1965).

Croon, H., 'Die Versorgung der Grossstädte des Ruhrgebietes im 19. und 20. Jahrhundert', in *Troisième Conférence Internationale d'Histoire Économique* (München, 1965).

Croon, H., 'Die wirtschaftlichen Führungsschichten des Ruhrgebietes in der Zeit von 1890 bis 1933', in H. Patze (ed.), *Blätter für deutsche Landesgeschichte* (Göttingen, 1972).

Croon H., and K. Utermann, *Zeche und Gemeinde* (Tübingen, 1958).

Däbritz, W., *Bochumer Verein für Bergbau und Gussstahlfabrikation in Bochum* (Düsseldorf, 1934).

Dennis, N., F. Henriques, and C. Slaughter, *Coal is our Life* (London, 1969 edition).

Desai, A. V., *Real wages in Germany* (Oxford, 1968).

Domansky-Davidsohn, E., 'Der Grossbetrieb als Organisationsproblem des Deutschen Metallarbeiter-Verbandes vor dem Ersten Weltkrieg', in H. Mommsen (ed.), *Arbeiterbewegung und industrieller Wandel* (Wuppertal, 1980).

Douglass, D., 'The Durham Pitman', in R. Samuel (ed.), *Miners, Quarrymen and Saltworkers* (London, 1977).

Douglass, D., and J. Krieger, *A Miner's Life* (London, 1983).

Dowe, D., 'The Workers' Choral Movement before the First World War', in *Journal of Contemporary History* xiii. ii (1978).

Eberlein, A., *Die Presse der Arbeiterklasse und der sozialen Bewegungen*, 5 vols. (Frankfurt a. M., 1970).

Eley, G., 'Defining Social Imperialism: Use and Abuse of an Idea' in *Social History* I. iii (1976).

Ely, G., *Reshaping the German Right. Radical Nationalism and Political Change after Bismarck* (New Haven and London, 1980).

Eley G., and K. Nield, 'Why does social history ignore politics?', in *Social History* v. ii (1980).

Evans, R. J. 'Politics and the Family: Social Democracy and the Working-class Family in Theory and Practice Before 1914', in R. J. Evans and W. R. Lee (ed.), *The German Family* (London, 1981).

Evans, R. J., 'Introduction: the Sociological Interpretation of German Labour History', in R. J. Evans (ed.), *The German Working Class 1888-1933: The Politics of Everyday Life* (London, 1982).

Evans, R. J., 'Religion and Society in Modern Germany', in *European Studies Review* XII. iii (1982).

Evans, R. J., 'Wilhelm II's Germany and the Historians', in R. J. Evans (ed.), *Society and Politics in Wilhelmine Germany* (London, 1978).

Feldman, G., *Army, Industry and Labor in Germany 1914-1918* (Princeton, 1966).

Ferenczi, I., 'International Migration Statistics', in W. F. Willcox (ed.), *International Migrations* (New York, 1929).

Festschrift zum 100-jährigen Bestehen der Gewerkschaft ver. Constantin der Grosse, Bochum (Essen, 1948).

Festschrift zum 100-jährigen Bestehen der Zechen Hannover und Hannibal (Bochum, 1947).

Field, J., 'British Historians and the Concept of the Labor Aristocracy', in *Radical History Review* xix (1978/9).

Fischer, I., 'Maurer- und Textilarbeiterstreiks in Augsburg 1899-1914', in K. Tenfelde and H. Volkmann (ed.), *Streik. Zur Geschichte des Arbeitskampfes in Deutschland während der Industrialisierung* (Munchen, 1981).

Fischer, W., *Die Bedeutung der preussischen Bergrechtsreform (1851-1865) für den industriellen Ausbau des Ruhrgebiets* (Dortmund, 1961).

Fischer, W., *Herz des Reviers: 125 Jahre Wirtschaftsgeschichte des Industrie-und Handelskammer-Bezirks Essen* (Essen, 1965).

Fischer, W., 'Konjunkturen und Krise im Ruhrgebiet seit 1840 und die wirtschaftspolitische Willensbildung der Unternehmer', in *Westfälische Forschungen* xxi (1968).

Foster, J., *Class Struggle and the Industrial Revolution. Early Industrial Capitalism in Three English Towns* (London, 1974).

Fricke, D., *Die deutsche Arbeiterbewegung 1869–1890* (Leipzig, 1964).

Fricke, D., *Die deutsche Arbeiterbewegung 1869 bis 1914. Ein Handbuch über ihre Organisation und Tätigkeit im Klassenkampf* (Berlin-Ost, 1976).

Fricke, D., *Zur Organisation und Tätigkeit der deutschen Arbeiterbewegung 1890–1914* (Leipzig, 1962).

Fricke, D., *Der Ruhrbergarbeiterstreik von 1905* (Berlin-Ost, 1955).

Friedberger, W., *Die Geschichte der Sozialismuskritik im katholischen Deutschland zwischen 1830 und 1914* (Frankfurt a. M., 1978).

Friedemann, P., 'Feste und Feiern im rheinisch-westfälischen Industriegebiet 1890 bis 1914', in G. Huck (ed.), *Sozialgeschichte der Freizeit* (Wuppertal, 1980).

Friedlander, D., 'Demographic Patterns and Socioeconomic Characteristics of the Coal-mining Population in England and Wales in the Nineteenth Century', in *Economic Development and Cultural Change* xxii (1973/4).

Fritsch, J., *Eindringen und Ausbreitung des Revisionismus im deutschen Bergarbeiterverband (bis 1914)* (Leipzig, 1967).

Frölich, P., *Rosa Luxemburg* (London, 1940).

Fülberth, G., 'Zur Genese des Revisionismus in der deutschen Sozialdemokratie vor 1914', in *Das Argument* (März, 1971).

Geary, D., *European Labour Protest 1848–1939* (London, 1981).

Geary, D., 'Identifying Militancy: the Assessment of Working-class Attitudes towards State and Society', in R. J. Evans (ed.), *The German Working Class 1888–1933* (London, 1982).

Geary, D., 'Radicalism and the Worker: Metalworkers and Revolution 1914–1923', in R. J. Evans (ed.), *Society and Politics in Wilhelmine Germany* (London, 1978).

Gelsenkirchener Bergwerks AG 1873–1913 (Düsseldorf, n.d.).

Gladen, A., *Geschichte der Sozialpolitik in Deutschland* (Wiesbaden, 1974).

Gladen, A., 'Die Streiks der Bergarbeiter im Ruhrgebiet in den Jahren 1889, 1905, und 1912' in J. Reulecke (ed.), *Arbeiterbewegung an Rhein und Ruhr* (Wuppertal, 1974).

Graf, H., *Die Entwicklung der Wahlen und politischen Parteien in Gross-Dortmund 1871–1957* (Hannover, 1958).

Gray, R. Q., *The Aristocracy of Labour in Nineteenth-century Britain* (London, 1981).

Grebing, H., *Geschichte der deutschen Arbeiterbewegung* (München, 1966).

Groh, D., 'Base-processes and the problem of organization: outline of a social history research project', in *Social History* IV. ii (1979).

Groh, D., 'Intensification of work and industrial conflict in Germany 1896–1914', in *Politics and Society* viii (1978).

Groh, D., *Negative Integration und Revolutionärer Attentismus* (Frankfurt a. M., 1974).

Gussstahlwerk Witten AG 1853–1954 (Witten, 1954).

Gutman, H. G., *Work, Culture and Society in Industrializing America* (Oxford, 1977).

Guttsman, W. L. *The German Social Democratic Party, 1875–1933* (London, 1981).

Hall, A., *Scandal, Sensation and Social Democracy. The SPD Press and Wilhelmine Germany 1890–1914* (Cambridge, 1977).

Harrison, R., 'Introduction' in R. Harrison (ed.), *Independent Collier: The Coal Miner as Archetypal Proletarian Reconsidered* (Hassocks, 1978).

Hartmann, K., *Der Weg zur gewerkschaftlichen Organization. Bergarbeiterbewegung und Kapitalistischer Bergbau im Ruhrgebiet, 1851-1889* (München, 1977).

Heinrichsbauer, A., *Harpener Bergbau AG 1856–1936* (Essen, 1936).

Heinrichsbauer, A., *Industrielle Siedlung im Ruhrgebiet* (Essen, 1936).

Hellfaier, K. A., 'Probleme und Quellen zur Frühgeschichte der Sozialdemokratie in Westfalen', in *Archiv für Sozialgeschichte* (1963).

Hellgreve, H., *Dortmund als Industrie- und Arbeiterstadt* (Dortmund, 1951).

Hemmer, H. O., 'Die Bergarbeiterbewegung im Ruhrgebiet unter dem Sozialistengesetz', in J. Reulecke (ed.), *Arbeiterbewegung an Rhein und Ruhr* (Wuppertal, 1974).

Henderson, W. O., *The rise of German industrial power, 1834–1914* (Wuppertal, 1974).

Hickey, S. H. F., 'Bergmannsarbeit an der Ruhr vor dem Ersten Weltkrieg', in H. Mommsen and U. Borsdorf (ed.), *Glück auf, Kameraden! Die Bergarbeiter und ihre Organisationen in Deutschland* (Köln, 1979).

Hickey, S. H. F., 'The Shaping of the German Labour Movement: Miners in the Ruhr', in R. J. Evans (ed.), *Politics and Society in Wilhelmine Germany* (London, 1978).

Hobsbawm, E. J., 'Class consciousness in history', in I. Meszaros (ed.), *Aspects of History and Class Consciousness* (London, 1971).

Hobsbawm, E. J., 'From social history to the history of society', in M. W. Flinn and T. C. Smout (ed.), *Essays in Social History* (Oxford, 1974).

Hobsbawm, E. J., *Labouring Men* (London, 1968 edition).

Howkins, A., 'Edwardian Liberalism and Industrial Unrest', in *History Workshop Journal* iv (1977).

Jackson, J. H., 'Overcrowding and Family Life: Working-class Families and the Housing Crisis in Late Nineteenth-century Duisburg', in R. J. Evans and W. R. Lee (ed.), *The German Family* London, 1981).

Jackson, M. P., *The Price of Coal* (London, 1974).

Jackson, R. T., 'Mining Settlements in Western Europe', in R. P. Beckinsale and J. M. Houston (ed.), *Urbanization and its Problems* (Oxford, 1968).

25 Jahre Arbeitnordwest 1904–1929. Herausgegeben aus Anlass seines 25 jährigen Bestehens vom Arbeitgeberverband für den Bezirk der nordwestlichen Gruppe des Vereins Deutscher Eisen- und Stahlindustrieller (Berlin, 1929).

100 Jahre Stahlform Guss (Bochum, n.d.).

Ein Jahrhundert Heinrichshütte Hattingen, 1854–1954 (Darmstadt, n.d.).

Jantke C., et al., *Bergmann und Zeche: die sozialen Arbeitsverhältnisse einer Schachtanlage des nördlichen Ruhrgebiets in der Sicht der Bergleute* (Tübingen, 1953).

Jasper, A. S., *A Hoxton Childhood* (London, 1971).

Joll, J., *The Second International 1889–1914* (London, 1974 edition).

Joyce, P., *Work, Society and Politics. The Culture of the Factory in later Victorian England* (London, 1982 edition).

Kalis, A., *Kirche und Religion im Revier: die Geschichte der Arbeiter- und Knappenbewegung im Ruhrgebiet* (Essen, 1968).

Kealey, M., 'Kampfstrategien der Unternehmerschaft im Ruhrbergbau seit den Bergarbeiterstreik von 1889', in H. Mommsen and U. Borsdorf (ed.), *Glück auf, Kameraden! Die Bergarbeiter und ihre Organisationen in Deutschland* (Köln, 1979).

Kerr C., and A. Siegel, 'The Interindustry Propensity to Strike: an International Comparison', in A. Kornhauser, R. Dubin, and A. M. Ross (eds.), *Patterns of Industrial Conflict* (New York, 1954).

Kertzer, D. I., *Comrades and Christians. Religion and Political Struggle in Communist Italy* (Cambridge, 1980).

Kirby, M. W., *The British Coalmining Industry 1870–1946* (London, 1977).

Kirchhoff, H. G., *Die staatliche Sozialpolitik im Ruhrbergbau 1871–1914* (Köln and Opladen, 1958).

Klessmann, C., 'Klassensolidarität und nationales Bewusstsein. Das Verhältnis zwischen der Polnischen Berufsvereinigung (ZZP) und den deutschen Bergarbeitergewerkschaften im Ruhrgebiet 1902–1923', in *Internationale wissenschaftliche Korrespondenz zur Geschichte der deutschen Arbeiterbewegung* (Juni 1974, Heft 2).

Klessmann, C., 'Polnische Bergarbeiter im Ruhrgebiet: Soziale Lage und gewerkschaftliche Organisation', in H. Mommsen and U. Borsdorf (ed.), *Glück auf, Kameraden! Die Bergarbeiter und ihre Organisationen in Deutschland* (Köln, 1979).

Klessmann, C., *Polnische Bergarbeiter im Ruhrgebiet 1870–1945* (Göttingen, 1978).

Koch, M. J., *Die Bergarbeiterbewegung im Ruhrgebiet zur Zeit Wilhelms II* (Düsseldorf, 1954).

Kocka, J., *Klassengesellschaft im Krieg* (Göttingen, 1978 edition).

Köllmann, W., *Bevölkerung in der industriellen Revolution* (Göttingen, 1974).

Köllmann, W., 'Die Bevölkerung Rheinland-Westfalens in der Hochindustrialisierungsperiode', in *Vierteljahresschrift für Sozial- und Wirtschaftsgeschichte* (1971).

Köllmann, W., 'Binnenwanderung und Bevölkerungsstrukturen der Ruhrgrossstädte', in *Soziale Welt* ix (1958).

Köllmann, W., 'Die Geschichte der Bergarbeiterschaft', in W. Först (ed.), *Ruhrgebiet und Neues Land* (Köln, 1968).

Köllmann, W., 'Industrialisierung, Binnenwanderung und "Soziale Frage" ', in *Vierteljahresschrift für Sozial- und Wirtschaftsgeschichte* (1959).

Köllmann, W., 'Vom Knappen zum Bergarbeiter: Die Entstehung der Bergarbeiterschaft an der Ruhr', in H. Mommsen and U. Borsdorf (ed.), *Glück auf Kameraden! Die Bergarbeiter und ihre Organisationen in Deutschland* (Köln, 1979).

Köllmann, W., 'The Population of Germany in the Age of Industrialism', in H. Möller (ed.), *Population Movements in Modern European History* (New York, 1964).

Köllmann, W., 'Urbanization in Germany at the height of the industrialization period', in *Journal of Contemporary History* (July, 1969).

Koszyk, K., *Anfänge und frühe Entwicklung der sozialdemokratischen Presse im Ruhrgebiet, 1875–1908* (Dortmund, 1953).

Koszyk, K., 'Die sozialdemokratische Arbeiterbewegung 1890 bis 1914', in J. Reulecke (ed.), *Arbeiterbewegung an Rhein und Ruhr* (Wuppertal, 1974).

Kraus, A., 'Gemeindeleben und Industrialisierung. Das Beispiel des evangelischen Kirchenkreises Bochum', in J. Reulecke and W. Weber (ed.), *Fabrik, Familie, Feierabend. Beiträge zur Sozialgeschichte des Alltags im Industriezeitalter* (Wuppertal, 1978).

Kraus, A., 'Wohnverhältnisse und Lebensbedingungen von Hütten- und Bergarbeiterfamilien in der zweiten Hälfte des 19. Jahrhunderts', in W. Conze and U. Engelhardt (ed.), *Arbeiter im Industrialisierungsprozess. Herkunft, Lage und Verhalten* (Stuttgart, 1979).

Krauss H., and H. Ostermann, *Verbandskatholizismus?* (Kevelaer, 1968).

Kuczynski, J., *Die Geschichte der Lage der Arbeiter unter dem Kapitalismus* (Berlin-Ost, 1961 onwards).

Langewiesche, D., 'Wanderungsbewegungen in der Hochindustrialisierungsperiode. Regionale, interstädtische und innerstädtische Mobilität in Deutschland 1880–1914', in *Vierteljahresschrift für Sozial- und Wirtschafts- geschichte* lxiv (1977).

Lee W. R., 'Germany' in W. R. Lee (ed.), *European Demography and Economic Growth* (London, 1979).

Leich, *Harpen und Harpener Bergbau. Ein Beitrag zur Heimatgeschichte* (Bochum, 1937).

Lidtke, V. L., 'August Bebel and German Social Democracy's Relation to the Christian Churches', in *Journal of the History of Ideas* (1966).

Lidtke, V. L., *The Outlawed Party: Social Democracy in Germany 1878–1890* (Princeton, 1966).

Lidtke, V. L., 'Social Class and Secularisation in Imperial Germany: The

Working Classes', in *Year Book of the Leo Baeck Institute* xxv (1980).

Linde, H., 'Die soziale Problematik der masurischen Agrargesellschaft und die masurische Einwanderung in das Emscherrevier', in H. U. Wehler (ed.), *Moderne deutsche Sozialgeschichte* (Köln, 1970).

Loth, W., *Katholiken im Kaiserreich. Der politische Katholizismus in der Krise des wilhelminischen Deutschlands* (Düsseldorf, 1984).

Lucas, E., *Arbeiterradikalismus: Zwei Formen von Radikalismus in der deutschen Arbeiterbewegung* (Frankfurt a. M., 1976).

Lucas, E., *Märzrevolution 1920*, 3 Bde. (Frankfurt a. M., 1970, 1973, and 1978).

Lützenkirchen, R., *Der sozialdemokratische Verein für den Reichstagswahlkreis Dortmund-Hörde* (Dortmund, 1970).

Marbach, R., *Säkularisierung und sozialer Wandel im 19. Jahrhundert* (Göttingen, 1978).

Mariaux, F., *Gedenkwort zum 100-jährigen Bestehen der Harpener Bergbau AG* (Dortmund, 1956).

Mariaux, F., *Gedenkwort zum 100-jährigen Bestehen der Industrie- und Handelskammer zu Bochum* (Bochum, 1956).

Marschalck, P., *Deutsche Überseewanderung im 19. Jahrhundert* (Stuttgart, 1973).

Marssolek, I., 'Sozialdemokratie und Revolution im östlichen Ruhrgebiet', in R. Rürup (ed.), *Arbeiter- und Soldatenräte im rheinisch-westfälischen Industriegebiet* (Wuppertal, 1975).

Martiny, M., 'Die politische Bedeutung der gewerkschaftlichen Arbeiter-Sekretariate vor dem ersten Weltkrieg', in H. O. Vetter (ed.), *Vom Sozialistengesetz zur Mitbestimmung* (Köln, 1975).

Mason, T. W., 'The Primacy of Politics', in S. J. Woolf (ed.), *The Nature of Fascism* (London, 1968).

Mattheier, K. W., 'Werkvereine und wirtschaftsfriedlich-nationale (gelbe) Arbeiterbewegung im Ruhrgebiet', in J. Reulecke (ed.), *Arbeiterbewegung an Rhein und Ruhr* (Wuppertal, 1974).

McLeod, H., *Class and Religion in the Late Victorian City* (London, 1975).

McLeod, H., 'Protestantism and the Working Class in Imperial Germany', in *European Studies Review* XII. iii (1982).

McLeod, H., *Religion and the People of Western Europe 1789-1970* (Oxford, 1981).

Medalen, C., 'State Monopoly Capitalism in Germany: the Hibernia Affair', in *Past and Present* lxxviii (1978).

Mitchell, B. R., *European Historical Statistics (1750-1970)* (London, 1975).

Mitchell, B. R., *The Fontana Economic History of Europe: Statistical Appendix, 1700-1914* (London, 1971).

Möllers, P., 'Die Essener Arbeiterbewegung in ihren Anfängen', in *Rheinische Vierteljahrsblätter* (1960).

Mommsen, H., *Bergarbeiter: Ausstellung zur Geschichte der organisierten Bergarbeiterbewegung in Deutschland* (Bochum, 1969).

Mommsen, H., 'Die Bergarbeiterbewegung an der Ruhr 1918-1933', in

J. Reulecke (ed.), *Arbeiterbewegung an Rhein und Ruhr* (Wuppertal, 1974).

Mommsen, H., 'Einleitung' and 'Soziale Kämpfe im Ruhrbergbau nach der Jahrhundertwende', in H. Mommsen and U. Borsdorf (ed.), *Glück auf, Kameraden! Die Bergarbeiter und ihre Organisationen in Deutschland* (Köln, 1979).

Mommsen, H., 'Soziale und politische Konflikte an der Ruhr 1905-1924', in H. Mommsen (ed.), *Arbeiterbewegung und industrieller Wandel* (Wuppertal, 1980).

Mönnich, H., *Aufbruch ins Revier, Aufbruch nach Europa. Hoesch 1871-1971* (Dortmund, 1971).

Barrington Moore, *Injustice. The Social Bases of Obedience and Revolt* (London, 1978).

Moring, K. E., *Die sozialdemokratische Partei in Bremen* (Hanover, 1968).

Moses, J. A., *Trade Unionism in Germany from Bismarck to Hitler, 1869-1933* 2 vols. (London, 1982).

Murphy, R. C., 'Polnische Bergarbeiter im Ruhrgebiet: Das Beispiel Bottrop', in H. Mommsen and U. Borsdorf (ed.), *Glück auf, Kameraden! Die Bergarbeiter und ihre Organisationen in Deutschland* (Köln, 1979).

Nettl, J. P., 'The German Social Democratic Party 1890-1914 as a political model', in *Past and Present* xxx (1965).

Nettl, J. P., *Rosa Luxemburg* (Oxford, 1966).

Nettmann, W., *Witten in den Reichstagswahlen des Deutschen Reiches 1871-1918* (Witten, 1972).

Neuloh O., and J. Kurucz, *Vom Kirchdorf zur Industriegemeinde. Untersuchungen über den Einfluss der Industrialisierung auf die Wertordnung der Arbeitnehmer* (Köln, 1967).

Neumann, W., *Die Gewerkschaften im Ruhrbegiet* (Köln, 1951).

Neville, R. C., 'The Courrières Colliery Disaster, 1906', in *Journal of Contemporary History* XIII. i (1978).

Niethammer L., and F. J. Brüggemeier, 'Schlafgänger, Schnapskasinos und schwerindustrielle Kolonie. Aspekte der Arbeiterwohnungsfrage im Ruhrgebiet vor dem Ersten Weltkrieg', in J. Reulecke and W. Weber (ed.), *Fabrik, Familie, Feierabend. Beiträge zur Sozialgeschichte des Alltags im Industriezeitalter* (Wuppertal, 1978).

Niethammer L., and F. J. Brüggemeier, 'Wie wohnten Arbeiter im Kaiserreich?', in *Archiv für Sozialgeschichte* (Bonn, 1976).

Nolan, M., *Social democracy and society: working class radicalism in Düsseldorf, 1890-1920* (Cambridge, 1981).

von Oertzen, P., 'Die grossen Streiks der Ruhrbergarbeiterschaft im Frühjahr 1919', in E. Kolb (ed.), *Vom Kaiserreich zur Weimarer Republik* (Köln, 1972).

Osterroth, N., *Otto Hue. Ein Lebensbild für seine Freunde* (Bochum, 1922).

Peerenboom, E., *Statistik der katholischen caritativen Einrichtungen Deutschlands*, 2 Bde. (Freiburg, 1924).

Pelling, H., *Popular Politics and Society in Late Victorian Britain* (London, 1979 edition).

Pounds, N. J. G., *The Ruhr: a study in historical and economic geography* (London, 1952).

Reekers S., and J. Schulz, *Die Bevölkerung in den Gemeinden Westfalens 1818–1950* (Dortmund, 1952).

Reulecke, J., 'Der erste Weltkrieg und die Arbeiterbewegung im rheinisch-westfälischen Industriegebiet', in J. Reulecke (ed.), *Arbeiterbewegung an Rhein und Ruhr* (Wuppertal, 1974).

Reulecke, J., 'Vom blauen Montag zum Arbeiterurlaub', in *Archiv für Sozialgeschichte* (Bonn, 1976).

Reulecke, J., 'Von der Dorfschule zum Schulsystem. Schulprobleme und Schulalltag in einer "jungen" Industriestadt vor dem Ersten Weltkrieg', in J. Reulecke and W. Weber (ed.), *Fabrik, Familie, Feierabend. Beiträge zur Sozialgeschichte des Alltags im Industriezeitalter* (Wuppertal, 1978).

Rimlinger, G. V., 'International Differences in the Strike Propensity of Coal Miners: Experience in Four Countries', in *Industrial and Labor Relations Review* XII. iii (1959).

Rimlinger, G. V., 'Die Legitimierung des Protestes. Eine vergleichende Untersuchung der Bergarbeiterbewegung in England und Deutschland', in W. Fischer and G. Bajor (ed.), *Die soziale Frage* (Stuttgart, 1967).

Ritter, G. A., *Die Arbeiterbewegung im Wilhelminischen Reich* (Berlin, 1959).

Ritter, G. A., 'Workers' Culture in Imperial Germany: Problems and Points of Departure for Research', in *Journal of Contemporary History* XIII. ii (1978).

Ritter G. A., and K. Tenfelde, 'Der Durchbruch der Freien Gewerkschaften Deutschlands zur Massenbewegung im letzten Viertel des 19. Jahrhunderts', in H. O. Vetter (ed.), *Vom Sozialistengesetz zur Mitbestimmung* (Köln, 1975).

Ross, R. J., *Beleaguered Tower: the Dilemma of Political Catholicism in Wilhelmine Germany* (Notre Dame, 1976).

Roth, K. H., *Die 'andere' Arbeiterbewegung und die Entwicklung der Kapitalistischen Repression von 1880 bis zur Gegenwart* (Essen, 1977).

Rothert, H., *Kirchengeschichte des westfälisch-rheinischen Industriegebietes vom evangelischen Standpunkt* (Dortmund, 1926).

Samuel, R., 'Quarry Roughs', in R. Samuel (ed.), *Village Life and Labour* (London, 1975).

Samuel, R., 'Mineral Workers', in R. Samuel (ed.), *Miners, Quarrymen and Saltworkers* (London, 1977).

Samuel, R., 'The Workshop of the World', in *History Workshop Journal* iii (1977).

Saul, K., *Staat, Industrie, Arbeiterbewegung im Kaiserreich* (Düsseldorf, 1974).

Saul, K., 'Zwischen Repression und Integration. Staat, Gewerkschaften und Arbeitskampf im kaiserlichen Deutschland 1884–1914', in K. Tenfelde and H. Volkmann (ed.), *Streik. Zur Geschichte des Arbeitskampfes in Deutschland während der Industrialisierung* (München, 1981).

Schieder, W., 'Religionsgeschichte als Sozialgeschichte', in *Geschichte und Gesellschaft* iii (1977).

Schmidt, A., *Lang war der Weg* (Bochum, 1958).

Schnadt, R. T., *Bochum. Wirtschaftsstruktur und Verflechtung einer Grossstadt des Ruhrgebietes* (Bochum, 1936).

Schneider, M., *Die Christlichen Gewerkschaften 1894–1933* (Bonn, 1982).

Schneider, M., 'Religion and Labour Organization: the Christian Trade Unions in the Wilhelmine Empire', in *European Studies Review* XII. iii (1982).

Schofer, L., 'Die Bergarbeiter in Oberschlesien', in H. Mommsen and U. Borsdorf (ed.), *Glück auf, Kameraden! Die Bergarbeiter und ihre Organisationen in Deutschland* (Köln, 1979).

Schofer, L., *The formation of a modern labor force. Upper Silesia, 1865–1914* (Berkeley, 1975).

Schofer, L., 'Patterns of Workers' Protest: Upper Silesia, 1865–1914', in *Journal of Social History* (1972).

Scholl S. H. (ed.), *Katholische Arbeiterbewegung in Westeuropa* (Bonn, 1966).

Schomerus, H., 'The Family Life-Cycle: A Study of Factory Workers in Nineteenth-century Württemberg', in R. J. Evans and W. R. Lee (ed.), *The German Family* (London, 1981).

Schomerus, H., 'Lebenszyklus und Lebenshaltung in Arbeiterhaushaltungen des 19. Jahrhunderts', and 'Saisonarbeit und Fluktuation. Überlegungen zur Struktur der mobilen Arbeiterschaft 1850–1914', in W. Conze and U. Engelhardt (ed.), *Arbeiter im Industrialisierungsprozess. Herkunft, Lage und Verhalten* (Stuttgart, 1979).

Schönhoven, K., 'Arbeitskonflikte in Konjunktur und Rezession. Gewerkschaftliche Streikpolitik und Streikverhalten der Arbeiterschaft vor 1914', in K. Tenfelde and H. Volkmann (ed.), *Streik. Zur Geschichte des Arbeitskampfes in Deutschland während der Industrialisierung* (München, 1981).

Schönhoven, K., 'Gewerkschaftliches Organisationsverhalten im Wilhelminischen Deutschland', in W. Conze and U. Engelhardt (ed.), *Arbeiter im Industrialisierungsprozess. Herkunft, Lage und Verhalten* (Stuttgart, 1979).

Schönhoven, K., *Expansion und Konzentration. Studien zur Entwicklung der Freien Gewerkschaften im Wilhelminischen Deutschland* (Stuttgart, 1980).

Schorske, C. E., *German Social Democracy* (Harvard, 1955).

Schuchman, A., *Codetermination: Labor's Middle Way in Germany* (Washington, 1957).

Schunder, F., *Tradition und Fortschritt. Hundert Jahre Gemeinschaftsarbeit im Ruhrbergbau* (Stuttgart, 1959).

Schwenger, R., *Die betriebliche Sozialpolitik im Ruhrkohlenbergbau* (München and Leipzig, 1932).

Scott W. H. *et al.*, *Coal and Conflict: a study of industrial relations at collieries* (Liverpool, 1963).

Shorter, E., and C. Tilly, *Strikes in France 1830–1968* (Cambridge, 1974).

Soziale Arbeit: BVG 1842–1942 (Hattingen, 1942).

Spencer, E. G., 'Between Capital and Labor: Supervisory Personnel in Ruhr Heavy Industry', in *Journal of Social History* (1975).;

Spencer, E, G., 'Employer Response to Unionism: Ruhr Coal Industrialists before 1914', in *Journal of Modern History* (1976).

Sperber, J., 'Roman Catholic religious identity in Rhineland-Westphalia, 1800–1870; quantitative examples and some political implications', in *Social History* VII. iii (1982).

Sperber, J., 'The transformation of Catholic associations in the northern Rhineland and Westphalia 1830–1870', in *Journal of Social History* (1981).

Spethmann, H., *Die geschichtliche Entwicklung des Ruhrbergbaus um Witten und Langendreer* (Gelsenkirchen, 1937).

Stearns, P. N., 'Adaptation to Industrialization: German Workers as a Test Case', in *Central European History* (1970).

Stearns, P. N., *Lives of Labour* (London, 1975).

Stedman Jones, G., *Languages of class. Studies in English working class history* (Cambridge, 1983).

Stedman Jones, G., *Outcast London* (London, 1976 edition).

Steinberg, H. J., 'Die Entwicklung des Verhältnisses von Gewerkschaften und Sozialdemokratie bis zum Ausbruch des Ersten Weltkrieges', in H. O. Vetter (ed.), *Vom Sozialistengesetz zur Mitbestimmung* (Köln, 1975).

Steinberg, H. J., *Sozialismus und deutsche Sozialdemokratie. Zur Ideologie der Partei vor dem I. Weltkrieg* (Bonn-Bad Godesberg, 1972 edition).

Steinisch, I., 'Der Gewerkverein Christlicher Bergarbeiter', in H. Mommsen and U. Borsdorf (ed.), *Glück auf, Kameraden! Die Bergarbeiter und ihre Organisationen in Deutschland* (Köln, 1979).

Die Steinkohlenbergwerke der vereinigte Stahlwerke AG: die Schachtanlage Bruchstrasse in Bochum-Langendreer (n.p., 1931).

Die Steinkohlenbergwerke der vereinigte Stahlwerke AG: die Schachtanlage Carolinenglück in Bochum-Hamme (n.p., 1930).

Die Steinkohlenbergwerke der vereinigte Stahlwerke AG: die Schachtanlage Dannenbaum in Bochum-Laer, 2 Bde. (n.p., 1937).

Die Steinkohlenbergwerke der vereinigte Stahlwerke AG: die Schachtanlage Engelsburg in Bochum (n.p., 1930).

Die Steinkohlenbergwerke der vereinigte Stahlwerke AG: die Schachtanlage Friedlicher Nachbar in Bochum-Linden, 3 Bde. (n.p., 1939).

Die Steinkohlenbergwerke der vereinigte Stahlwerke AG: die Schachtanlage Prinz Regent in Bochum-Wiemelhausen, 2 Bde. (n.p., 1939).

Tampke, J., 'The rise and fall of the Essen model', in *Internationale wissenschaftliche Korrespondenz zur Geschichte der deutschen Arbeiterbewegung* (Juni 1977, Heft 2).

Tampke, J., *The Ruhr and Revolution. The Revolutionary Movement in the Rhenish-Westphalian Industrial Region 1912-1919* (London, 1979).

Tampke, J., 'Die Sozialisierungsbewegung im Steinkohlenbergbau an der Ruhr' in H. Mommsen and U. Borsdorf (ed.), *Glück auf, Kameraden! Die Bergarbeiter und ihre Organisationen in Deutschland* (Köln, 1979).

Taylor, A. J., 'The Coal Industry' in D. H. Aldcroft (ed.), *The Development of British Industry and Foreign Competition* (London, 1968).

Tenfelde, K., 'Arbeiterschaft, Arbeitsmarkt und Kommunikationsstrukturen im Ruhrgebiet in den 50er Jahren des 19. Jahrhunderts', in *Archiv für Sozialgeschichte* xvi (Bonn, 1976).

Tenfelde, K., 'Der bergmännische Arbeitsplatz während der Hochindustrialisierung', in W. Conze and U. Engelhardt (ed.), *Arbeiter im Industrialisierungsprozess. Herkunft, Lage und Verhalten* (Stuttgart, 1979).

Tenfelde, K., 'Bergmännisches Vereinswesen im Ruhrgebiet während der Industrialisierung' in J. Reulecke and W. Weber (ed.), *Fabrik, Familie, Feierabend. Beiträge zur Sozialgeschichte des Alltags im Industriezeitalter* (Wuppertal, 1978).

Tenfelde, K., 'Bildung und sozialer Aufstieg im Ruhrbergbau vor 1914', in W. Conze and U. Engelhardt (ed.), *Arbeiter im Industrialisierungsprozess. Herkunft, Lage und Verhalten* (Stuttgart, 1979).

Tenfelde, K., 'Konflikt und Organisation in einigen deutschen Bergbaugebieten 1867-1872' in *Geschichte und Gesellschaft* ii (1977).

Tenfelde, K., 'Die "Krawalle von Herne" im Jahre 1899', in *Internationale wissenschaftliche Korrespondenz zur Geschichte der deutschen Arbeiterbewegung* (März 1979, Heft 1).

Tenfelde, K., 'Linksradikale Strömungen in der Ruhrbergarbeiterschaft 1905 bis 1919', in H. Mommsen and U. Borsdorf (ed.), *Glück auf, Kameraden! Die Bergarbeiter und ihre Organisationen in Deutschland* (Köln, 1979).

Tenfelde, K., 'Mining Festivals in the Nineteenth Century', in *Journal of Contemporary History* XIII. ii (1978).

Tenfelde, K., 'Probleme der Organisation von Arbeitern und Unternehmern im Ruhrbergbau 1890-1918', in H. Mommsen (ed.), *Arbeiterbewegung und industrieller Wandel* (Wuppertal, 1980).

Tenfelde, K., *Sozialgeschichte der Bergarbeiterschaft an der Ruhr im 19. Jahrhundert (1815-1889)* (Bonn-Bad Godesberg, 1977).

Thomas, K., *Religion and the Decline of Magic* (London, 1982 edition).

Thompson, E. P., 'Eighteenth-century English society: class struggle without class?', in *Social History* III. ii (1978).

Thompson, E. P., *The Making of the English Working Class* (London, 1968 edition).

Thompson, E. P., 'Time, work-discipline and industrial capitalism', in

M. W. Flinn and T. C. Smout (ed.), *Essays in Social History* (Oxford, 1974).

Timm, W., *Der Bergarbeiterstreik 1889 und die Anfänge der Arbeiterbewegung in Unna* (Unna, 1969).

Volkmann, H., 'Organsation und Konflikt. Gewerkschaften, Arbeitgeberverbände und die Entwicklung des Arbeitskonflikts im späten Kaiserreich', in W. Conze and U. Engelhardt (ed.), *Arbeiter im Industrialisierungsprozess. Herkunft, Lage und Verhalten* (Stuttgart, 1979).

Wallraff, H. J., 'Die Belastung einer Gewerkschaft durch ideologische Differenzen: Spannungen innerhalb der christlichen Gewerkschaftsbewegung in den Jahren 1900–1914', in H. O. Vetter (ed.), *Vom Sozialistengesetz zur Mitbestimmung* (Köln, 1975).

Weber, W., 'Der Arbeitsplatz in einem expandierenden Wirtschaftszweig: Der Bergmann', in J. Reulecke and W. Weber (ed.), *Fabrik, Familie, Feierabend. Beiträge zur Sozialgeschichte des Alltags im Industriezeitalter* (Wuppertal, 1978).

Wehler, H. U., *Bismarck und der Imperialismus* (Köln, 1969).

Wehler, H. U., 'Die Polen im Ruhrgebiet' in H. U. Wehler (ed.), *Moderne deutsche Sozialgeschichte* (Köln, 1970).

Wehler, H. U., *Sozialdemokratie und Nationalstaat* (Göttingen, 1971).

Werner, G., *Ein Kumpel. Erzählung aus dem Leben der Bergarbeiter* (Berlin, 1929).

Westfälische Allgemeine Zeitung (30. 5. 1972).

Wiel, P., *Wirtschaftsgeschichte des Ruhrgebietes* (Essen, 1970).

Williamson, B., *Class, Culture and Community: a Biographical Study of Social Change in Mining* (London, 1982).

Wolcke, I. D., *Die Entwicklung der Bochumer Innenstadt* (Kiel, 1968).

Wrigley, E. A., *Industrial growth and population change: a regional study of the coalfield areas of north-west Europe in the later 19th century* (Cambridge, 1962).

Zeender, J. K., 'The German Centre Party 1890–1906' in *Transactions of the American Philosophical Society* lxvi (1976).

Zehnter, G., 'Sie vertraten Bochum im Reichstag', in *Ruhr-Nachrichten* (1961).

Ziranka, J., *Die Auswirkungen von Zechenstillegungen und Rationalisierungen im Steinkohlenbergbau auf die Wirtschaftsstruktur ausgewählter Gemeinden im niederrheinisch-westfälischen Industriegebiet* (Köln and Opladen, 1964).

Zwahr, H., *Zur Konstituierung des Proletariats als Klasse. Strukturuntersuchung über das Leipziger Proletariat während der industriellen Revolution* (München, 1981).

Unpublished Books and Theses

Aumann, B., *Die Bergarbeiterbewegung im rheinisch-westfälischen Industriegebiet im Spiegel der regionalen Presse* (Staatsexamarbeit, Bochum, 1973).

Crew, D., *Industry and Community: the social history of a German town 1860-1914* (Ph.D. thesis, Cornell, 1975).

Hemeyer, K. H., *Der Bochumer Wirtschaftsraum von 1840 bis zur Jahrhundertwende* (Diplomarbeit, Bochum 1960).

Hickey, S. H. F., *Class conflict and class consciousness: the emergence of the working class in the Eastern Ruhr 1870-1914* (D.Phil. thesis, Oxford, 1978).

Kliss, G., *Die Wanderung der Ostpreussen nach Bochum um die Jahrhundertwende im Zuge der Ost-West-Wanderung* (Seminararbeit, Bochum, 1971).

Siegel, A., *Mein Lebenskampf. Das Schicksal eines deutschen Bergarbeiters* (MS, Bochum, 1931).

Index